South Asian Religions

The religious landscape of South Asia is complex and fascinating. While existing literature tends to focus on the majority religions of Hinduism and Buddhism, much less attention is given to Jainism, Sikhism, Islam or Christianity. While not neglecting the majority traditions, this valuable resource also explores the important role which the minority traditions play in the religious life of the subcontinent, covering popular as well as elite expressions of religious faith. By examining the realities of religious life, and the ways in which the traditions are practiced on the ground, this book provides an illuminating introduction to Asian religions.

Karen Pechilis is NEH Distinguished Professor of Humanities and Chair and Professor of Religion at Drew University, USA. Her books for Routledge include *Interpreting Devotion: The Poetry and Legacy of a Female Bhakti Saint of India* (2011).

Selva J. Raj (1952–2008) was Chair and Stanley S. Kresge Professor of Religious Studies at Albion College, USA. He served as chair of the Conference on the Study of Religions of India and co-edited several books on South Asia.

South Asian Religions

Tradition and today

**Edited by Karen Pechilis
and Selva J. Raj**

Routledge
Taylor & Francis Group

LONDON AND NEW YORK

First published 2013
by Routledge
2 Park Square, Milton Park, Abingdon, Oxon OX14 4RN

Simultaneously published in the USA and Canada
by Routledge
711 Third Avenue, New York, NY 10017

Routledge is an imprint of the Taylor & Francis Group, an informa business

British Library Cataloguing in Publication Data
A catalogue record for this book is available from the British Library

Library of Congress Cataloging in Publication Data
South Asian religions : tradition and today / edited by Karen Pechilis and Selva J. Raj.

  pcm
1. South Asia--Religion. I. Pechilis, Karen, editor of compilation.
II. Raj, Selva J., editor of compilation.
BL1055.S655 2012   200.954--dc23
2012033975

ISBN: 978-0-415-44851-2 (hbk)
ISBN: 978-0-415-44852-9 (pbk)
ISBN: 978-0-203-07993-5 (ebk)

Typeset in Sabon
by Bookcraft Ltd, Stroud, Gloucestershire

Contents

List of illustrations

Figures

Maps

List of contributors

Sunil Goonasekera has taught sociology at the University of Peradeniya, Sri Lanka, and anthropology and religion at the University of California, San Diego, and Bowdoin College, Maine. His areas of research include religion, art, law, political violence in South Asia, and pilgrimage studies. His publications include *George Keyt: Interpretations* (Institute of Fundamental Studies, 1991); *Walking to Kataragama* (International Centre for Ethnic Studies, 2007); and many journal articles and chapters in books.

Nathan Katz is the Bhagwan Mahavir Professor of Jain Studies and Director of the Program in the Study of Spirituality at Florida International University. He is co-editor of the *Journal of Indo-Judaic Studies* and among his fifteen books are: *Spiritual Journey Home: Eastern Mysticism to the Western Wall* (KTAV, 2009); *Indo-Judaic Studies for the Twenty First Century: A View From the Margin* (editor-in-chief, Macmillan, 2007); *Who Are the Jews of India?* (University of California Press, 2000); *The Last Jews of Cochin: Jewish Identity in Hindu India* (University of South Carolina Press, 1993); and *Buddhist Images of Human Perfection* (Motilal Banarsidass, 1983).

M. Whitney Kelting is Associate Professor of Religious Studies at Northeastern University. She is the author of two books, *Singing to the Jinas: Jain Women, Mandal Singing and the Negotiations of Jain Devotion* (OUP, 2001) and *Heroic Wives: Rituals, Narratives and the Virtues of Jain Wifehood* (OUP, 2009). Her two current book projects examine the intersection between gender, prestige and modernity in the Jain community: the first is centered on temple patronage and masculinity and the other on motherhood.

Joseph Marianus Kujur is the Assistant Research Director and Head of the Tribal Unit of the Indian Social Institute, New Delhi. As a Visiting Researcher at the Center for Latin American Studies, Georgetown University, Washington, DC, he was engaged in a study of identity formation of indigenous peoples in India and Bolivia. Dr. Kujur has to his credit more than thirty research papers in national and international journals and he is the co-editor of five books including *Margins of Faith: Dalit and Tribal Christianity in India* (SAGE, 2010), and *Indigenous People of India: Problems and Prospects* (Indian Social Institute, 2007).

Vasudha Narayanan is Distinguished Professor and Chair, Department of Religion, at the University of Florida and a past President of the American Academy of Religion. Her fields of interest are the Hindu traditions in India, Cambodia and America; visual and expressive cultures in the study of the Hindu traditions; and gender issues. She is currently working on Hindu temples and traditions in Cambodia. She is the author or editor of seven books including *The Life of Hinduism* (University of California, 2006) and *Hinduism* (The Rosen Publishing Group, 2010), and numerous articles, chapters in books, and encyclopedia entries. She is also an Associate Editor of *Brill's Encyclopedia of Hinduism* (Brill, 2009). Her research has been supported by grants and fellowships from several organizations including the Centre for Khmer Studies, the American Council of Learned Societies, National Endowment for the Humanities, the John Simon Guggenheim Foundation, the American Institute of Indian Studies/Smithsonian and the Social Science Research Council.

Karen Pechilis is NEH Distinguished Professor of Humanities and Chair and Professor of Religion at Drew University. Her research areas are histories and literatures of devotional Hinduism in South India, with a special focus on female religious authorities. Her previous books are: *The Embodiment of Bhakti* (OUP, 1999), the edited volume *The Graceful Guru: Hindu Female Gurus in India and the United States* (OUP, 2004) and *Interpreting Devotion: The Poetry and Legacy of a Female Bhakti Saint of India* (Routledge, 2011). Her current project is focused on women, devotion and ethnography.

Karen G. Ruffle is assistant professor in the Department of Historical Studies and the Department and Centre for the Study of Religion at the University of Toronto. Her research and teaching interests focus on various aspects of Islam, including Muslim devotional texts, ritual practice and gendered constructions of holiness in Shiʻism. Ruffle's first book, *Gender, Sainthood, and Everyday Practice in South Asian Shiʻism* was published in 2011 by the University of North Carolina Press. She has published numerous essays on Fatimah al-Zahra in Shiʻi religious thought and practice and is currently working on a larger book project examining the ways in which the Prophet Muhammad's daughter's body, gender and sexuality are imagined and deployed in religious literature, ritual and material culture.

Pashaura Singh is Professor and Dr. Jasbir Singh Saini Endowed Chair in Sikh and Punjabi Studies at the University of California, Riverside. His publications include *The Guru Granth Sahib: Canon, Meaning and Authority* (OUP, 2000), *The Bhagats of the Guru Granth Sahib: Sikh Self-Definition and the Bhagat Bani* (OUP, 2003) and *Life and Work of Guru Arjan: History, Memory and Biography in the Sikh Tradition* (OUP, 2006). In addition, he has edited four volumes, the most recent one being *Sikhism in Global Context* (OUP, 2011).

M. Thomas Thangaraj retired in 2008 as Professor Emeritus of World Christianity at Candler School of Theology, Emory University, Atlanta, GA. He taught at Tamilnadu Theological Seminary in Madurai, India, for several years before his move to Emory in 1988. He has widely published in Tamil and English, and his publications include: *The Crucified Guru: An Experiment in Cross-Cultural Christology* (Abingdon, 1994), *The Common Task: A Theology of Christian Mission* (Abingdon, 1999), "Indian Christian Tradition," in *Religions of South Asia: An Introduction*, edited by Sushil Mittal and Gene Thursby, New York: Routledge, 2006, pp. 185–98, and "Religious Pluralism, Dialogue, and Asian Christian Responses," in *Christian Theology in Asia*, edited by Sebastian C. H. Kim, Cambridge University Press, 2008, pp. 157–78. He is currently at Boston University School of Theology, Boston, MA, as their Visiting Professor of Global Christianity.

Introduction

In a Shared World: Selva J. Raj and the study of religion

Karen Pechilis

This book was originally conceived and developed by Professor Selva J. Raj, our beloved colleague whose untimely death on March 15, 2008 left a heart-shaped hole in the universe for many of us. He had two co-edited books under his belt (and three more in progress), but the present volume was to be his first textbook-style publication. In a review article published in 2005, Selva spoke of his frustration in finding a good textbook on Asian religions:

> finding accessible textbooks on Eastern religions is a major challenge. Even more challenging, or should I say disappointing, is the task of finding texts that treat South Asian religions adequately and comprehensively. As I continued to teach more survey courses in the next nine years, I discovered to my dismay that there is not a single world religions textbook that acknowledges the existence or the complexities of South Asian minority religious traditions. I am still waiting for that elusive textbook![1]

The short answer is, he decided to produce it.

Selva's main contention was that the textbooks to date contained a "bias" in their lack of coverage of the "minority" religions of Islam and Christianity, while Sikhism and Jainism received greater coverage; yet Muslims and Christians are much more numerous in India.[2] To the argument that Jainism and Sikhism originated in India, Selva countered that Islam and Christianity were thoroughly indigenized, by virtue of their antiquity on the subcontinent as well as their association with two monumental political and cultural powers that had ruled much of India: Islam as the religion of the sultanates and the Mughal emperors (ca. 1200–1700 CE), and Christianity as the religion of the British colonialists and empire (ca. 1757–1947 CE):

> Additionally, both Christianity and Islam have long been and continue to be an integral part of the South Asian religious landscape, the former from the beginning of the common era and the latter from the eleventh century, long before the birth of Sikhism. More important, these indigenized religions have played a vital role not only in defining the religious, cultural, and political history of the subcontinent but also in shaping the content and character of religious life and practice in South Asia, including the dominant religions of the land.[3]

He supported his thesis that textbooks on India need to cover Islam and Christianity by pointing to contours in Indian Christianity (Christianity was his field of research) that are distinctive to India, thus demonstrating "the coexistence, interface, and cross-fertilization of multiple traditions" in India; by observing that many studies of Indian religions favored elite, rather than popular formulations, when it is instead often in the popular arena that one sees such cross-fertilization; and by extending his argument to promote the necessity of including folk traditions in surveys of Indian religions. Ultimately, his was an argument for a comprehensive textbook that would represent "religiously complex and pluralistic South Asia."[4]

I very much agree with Selva that this textbook's comprehensiveness is valuable to both teacher and student: here, everything is in one place in accessible, conscientious presentation by scholars who are experienced teachers and researchers. Each article discusses the major themes of identity, practice, and current issues. This discussion is followed by questions for discussion, a list of about ten key terms with definitions, and a list of recommended resources. The authors were asked to put a limited number of accessible sources in the recommended resources section as a "next step" for researching the religious tradition. Since it is a goal of this book to be accessible, let me note here that the scholarship represented in the articles is based on the scholar's own research plus her or his extensive review of scholarship in the field, but not all of these sources will be listed.

Several distinctive features of this volume especially reflect Selva's vision, including: the pioneering inclusion of a chapter on tribal religions; chapters on Islam and Christianity; the mindfulness of contributors in representing both elite and popular dimensions of religion; the contributors' discussion of practice, as well as precept, as constitutive of religious experience; the invitation the volume makes to teachers and to students to engage in critical thinking by discerning dominant streams in each tradition and nuances that challenge them; and the emphasis on developing comparative thinking by identifying similarities and differences across South Asian religions, including those that originated in areas in which Abrahamic axioms dominated the conversation.[5]

This volume encourages students to understand South Asia through its historical and present-day conversations in religion. Geographically, South Asia is variously defined: the United Nations currently groups the countries Afghanistan, Bangladesh, Bhutan, India, Iran (Islamic Republic of), Maldives, Nepal, Pakistan and Sri Lanka under the designation Southern Asia,[6] while the South Asian Association for Regional Cooperation is constituted by a charter among the nations of Bangladesh, Bhutan, India, Maldives, Nepal, Pakistan and Sri Lanka.[7] All of these countries have their own distinctive cultural identities, including religious identities. India is geographically the largest country in the region and the most populous; although there is political sensitivity in some quarters on the predominant role India plays in the region, for our purposes it is significant that India is a large country with a distinguished multicultural history and present. India's identity as a country where many religions have co-existed in part explains its importance in the field of history of religions, and the attraction it has for researchers in religion.

Most of the authors in this volume have performed their research in India and their articles are thus grounded in their research experiences in India. The exception is Professor Goonasekera's article on Buddhism, which takes as its focus Sri Lanka and considers aspects of Tibet on a comparative basis, for these two countries have continuously preserved Buddhism since the medieval period when the Buddhist community declined in India. Although all of the authors need to have the detail of research in a specific location and time in order to support their discussion, religion in a specific place and time participates in definitions across regions that are characteristic of the religion as a whole. The connections and tensions between micro and macro exist in religion as in other fields, and Selva was very well acquainted with them in his studies of Christianity in India, as his research focused on rituals in small towns in south India that were meaningful in the overlapping areas of "rural south Indian Christianity," "south Indian Christianity," "Indian Christianity," "South Asian Christianity," and "Christianity."

What is distinctive about the status of religion in the South Asian region, and even Asia more generally, is that it has a long history of the co-existence of diverse religions. This is not to say that all religions have the same cultural influence in all areas. Tribal religions may have had a presence over the entire Indian subcontinent prior to any of the other religions—tribals call themselves *adivasi*s, or "original inhabitants"—but many are now confined to forested areas that are officially accorded protection by the government. Some religions are influential through large numbers of adherents, such as Hinduism in India or Buddhism across Asia. Some religions are traditionally concentrated in certain regions, such as Jainism in the Indian state of Gujarat, Sikhism in the Indian state of Punjab, Hinduism in the central tea zone and northern region of Sri Lanka, Buddhism over much of Sri Lanka, and Christianity in the Indian state of Kerala. Some religions were powerful through their association with rulers, such as Islam in Mughal India and in Pakistan and Bangladesh, and Christianity in India's major English colonial cities of Delhi, Calcutta (Kolkata), Madras (Chennai), and Bombay (Mumbai). However, overall what we do not find in the history of religion in Asia is one religion predominating to the exclusion and even extinction of other religions, such as one finds in the religious history of Europe and the Middle East.[8]

Instead, in South Asia there was an exchange among distinctive points of view that held as central different views of the sacred; for example, divine multiplicities, or one God, or extraordinary human leaders whose lives were foundational in establishing the tradition for a particular historical era. Constituting, and sharing, a pluralistic context, Tribal religions, Vedism (early Hinduism), Jainism, and Buddhism originated in India a long time prior to the common era; Hinduism, Christianity, and Judaism were all represented by flourishing communities on the subcontinent by the fourth century CE and Islam by 1000 CE; and Sikhism originated in India in the fifteenth century CE. All of the religions were mutually influential in the South Asian context; in contrast to European and Middle Eastern history, the belief in one God found itself in dialogue with well-established, literate traditions that contextualized and shaped the religious discourse. As Diana Eck discusses in her classic book, *Darsan: Seeing the Divine Image in India*:

> In entering into the Hindu world, one confronts a way of thinking which one might call "radically polytheistic," and if there is any "great divide" between the traditions of India and those of the West, it is in just this fact. Some may object that India has also affirmed Oneness as resolutely and profoundly as any culture on earth, and indeed it has. The point here, however, is that India's affirmation of Oneness is made in a context that affirms with equal vehemence the multitude of ways in which human beings have seen that Oneness and expressed their vision. Indian monotheism or monism cannot, therefore, be aptly compared with the monotheism of the West. The statement that "God is One" does not mean the same thing in India and the West. At virtually every level of life and thought, India is polycentric and pluralistic.[9]

Religions of South Asia, and most particularly India as a cradle and home for multiple religions, wrote a different script than the one with which students of European or Middle Eastern religions are familiar. Tribal religions very much contributed to India's pluralistic script, informing Hinduism and, in a different key, Islam and Christianity through the negotiation of past and present in the conversion process. This is why, in my opinion, religions of South Asia might most fruitfully be studied as a pluralistic grouping in a geographical location, rather than as singular religions, since the ethos over centuries was a model of shared yet distinctive paths, rather than a model of singularity. This textbook highlights this important nature of South Asian religions.

This returns me to Selva, who wrote a different script for the study of religion than the one that those of us in his generation had inherited. Four areas stand out as his special contributions to changing the culture of academia—or at least the study of South Asian religions' corner of it: collaboration, self-reflection, vividness of observation, and a lightness of heart.

Be collaborative

Selva once told me that his given name was "Selvaraj," and that he split it into two to create a US-style first and last name. I never asked about the middle initial—it's one of the strange aspects of being close friends that you one day realize how much you didn't ask. Knowing Selva, he might in a moment of play have made it up, since it was a signifier with modest consequence. His given name "Selvaraj" translates to "the king of wealth," in the sense of material riches first and foremost but also in the extended meanings of "flourishing state," "beauty," "experience of happiness," and even "learning."[10] Selva was all of these things, and his special gift was to share them with others. As an educator, Selva firmly believed that students enrich themselves and make their lives beautiful though learning, and so do colleagues. He was very much appreciated as such at the marvelous Albion College, where he had been appointed for a second term as the prestigious

Stanley S. Kresge Scholar of Religious Studies. For Selva, study revealed riches to be shared.

Many of Selva's students and colleagues point to his warm inclusiveness as his most prominent and admired characteristic. I am convinced that his inclusive approach was important for the way in which he rewrote the script for the study of religion. He brought people together to investigate important topics in the study of religion; his first book was a groundbreaking co-edited volume on popular Christianity, and this was followed by four more co-edited volumes on the nature of vows, the South Asian Christian diaspora, the status of miracles in the modern world, and the category of sacred play.[11] These books are collaborative in two ways: the co-editorship of the volumes and the diversity of contributors in them, from younger scholars to established scholars.

Several of these collaborative volumes emerged from the Conference on the Study of Religions of India (CSRI). Selva brought his skill at collaboration to his role as Chair of the CSRI. To make the conference more inclusive he changed its name, which opened the conference to greater participation of a diversity of scholars. For more than 25 years it had been the Conference on Religion in South India (CRSI), focusing on South India only. Selva's change of the name indexed his inclusive approach, and brought in scholars studying all religions and regions of India, appropriately emphasizing the pluralistic script characteristic of South Asia.[12] It is also a mark of Selva's emphasis on collaboration that he generously invited other scholars besides himself to co-edit volumes from presentations at the conference.[13]

What Selva's approach underscored to me was that there was a different way of doing scholarship than that which in my view had been promoted in the academy. The established approach had been agonistic; it was combative, especially in the sense of striving to overcome in argument. Selva's approach emphasized building; it prioritized learning from others, especially in the sense of gaining insights from others on which to build one's own perspective while acknowledging those insights from others. Collaborative work is work done with, not against, others. Collaborative work can result in co-edited volumes and collections, but it can also inform work done independently, in which one's narrative constructively and with acknowledgement builds on the work of others, rather than taking a combative stance to the work of others. In one's independent work, one approaches a source saying: what can this contribute to my study? As Selva demonstrated in his teaching and scholarship, collaboration brings out the best in everyone by recognizing a multiplicity of productive contributions.

Engage in self-reflection

Selva participated in a panel I put together on "Encounters in Ethnography Today" at the 2007 American Academy of Religion (AAR) Annual Meeting, the last AAR he was able to attend before his untimely death in spring 2008. In his presentation, he engaged in reflections that were "intentionally anecdotal and autobiographical—something that I have fiercely avoided for much of my academic career—that hopefully will stimulate some theoretical reflection."[14]

Selva's linking of autobiographical reflection with theoretical reflection is important.

In his remarks, Selva reflected on his experience in graduate school at the University of Chicago Divinity School, where he was studying History of Religions, in particular the responses his status as an "ordained Catholic priest with part-time pastoral commitments in a blue-collar parish" engendered:

> It didn't take long to realize that many in Chicago were then openly skeptical and suspicious – if not disdainful – of scholars with official ties to established religions. Particularly, the radical wing in the History of Religions regarded such scholars as no more than "crypto-theologians" or "theologians in wolf's clothing" or "closet theologians." Even as I resented the pejorative label and its implicit indictment of my capacity for intellectual neutrality, I was also aware that in some ways, I was an academic anomaly. First, unlike many of my peers who studied the exotic other, I chose the uncommon terrain of ethnographic research on Christianity. Second, I was an official insider contemplating ethnographic study of [my] own tradition that was an anathema and a sacred taboo. Not surprisingly, I came to regard my religious biography as a serious academic liability, taking great pains to shield it.[15]

I would have liked to have had an extended conversation with Selva about the reflections he presented; since that is no longer possible, I will have to think aloud here, without the benefit of his response. I do recall the kind of dynamic of which Selva spoke, and I unfortunately had the attitude he describes at that time, even though Selva and I were friendly in graduate school and became closer after graduation. One dimension of the issue is that one has to unlearn some things from graduate school, including the imposed competition. Another dimension is that then, as now, the theological study of religion has much more of a presence in the popular imagination of the study of religion than the historical and cultural study of religion—we historians and culturalists have only to mention to a non-academic person that we study religion and nearly uniformly the answer back assumes that we study theology. In my experience this has not changed over the past 25 years, and if we look at the institutionalized graduate study of religion—in divinity schools, in theological schools, sequestered from liberal arts (a legacy of I. Kant's 1798 *Conflict of the Faculties*)—it is not hard to see why the identity of the study of religion *as* theology is so prominent in the popular imagination. So our reaction as graduate students had to do with a real and perceived minority defining itself against a hegemony.

But we needed more nuance than that, and Selva was a scholar who pointed this out in thoughtful and productive ways. I believe it was at one of the AAR conferences in the latter half of the 1990s when I heard Selva deliver a paper in which he passionately, and with carefully constructed reasoning, argued that the study of Christianity in India was a necessary and important part of the study of religion in India and South Asia. I recall being surprised by the informed passion in Selva's voice, as though I were seeing a new side of him, and being very impressed that he made the point so impeccably and convincingly.[16] Now I can more clearly see that his autobiography informed his passion and his argument in a sophisticated way, which resulted in his theoretical stance that the study of Christianity in India needed to be included in the study of South Asian religions because it both shaped, and was shaped by, the history of religions in South Asia. His approach was not at all something along the lines of "I exist, and so I deserve to be studied/represented/the recipient of public attention"; instead, his argument was a theoretical one impassioned by his life experience, along the lines of "the study of Christianity in India contributes to our understanding of religion in South Asia."

Nor was Selva's argument based on a simplistic notion of an "insider" who is opposed to an "outsider." Selva's own life story would not permit this simplicity; as he discussed in his paper at the ethnography panel, he left the Catholic priesthood in 2000, thereby changing his status of ecclesiastical insider to one of ecclesiastical outsider. This change in status raised both logistical and ethical issues for him. For example, when he was among his former priestly colleagues such issues involved his not being entitled to stay at official ecclesiastical lodgings during his fieldwork endeavors, and his grappling with whether or not he could accept hospitality from current priests based on his former status of priest. When he was among his lay informants, he wondered whether or not he should explicitly reveal his change in status to them, or let them keep their presuppositions about him, which ranged from some people's belief that he was still a priest to others' assumption that he was "no different from any local Tamil." Significantly, Selva framed these issues in terms of his *study* of religion; specifically, his performance of ethnographic fieldwork to understand and interpret rural south Indian Christianity. At no time did Selva suggest that his status (or former status) of Catholic priest automatically entitled him to be viewed as an academic scholar of religion. As he put it, it is the "critical credentials" that make the scholar, which are based on academic study in dialogue with life experience.[17]

I believe that preeminent current theorist of religion Jonathan Z. Smith has helpfully distinguished two different approaches to understanding religion that help us to nuance the issue of perspective beyond the oft-heard oppositions between theologian and historian or culturalist, and between insider and outsider. He describes the fundamental issue of perspective in religion as either based on presence or based on representation:

> The history of the history of religions is not best conceived as a liberation from the hegemony of theology—our pallid version of that tattered legend of the origins of science, whether placed in fifth-century Athens or sixteenth-century Europe, that depicts science progressively unshackling itself from a once regnant religious world-view. Our variant of this twice-told tale needs to be set aside, not because such a claimed liberation has been, in so many moments of our history, an illusion, but rather because this way of retelling the tale occludes a more fundamental issue that yet divides us. In shorthand form, this is the debate between an understanding of religion based on *presence* and one based on *representation*.[18]

Smith indicates further that an understanding of religion based on presence is one that assumes: that religion is unique or *sui generis* in terms of both human culture and scholarly study; that religion is "reality"; that language is self-evident and transparent; that the goal of study is to discover a universal principle or idea; and that the method of study "denies the legitimacy of translation, and the cognitive value of difference." In contrast, an understanding of religion based on representation assumes: that religion is an interrelated aspect of human culture and an interrelated discipline of scholarly study; that religion is an intellectual category; that language is a cultural construction; that the goal of study is to propose generalizations; and that the method of study is to engage in translation in which the unknown/unfamiliar is critically approached through the known/familiar.[19]

Significantly, these two modes of understanding (presence and representation) do not characterize different specializations within the study of religion; rather, they are modes of thought found across the study of religion. Thus, there is no inherent opposition between, say, theology and history, but there is an opposition between people who view religion as unmediated experience and those who view religion as experience that is inextricably tied to linguistic conceptualization and expression:

> [T]he central debates within the study of religion revolve around the relations of language and experience. Questions as to whether experience can ever be immediate or is always mediated? Whether we can experience a world independently of the conventional ways in which it is socially represented? Whether the *re-* of re-presentation remains always at the level of re-presentation? Such questions constitute the serious theoretical matters that sharply divide us in ways that cut across conventional, essentially political, divisions such as historians of religions and theologians.[20]

To undergraduate students, I often suggest that a way to characterize the opposition Smith describes in a manner that provides a very basic and accessible point of entry is to view an understanding of religion based on *presence* as primarily consisting of discourses that seek to instruct others on how to *be* religious (that is, to obtain religious experience); in contrast, an understanding of religion based on *representation* primarily consists of discourses that are *about* religion in their explanation of aspects of religion (that is, to understand what religious people say about their religious experiences as part of their cultural context). Selva's and Smith's reflections encourage us to engage in self-reflection and self-awareness of the kind of discourse we are creating with our oral discussion of and written ideas on religion.

Observe vividly

The history of religions method of study has traditionally been dominated by textual criticism. The identification of the field as "history" contributes to the bias; texts from many centuries ago have survived, including those that seem to be reliable copies of very ancient texts. The Vedas of Hinduism are oral texts that have been meticulously preserved for millennia sheerly by controlled oral transmission. Works of art used in ritual, such as Buddha images at *stupas* (memorial structures over Buddhist relics), images of Jinas on monastery walls, and Hindu sculptures of deities in temples are also extant from past centuries and help us to imagine the history of religions in South Asia. These locations where art is found also often contain inscriptions carved into the rock, which also contribute to our historical knowledge.

Scholars who work with historical materials certainly travel to the sites under study, such as sites where there are manuscripts or copies of texts, sites where certain events happened in the past, and sites where monuments and religious buildings are extant. But the method of performing fieldwork at a site, in which the inquiry and analysis are primarily based on what people say about their culture as they live within it, is less well represented traditionally in the history of religions field, although it is a growing method. Selva was a scholar who primarily performed ethnographic fieldwork rather than historical analysis with texts. The method of ethnography involves fieldwork at a given time that is the "present" for both ethnographer and informant in the culture under study. Ethnography, or "writing culture," is thus primarily concerned with the present rather than history, though it preserves that "present" interaction and observation like a fly in amber for future generations, to whom it can read as history. What historians of religion such as Selva bring especially to the performance of ethnography is that they are concerned with understanding how their informants connect events in the present with traditional beliefs and practices in religion, and thus, distinctive from other ethnographers, historians of religion who practice ethnography reveal the complex relationships between present and past in their scholarly writings.

For example, in his research on the shrine to St. John de Britto in southern India, Selva discussed the pilgrims' connection of the present-day practice of sacrificing animals with the traditional story that Britto became so powerful that he threatened a local king's power, and so the king had him beheaded; Britto's followers understood this as his martyrdom, which effected his transformation into a saint.

> The extraordinary sacral powers of St. John de Britto and his martyrdom site have transformed the remote village of Oriyur into a famed regional pilgrimage center. Tens of thousands of pilgrims and devotees of diverse religious affiliations from all over Tamil Nadu go on annual pilgrimage to this sacred site, where animal sacrifice is a regular feature … Wednesdays are considered particularly auspicious for animal sacrifices, since the martyr was beheaded on a Wednesday. Thus it would not be unusual to find, on any Wednesday, a group of pilgrims offering animal sacrifices at the shrine.[21]

Selva's fieldwork study of ritual reminds us that when we are studying living tradition by the ethnographic method we are primarily studying living memory; a memory on the part of participants that brings to the fore aspects of history that are most meaningful to them as they engage with their present world. The act of decapitating an animal in the present day recalls the act of Britto's beheading

long ago as it repeats the historical act in a new way in order to commemorate, celebrate, honor, and access the saint's holy power. Further, as Selva also
discusses in the article, the living memory engages its context: the choice of
animal sacrifice resonates with the Hindu Indian context, with its past tradition
of animal sacrifice in the Vedas to present-day animal sacrifice in villages and
those in celebration of the goddess, especially Kali.

Increasingly in his work, Selva enhanced the lucidity of explanation in his
ethnographic writing with a vividness of description, and his language became
exceptionally visual. I was mesmerized at an American Academy of Religion
conference presentation he gave on roadside shrines because of such descriptions, as I was also at his presentation at the Conference on the Study of Religions
of India in 2007 on the *kumpitusevai* tradition at the shrine of St. Anthony at
Puliampatti. Hearing him describe the scene, I felt I was there with him. His
analysis of the *kumpitusevai* tradition has recently been published in Knut
Jacobsen's edited volume on *South Asian Religions on Display*; the specificity
of his language in phrases such as the "fervent cries," the "downpour of devotion," and the prostrating people on the "filthy gravel" streets creates a vivid and
experiential description:

> As the *chaparams* [palanquins, one of which contains the statue of St.
> Anthony and the other a statue of Mary] are lifted skyward to the accom-
> paniment of fervent cries and loud chanting of Anthony's name, dozens
> of boys and girls throw baskets of salt, pepper, and marigold petals at his
> statue. Caught totally off guard by the sudden downpour of devotion, I was
> completely drenched in the "shower of salt and pepper". As the procession
> inches its way through worshipping crowds, there are periodic and desig-
> nated stops along the route, predetermined by the parish council and secured
> as a ritual privilege on the basis of convention, competition, status, and rank.
> At each stop, devotees, who secured this right at the public meeting, offer
> garlands, gold chains, and other votive offerings to the saints. Each time
> the *chaparam* is lifted above the ground, the "salt shower" is repeated with
> abandon as cries of "uppu malai" reverberate.
>
> The procession slowly moves past the shrine as drummers and pipers play
> devotional music. Standing right behind the *chaparams* is a select group of
> over a hundred devotees. Walking five abreast, these devotees fully prostrate
> themselves on the gravel streets for a few seconds – totally unmindful of the
> filth on the streets – stand up and walk about ten yards and prostrate them-
> selves again, repeating this ritual every five minutes. This pattern continues
> for the entire four-hour procession.[22]

Be light of heart

I believe that the single-most characteristic that enabled Selva to be collaborative, to engage in productive self-reflection, and to be vivid of observation was his
lightness of heart. "Lightness of heart" does not mean that he did not take things
seriously; it means that he undertook and accomplished his work of teaching,

fieldwork, and scholarship with a knowing sensitivity to the play of human relationships. The multiplicity of ideas, his own and from those with whom he collab-
orated, were to be considered, discussed, and revised in a process that could be
characterized as "serious play." He could almost have been describing his own
approach when he portrayed a couple's ritualized mock "auction" of their baby at
the shrine of St. Anne at Arulnandapuram, in fulfillment of a vow they made to
the saint to give *her* their baby should they be fortunate enough to give birth to
one. Selva analyzed the event as the interplay of levity and seriousness:

> The auctioneer knew well that he was presiding over a pretend auction
> that has serious implications. Members of the assembly were serious about
> making bids on the child knowing that they would never make the final
> bidding. Yet they played a crucial role insofar as they helped the parents
> fulfill their promise to pay off the debt. The parents initiated the auction
> confident in the knowledge that they would not in fact lose the baby even
> if the ritual caused some internal anxiety. According to devotees, the saint
> also knew that she would not get the baby, as did the priests and church
> officials. With the exception of the screaming baby—the central character in
> this ritual drama who was blissfully innocent of the multiple and multilay-
> ered negotiations and deals—everyone knew it was a pretend auction. Yet
> the auction was conducted with dead seriousness.[23]

A good-natured mirth appeared in his scholarly writings, often through allit-
erative phrases he would coin, such as "downpour of devotion" in the passage
quoted earlier. He playfully described his sense of his bimodal existence as he
commuted between his graduate classes in religion on the elite campus of the
University of Chicago and his pastoral work at a parish in a blue-collar neighborhood of Chicago as "between the ivory towers of the academy and the mundane
pastoral realities on the ground, between Bloomingdale's and Kmart as it were."[24]
We can also point to his idea of "cocktail communitas," which he discussed in an
analysis of the shrine of John de Britto at Oriyur, in which he examined Victor
Turner's thesis on pilgrimage:

> Curiously, while caste identities and class distinctions are carefully preserved
> and consciously displayed, pilgrims' religious identities and delineations
> remain quite fluid, both during and beyond the pilgrimage experience.
> These facts suggest that caste identities and class distinctions are not entirely
> repressed nor obliterated but in fact reinforced in pilgrimage contexts, which
> compels us to distinguish between a superficial feeling of solidarity, a kind
> of "cocktail communitas", and the actual breakdown of social groups. It is
> this "cocktail communitas" that is most visible among the pilgrims at the
> shrine of John de Britto.[25]

A further example would be Selva's description of devotees currently in search
of a guru (who is viewed as an embodiment, or *avatar*, of god) in the American
context as "avatar-tourists."[26] It was his gift to recognize the playful–serious

approach in others, too. For example, in explaining the "cultural role reversal" he observed among the devotees of the female guru Ammachi, with Euro-devotees more conspicuously dressing in Indian style than many Indo-devotees, he quoted one devotee as remarking: "The Anglos seem more Indian than the Indians and the Indians seemed more Anglo and less Indian."[27] In describing the variety of interpretations of Ammachi's *devi bhava*, he observed that the traditional significance of her performance is that she becomes the goddess and dances, but for at least some in the audience, in the words of one devotee, the performance is "a spiritual disco night" for devotees.[28] His playful use of such phrases also communicates the serious point that Selva was a scholar who was not afraid to call it as he saw it.

Through his style and grace, Selva changed my experience of the study of religion in the academy for the better, and I wish his illuminating self were still here. Many other colleagues feel this way, too. When Selva passed away, the plans for this volume, including the nature of its content, the identity of the scholars who would contribute articles, and the identity of the publisher were set, but none of the writing had yet been undertaken. I thank the generosity of the contributors to this volume, who agreed to carry on with the work in honor of Selva; it has been a pleasure and a fruitful learning experience to share this collaboration initiated by Selva with them. I also thank the executors of Selva's estate, his colleague at Albion College Bindu Madhok and her husband George Strander, for supporting the continuation of this project. I also thank Routledge, especially Lesley Riddle, Senior Publisher of Religion and Anthropology, and Katherine Ong, Senior Editorial Assistant of Religion and Anthropology, for continuing the press' participation in this project. I hope that future scholars of South Asian religions may be also be inspired by Selva's work and build on his collaborative scholarly legacy; that would be most fitting.

Recommended resources

Each chapter of this volume includes a section on recommended resources. Here, I provide not a comprehensive list but selected resources for primary texts, film, and literature that I and others have found helpful for the study of religions of South Asia, especially in the classroom.

Anthologies

The Religions in Practice series from Princeton University Press, which includes the following five volumes, contains primary readings from South Asian traditions beyond central classical texts, providing a window onto more popular iterations of religious belief and practice.

Religions of India in Practice, ed. Donald S. Lopez, Jr., 1995.
Buddhism in Practice, ed. Donald S. Lopez, Jr., 1995.
Religions of Tibet in Practice, ed. Donald S. Lopez, Jr., 1997.
Asian Religions in Practice: An Anthology, ed. Donald S. Lopez, Jr., 2002 [1999].

Islam in South Asia in Practice, ed. Barbara D. Metcalf, 2009.

An Anthology of Sacred Texts by and about Women, ed. Serinity Young, New York: The Crossroad Publishing Company, 1994. This volume contains translations of primary texts by and about women from religions across the globe.

Sources of Indian Tradition, Vols. 1 & 2, New York: Columbia University Press, 1988. These volumes, which provide translations of selected primary sources from classical to modern India, were originally published in 1988 and are soon to appear in updated editions.

Films

Ashura at Skardu. Directed by John R. Perry. Chicago, IL: University of Chicago. DVD and study guide, 2006.

> Since the eighteenth century, the region of Baltistan in the Karakoram mountain range of Pakistan has been predominantly Shiʻa. On the tenth of Muharram (ʻAshura), the Shiʻa of Skardu town perform bloody *matam* with whips and chains to demonstrate their loyalty to Imam Husain.

Banaras Muharram and the Coals of Karbala. Directed by Marc J. Katz. Madison, WI: University of Wisconsin Center for South Asia. DVD, 2004.

> Focusing on the Muharram possession ritual in which the spirit of Imam Husain's nephew Qasem ("the bridegroom of Karbala") inhabits the body of a young man in Banaras, India, this documentary highlights the myriad ways that Hindus, Sunni and Shiʻi Muslims have shaped Muharram ritual in this North Indian city.

The Frontiers of Peace: Jainism in India. Written and produced by Paul L. Kuepferle, produced by Barry Lynch. Documentary for the British Broadcasting Corporation, VHS, 1986. Distributed as DVD by University of Wisconsin-Madison, 2004.

> Set in Ahmedabad, Gujarat, this documentary explores Jainism, its beliefs and practices. Interviews with a Jain industrialist, a Jain nun, and a Jain monk explore the respective paths of laypeople and monastic members of the religion.

Ganges. Directed by Tom Hugh-Jones. Documentary for the British Broadcasting Corporation. DVD, 2008.

> This feature-length film explores India's most sacred river in three parts that respectively focus on its origins in the Himalayan mountains, its path through India's central plains, and its joining to the sea in Calcutta. Mainly focuses on the river's environmental impact though engages cultural perspectives on the river.

Gurdwara: House of the Guru. Directed by Roy Hayter. Produced by Roy Hayter, Hugh J. M. Johnston, David Pettigrew, and Jon Stoddart. Vancouver: Temple Films Ltd. Distributed by Image Media Services, Richmond British Columbia. VHS, 1992.

> This short film examines Sikh religious tenets, social life and family values in a Canadian setting.

Haro Hara: Pilgrimage to Kataragama Sri Lanka. Directed and produced by Samuel Holt, cinematographer and producer Ethan Higbee. Distributed by Nomad Productions. DVD, 2007.

> This feature-length documentary, shot in 2003 and 2004, follows a group of Tamil Hindu pilgrims as they journey to Kataragama, a pilgrimage town in southern Sri Lanka that attracts Buddhist, Hindu, and Muslim pilgrims.

I Am a Sufi, I Am a Muslim. Directed by Dirk Duman. Distributed by Films for the Humanities. DVD, 2005.

> Although focusing on Sufism across the Islamic world from Turkey to India, this documentary devotes considerable attention to *qawwali*, devotional music that draws the devotee closer to God, and its premier performer, the late Nusrat Fateh Ali Khan (d. 1997).

In the Name of God (Ram Ke Naam). Cinematographer and editor Anand Patwardhan. Distributed by First Run Icarus Films. VHS, 1992.

> This documentary-style film explores the rise of Hindu fundamentalism in India and its role in the destruction of the historic Babri mosque in Ayodhya in 1992.

The Last Jews in Calcutta: Albert Jacob's Journey to the City of his Birth, 1995. Produced and directed by Larry Frisch.

> This film traces a visit back home by Albert Jacob, now of London. "The first and last video ever produced" about Kolkata's expiring Jewish community visits the synagogues, schools, hospitals, and cemeteries that are the basis for reminiscences of holidays and personal communal history.

Next Year in Jerusalem. Written, directed and produced by Chetan Shaw, Cintel Communications, Madras, 1991.

> This film was shot in Kochi's Jew Town in 1984. Highlights include an interview with the then 84-year-old Stattu Koder, the community's leader, and his wife, Gladys; a look at the Koders' Seder; wine-making in the home of Gummy and Reema Salem, and a Kochini wedding.

Puja: Expressions of Hindu Devotion. Produced and edited by A. C. Warden, written by Nathan Antila. Distributed by the Arthur M. Sackler Gallery of the Smithsonian Institution. VHS, 1996.

> This very short instructional film was made to accompany an exhibition of the same title held at the Sackler Gallery in 1996. It introduces viewers to *puja*, or worship with images, a mainstream practice in Hinduism. It also includes interviews with younger and older devotees to explain central concepts. The Sackler Gallery has an online resource for understanding *puja*: Guide for Educators, http://www.asia.si.edu/pujaonline/puja/lesson_ contents.html

Rafting to Bombay. Directed and produced by Erez Laufter. Distributed by Erez Laufter Films Tel Aviv. DVD, 2009.

> Tells the little-known story of Jewish refugees who found a safe haven in Mumbai, India, during World War II, through the personal history of the filmmaker's father. While filming the father's return to Mumbai, the 2008 attacks took place, and the film reflects on the terrorist takeover of Chabad House.

Shalom Bombay. Directed and produced by Alex Hayim, 1998.

> A documentary about the Bene Israel Jews and the Baghdadi Jews of Bombay, this film mixes Jewish sites in and around Mumbai with recollections about "the good old days" with a cross section of India's largest Jewish community.

The Story of India. Written and presented by Michael Wood. Distributed by PBS Home Video, a department of the Public Broadcasting Service. DVD, 2008.

> A thoughtful overview of Indian history in six hour-long parts, from its very early history to the present day. Buddhism is profiled in the early history BCE, Hinduism in the early centuries CE, and Islam in the Mughal era of the Middle Ages. Also includes discussion of the Silk Road and the Independence movement. PBS has an online guide and educational materials for this film at: http://www.pbs.org/thestoryofindia/

Literature

Bama. *Karukku.* Translated by Lakshmi Holmström. New York: Oxford University Press, 2011, 2nd revised edition [New Delhi: Macmillan India, 2000]. An autobiographical account by the renowned Dalit author, in which she explores the tensions of caste in Indian Catholicism.

Blank, Jonah. *Arrow of the Blue-Skinned God: Retracing the Ramayana through India.* Boston, MA: Houghton Mifflin and London: Penguin Books, 1992. A journalist traces the route of the hero Rama from India's classic epic across India and Sri Lanka, making observations on culture and religion along the way.

Dalrymple, William. *Nine Lives: In Search of the Sacred in Modern India*. New York: Alfred A. Knopf, 2010. A journalist profiles the lives of nine religious people in India today, including a bard who recites traditional epics, a female Sufi devotee, a Tibetan monk, and a Tantric goddess worshipper.

Devi, Mahasweta. *Imaginary Maps*. Translated by Gayatri Chakravorty Spivak. Abingdon, Oxford, UK: Routledge, 1994. These short stories explore the beliefs and practices of tribals in the context of their marginalization in India.

Ezekiel, Nissim. *Collected Poems*. With a Preface by Leela Gandhi and an Introduction by John Thieme. New York: Oxford University Press, 2006, 2nd ed. Nissim Ezekiel is regarded as one of India's foremost English-language poets, playwrights, and essayists of the 20th century. His much-anthologized poems reflect modern Indian life in Mumbai from the perspective of a member of India's tiniest minority. In some cases, this marginality is subtle and, in others, his Bene Israel heritage is in the foreground.

Feinberg, Leonard. *Waking the Tiger: A Novel of Sri Lanka*. Santa Fe, NM: Pilgrims Process Inc., 2005. Set in 1950s Sri Lanka, a fictional story of the rising tensions between ethnic, religious, and political groups on the island.

Mehta, Gita. *A River Sutra*. New York: Vintage, 1994. A fictional story about a man who is caretaker of a pilgrimage resthouse and the many religious people he meets in that capacity, from a Jain monk to a Sufi singer to a Hindu ascetic.

Reza, Rahi Masoom. *The Feuding Families of Village Gangauli*. Translated by Gillian Wright. New Delhi: Penguin, 1994. A story of the people of the village Gangauli in which caste, religious identity, and the *zamindari* system of land ownership were turned upside down during World War II and the Partition of India and Pakistan in 1947.

Rushdie, Salman. *The Enchantress of Florence*. New York: Random House, 2008. An imaginative comparison of the contemporaneous cultural heights achieved in Mughal India and Renaissance Italy through a mysterious blond man's appearance at the palace of the Mughal emperor Akbar at Fatehpur Sikri and his adventures in Florence amidst Machiavelli and the cousins Vespucci.

Art online

Accessible resources for the study of South Asian art

American Institute of Indian Studies, Center for Art and Archaeology, Delhi; art and archeology of India, dsal.uchicago.edu/images/aiis/database.html

Asia Society, New York; highlights from the Mr. and Mrs. John D. Rockefeller 3rd collection of fine art from Asia, http://www.asiasocietymuseum.org/

British Library, London, online collection of illuminated manuscripts, http://www.bl.uk/onlinegallery/index.html

British Museum, London; collection database search, http://www.britishmuseum.org/research/search_the_collection_database.aspx

Huntington Archive of Buddhist and Asian Art, Ohio; http://huntingtonarchive.osu.edu

Metropolitan Museum of Art, New York; timeline of South and Southeast Asian art history, http://www.metmuseum.org/toah/world-regions/#/06/South-Southeast-Asia; collection database search, http://www.metmuseum.org/works_of_art/collection_database/

Rubin Museum of Art, New York; provides extensive educational materials for current and past exhibitions on religious art of the Himalayas, http://www.rmanyc.org/, and a link to Himalayan Art Resources, an online educational database with 45,000 images, http://www.himalayanart.org/

Notes

1   Selva J. Raj, "The Quest for a Balanced Representation of South Asian Religions in World Religions Textbooks," *Religious Studies Review* 31: 1 & 2 (2005): 14–16. This issue of *Religious Studies Review* contains reviews of textbooks in several fields within the study of religion. Since my essay is a personal tribute to Professor Raj, I will refer to him as Selva throughout this essay. Let me take this opportunity to remind students that in academic papers the convention is to use a title (e.g. Professor Raj argues that…) or the scholar's last name (e.g. Raj argues that…) when describing or analyzing that scholar's work in your own work.

2   The Census of India of 2001 provides the following numbers: Total Persons: 1,028,610,328; Hindus: 827,578,868; Muslims: 138,188,240; Christians: 24,080,016; Sikhs: 19,215,730; Buddhists: 7,955,207; Jains: 2,177,398; Other: 6,639,626; http://www.censusindia.gov.in/Tables_Published/C-Series/C-Series_link/c15_india.pdf. Information on religious populations from the Census of India of 2011 has not been released at the time of this writing.

3   S. Raj, "The Quest," p. 14.

4   Direct quotations are from Raj, "The Quest," p. 15.

5   Critical thinking and comparison in relation to textbooks is a theme of Steven W. Ramey's engaging article in which he constructively promotes the use of a textbook in the classroom, "Critiquing Borders: Teaching About Religions in a Postcolonial World," *Teaching Theology and Religion* 9:4 (2006): 211–20, esp. p. 213.

6   http://millenniumindicators.un.org/unsd/methods/m49/m49regin.htm

7   http://www.saarc-sec.org/SAARC-Charter/5/ (Afghanistan joined in 2007).

8   The official policy of a state religion in the South Asian countries of Bhutan (Buddhism) and Pakistan (Islam) is a modern development.

9   Diana L. Eck, *Darsan: Seeing the Divine Image in India*, 2nd ed., Chambersburg, PA: Anima Books, 1985, p. 24.

10 Definition of "celvam" (which is the Tamil for Selva) in the *Tamil Lexicon*, p. 1610, http://dsal.uchicago.edu/cgi-bin/philologic/getobject.pl?c.5:1:3314.tamillex

11 Selva J. Raj and Corinne G. Dempsey, eds., *Popular Christianity in India: Riting between the Lines*, Albany, NY: SUNY Press, 2002. Selva J. Raj and William P. Harman, eds., *Dealing with Deities: The Ritual Vow in South Asia*, Albany, NY: SUNY Press, 2006. Knut A. Jacobsen and Selva J. Raj, eds., *South Asian Christian Diaspora*, Surrey, UK: Ashgate, 2008. Corinne G. Dempsey and Selva J. Raj, eds., *Miracle as Modern Conundrum in South Asian Religious Traditions*, Albany, NY: SUNY Press, 2009. Selva J. Raj and Corinne G. Dempsey, *Sacred Play: Ritual Levity and Humor in South Asian Religions*, Albany, NY: SUNY Press, 2010.

12 A brief history of the original conference is at http://www.luc.edu/csri/about.shtml; current information on the CSRI is at http://www.luc.edu/csri/index.shtml

13 Tracy Pintchman and Corinne G. Dempsey are co-editing a volume entitled *Sacred Matters: Material Religion in South Asian Traditions*, based on the 2006 Conference theme, "Material Religions in South Asian Traditions," and Karen Pechilis and Barbara Holdrege are co-editing *Refiguring the Body: Embodiment in South Asian Religions*, based on the 2007 Conference theme, "Religion and the Body in Indian Religions."

14 His presentation, lightly edited, was entitled "The Tie that Binds: Connecting Biography and Ethnography" and was published with other papers from the panel in a special section of *Method & Theory in the Study of Religion* 21 (2009): 73–77; the quote is from p. 73.

15 Raj, "The Tie that Binds," pp. 74–75.

16 I cannot recall the date of his presentation, and it may have been presented at a session under the Society of Hindu-Christian Studies, which holds its meeting conjointly with the AAR meeting, http://www.hcstudies.org/about.html. Selva discusses the reactions he received from scholars when he suggested that the Religion in South

Asia Section of the AAR ought to include papers on Indian Christianity in its conference offerings in his essay, "The Quest for a Balanced Representation of South Asian Religions in World Religions Textbooks," p. 15.

17 The quotations in this paragraph are from Raj, "The Tie that Binds," pp. 75 and 77, respectively.

18 Jonathan Z. Smith, "A Twice-Told Tale: The History of the History of Religions' History," in Jonathan Z. Smith, *Relating Religion: Essays in the Study of Religion*, Chicago, IL: University of Chicago Press, 2004, pp. 362–74; pp. 362–3.

19 Ibid., esp. pp. 366–7, 369, 371; quotation on p. 372. Smith discusses aspects of the distinctive ideals of the Enlightenment and the counter-Enlightenment as contributing sources for the two understandings of religion, and he stresses the relevance of modern linguistic theory.

20 Ibid., p. 366.

21 Selva J. Raj, "Transgressing Boundaries, Transcending Turner: The Pilgrimage Tradition at the Shrine of St. John de Britto," in Selva J. Raj and Corinne G. Dempsey (eds.) *Popular Christianity in India: Riting between the Lines*, Albany, NY: SUNY Press, 2002, pp. 85–111; p. 87.

22 Selva J. Raj, "Public Display, Communal Devotion: Procession at a South Indian Catholic Festival," in Knut Jacobsen, ed., *South Asian Religions on Display: Religious Processions in South Asia and in the Diaspora*, New York: Routledge South Asian Religion Series, 2008, pp. 77–91; p. 83.

23 Selva J. Raj, "Shared Vows, Shared Space, and Shared Deities: Vow Rituals among Tamil Catholics in South India," in Selva J. Raj and William P. Harman (eds.) *Dealing with Deities: The Ritual Vow in South Asia*, Albany, NY: SUNY Press, 2006, pp. 43–64; p. 56.

24 Selva J. Raj, "The Tie that Binds," p. 74.

25 Selva J. Raj, "Transgressing Boundaries, Transcending Turner," p. 106.

26 Selva J. Raj, "Ammachi: The Mother of Compassion," in Karen Pechilis (ed.) *The Graceful Guru: Hindu Female Gurus in India and the United States*, New York: Oxford University Press, 2004, pp. 204–18; p. 210.

27 Ibid., p. 209.

28 Ibid., p. 213.

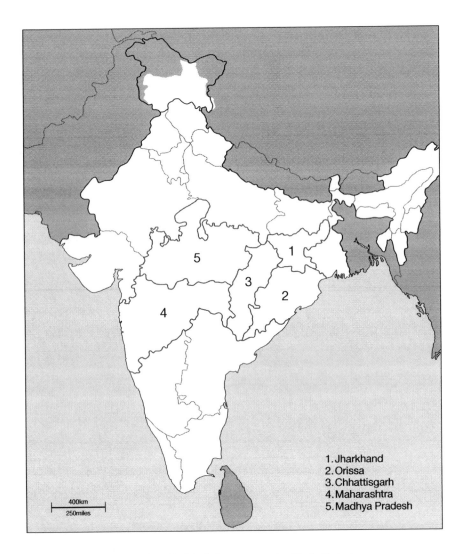

1. Jharkhand
2. Orissa
3. Chhattisgarh
4. Maharashtra
5. Madhya Pradesh

400km
250miles

Map 1 Prominent places in Tribal Religions as practiced in India today

1   Tribal religions in India

Practicing tradition today

Joseph Marianus Kujur

Introduction

The terms tribes, indigenous people, Adivasis, or the original settlers of the land
are often synonymously used for what are believed to be the earliest populations in India, despite conceptual problems. Most commonly, the generic term
for the religions of the tribes in India is "Adi," which literally means "beginning."
Defining the religions of tribals, Ram Dayal Munda says,

> By Adi-dharam we mean the basis, the roots, the beginnings (*adi*) of the reli-
> gious beliefs of the Adivasis, the first settlers of India. Such beliefs have been
> variously known as: animism, animistic religion, primitivism, primitive reli-
> gion, aboriginal religion, nature religion, *adivasi* or *janjati dharam, sarna
> dharam, sari dharam, sansari dharam, jahera dharam,* bongaism, etc.[1]

The Indian tribes, the indigenous people of the land (the widely used term for
this is "autochthonous"—"of the land"), are believed to be the earliest settlers in
the Indian peninsula. They are called "Adivasis" in some parts of India, which
means "original inhabitants." In spite of the diversity among tribes in India, most
of them follow the traditional faith and thus have a similar pattern of religious
beliefs and practices, which is very different from that of the non-tribes. Since
there are innumerable tribal traditions, the focus here is on some major traditions
in central and eastern India.

At the outset of this chapter, three assumptions need to be clarified: first, tribals,
although demographically non-dominant in India, are culturally distinct from
non-tribal groups and are threatened to be assimilated by dominant traditions;
second, rather than their characterization by homogeneity, tribes are marked by
their diversity and pluralism, and hence there are as many tribal religions in India
as there are tribes; and third, religion is only one of the many aspects of tribal
identity. Language, territoriality, social organization, economy, cultural ethos,
philosophy, worldview, political consciousness, arts and aesthetics, are other
aspects of their identity.

When the British ruled India as a colony, they tried to classify information about the tribals by conducting censuses in tribal areas. J. A. Bains, the
Commissioner of the Census of 1891, classified in the report the castes according

to their traditional occupation. He included a subheading called "Forest Tribes" under the category of "Agricultural and Pastoral Castes." The number of tribals who were put in the category of "Forest Tribes" was estimated to be nearly 16 million during the census. In the Census Report of 1901, they were classified as "Animists" and in 1911 as "tribal animists or people following tribal religion." In the Census Report of 1921, they were specified as "Hill and Forest Tribes" and their number was estimated to be 16 million. The Government of India Act of 1935 designated the tribal population as "Backward Tribes." However, in the Census Report of 1941, they were classified as "Tribes" only and their total population was estimated to be 24.7 million.

In contemporary times, the term tribe, according to Western writers, generally means "an ethnic group, geographically isolated or semi isolated, identified with one particular territory and having distinct social, economic and cultural traditions and practices." There are no criteria in the Constitution to define and specify the Scheduled Tribes. According to Article 36(25) of the Constitution, Scheduled Tribes means "such tribes or tribal communities or parts of or groups within such tribes or tribal communities as are deemed under Article 342 to be Scheduled Tribes for the purposes of this Constitution." There is also provision in the law to authorize the Parliament to include or exclude from the list of Scheduled Tribes "any tribal community or part thereof in any State or Union Territory." The concept of a tribe, in the post-independence period, has undergone a change from that of a political unit of olden days to a group of people identified with poverty and backwardness.[2] The tribal population of the country, as per the 2001 census, was 84.3 million, constituting 8.2 percent of the total population of India. More than half of the Scheduled Tribe population was concentrated in the states of Madhya Pradesh, Chhattisgarh, Maharashtra, Orissa, Jharkhand and Gujarat.[3]

Tribal religions in India: Identity

Classification has been a major issue in understanding tribal populations. Sir Herbert Risley classified the Indian population into seven racial types, of which the three fundamental races are Dravidian, Mongoloid and Indo-Aryan. The other four secondary races are Cytho-Dravidian, Aryo-Dravidian, Mongolo-Dravidian and Pre-Dravidian. J. H. Hutton is of the view that Negrito races were the original occupants of India although the Negroid was absent from Risley's classification. According to the classification of the Indian people by Hutton, Guha and Majumdar, there are six main races with nine subtypes, namely the Negrito; the Proto-Australoid; the Mongoloid—Palaeo-Mongoloids, Tibeto-Mongoloids; the Mediterranean—Palaeo-Mediterranean, Mediterranean, Oriental; the Western Brachycephalis—Alpinoid, Dinaric, Armenoid; and the Nordic. B. S. Guha, in 1952, summed up his conclusions as regards the racial composition of tribal India in terms of first, Negrito strains, such as the Kadar, the Irula and the Paniyan of South India with frizzly hair; second, the Proto-Australoid group to which the tribes of Middle India belong; third, the Brachycephalic Mongoloids of North Eastern India with typical features of the face and eye; and a slightly different Mongoloid type with medium stature, high head and medium nose living in Brahmaputra valley. Majumdar, however, does not support the theory of an ancient Negrito strain in India as he finds no evidence for it.[4]

Taking a lead from the above classifications, Verma observes that the tribes in India can be broadly classified into three stocks, namely the Negritos, the Mongoloids and the Mediterranean. The Negritos, believed to be the most ancient inhabitants of the Indian Peninsula, have almost disappeared. Their traces are found among the Onge, the Great Andamanese, the Sentinelese, and the Jarwa tribes of the Andaman and Nicobar Islands, and also among the Kadar, the Irula and the Paniyan tribes in Kerala. They can be identified by their dark skin, curly hair, broad nose and medium height.

The Mongoloids are represented by the tribes of the Sub-Himalayan region. They may be further divided into two categories, namely, the Palaeo Mongoloids and the Tibeto Mongoloids. The Palaeo Mongoloids are represented by the tribes of Assam, Meghalaya, Mizoram, Nagaland and Manipur. The Tibeto Mongoloids are represented by the tribes of Sikkim and Arunachal Pradesh. They are believed to have migrated from Tibet. They belong to the Monkhmer and Tibeto-Burmese language families.

The third group of tribes, identified as the Mediterranean people, form a bulk of the tribal population in India. They are generally known as the Dravidians. However, Dravidian is also a name of the linguistic family spoken by these people. The tribes of the Dravidian stock, such as the Gonds, the Kandhs and others, are found in the Chotanagpur Plateau, the Rajmahal Hills region, the Aravalli ranges, the Central Vindhyachal, the Deccan Plateau region and in the Nilgiri Hills. Some of these groups are found in Bangladesh also. The Dravidian language in south India has Tamil, Telugu, Malayalam and Kannada as its repre-sentatives. In Central India traces of Dravidian language are found among the Oraons, the Gonds, the Mundas, the Malers, the Khonds and some other tribes. There are two stocks of the Dravidians: firstly, the Kolarians who speak a dialect called Mundari, and secondly, the Dravidians proper whose languages are repre-sented by Tamil, Telugu, Malayalam and Kannada. The Mundas, the Santhals, the Oraons and other tribes inhabiting Chotanagpur Plateau region belong to the Kolarian stock.[5]

While a four-caste structure is the hallmark of the Hindu society, the tribals do not fit into the caste system. Due to factors such as the tribals' isolation in hills and forests, their subsistence-level agriculture, and their lack of contact with dominant cultures, they are widely viewed as economically and culturally back-ward people vis-à-vis the so-called advanced and cultured or civilized society in India.[6] However, tribals themselves identify with their own distinctive religious and cultural beliefs and practices.

The origin of the tradition—The Oraon myth

In the beginning there was water everywhere. Hence, there was consultation of the heavenly court, including Dharmes (Supreme Being of the Oraon Tribe), old

Mother Sita (Consort of Dharmes), and Mahado (Manifestation of Dharmes), on how to make the earth. A maid-servant was giving a massage to Mother's body and in the process some dirt came out. A Golden Kilkila (kingfisher bird) was created out of the dirt to go to the subterranean world in search of the seed of the earth. The Kilkila brought the seed of the earth. The earth was formed by churning the mud in the seven seas and sixteen currents. Sita asked Dharmes to take a walk on the earth. Dharmes went out on the back of the Hansraj horse. Sita asked Dharmes to make human beings. However, when Dharmes made the clay figures, the Hansraj horse trampled them. In order to guard the clay figures Dharmes made two dogs called Chaonra-Bhaonra and Lili-Bhuli. When the figures were dried, life was blown into the clay figures. Dharmes made humans and other beings. Dharmes provided food for everyone. As human beings multiplied they started searching for their own food. Dharmes went hunting with the falcon called Bhandi-Besra and the Chaonra-Bhaonra dogs. He found human excreta everywhere and was disgusted. Human beings were indulging in polluting the earth. Hence, Dharmes sent a Rain of Fire for seven days and seven nights and destroyed everything.

During the Rain of Fire Sita hid Bhaya-Bahin (brother and sister) in her locks and they were saved. Dharmes again sent rain to carry away the ashes and the earth was flooded with water. Sita asked him to plough. He did so and hence the flood became rivers. God felt hungry but there was nothing to eat as he had destroyed everything. Sita told him about Bhaya-Bahin in the lowland field. Dharmes went to find them along with his dogs. Dharmes brought them home where they grew up. Sita asked Dharmes to teach them some profession. Dharmes sent them to Mahado, who had an axe for clearing the forest. Mahado created day and night and gave them seeds of grain, corn and bottle gourd. When the crops were attacked by insects, Dharmes sent them to Mahado to perform the *Danda-Katta* ceremony to neutralize the effects of the Evil Eye and Evil Mouth. This "splitting the branch ceremony," also known as *Bhelwaphari* (splitting the Bhelwa branch) and *Palkansna* (breaking the teeth), is a ritual sacrifice exclusively for the Supreme Being. Then Bhaya-Bahin were taught to prepare rice beer. When they slept at night with a log between them they were like brother and sister. But when under the influence of rice beer, Dharmes removed the log and they acted like husband and wife. Hence procreation started.[7]

Primal vision of cosmos and human

The myths of the tribes reveal the primal vision of cosmos and human beings. The "Man" in the myth of origin is not an individual. He is the Man, representative of all mankind. The emerging message is the harmony between the Supreme Being, human beings and the world/nature, which is the foundation of the tribal worldview. In the myth there is also a process of creation, destruction and restoration. There is a promotion of ecological concerns. The genesis myth of the Oraon is similar to those of the Munda, Kharia, Ho, Santhal and hundreds of other tribes in India irrespective of their diverse manifestations. All the myths invariably reveal the Supreme Being as all goodness, omnipotent and powerful. He is the creator, sustainer and destroyer. The catechesis is that he should be revered and worshipped. It is believed that the Supreme Being himself has instituted marriage, family and community and hence they are sacred and their sacredness has to be maintained. The Supreme Being also teaches human beings the art of living.

The myth of origin manifests the unmanifest. However, the manifest remains unqualified. It is expressed only metaphorically in terms of primordial water, which is a symbol of chaos and death for tribals. Kullu interprets the primordial water in the Kharia myth of origin as a source of crab, which symbolizes the presence of life in the very midst of death. In a similar way, spirits, humans and animals are only creatures and creators of the second order and are not themselves omniscient and omnipotent.[8]

The tribal worldview has no gap between knowledge and existence. Life is understood in its entirety. The knowledge of the Supreme Being, the world and human beings' existence are understood as a whole and not as separate entities. The universal knowability is believed to be the prerogative of the transcendent Supreme Being. The tribal myths of origin reveal that the transcendent Supreme Being is the ultimate source of human knowledge and the humans and creatures are his collaborators. Saraswati is of the opinion that humanity is not unique in the possession of knowledge, as the primordial knowledge at the beginning of creation came to human beings from birds and animals.[9] Different tribal myths describe the creatures' part in creating the world. There is collaboration of creatures, such as crab, bird, earthworm, tortoise etc., cooperating with the Supreme Being in the sacred task of creation of the earth. However, the role of the Creator and creatures is clear. The Supreme Being is the creator, the creatures only cooperate. In the Oraon myth of origin the bird, dogs, horses, earthworm, locusts, etc. are collaborators. The characters of the myths are from the invisible and visible world of nature.

Outlook of the tribal religions

The tribal religions have some challenging aspects. For instance, despite being a relatively egalitarian society with equality between men and women, most of the tribal religions do not permit the presence of married women in their traditional place of worship, which is called "Sarna" or "Jaher" in central India. Similarly, the ritual priesthood is restricted to male members of the community. A woman as a general norm cannot be the religious head of a tribe in a village. Oftentimes, tribal religion is also associated with witchcraft or black magic. These are some of the challenging issues with regards to the universality of the tradition. However, the human values that the tribal religions in India promote are universal in nature. Communitarianism, respect and reverence for nature, collective consciousness in decision making processes and day-to-day responsibilities, etc. are the most valued universal features the tribal religions promote.

Distinction between tribal and other traditions

Tribal epistemology

Experience is the starting point to analyze the hermeneutics of the tribal religious consciousness. Oral tradition as encapsulated in the traditional myths is the foundation of tribal epistemology. There is no dichotomization and compartmentalization of tribal religion and culture (that is, separation between or isolation of religion and culture), and they are inseparably interwoven with their beliefs and practices, rites and rituals, and signs and symbols. The tribal religion is devoid of abstract dogmas and doctrines. It has no written scriptures as in other established religions like Christianity, Hinduism and Islam. Tribals have traditional myths to unravel the mystery of the supernatural, cosmos and origin. Their oral tradition as a crystallized body of collective knowledge is transmitted from one generation to another over centuries. Myth is an entry into the unthought and unthinkable. As a vehicle, myth takes one from the visible to the invisible, from the thought and thinkable to the unthought and unthinkable, from the seen to the unseen. Myth, according to Mundu, is the "story of life in general and human life in particular."[10] The myth at once takes us to primordial times and makes us challenge the present understanding of the human condition. Myths and rites are valid here and now, and they are given for all times to come.[11] The myths of creation, destruction in the Rain of Fire, restoration and propagation of life, division of time, origin and purpose of marriage, sickness, sacrifice, organization of the community, etc. all manifest existential realities of life.

Holistic spirituality

The spirituality of tribals can be understood in terms of their relationships with nature, one another, and the supernatural. Their relationship with nature (land, forest, water) is marked by a symbiosis. This relationship is harmonious and accommodative and not exploitative and oppressive. For instance, when they cut trees they cut them in such a way that new shoots come up soon and the species is not destroyed. Similarly, their traditional hunting takes place at a time when there is no breeding season for the animals. There is no rampant and indiscreet hunting of the animals. There is co-existence and no subjugation. Since the notion of ownership of land is collective, natural resources are non-commodifiable, non-transferable and non-saleable. There is collectivity in the traditional economic structure of the tribes and not individualism, thereby promoting cooperation and decentralization.

The central values of the tribal social organization are egalitarianism, man–woman relative equality, dignity of labour, communitarianism, mutual sharing and village cooperation. The traditional political relationship is characterized by self-rule, participatory and democratic governance, and decision by consensus. The religious relationship of the tribes is marked by their sense of harmony with the divine, community and creation. This triangular communion is the hallmark of tribal religions in India.

Similarities with other traditions

Belief in the supernatural

Belief in the supernatural is one of the most common beliefs of different faiths, not only of South Asia but across the world.

Contrary to the popular notion that tribals are polytheists, most of the tribal communities in India believe in one Supreme Being, who is called by various names by different tribes. The Supreme Being is called Dharmes in the Oraon religion, Singbonga in the Munda religion, Ponmesor in the Kharia religion and Thakur Jiu in the Santhal religion. He is also the creator of life—spirit, human, animal and plant. The Supreme Deity is friend and father to the good and the invisible guardian of law and morality. He is interested in the welfare of his creatures. God is the giver of knowledge and wisdom. He teaches the first human couple how to work, cultivate, take care of the crops, worship, lead a moral life and ward off evil spirits. The tribal God is believed to transcend and control all other gods and ghosts, and supernatural powers. Although their Supreme Deity is named after the sun (Biri-Belas/Sun King in the Oraon tribe), the Deity is not simply identified with the sun and tribal worship cannot be simply equated with nature worship as many would like to do.[12] The tribal God is above all created beings.[13]

Immortality of soul and the spirit-world

Tribals believe in the immortality of the soul. They believe that in the afterlife the soul requires food and other materials for sustenance. They believe that humans, non-human beings, animals and plants have souls. In the tribal worldview there are three kinds of spirits: the benevolent spirits, called *manita bonga*s or *deota*s; the malevolent spirits, known as *banita bonga*s; and the neutral spirits. The first category of spirits is believed to be good by nature. The second class of spirits are bad, who are appeased and propitiated. The third kind of spirits can do good or evil. They have to be kept tamed. The ancestor spirits, village spirits, class spirits, clan spirits and household spirits are *manita*. The *banita* spirits are of those dying unnatural death and are not worshipped but are only propitiated by the witch-finders.

The criteria of communion and salvation

Communion with the divine

In the hierarchy of the supernatural beings spirits do not occupy a place as high as that of the Supreme Being. Hence, the spirits are only propitiated and placated but not worshipped. Thus in the tribal religion the notion of liberation is understood as communion with the Supreme Being in the afterlife. Eternal happiness for the tribal is a possibility only in and through the Supreme Being and their ancestors. This is the final state of communion, liberation and fulfillment tribals hope for.

Communion with community

There are two dimensions of communion in the tribal worldview—a communion with the community while on earth; and a communion with ancestors after death. A communion with the tribe implies that one is in harmony with the society. If a tribal is perceived to be a violator of the norms of the community resulting in disharmony, rupture and disintegration, one is ostracized or excommunicated from the tribe. Moreover, a tribal's communion with the community while on earth determines whether one will be in communion with the ancestors after death. If a person dies in a state of ex-communication, one is considered to be "outside" the tribe, and by virtue of one's ostracism one cannot get a communal burial.

Communion with nature

Tribes are symbiotically related with nature. There is a relationship of harmony, respect and reverence between human and nature. They believe that natural resources—land, forest and water—are a gracious gift of the Supreme Being of which they are stewards and not owners. Hence, social responsibility in the preservation, protection and promotion of the earth is emphasized. Minz points out that by space it is meant that everything is integrally related to one another. Hence, no one can cut a tree without supplementing its loss. No animal can be hunted and killed indiscriminately. Animals should be hunted outside the

Figure 1.1 Celebration of the Feast of Karam in which the Karam branch from the Karam tree symbolizing the Karam deity is venerated. Photo by Dr Alex Ekka.

breeding season and not indiscriminately. The principle behind such a practice is that the balance between human and nature has to be maintained. The attitude of reciprocity avoids confrontation and subjugation. Their belief in the spirit-world defines their "reciprocity" and the concept of nature as their "relative" facilitating to "treat their relatives with respect, and deal with them justly be they other human beings, trees, animals and insects, water, air or sunshine."[14]

Tribal religions of India: Practice

Religious functionaries and heads of the families perform various sacrifices during festivals and rites of passage. The religious heads known as Pahan in the Munda tribe and Mahato in the Oraon tribe are required only when the sacrifice is offered on behalf of the community. They are considered as mediators between the supernatural beings and community. These religious functionaries are not as prominent as the priests of the Hindu, Muslim and Christian communities. The heads of the families and any adults can validly offer sacrifices at the level of the family. The popular forms of religion are in practice. There is no real issue about the tribal religions being elite or popular. The folk traditions of the tribes continue in everyday life. However, in the last few years there have been efforts by some groups to formalize the traditional religion.

The *Danda-Katta* ritual is performed by any elder and not necessarily by the priest before important undertakings, such as ploughing, sowing, harvesting and hunting expeditions. The purpose of the ritual is to thank Dharmes, to beg and implore him for mercy and blessing, and to obtain God's protection against the effects of the evil eye and the evil mouth. While breaking the egg, which is the symbol of the purity of the gift, the prayer in Oraon is recited by the village priest or the head of the family in the following words:

> God, Dharmes above,
> The Elders or Panches here below!
> You, Dharmes are our Father.
> Take care of whichever spirits we have overlooked!
> Our eyes do not see, Your eyes see.
> You alone are Father,
> Do Thou take care (restrain them)![15]

Some of the materials used during the ritual are highly symbolic. The egg is a sacrificial life without an opening; hence it is a pure gift. The unbleached rice is also considered to be pure. The *bhelwa* (botanical name *Sembacarpes anacardium*) twig is split into two parts, the first symbolizing the sky and the second, the earth. Its juice is a poisonous oil and it is believed that it can destroy evil. In day-to-day experience some people are observed to be allergic even to the shade of the *bhelwa* tree and hence they avoid going under it. The *bhelwa*, which is a tree celebrated in myth, exists in some parts of India, and is considered to be pure and holy. During the *Danda-Katta* ceremony a diagram with seven arches is constructed on the ground. The seven arches of the diagram represent the seven corners of the world. Three colors are used to make the diagram and each of them is significant. The red, black and white are the three principal colors of the rainbow, the most potent weapon of the tribals' bow, to strike the enemy with. The entire diagram is the universe, which represents God's omnipresence. The Supreme Being is the benevolent Spirit. Everything good is attributed to Dharmes and the ancestors. The evil eye and the evil mouth are considered to be the sources of all evil. The *Danda-Katta* ceremony, which is believed to be divinely instituted, is meant to ward off the evil eye and the evil mouth.[16]

Rites of passage

The initiation rite

The initiation rite is popularly called *chathi*. It is performed, firstly, for purifying the mother who is considered defiled by conception and childbirth; secondly, for naming the child; and, thirdly, for officially incorporating the child into the tribe. The child in some tribes is believed to be a reincarnation of his/her grandparents. A male child is considered to be a reflection of his grandfather and a female child that of her grandmother. As part of the ritual, a leaf cup with rice beer is taken. A village elder drops three grains of rice into the leaf cup while pronouncing the name of an ancestor whose name he wants to give to the child. If the three grains floating on the water touch one another, the child is named after the ancestor in whose name the grains were dropped.

The marriage ceremony

In the first type of marriage among some tribes, the marriage ceremony takes place in the house of the bride. In the second type, the marriage is celebrated in the house of the bridegroom. At the marriage site of the bride, various symbols of a new house, including a curry stone, a yoke, a small bundle of hay, etc., are kept on a new mat. There is marking with vermillion by the boy on the bride's forehead. As soon as this is done, water is sprinkled on the couple while invoking the divine blessing. There are elaborate rituals of marriage, but the main message is that there is an alliance made between a boy and a girl and also between their villages and relatives.

Ritual of the dead

Some tribal communities in India perform double obsequies for their dead. According to Dehon, there are two main rituals of the deceased: firstly, calling back the light shade of the departed into the house; and secondly, the *koman* or the reuniting of the heavy shade with the shades of their ancestors; both rituals are reminiscent of the tribe's communion with the ancestors and the Supreme Being.[17] The bodies of those who died before the sprouting of rice plants are burnt. Those who die later are temporarily buried. In the beginning of January, all the bones of the persons who have died in the course of the year are carried

Figure 1.2 Unmarried girls breaking their three days' fast to mark the Karam feast, praying for good husbands, their motherhood, protection of their brothers and for prosperity. Photo by Dr Alex Ekka.

in a procession with singing and dancing and then are consigned to their respective clan ossuaries. The feast is called *jangtopa* or *hargari* (burying the bones). Strangers, children and people dying a violent death by murder, suicide and drowning, and women in childbirth, are not given a second burial in the clan ossuary.

Authoritative forms in the tradition

Tribal religions are strongly communitarian. Hence, the community's decision by consensus is the general norm and authoritative form in the tradition. People are the text and the context. The *Sarna* (sacred grove) is the sacred space for them where they perform their communal rituals. They have no structures like temples, mosques and churches for their worship. The entire universe is the worshipping place for them. Customary laws transmitted from one generation to another by word of mouth are their authoritative forms.

Tribal religions in India are not hierarchical. They are relatively less institutional than other traditions. In spite of charismatic and prophetic leaders in different tribes at different points in history, communitarian leadership is viewed with dignity and respect. The duties of the tribal religious functionaries are, firstly, to sacrifice to the Supreme Being and spirits in the name of the community so as to be saved from distress; and, secondly, to bring the much desired harmony in the universe among human beings, nature and other created beings. It may appear that tribal priesthood is as hierarchical as in other religions. However, there is a relative egalitarianism in tribal religion in the sense that the priest represents the tribal religion of his village and that he does not take single-handedly any decision on religious matters. Every religious decision is taken by consensus and from that point of view the priest is there only to facilitate the smooth functioning of the religion rather than for asserting his authority. Priests are believed to be divinely elected to transmit the ritual knowledge to the tribe. Every tribe has its own village priest. Among some of the major tribes priesthood is hereditary and is confined to the family of the first settlers of a village. Only married men are entitled to occupy the office of the priest. In case the priest does not have a male issue, a priest can be elected from some other clan from among the first settlers. A tribal priest is responsible for the religious activities of the village and offers sacrifices to the deities in the name of the village.[18] The head of the tribal family can also offer sacrifice to the household spirits.

Tribal religions: Current approaches

Identity of tribal Christians and Sarna people

The "tribal" identity of the tribal peoples who have become Christians has been challenged at regular intervals by a section of the Sarna people, who still adhere to their traditional faith. The Hindutva forces (Hindu nationalist groups), while supporting the Sarna challenge to the Christians' tribal identity, claim that the tribals are indeed Hindus. The Sarnas, however, in the systematization of their prayer assert that they are distinct from the Hindus. The tribal Christians also assert their tribal identity. The Oraons argue that there is no loss of the Oraon identity in dropping one's traditional Oraon religion either individually or collectively. In spite of a change in their religious identity the Oraons remain "Oraons." In this regard Xaxa observes that despite the fact that tribes are in transition, as in the case of Oraons who speak various tongues and practice different religions, have variety of occupations, etc., they continue being Oraons "in some socially significant sense" without losing their distinctive identities.[19]

Problem of suffering and evil

The world of tribal religions appears at first sight to be a world of magic and sorcery. However, the concept of divine reward and punishment also greatly influences the experience of evil in its various forms. Tribals believe that mystical powers or curses can affect their crops, animals and family. Natural disasters seem more devastating if they are believed to be either the result of some malicious will or evidence of divine displeasure. Some of the traditional practices to ward off evil are as follows: *Deonraism* is the practice of divination performed by a *deonra* who is a specialist in witch-detection. *Niksari* is a ritual in which the *deonras,* equipped with the iron-cone called *singhi* and accompanied by two of his pupils, carrying a lamp, two antelope horns and an earthen pot, go to the house of the votary. The ritual that follows is performed until the evil spirit is subdued. *Kansphandi* is a ritual performed when the same sickness keeps recurring despite *Niksari.* The Oraons take the recurrence of the same sickness as a foul play by the witch. In such moments the *Ojha* (witch doctor) works throughout the night. Once he detects the witch the whole village goes to her house, abuses her and even kills her. *Rog Khedna* literally means driving the sickness. They attribute small regular ailments to alien spirits. The women assemble with an old mat, old broom and broken pots. They go to the border of the village to "throw the sickness out" of the village. *Jharni* is the "sweeping out" of the small sicknesses from the body of the sufferer.

However, witch-finding and *deonraism* is not the only way of dealing with suffering and evil. Tribals offer sacrifices in times of festivals and sicknesses, suffering and calamities. They offer prayers and sacrifices at the following festivals: *Sarhul*—the feast of the mystical marriage of the Sun god (Bhagwan) with the Goddess earth (Dharti-mai); *Kadleta*—to prevent the animals from destroying the crops; *Khalihani*—feast previous to the threshing of the paddy; *Hariyari*—to ward off sicknesses and insects that could attack the crops; and *Nowakhani*—feast of the new rice.

Figure 1.3 Tribals dancing to the drum beats and seasonal songs. Life is a celebration for them. Photo by Dr Alex Ekka.

Current academic approaches

The anthropological and sociological approaches to the study of tribal religions in India were significant even before the independence of the country. Initially tribal religions were described as animistic. Some thinkers conceived of tribal religion as a form of Hinduism. Risley, for instance, as early as 1916, found it difficult to demarcate between Hinduism and animism. Indian sociologist G. S. Ghurye, too, suggested that primitive tribes of India were part of the Hindu social structure. He went to the extent of calling tribes "backward Hindus."[20] N. K. Bose in his paper "The Hindu Method of Tribal Absorption" (1941) also speaks of the impact of the Hindu great traditions on the Juang tribals in the state of Orissa.[21] Among the contemporary anthropologists André Béteille (1986) holds a similar position.

According to scholar Karma Oraon, in the context of central India the concepts of bongaism (Majumdar 1950) and sacred complex (Vidyarthi 1963) were developed while studying the primitive tribes of the region. The concept of bongaism means "a power that pervades all space." Further, it is believed that bongas (spirits) are indefinite and impersonal and can take any shape or form. This power is said to give life to all animals and plants, to bring rain, storm, flood, cold, etc. It is also believed to destroy evils, stop epidemics, cure diseases, to give currents to rivers, and strength to tigers, bears and wolves. Oraon points out that Vidyarthi (1963), while studying the Maler, proposed that the essence of tribal religion can be known through the organization of their sacred complex. According to him sacred performances were observed at different sacred centers by the sacred specialists and people of the tribe. S. C. Roy made a study of the Oraon tribe as early as 1915. His books *The Oraons of Chota Nagpur: Their History, Economic Life and Social Organization* (1984 [1915]) and *The Oraon Religion and Customs* (1928) describe religious beliefs and traditions of the Oraons.[22]

In contemporary times tribal thinkers have tried to spell out what their religion is and their articulations in many ways assert their distinct identity. John Lakra (1997) in his paper "Rewriting Tribal Anthropology" debunks the notion of labelling tribal religion as animistic and argues that they have a religious system that reveals their monotheistic beliefs which have so far been overlooked by anthropologists.[23] Munda[24] and Munda and Manki[25] in their books drive home the point about the typical religious beliefs and practices of the tribals with special reference to the Munda tribe. Anthropologists like Virginius Xaxa,[26] Agapit Tirkey[27] and Boniface Tirkey[28] also subscribe to the idea of distinct identity of the tribals with their own values, norms, beliefs and practices.

Discussion questions

1 What are the main characteristics of tribal religions in India?
2 How is tribal religion in India different from other religious traditions?
3 What are the similarities between tribal religion and other traditions in India?

Key terms

Ādivāsi—"Adi" literally means ancient times or beginning, and "vasi" settler. Adivasis claim to be the original settlers of the land.

Bīri-Belas—This Oraon expression is used for the Supreme Being, which literally means "sun king." This symbolizes the power and the glory of the Supreme Being. The Oraons are not sun-worshippers. However, they see the image of the Supreme Deity behind the sun.

Bongās—Bongas are spirits that can take any shape or form. This power is believed to pervade all space.

Ḍaṇḍa-kaṭṭa—This ritual is performed by an elder before any important undertakings, such as agricultural activities, hunting expeditions and rites of passage. Through this ceremony the Oraon tribals invoke blessings and protection of the Supreme Being.

Deoñṛa—A deonra is a witch-doctor specializing in witch-detection and protection and cure of the victims of witchcraft.

Hāṛgaṛi—"Har" means bones and "gari" means "burying." Hence, in the annual feast of the "Burying of Bones" sometime in January, the bones of all the deceased during the course of the year, are collected, carried in a procession and are consigned to their respective clan ossuaries.

Niksāri—Niksari literally means "taking out" of the sickness from a house or a village.

Nowākhāni—This feast of the "new rice" is the last of the agricultural feasts, which is celebrated after all agricultural operations of the year are over.

Sarnā—It is a place of worship for the tribals practicing their traditional religion. This is also a generic term of tribal religions, primarily of central India.

Notes

1 Ram Dayal Munda, *Adi-Dharam: Religious Beliefs of the Adivasis of India*, Chaibasa: Sarini and Birsa, 2003, p. 3. The terms "animism" and "bongaism" refer to belief in spirits; the phrase *janjati dharam* means "tribal religion," and the other phrases translate to "traditional religion."

2 Statistical information and quotations in this and the preceding paragraph are from R. C. Verma, *Indian Tribes through the Ages*, New Delhi: Publication Division, Ministry of Information and Broadcasting, Government of India, 2002, pp. 8–10.

3 Ministry of Tribal Affairs, "The Scheduled Tribes and the Scheduled Areas," in *Annual Report 2006–07*, New Delhi: Ministry of Tribal Affairs, Government of India, 2007, p. 22.

4 Information in the paragraph is from http://www.sociologyguide.com/types-of-society/race.php

5 The information in this and the preceding two paragraphs is from Verma, *Indian Tribes*, pp. 5–6.

6 Nirmal Minz, "Tribal Identity in India," *Religion and Society* 25 (March, 1978): 70–9.

7 John Lakra, "The Genesis of Man: The Uraon Myth," *Sevartham* 9 (1984): 33–55.

8 Paulus Kullu, "Tribal Culture—Religion in Practice," *Sevartham* 18 (1993): 15–33, p. 18.

9 Baidyanath Saraswati, "Tribal Cosmogony: Primal Vision of Man and Cosmos," in B. Saraswati (ed.) *Tribal Thought and Culture*, New Delhi: Concept Publishing Company, 1991, pp. 63–79.

10 John B. Mundu, *The Ho Christian Community: Towards a New Self-Understanding as Communion*, Delhi: Media House, 2003, p. 30.

11 A. Van Exem, *The Religious System of the Munda Tribe: An Essay in Religious Anthropology*, St. Augustin: Haus Völker und Kulturen, 1982, pp. 22–3.

12 John Lakra, "Rewriting Tribal Anthropology," *Sevartham* 22 (1997): 11–28, p. 20.

13 S. C. Roy, *The Oraons of Chota Nagpur: Their History, Economic Life and Social Organization*, Ranchi: Man in India Office, 1984 [1915], p. 23.

14 Nirmal Minz, "The Adivasi Perspectives on Ecology," in Andreas Nehring (ed.) *Ecology: A Theological Response*, Madras: The Gurukul Summer Institute, 1993, pp. 67–88; p. 69.

15 This refers to people invoking the Supreme Being for protection and for taming the spirits and so that they do not harass them. This translation is from Boniface Tirkey, *Oraon Symbols*, Delhi: Vidyajyoti, 1983, p. 28.

16 Boniface Tirkey, *Oraon Symbols*; and Boniface Tirkey, *The Smiling Uraon*, Patna: Navjyoti Niketan, 1989.

17 P. Dehon, "Religion and Customs of the Uraon," in *Memoirs of the Asiatic Society of Bengal*, Vol. I, No. 9, Communicated by E. A. Gait, I. C. S., 1906, pp. 121–81.

18 A. Parapullil, "Tribal Theology," *Sevartham* 2 (1977): 27–52, p. 46.

19 V. Xaxa, "Transformation of Tribes in India," *Economic and Political Weekly* 34: 24 (June 12–18, 1999): 1519–24.

20 G. S. Ghurye, *The Scheduled Tribes*, Bombay: Popular Prakashan, 1963 [1953], p. 19.

21 N. K. Bose, "The Hindu Method of Tribal Absorption," *Science and Culture* 7 (1941): 188–94.

22 Information and quotations in this paragraph are from Karma Oraon, *The Specturm of Tribal Religion in Bihar: A Study of Continuity and Change among the Oraon of Chotanagpur*, Varanasi: Kishor Vidya Niketan, 1988, pp. 7–8.

23 John Lakra, "Rewriting Tribal Anthropology," p. 20.

24 Ram Dayal Munda, *Adi-Dharam: Religious Beliefs of the Adivasis of India*, Chaibasa: Sarini and Birsa, 2003.

25 Ram Dayal Munda and Ratansingh Manki, *Adi-Dharam: Religious Beliefs of the Adivasis of India* (Hindi), New Delhi: Rajkamal Prakashan, 2009.

26 Virginius Xaxa, *State, Society, and Tribes: Issues in Post-Colonial India*, New Delhi: Pearson Longman, 2008.

27 Agapit Tirkey, "Khalihani: Ritual and Myth" *Sevartham* 13 (1988): 17–25; Agapit Tirkey, "Hariari: The Festival of Green Paddy Plants," *Sevartham* 15 (1990): 65–74; and Agapit Tirkey, "The Origin of Evil Spirits," *Sevartham* 18 (1993): 35–9.

28 Boniface Tirkey, *Oraon Symbols*, Delhi: Vidyajyoti, 1983; and Boniface Tirkey, *The Smiling Uraon*, Patna: Navjyoti Niketan, 1989.

Recommended resources

Béteille, André. "The Concept of Tribe with Special Reference to India." *The European Journal of Sociology* 27 (1986): 297–317.

Khanna, Madhu. "Feminine Presence: The Case of Santal Tribe." In Arvind Sharma (ed.) *Women in Indian Religions*, New Delhi: Oxford University Press, 2002, pp. 201–35.

Munda, Ram Dayal. *Adi-Dharam: Religious Beliefs of the Adivasis of India.* Chaibasa: Sarini and Birsa, 2003.

Saraswati, Baidyanath. "Tribal Cosmogony: Primal Vision of Man and Cosmos." In B. Saraswati (ed.) *Tribal Thought and Culture*, New Delhi: Concept Publishing Company, 1991, pp. 63–79.

Verma, R. C. *Indian Tribes through the Ages*. New Delhi: Publication Division, Ministry of Information and Broadcasting, Government of India, 2002.

Xaxa, V. "Transformation of Tribes in India." *Economic and Political Weekly* 34:24 (June 12–18, 1999): 1519–24.

Xaxa, Virginius. *State, Society, and Tribes: Issues in Post-Colonial India.* New Delhi: Pearson Longman, 2008.

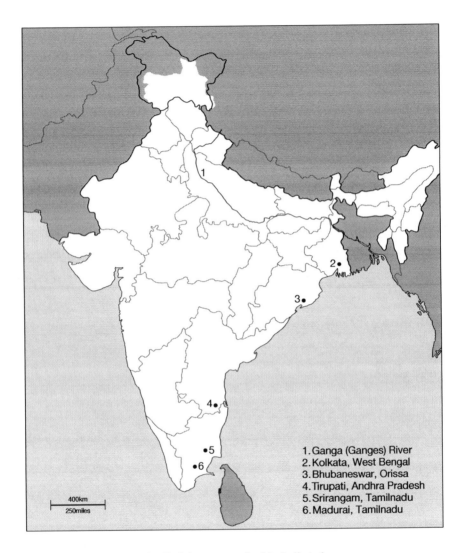

1. Ganga (Ganges) River
2. Kolkata, West Bengal
3. Bhubaneswar, Orissa
4. Tirupati, Andhra Pradesh
5. Srirangam, Tamilnadu
6. Madurai, Tamilnadu

Map 2 Prominent places in Hinduism as practiced in India today

2 Hinduism

Practicing tradition today

Vasudha Narayanan

Introduction

The word "Hindu" has been used largely since the nineteenth century and has become popular only since the twentieth century. It is used as a convenient umbrella term now, and in retrospect, for hundreds of communities and social divisions, as well as for diverse beliefs and practices of people who lived in South Asia and in many parts of the world for more than two thousand years. The term is used as an anachronism for phenomena from several millennia brought under this rubric, and serves as a contemporary label used by almost a billion people today to describe themselves and their multiple histories.

Much of what we call "Hindu" has its origins in South Asia, but people worshipping the deities and following practices which are accommodated generously by this word have lived in Southeast Asia from the beginning of the common era, and in Africa, Europe, and the Americas since the nineteenth century. Many practices associated with this tradition like meditation, worship, ritual calendar calculations, iconography, performing arts, and social divisions, as well as beliefs such as *karma* and reincarnation, are also shared with other religions that originated in South Asia such as Jainism and Buddhism. The boundaries between a few Hindu, Jain, and Sikh communities in some contexts are porous; for instance, the Buddha is sometimes revered as an incarnation of the Hindu deity Vishnu; and social divisions known as the "caste system" generally associated with the Hindu traditions are prevalent among Christians and members of other faith groups in India.

Since the twentieth century, Hindus are noted for saying: "Hinduism is more than a religion; it is a way of life." While this statement can be interpreted in multiple registers, we know that this articulates their recognition that what they think of as "religion" may not be considered under that rubric in other parts of the world. Thus, Hindus may say that their religious worldview encompasses, amongst other practices, an attention to food, song and dance, astrology and auspicious times, pilgrimage, and healing. Within the Hindu traditions, religion, art, and culture often merge seamlessly.

Hinduism: Identity

Location and numbers

Most Hindus live in South Asian countries, particularly India. About 80 percent of India's population (estimated at 1.21 billion) is estimated to be Hindu. There are, however, sizeable numbers in other countries in the region, especially Nepal and Bangladesh, as well as in Singapore and Indonesia in Southeast Asia. Large numbers have migrated since the nineteenth century to the Caribbean, Africa, Europe, and the Americas, and a sizeable number are now in the "second" diaspora, having moved from one home-location to another. Because Hinduism is not a congregational religion and Hindus are not (for the most part) affiliated to a temple for membership and regular worship, their numbers in other parts of the world remain approximations.

History

An important part of one's identity is one's perception of a shared history one may have with others. There are many histories of Hindus and Hinduism; some trace the history of the universe and in large cosmic terms, and others, at a very local, community-based level. Most Hindus know through history textbooks, and not necessarily practice, that the origins of their tradition may be projected back to the civilization that existed on the banks of the river Indus in the second (or possibly third) millennium BCE. Scholarly accounts of Indian history do not, in general, discern significant and explicit connections between the Indus Valley Civilization and Hindu practices today but do note a number of possible similarities. One such example is a seal from the Indus Valley Civilization in which a person is sitting in a position similar to one seen in the practice of yoga. The relationship between this civilization and the Indo-European people who composed the Vedas, the earliest religious texts in India, has been much debated in last few decades.[1]

Starting around 1500 BCE, and possibly earlier, four collections of texts were composed over several hundred years. These are known as the Vedas, and acknowledgement of their sanctity has long been the cornerstone of communities which we call "Hindu" in retrospect. The meaning of the term "Vedas" is not fixed. In the broadest sense, they may be all that is sacred in tradition and, to some, may represent the transformative wisdom through which one knows one's relationship with the universe and the Supreme Being. On a more local level, the term refers to four collections of poetry charged with power, sacrificial formulae, and philosophical texts known as *aranyaka* ("books to be read in the forest") and *Upanishad* ("sitting near [a teacher]"). Although most parts of the Vedas are not in daily use, some hymns are in regular use in domestic and temple rituals. Some sections of the *Upanishads* are also recited in south Indian temples, and all of them form an important foundation for the later philosophical interpretations known as *Vedanta* ("end of the Vedas").

While the Vedas are technically deemed to be the most important sacred texts, most Hindus are not well acquainted with them. The devotional lives of Hindus for about two millennia—and in some cases, much longer—have centered on deities who appear in two epics, the *Ramayana* (the story of Rama) and the *Mahabharata* ("[descendants] of the Great Bharata" or "the Great Bharata of India"), and in books called *Puranas* ("ancient lore") as well as deities who are only locally known in an area or community. The *Mahabharata*, which is said to be the longest poem in the world, contains eighteen chapters which are taken out and published as a separate treatise called the *Bhagavad Gita* ("Sacred Song" or "song of the sacred Lord"). The *Bhagavad Gita* has been one of the most beloved books for generations of educated Hindus and one of the most influential books in the traditions, but not particularly well known directly among many communities. Nevertheless, the philosophical concepts from this book are probably the best known among the Hindu traditions.

Most of the deities known who are worshipped today are connected with the epics and also with books called the *Puranas*. Although there are dozens of books in this category, about eighteen are said to be important; and there are many lists of which eighteen of the *Puranas* are most significant. While all these books, as well as the books on *dharma* or right behavior are in Sanskrit (sometimes called a "dead" language because it has not been a regularly spoken language in millennia), Hindus also revere many texts in vernacular languages and hold them to be as sacred as, if not more than, the Sanskrit ones. The epics and stories from the *Puranas* have been known and transmitted in the multiple histories articulated by Hindus in different parts of the Indian subcontinent and in many parts of the world.

Deities

Hindus believe in many manifestations of the divine, and many articulate their identity by association with a community which worships a particular deity. Thus the Vira Shaivas, who follow the teachings of Basava, a twelfth century philosopher, social reformer, and religious leader from the area known as Karnataka today, hold Shiva as the Supreme Being. The Vaishnavas—and they are subdivided into many smaller groups based on region, philosophical allegiance, language, and caste—are named so because they worship Vishnu. While most Hindus say they are monotheistic, in practice, their temples and domestic altars have multiple deities. Some say that all deities are manifestations of one Supreme Being; others say there are many, but the one they worship is the form they like best. The Supreme Being is said to be ineffable and beyond name, gender, and form by some Hindu texts. Other Hindus think of the Supreme Being as the perfect man or as a primordial mother. Yet others worship the divine one as half man, half female or as a family of deities. Divinity is perceived in many shapes and forms, human, animal, trees, and as combinations of these beings; this comes from their recognition that not only is the divine beyond gender and name, but beyond number as well. Both monotheism and polytheism, then, by some Hindu interpretations, are expressions of a finite mind. While the Supreme Being is beyond thought, most Hindus believe that s/he manifests him/herself periodically on earth to protect the good and destroy evil, a concept most famously articulated in the *Bhagavad Gita*.[2]

Among the best known deities in Hinduism are Vishnu, Shiva, Lakshmi, Parvati/Durga, Ganesha, Murugan, and Hanuman, as well as Rama and Krishna. Many Hindus think of Rama and Krishna as incarnations (*avatara*) of Vishnu; even here, however, there is no agreement, and some, like the followers of Chaitanya (fifteenth century religious leader), think that Krishna (and not Vishnu) is the Supreme God. Sometimes a deity, like Murugan, the son of Shiva and Parvati, is closely associated with people who speak a particular language (in this case, Tamil) and the culture of those people. Tamil-speaking people from India, Sri Lanka, and Malaysia hold this god (who is hardly known in northern India) as the Supreme Being and make pilgrimages to his temples.

Many Hindu deities have traveled well. Icons of Brahma, Vishnu, Shiva, Hari-Hara, Ganesha, Skanda, Nandi (a bull sacred to Shiva), Garuda (the eagle mount of Vishnu), the "nine planets" (personifications of some heavenly bodies including the sun and the moon), and other deities have been found all over Southeast Asia.

Some of the most popular stories a child will hear, the songs she will learn, or the dances she will see will be connected with two *avatara*s of Vishnu, Rama and Krishna. The story of Rama is narrated fully in the Sanskrit *Ramayana* ("the way of Rama"), an epic story composed around the fifth century BCE. The *Ramayana* has been an integral part of Hindu culture; it has been told and retold, the focus of song and dance, and the source of inspiration and consolation for centuries. Rama is married to Sita, a beautiful princess. In popular understanding, Sita is the incarnation of the Goddess Lakshmi. As Lakshmi and Vishnu are inseparable, she incarnates every time Vishnu comes down to earth. Rama is exiled because of a family intrigue; Sita and Lakshmana,

---

Krishna

Krishna is considered to be the eighth or ninth incarnation of Vishnu—depending on which text one reads—and is dearly beloved in India and in many parts of the world where the International Society of Krishna Consciousness (ISKCON, more popularly known as the Hare Krishnas) and other Hindus live. Children are told about Krishna's divine birth, his magical childhood, his mother's and foster mother's affection for him, his mischievous pranks, his dancing the autumnal moonlit nights away with the young cowherd girls he grew up with, and his philosophical counsel to his cousin and peer, Arjuna, on the battlefield. The enchanting evenings of dance are emulated in autumn in some communities in India through a folk dance called *raas* from the state of Gujarat; his battle to destroy the forces of evil are celebrated annually in south India during the festival of Deepavali in south India.

Figure 2.1 Radha-Krishna in Odissi dance. Photo taken by Vasudha Narayanan.

Rama's brother, accompany him to the forest. Here, Ravana, a king of Lanka, lusting after Sita, kidnaps her. After an epic battle, in which Rama is helped by Hanuman, a wise, divine monkey—who is also a popular deity for Hindus— Ravana is killed, and Sita returns to Rama. Rama and Sita then return home to Ayodhya and are coronated. Rama's rule of the kingdom is held to be paradigmatic, as is his filial piety, the loyalty of Sita, and the devotion and service of Hanuman. Hindus from many middle class households in northern India have copies of medieval versions of the *Ramayana* in their houses and occasionally have uninterrupted readings of the text in the Sanskrit or vernacular versions at home. Classical music, popular songs, dances, and, above all today, television shows, portray stories from his life, and many young men and women are named after characters in the epics.

Figure 2.2 Radha-Krishna icons at ISKCON temple, Alachua, Florida. Photo taken by Vasudha Narayanan.

Unlike medieval India, where most temples were sectarian—in that they held one particular deity such as Vishnu, Shiva, Durga, or their local manifestations as most significant—Hindu temples around the world frequently have an array of multiple deities. It was common practice in Southeast Asia to have Shiva, Vishnu, and manifestations of the goddess (Devi) all in the same building after the ninth century CE. We see this multiplicity in temples in most temples in Europe and the Americas. An important exception is the temple-building program of the Swaminarayan sect among immigrant "Gujarat-origin" Hindus and the Hare Krishna temples among Euro-American Hindus. While traditions relating to local goddesses like Mariamman (popular in the Indian state of Tamilnadu) are seen where indentured workers traveled (such as Guyana), by and large, many of the temples in the United States of America and Canada have pan-Hindu deities who are recognizable in many parts of the Hindu landscape. Many of the deities in south India have very local names and are seldom known by generic names such as Vishnu, Shiva, or Parvati; thus, the Goddess who reigns from her temple in Madurai is called "Meenakshi" ("she with fish-shaped eyes"). "Local" deities who are popular in the Americas include Lord Venkateswara ("Lord of the Venkata Hills"), a manifestation of Vishnu who is enshrined in dozens of temples, Murugan from Tamilnadu, as well as Ayyappan, a deity worshipped in Kerala, India.

Social divisions

One can seldom find a generic Hindu in India; Hindus belong to a caste, community, sectarian group, all of which are further subdivided along linguistic and geographic lines. However, the texts and practices of Hinduism have been mined for "universal" messages which have been disseminated as not belonging to any one religion but to all human beings. Thus, at any time, Hindus may be members of distinct community, caste, and language groups, but at other times, think of their tradition as "eternal" and "timeless."

It is said that the four classes (*varna*-s, literally, "colors") of society came from an initial cosmic sacrifice that is spoken of in the Rig Veda. Although the textual sources speak of four major classes, that is, the priestly Brahmins, royalty and warriors, merchants and producers, and finally the "servants," there are actually thousands of castes in Hinduism and other religions of India. It is not clear if the simple fourfold structure ever existed—but what we have now is a plethora of endogamous social and occupational divisions, and hundreds of *jati*s ("birth groups") in India. People regularly identify themselves by their *jati*. Ritual practices, dietary rules, and sometimes dialects differ among the castes. Deviation from caste practices in past centuries sometimes resulted in one's being excluded from the caste.

The word "caste" comes from the Portuguese, who used "casta" to refer to the various sections of Hindu society. The modern word "caste" signifies both the four broad *varna*s and the minutely divided *jati*s, although Western scholars sometimes translate *varna* as class and *jati* as caste. Hindu society is marked by hierarchies including caste, gender, age, piety, and practices like meditation, devotional singing, or dietary control. In the past, with the exception of Brahmanical castes and customs, the caste system was transformed and became diluted in Hindu communities outside India.

Large numbers of people (estimated as 16.2 percent of the Indian population in the 2001 census)[3] excluded in this classification formed many groups loosely called "outcaste" in English or "scheduled castes" in the modern administrative jargon of India. In some parts of India, several of these communities call themselves Dalit or "oppressed."

Although religion forms a useful way of identifying groups, there are other social factors perceptible in the organization of immigrant communities in many parts of the world. Broad divisions are seen among Hindus who come from different *geographic areas*; thus, Hindus from north India, south India, Sri Lanka, Trinidad and Tobago, South Africa, and so on, tend to form separate communities if there is a large enough population in the place of residence. A further subdivision for the Indian communities is by way of *language group*; such groups include the Tamil Sangam ("Society of Tamil People"), Kannada Koota (the Kannada [People's] Group), and the Gujarati Samaj (the Gujarati Society).

Religious identity was also connected with *dharma,* a concept that is central to the understanding of the Hindu traditions. *Dharma* has many meanings, including "duty," "righteousness," and "ethics." There is a common *dharma* to all humanity—these are virtues like non-violence, compassion, generosity, and gratitude. There is also a *dharma* that was considered to be specific to one's caste and station in life. Finally, there is a *dharma* that leads one to liberation from the cycle of life and death. Actions, in the Hindu, Jain, or Buddhist traditions, are said to incur *karma* for a human being. In Hinduism, "karma" (literally, "action") has come to mean the results of good and bad deeds performed by a human being and which, to some extent, determines the quality of life both now and in later births. According to the *Bhagavad Gita*, one gets liberation from the cycle of life and death when one's *karma* ends and one has, literally, a zero *karma* balance. This may be done through detached action, that is, acting without expectation of reward or fear of punishment; through knowledge; and through devotion. Other Hindus believe that through devotion and surrender, one gets the saving grace of the Supreme Being which stops the cycle of rebirth. Hinduism is a very life affirming society, and Hindu *dharma* speaks about one's obligations to the community.

Texts on *dharma* have always been only selectively followed, and local customs have tempered the rule of the books. In some parts of India, *dharma* texts such as the *Manu Smriti* were not well known, and certainly large parts of it were ignored.[4] While the Hindu traditions are portrayed—and quite correctly in some instances—as being hierarchical and codified in very strict ways, the system has built-in mechanisms to allow for dynamic reinterpretation. This "wiggle" room can serve and has served to legitimate progressive action. The traditional sources of *dharma*, or righteous action, are flexible enough to allow room for innovative action. The Vedas; the tradition of the epics and *Purana*s; actions of the righteous; and finally to do what is "dear to one's soul," that is, to act after much thought and according to the dictates of one's conscience, are said to be the sources of *dharma*.[5] The last of these sources provides the mechanism and avenue by which women, or anyone who may feel marginalized, can appropriate, redefine, or come up with new rituals.

Hinduism: Practice

Most Hindus learn about their religion through stories, music and dance, going to temples, and participating in rituals. Holy places, rituals, and stories are the first entry points and, for many, all of the religion that they will get in life. In general, most Hindus living in India may not consider doctrines and belief systems as central to their tradition; performance and practice of rituals, however, are most important. One may say that belief in a historical unfolding of events and bearing testament to creeds are less important to Hindus than pilgrimages at certain points in one's life; watching and hearing stories being performed through music and dance; fasting and feasting at the appropriate moments of the lunar calendar; and celebrating festivals.

Three important points have to be made before we discuss the religious practices of Hindus. The first is one that has been apparent in our discussions so far: that there is an enormous diversity in religious practices, and there is a great deal of variation between communities and regions. Second, local custom and practices trump textual descriptions and details of rituals and practices, and this has also been upheld by the Supreme Court of India. Finally, and what is of immediate concern to us now, is that notions of auspiciousness and inauspiciousness on the one hand, and purity and pollution on the other, are integral to the understanding of much of Hindu practices.

Auspiciousness and purity

The "auspicious" and "inauspicious" form important categories in the practice of the Hindu tradition, and while they sometimes intersect with the pole of ritual purity and impurity, they are quite distinct. In general, and in popular understanding, life-promoting rituals and those that increase a person's well-being are considered auspicious; those associated with death are inauspicious.

The axis of purity and pollution is different from that of auspiciousness and inauspiciousness, but the categories have fuzzy boundaries and sometimes intersect. Death brings ritual impurity to a family and is also inauspicious. The occasion of childbirth is happy and "auspicious"; nevertheless, some communities hold that the birth of a child (possibly because it is accompanied by a considerable loss of blood) is ritually defiling and polluting to the entire family. Thus, what is pure may not always be auspicious; what is auspicious may be polluting. What is important to bear in mind is that these notions of purity are not directly connected with feelings of inner purity, virtue, or sinfulness. Ritual impurity happens in any number of ways—through menstruation, death, and so on—and, through the passage of time or through bathing and physical cleansing, purity is restored.

Most Hindus reiterate the centrality of "auspiciousness" in their religious practice, and this term is used as a shorthand word for half a dozen terms in Sanskrit and in other languages which have overlapping meanings. In some cases, they are used as synonyms and, in others, in distinctive ways. Generally, the term indicates the potential and power to bring about good fortune and a good quality of existence. Auspiciousness on the earthly level is life promoting, and in this context, death is considered to be inauspicious. However, from a different perspective, in devotional milieu, death is considered not as an end to life, but as an act by which the soul is liberated from the cycle of life and death and achieves the best state of existence possible. Thus, from a theological perspective, the virtuous path that leads to liberation is the highest form of auspiciousness.

Hindus consider certain people, animals, rituals, symbols, qualities, foods, smells and sounds, places, dwellings, and above all, times of the day, week, or year, as "auspicious." They arrange their lives with an eye on auspicious times, start new writing enterprises with symbols of auspiciousness, and use the words *sri* or *srimati*, which have the dominant meanings of good fortune and auspiciousness, as a prefix for names of people and places. Auspicious times have potential; auspicious people, places, and objects have the *contagious* quality of spreading good fortune; thus, association with objects of auspiciousness or starting ventures in times deemed by astrologers to be auspicious leads to prosperity and success. The layout of land in terms of depressions and elevations, the direction of an entrance to the house, or the placement of rooms can make places auspicious or inauspicious and has led to the whole traditional branch of knowledge called *vastu sastra*. In other words, these phenomena, whether they occur by themselves or are brought about by actions of people, are still part of the natural rhythm of the universe, and by seizing the opportunity, one can realize happiness. Times, too, depending on the concatenation of planets and stars, or those that are traditionally connected with ancestors, may be inauspicious.

Calendar

Hindu calendars are lunar but adjusted to the solar year, so like Easter or Yom Kippur, they come at the same time of the year, though not on the same dates. Many of the festivals celebrated at home occur on dates calculated according to the phases of the moon. Most Hindus celebrate the traditional new year in March or April, but some, like those from the state of Gujarat, celebrate it in autumn.

Hindus all over the world do not have a common New Year's Day. There are at least three popular new year's days in the Hindu calendar. People from many parts of South and Southeast Asia, including Tamilnadu, Punjab, Assam, Kerala, Bengal, and Sindh, as well as residents of the predominantly Buddhist Cambodia, Thailand, Burma, and Laos, celebrate the beginning of the new year between April 13 and 15. Many communities in this "monsoon" basin worked off shared cultural matrices in the first millennium of the Common Era and began to share a common calendar. The celebration of the new year has more to do with community, language, and region than with religious affiliation.

Ugadi (from the Sanskrit *yuga adi*, literally, "beginning of an eon"), the new year for Hindus from the states of Maharashtra, Andhra Pradesh, and Karnataka, is celebrated the day after the new moon that occurs near the vernal equinox in March. People from the region of Gujarat, on the other hand, celebrate new year's day soon after Deepavali, the festival of lights which falls on the new moon day between mid-October and mid-November.

The Hindu calendar is divided into auspicious times with many rules governing the potential of every moment. There are many systems of calculating the potential of the daily planetary configurations based on texts, oral traditions, and local practices; astrologers work with traditional systems of calculations as well as computers. While we can speak of certain generalities, the many rules and local variations make it impossible to say which days or months are auspicious. In general, the waxing half of the moon and the six months when the sun travels north—from winter to summer solstice (*uttarayana punyakala*)—are considered good, but, obviously, weddings take place through the year except for a couple of months.

In South and Southeast Asia, the fortnight of the waning moon that comes between mid-September and mid-October is an inauspicious time, dedicated to ancestors (*pitr paksha*), and no auspicious event takes place then. In some areas, particularly the south of India, Tuesdays and Saturdays are considered inauspicious for weddings; some Hindus think of Tuesdays as particularly malefic and think that it is to avoid its negative tendencies that it is ironically named with a euphemism, *mangalavara*, or the "auspicious day of the week." Apart from months or certain fortnights, some days connected with specific phases of the moon, such as the eighth day (*astami*) in a lunar cycle, and major events like eclipses, may be considered to be inauspicious. In each day of the week, there are specific hours (*rahu kalam*) which are inauspicious as well, and these are known by heart or read in daily calendars which are sold all over India. Since these hours are technically connected with the time of sunrise, and sometimes latitude and longitude, calendars printed or websites maintained by some Hindu temples in the United States of America calculate these times for the North American continent.

Horoscope and astrology

Jyotisha, "the knowledge of the lights or stars," was a form of astronomy–astrology to do with determining auspicious and inauspicious times, casting of horoscopes, etc. In ancient India, it was considered to be a distinct branch of knowledge which was an ancillary to the study of the Vedas (*vedanga*). It is very much connected with the practice of the Hindu tradition.

Many Hindu communities have a practice of having a child's horoscope cast as soon as it is born, and the particularities of this time of birth may determine everything from its name to when all the important rituals in his/her life are conducted. In some castes and communities, this may be used in later years to be "matched" with a potential matrimonial mate. Hindus from some regions connect the time and date of a child's birth with the almanac, and the child's name may be chosen to have a numerical value or start with a syllable harmonious with this moment of birth. The movement of the planets and stars are studied in detail, and when a person experiences, say, a series of setbacks in his/her career, or is not able to find a right partner in life, an astrologer may be consulted. The astrologer checks the position of the planets in one's horoscope, and then recommends a series of remedies to alleviate the problem.

Many south Indian temples, following a custom that began to be popular towards the end of the first millennium CE (primarily in centers now present in the state of Orissa), have a shrine for the personification of the "nine planets" (*navagraha*). Devotees propitiate these nine planets regularly in an effort to ward off evil influences and maximize the good vibrations. In the state of Tamilnadu, there are many temples dedicated to these "nine planets"; elaborate rituals are held here whenever a planet leaves one astrological sign and moves to another. These nine planets are not completely congruent with Western lists of "planets"; the Indian list excludes the Earth, and includes the Sun, the Moon, Venus, Mercury, Mars, Jupiter, Saturn, and two "planets" called Rahu and Ketu, identified as the "ascending and descending nodes of the moon." Apart from times that are commonly good or bad for all (the criteria being different in the various regions of India), there are specific times according to one's own detailed horoscope which affect one positively or adversely.

In orthoprax households, where marriages are "arranged," horoscopes of the potential bride and bridegroom are matched before they even meet each other.

This is said to ensure compatibility of personalities and to balance out good times and bad in the course of the married life. The first such compatibility match is with the "star" that a person is born under. This is determined by where the moon is at the time of one's birth. Twenty-seven constellations are recognized as "birth stars." After looking at the fit by considering caste, community, sub-sect, and, in some cases, a grouping called *gotra* (a subgroup whose members are, by patrilineal reckoning said to be followers of one of the holy seers mentioned in the Vedas), one then comes to the issue of compatibility of stars. By a quick reckoning, one can figure out if the star of the potential mate is compatible with them. If all these fit, then one takes it a step further to see if the horoscopes match in detail.

Even the millions who do not keep tabs on or observe the day-to-day rhythms of the calendar, definitely get the local astrologer to tell them the precise time when they should move into a house or office, start an important journey, job, or venture, and get married—and it does not matter whether one is in Singapore, Silicon Valley, or Singavelkundram (a small town in south India). One of the few things one can say about Hindus, despite their diverse beliefs and practices, is that most of them calculate or seek a ritual specialist to calculate auspicious times to enact the significant events of their lives; the central rituals of a wedding, for instance, invariably take place at the precise time when particular sets of planets and stars come into a propitious alignment and are most favorable to the bride and bridegroom.

The home altar

The home is the center for many religious activities in the Hindu tradition. Many of the sacraments, rituals, and festivals are conducted at home and, from some perspectives, a Hindu can be considered to be very religious without ever having to leave it. It is here that the first awareness of one's religious tradition begins—and for many it shapes it completely. Spatially, one may have a special room, or at least an altar set apart for worship (*puja*); temporally, several days in a year may be spent in the celebration of major ritual festivals. Religious rituals associated with birth, puberty, pregnancy, and death also take place at home.

A child's earliest exposure to its religious tradition comes from seeing daily rituals at the *puja* altar. Here are many pictures and images, local gods and goddesses, as well as those brought as souvenirs from distant pilgrimages that someone in the family may have taken. Every day, or even twice a day, the mother may light an oil lamp in front of this altar. The woman may draw symmetric geometric designs with rice flour in front of the altar or in front of the house. These patterns are also drawn outside shrines in south Indian temples. Interestingly enough, the *svastika* (from the Sanskrit "*su + asti*" or "well-being") and what is now popularly known as the "star of David" are both traditional Hindu motifs, having religious significance, and are drawn in many households and reproduced in religious pamphlets or even wedding invitations. Family members may recite prayers regularly in front of the shrine; there may be copies of holy texts or prayer books that people may read or recite. Red powder, known as the *kumkum*, may be taken from the altar and placed on one's forehead. Flowers and fruits may be offered to the deities in the altar and then used by the devotee. It is from these simple acts of piety and reverence that a child's practice of Hindu culture begins. The home altar, the *puja* cabinet, or room serves as a lightning rod for the Hindu's perception of divinity.

Life cycle rituals

The lunar calendar is adjusted to the solar calendar, so festivals, birthdays, and death anniversaries which are calculated in terms of astronomical phenomena occur at the same time of the year. While the number of life cycle rituals and the manner in which they are celebrated depends on the community as well as on financial means, the two sacraments common across all divides are weddings and funeral rituals. Life-enhancing, auspicious rituals include pre-natal rites; naming a baby; giving the first solid food to a child; birthdays, especially the first, sixtieth, and eightieth; and weddings.

Wedding rituals

In the Hindu tradition, the wedding ritual is considered to be a *samskara* ("to make perfect") and is considered to be a sacrament. The wedding (*shubha vivaha*; *kalyana*) is the most auspicious event in one's life and every ritual connected with it, starting from the planning to buying of clothes, will be done at auspicious times. During the ritual itself, music from auspicious instruments (*nadaswaram* in south India, *shehnai* in north) is played loudly, especially at the central moments of the sacrament, to drown out all inauspicious sounds like sneezes.

The texts on *dharma*, which hold an "upper" caste male as the norm, say that a man has an obligation in life to marry, raise children, and fulfill his debts to his community. A woman and her husband are partners in fulfilling religious obligations, partners in the acquisition of wealth and fortune, and partners in the enjoyment of sensual pleasures. Thus, through a marriage, a man and a woman become companions in the pursuit of spiritual and material goals. In most communities within the Hindu tradition, a man can only perform important religious rituals—like conducting the wedding of a daughter—if his wife is by his side.

Weddings in India may last several days, and there is an atmosphere of a county fair, with people streaming in and out, greeting each other, and getting something to eat, even while the wedding rituals are being conducted for the couple under a canopy. In more recent years, wedding rituals have been shortened to a day or so in India and are considerably shorter in other countries. Pre-wedding rituals which begin a day or two before the actual event may include "secular" rituals like painting the bride's hands—as well as those of her family and women friends—with *mehendi* (henna) and also prayers to Lord Ganesha, one of the most popular deities of Hindu India. With his elephant head and beaming smile, Ganesha is said to remove all obstacles from one's path. Hindus worship him before the commencement of any journey, examination, ritual, or job.

Figure 2.3 Wedding couple in Karnataka. Photo taken by Vasudha Narayanan.

The wedding rituals almost always take place in front of a specially kindled fire (*agni;* cognate with the English word "ignite"). Most of the significant Hindu sacraments are to take place only near a sacred fire. Early Vedic rituals were done around an altar of fire. The sacred fire is lit during those mile markers of growth and aging—aging which begins in one's pre-natal days. Fire is the eternal witness to life and to the major sacraments of life. A wedding is valid only if the couple is married in front of a fire; *agni* is said to be the eternal witness to this sacrament. While fire is considered to be indispensable for the wedding ritual, like all else in the Hindu tradition, there are exceptions, and in some communities—like the Coorgis of south India—a fire is not lit for weddings. Local customs frequently supersede the laws according to the texts on *dharma.*

Although the order of the rituals differs in many parts of India, there are many common rites. The bride and bridegroom exchange garlands; the bridegroom clasps the right palm of the bride at the auspicious moment; and the couple take seven steps together. In the southern states, the bridegroom ties a "thread of auspiciousness" (*mangala sutra*) around the neck of the bride as a symbol of their marriage, saying, "This is a sacred thread [which is a symbol] of my long life. I fasten it around your neck. O beautiful lady! O lady with auspicious qualities! May you see a hundred autumns [with me]." In northern India, the bridegroom anoints the bride's forehead with a red powder called *sindur*; this is the symbol of her married status.

Many of the mantras recited during the wedding ritual are from the Rig Veda and have been used in Hindu weddings for over three thousand years.

May all the guests present here unite our hearts! May we be calm and united! May we be peaceful and unite together like the rivers mingling (in the ocean and losing their separate identities). May we be like breaths united with the body. May we be united like the Lord and his creation. May we be united like the teacher and his disciple. May we love each other and be loyal to each other through our lives![6]

The central ritual of the wedding itself is the holding of hands (*panigrahana*) and the taking of the seven steps around the fire (*saptapadi*). After taking the seven steps, the bridegroom tells the bride:

You have taken seven steps with me; be my friend. We who have taken seven steps together have become companions. I have attained your friendship; I shall not forsake that friendship. Do not discard our relationship. Let us live together; let us think together. We have come to a right and fitting stage of our lives; let us be happy and prosperous, thinking good thoughts. Let there be no difference in our hopes and efforts; let us attain our desires. And so we join ourselves (our lives). Let us be of one mind, let us act together and enjoy through all our senses, without any difference. You are the song (Sama) I am the lyric (Rig), I am the song, you are the lyric. I am the sky, you are the earth. I am the seed; you shall bear my seed. I am thought; you are speech. I am the song, you are the lyric. Be conformable to me; O lady of clear, sweet words. You who are so precious, come with me; let us have children and attain prosperity together. May there be auspiciousness.

It is after taking the seven steps together that the bride and bridegroom are considered to be officially married. *Manu Smriti*, one of the important books on *dharma* says: "The Vedic mantras for the wedding ritual of the joining of hands mark the attainment of the wife; but wise people say that the [sacrament] is sealed in the seventh step."[7] In the concluding rituals, the bride and the bridegroom are blessed by the elders in the community.

Funeral rituals

While weddings are auspicious from the viewpoint of most Hindus, death and funeral rituals are all inauspicious and impure. The ritual impurity is *contagious*—if there is a death in the family or even if one goes to a funeral, one is considered to be impure. A cleansing bath or pouring water over one's head is said to ritually cleanse the person from this impurity. While the texts on *dharma* wax eloquent on this purity and pollution and one observes it in practice, from the viewpoint of one who wants liberation, death is indeed auspicious.

Most Hindus—and again, there are exceptions as in the Vira Shaiva/Lingayat community—cremate the dead. The cremation takes place very soon after death and in many cases within a day. The body is washed by the women in the house, and the forehead is anointed with sacred marks. The dead body is laid on a bier, and the family priest begins the rituals at home itself. Family and friends garland the body and frequently bow down in respect, facing south. The south is considered to be the direction of death. At the cremation ground, the pyre is lit; the ashes are collected the next day and eventually immersed in the ocean or in a river. Immersion of some parts of the ashes, at least, in the holy river Ganga is considered to be particularly meritorious.

In almost all cases, it is the son, or a close male relative, who does the funeral rites. In some areas, women do not even go into the cremation ground. However, occasionally, in some families where there are no sons, the daughters have been known to do the funeral rites. There has been precedence for this; in the Vedic times, a man sometimes appointed a daughter as a *putrika* (a daughter who functions like a son in ritual matters). This daughter (or sometimes her son) officiated in funerals.[8] While this does not take away from the patriarchal structure and norm, it showed that the gender issues in this ritual were more fluid than the practice in recent centuries.

Most Hindus believe that the soul is immortal. The soul is encased in a human body which perishes, but the *atman* or soul is imperishable. At death, one merely discards one's body and eventually takes on another. The classical location of this doctrine is in the holy text, the *Bhagavad Gita*. Composed around 200 BCE or a little later, it is a text in which Krishna instructs his cousin Arjuna (who is understood by Hindus who are familiar with this text as a paradigmatic seeker) on the nature of the human soul, God, and how one can reach liberation. In verses that are still recited at funerals, Krishna describes the human soul as being beyond the reach of human senses and thought; it is not affected by the sense organs or physical nature and is removed from it. Just as a human being casts off old clothes and wears new ones, so too does a soul discard bodies and assume new ones. Thus, the soul inhabits bodies that are born and that die. This continues through the ages until the soul is finally liberated from the cycle of births and death. The soul does not die when the body dies; it is never born and never killed. In later centuries, some Hindu texts also explicitly speak of the soul as being beyond gender.

In the course of the *Bhagavad Gita*, Krishna describes three ways to liberation (or as some Hindus believe, three aspects of one way to liberation) from the cycle of births and death. These are the way of action, the way of knowledge, and the way of devotion. Each way (*marga*) is spoken of also as a discipline (*yoga*). The way of action (*karma yoga*) entails the path of unselfish action; one must do one's duty, but it should not be done either out of fear of punishment or hope of reward. The right action should be done without expectation of praise or blame. For example, one is to study or do good acts because it is correct to do so—because it is one's duty (*dharma*) to do so, not because other people will pat you on your back or give you an award. Indeed, on one level (according to other books in the Hindu tradition), even the *karma* one gets from performing good deeds is ultimately bad and causes bondage because to enjoy the good *karma*, one has to be reborn. Pillai Lokacharya, a thirteenth century Hindu philosopher, calls good *karma* "golden handcuffs." Therefore, one is to act according to one's *dharma*. Krishna urges Arjuna to act without any attachment to the consequences. Then evil will not touch such a person, just as water does not stick to a lotus leaf. All actions are to be offered to Krishna. By discarding the fruits of one's action, one attains abiding peace.

Krishna also talks of the way of knowledge (*jñana yoga*): knowledge may lead to transforming wisdom that destroys one's past *karma*. The point of enlightenment is an insight into the real nature of the universe, divine power, and the human soul. Later philosophers say that when one hears scripture, asks questions, clarifies doubts, and eventually meditates on this knowledge, one achieves liberation. Krishna tells Arjuna that just as fire reduces firewood to ashes, so, too, does the fire of knowledge reduce all *karma* (actions) to ashes.

The third way is the most emphasized throughout the *Bhagavad Gita*: the way of devotion (*bhakti yoga*). If there is a general amnesty program offered to those who sin, those who have a karmic overload, it is through the way of devotion. It is the way of devotion, as expressed through acts of worship, performances and rituals, which has dominated the Hindu traditions for the last two millennia.

Festivals

The Hindu calendar is filled with festivals. Many are local; some are recognized by Hindus all over the world. Navaratri, the festival of "nine nights," (also known as Dasara) and Deepavali, the festival of lights, are two of the best known celebrations in the Hindu world. Pongal, a festival celebrated in mid-January, is a huge holiday, but only in the state of Tamilnadu, and is a good example of local days of feasting.

Figure 2.4 Women from Gujarat praying during Navaratri, Gainesville, Florida. Photo taken by Vasudha Narayanan.

Dasara (Sanskrit: "ten days" or "destroying ten sins") is technically another name given for the Navaratri ("nine nights") festival, but sometimes restricted to denote the "Great Ninth" (*maha navami*) and the "Victorious Tenth" (Sanskrit: *Vijaya dasami*; Bengali: *Bijoya*) days of the celebrations. The concluding ceremonies of this festival commemorate either the victory of Durga over the buffalo demon Mahisha or Rama's conquest of Lanka in the epic *Ramayana*. These victories are interpreted literally and symbolically in rituals. On the ninth day, warriors worship their weapons (*ayudha puja*), and by extension, craftsmen and other workers venerate their tools and implements; others understand the stories as denoting triumph of knowledge and learning over the darkness of ignorance. In parts of south India, educational materials (books, pens, pencils, and today, computers and disks) and musical instruments are dedicated to Saraswati, the goddess of learning and the performing arts. Finally, on the last day (the "Victorious Tenth" day dedicated to the Goddess Lakshmi in south India), there is a multidimensional celebration: new learning, especially of the performing arts, takes place, along with the honoring of music and dance teachers.

Deepavali (literally, "necklace of lamps"; popularly known by the vernacular *diwali* in some parts of India) is celebrated on the eve of the new moon that falls between mid-October and mid-November. While it is celebrated by most Hindus, the reasons and the stories connected with it differ in the various regions. The many ways and many reasons for the celebration of this festival give us some idea of the diversity of the Hindu tradition. There are many, many regional variations; but what is common here, is that most Hindus (though not all) *do* celebrate that day. Hindus, from those in some parts of northern India, believe that Lord Rama returned to Ayodhya after his victorious battle with the evil Ravana that day, and that the kingdom lit lamps all over to mark the celebrations. In other parts of India, it is believed that Lord Krishna fought a long battle with Narakasura ("demon of hell") and won the battle on the dawn of this new moon day. To

---

Nine Nights Festival in Bengal

People who hail from Bengal craft gigantic icons of the goddess Durga and other deities, and consecrate and worship them during the nine nights of the Navaratri festival; on the tenth day, the animating life that is believed to reside in them is said to depart, and the images, after being taken in a day-long procession, are submerged in a river or pond. Conducted in every neighborhood in Kolkata, it is also celebrated this way wherever Bengalis congregate around the world. Hindus from the state of Gujarat celebrate the creative energies of the mother goddess at this time of the year. Among other rituals, women dance around a clay jar which houses a lamp symbolic of the light of creation and wisdom. This dance, known as the *garbha*, literally, "womb," is indicative of the creative power of the supreme female principle, the goddess.

celebrate this victory of good over evil, Hindus in every home let off fireworks, to emulate the noise of the war that Krishna waged against evil, and light lamps to display the victory of light over the forces of darkness. Special sweets and candies are made at home; new clothes are bought and worn. In some parts of south India, Hindus believe that the sacred river Ganga is spiritually present in all the waters. Early on the morning of Deepavali, even before dawn, people take a special ritual bath using oil and fragrant herbs, and some communities greet each other with the rhetorical question: "Have you bathed in the waters of the Ganga?" Bathing in this river is said to purify a human being and one begins this day with this physical and mental purity. Hindus from the Gujarat region celebrate their new year at this time of the year (most other Hindus, as noted earlier, celebrate it in March or April).

Hindus from Punjab spend the nights in ritual gambling, with cards, and invite Lakshmi, the goddess of good fortune, to their houses. In most parts of India, gifts of dried fruits and sweets are given to friends, and cash bonuses are given to employees. In some Krishna-worshipping communities in northern India, one of the grandest festivals involving ritual food is the *Annakut* ("mountain of food"), which is celebrated soon after Deepavali. Dishes of cooked food are arranged in tiers like a mountain to resemble Mt. Govardhan, which was lifted by Krishna to protect his devotees. Whether elaborate like this celebration, or as simple as the offering of a piece of fruit, the *prasada* (literally, "favor" or "grace"; it refers here to the food blessed as an offering to the deity) is said to be filled with divine grace.

The festival of Pongal (mid-January) in Tamilnadu is centered on the ritual food of *pongal*, of which there is both a savory and a sweet variety. This is sometimes called a harvest festival and a festival of thanksgiving and veneration of the Sun god. It marks the beginning of the sacred time when the sun starts going north (*uttarayana punyakala*) in the Hindu calendar. Pongal literally means "flowing over" and refers to the flowing over of prosperity in a home or community. The rice, milk, and jaggery are cooked in a pot facing east at an auspicious time around Pongal day which falls ordinarily on January 14 or 15. The boiling of the milk and its overflow symbolizes the abundance and prosperity that is prayed for in the following year.

Domestic rituals

Vratas: The lunar calendar, food, feasting, and fasting

Apart from festivals, every lunar cycle is marked with days of fasting and feasting at home. On the eleventh day after new moon (*ekadashi*), many people, especially the followers of the god Vishnu, abstain from eating grains. Fasts, as many rituals, come in various forms: some involve abstinence from all food and water; some involve abstinence from grain only (as is done by women in the state of Maharashtra during the Navaratri rituals); and some involve not eating certain vegetables like eggplant, which are considered to be filled with seeds, and therefore, potential life forms. Women in many parts of India observe special days of fasting and feasting in connection with votive rituals called *vratas*.

These rituals, which involve a day (or more) of strict fasting, are done in honor of specific goddesses and for various purposes.[9] Women, from some areas like Uttar Pradesh and Punjab, dressed in their wedding finery observe the *karva chauth* fast, which usually comes soon after Navaratri. They fast from dawn to dusk and break their fast after seeing the rising moon. This fast is undertaken on the fourth day of the waning lunar cycle between October and November and is done to pray for and to preserve conjugal happiness. Other fasts are done for the welfare of the family. There are regular fasts like *ekadashi*, which men and women observe, and special ritual fasts which only women observe. While some of these ritual fasts occur in a patriarchal context (prayers for the husband or son), some scholars and some women see these as, in fact, empowering to women. Seen from this perspective, when women undertake the fasts, it gives them some sense of control and power over other people's welfare and well-being. The fasts are broken with special foods, and each may be distinctive to the community or to the fast that is being observed.

Consuming *prasada* is also a central part of many domestic votive rituals known as *vrata*s. Of the hundreds of *vrata*s in Hinduism, the one dedicated to Satyanarayana has perhaps been the most popular since the second half of the twentieth century. During the ritual, the story of the *vrata* is narrated in Sanskrit, or more often in a regional language, or even English; offerings of light, incense, water, and food are made, and after the final waving of lights, the blessed food (*prasada*) is consumed by the family and friends. Consuming this *prasada* is a central feature of the ritual. Ordinarily, a particular kind of sweet with five ingredients is made for the occasion. In more informal varieties of the ritual, after the lighting of lamps and incense, the story is read, and the *prasada* is distributed to all. In some of them, the protagonist loses faith, forgets, lies, or does not live up to his/her words, or shows disrespect to the deity by not consuming the *prasada* and soon experiences the wrath of the lord.

Food and diet

Perceptions of and activities dealing with ritual food in the Hindu traditions can only be understood in the larger context of ideas of food in everyday life, body, health, purity, auspiciousness, and one's relationship with the deities, ancestors, and fellow human beings. Food is central to the practice of the Hindu tradition; next to a wedding, it is this topic that commands the most space and energy of the writers of the texts on *dharma*. There are many rules and regulations connected with food in ritual contexts in domestic and temple spaces. Although treated at length in texts on *dharma* and those on medicine and health, these rules and regulations are transmitted primarily through oral traditions, known and adapted through custom and practice.

While some of the rules and customs are fairly commonly known and followed, there is, as in every other matter, considerable variation and diversity depending on economic class, caste, community, and region on the one hand, and time of year, month, ritual calendar, which is based on the phases of the moon and position of stars, as well as special occasions, on the other.

Food is ceremoniously or symbolically offered to ancestors, deities, birds and beasts, guests, and other human beings—and sometimes all of the above—before orthoprax Hindus eat. In many communities, food cooked daily is ritually offered at the home altar and then consumed; in such cases, the line between food consecrated in temples and at home is blurred. Discussions on food in domestic ritual contexts in texts of *dharma* include how many times one could eat food; recommended and forbidden foods; the nature of the cook and giver; causes for ritual defilement of food; consuming of meat and alcohol; and ritual protocol before, during, and after eating of a meal.[10]

Many dietary regulations and rituals surrounding food and eating still continue in Hindu families all over the world, and one would be hard pressed to find Hindus who are not bound by at least some rules, at least on ritual occasions. Orthoprax Hindus may be more stringent in their degree of compliance with the regulations concerning ritual food. The fortnightly, monthly, and annual calendars have dates and phases of the moon which involve fasting or feasting at appropriate times. There are technical differences in many kinds of fasts; those that involve abstention from rice, from all grain, from all food, and the intentions behind and times of the fast are all said to have effect on the results. In some cases, observing the right kinds of fast at the correct times (like abstaining from rice, indeed, all grain on the eleventh day of the waxing or waning moon) are said to have the efficacy to give one liberation from the cycle of life and death.

Underlying the general rules of food and eating rituals are notions of purity/impurity and auspiciousness/inauspiciousness; traditional ideas of the body, mind, and health; as well as many theological concepts. Most Hindus may observe the rules and regulations periodically (for example, a particular day of the week) or at least on a few ritual occasions.

Physical or ritual purity and food

All ritual food is to be prepared with various levels of physical purity. Bathing in the morning, before the preparation of any ritual food or everyday food, is *sine qua non,* and in both custom and texts, this is taken for granted. In addition to this, men and women may observe a more strict form of ritual purity in cooking for specific kinds of rituals like ancestral rites. Food is served and eaten with the right hand; the left is considered impure and inauspicious.

In popular understanding and by fitting a template from philosophical discourses on what we eat, food, like people and even deities, is said to have propensities to bring about purity (*sattva*); sloth and stupor (*tamas*); and energy and passion (*rajas*). While this is not clearly discussed in the early texts on *dharma*, in popular practice many Hindus understand food to have these propensities; thus, meat and fowl may be thought of as having *rajas*; stale food and liquor as giving rise to *tamas;* and so on. In general, dairy products (with the exception of cheese) were considered to be *sattvic*. Lentils and most fruits (but certainly not all vegetables and spices) are said to belong to the category of *sattva*. The lentils, vegetables, types and number of dishes cooked, and the order in which they are served are all decided with what is considered to be auspicious by that community; and there is considerable variation in this. Certain flavors, spices, and vegetables, for instance, are associated with death/ancestral rituals, and not used for weddings. Here too, the difference between purity and auspiciousness is seen; while only "pure" foods may be used for death and ancestral rituals (a list which would not include, for instance, fish, fowl or meat, or even onions and garlic), the menu for a wedding is auspicious but does not have to be "pure."

There are other categories taken into consideration for health and well-being. One such category is the Ayurvedic division known as *kapha, pitta,* and *vata,* which are very loosely translated as propensities for phlegm, bile, and wind. Food classified in these categories is consumed at specific times of the season or according to perceived health needs.

Contrary to popular perception, most Hindus are not vegetarian; however, certain castes and communities may avoid the eating of fish, fowl, and meat in general, or on ritual occasions, or on some days of the week dedicated to the deity or spiritual teacher of their choice. From the Brahmanical perspective, the "higher" castes were more pure and therefore had more pure foods, and were likely to be vegetarians. However, members of some sectarian Vaishnava and Shaiva communities, no matter what their *jati,* think that devotion to Vishnu or Shiva imbues them with more purity than that conferred by caste, and are also very strict in regulations about purity in food. Again, there is diversity; Brahmans in the Konkan region on the west coast or Bengal, for instance, regularly eat fish; the ritual food of Kashmiri (Brahman) Pandits ranges from regularly including mutton to complete avoidance of impure foods such as garlic and onions.

Most texts spend a considerable amount of time on forbidden foods, which varied through the different time periods, regions, and between authors. In addition to avoiding meat, fowl, fish, and eggs, several other vegetables and spices like onions, garlic, and mushrooms are not considered to be part of a "pure" diet by many followers of Vishnu; early texts on *dharma* have a blanket decree against these foods. Food and eating, then, even with the advent of modernity, continue to be a central part of the religious, everyday lives of Hindus. Hindus grow up with various degrees of dietary regulations depending on their social position and degrees of secularization, and the guidelines discussed in texts of *dharma* and conditioned by practice of one's community and family form part of one's lifestyle. With accelerated modernization and secularization, these dietary regulations have been relaxed considerably in many households, but it would be commonplace to find Hindus who follow at least a few regulations without even thinking about it. Many of these rules and regulations and their interconnection with modern dilemmas, like the use of genetically modified foods, are being discussed by Hindus.

Worship

Temples and shrines

Hindu temples have several functions and identities. They have a cosmological identity, and devotees may understand the tower to represent Mount Meru, a mythical mountain which is the *axis mundi* in Hindu and Buddhist cosmology. But temples also have multiple national identities; for example, some think of themselves as Indo-Guyanese-American institutions. Some temples are explicit about their ethnic identities and cater to Telugu, Tamil, or Gujarati people, and yet others have pronounced sectarian identities in that they are devoted to Vishnu (Vaishnava) or to Shiva (Shaiva).

Mountains, groves, rivers, towns, cities, and forests are all sites of hierophany (a manifestation of the sacred) in the Hindu tradition. Although the entire South Asian subcontinent is considered to be holy, thousands of places claim a special status and have been visited by pilgrims for centuries. Many Hindus believe that they can get liberation just by visiting a sacred place or by bathing in a holy river. Temples were built with great care, and according to strict regulations, facing specific auspicious directions, and many of them are theologies in stone. These temples and shrines display the embodied cosmologies of Hinduism, and some were built with precise astronomical coordination.

The temples were centers of piety and centers of power; they were also economic hubs and a nexus for cultural activities. Replication of holy places and sacralizing new territories has been a hallmark of Hindu migration, and the names of Indian holy places are found in Southeast Asian countries.

According to texts and oral traditions, a temple may represent either the body of the Cosmic Person, or be regarded as a physical extension of the Supreme Being. In other traditions, the temple is likened to a cosmic mountain, like the gigantic Kailasha described in the *Purana*s. Others consider the temple to be an

Figure 2.5 Pilgrims en route to the Melmaruvatur temple near Chennai stop at the Thanjavur temple in Tamilnadu. Photo taken by Vasudha Narayanan.

abode of God, like Vaikuntha or Heaven. In an extension of the body metaphor, the tower or the uppermost structure is called a *shikara* (crest of a mountain or head), and the main shrine, which is in the innermost recesses of the temple is the womb-house (*garbha griha*).[11]

Most temples in India are characterized by intricate carvings and sculptures on walls and towers. Many of them are decorative; some were put there to ward off the evil eye.

Many of the small temples may be little more than a single shrine, sometimes jutting out into a crowded, urban street. There may be a single room with a deity installed inside, and at appointed times, a *pujari* or ritual priest will stay there and, if asked, will light a camphor flame in front of the deity. Some north Indian temples resemble houses and may be tucked away in residential and shopping complexes, indistinguishable from the architecture around them. Other temples, like the Lingaraja and the Ranganatha temple complexes in Bhubaneswar and Srirangam, respectively, are elaborate structures, spanning several acres with several towers.

Older temple complexes were built for a family of deities and had multiple shrines in one compound. Temple rituals and distribution of honors were financed by the offerings and endowments of the devotees. Many women made such endowments in their own names, and it seems possible that many of these were either from royal families or from courtesans attached to temples. Devotees did not and do not visit all, or even most of, the shrines in large temples. The temple complex is like a buffet table; worshippers will walk in, pick and choose which deities they want to worship that day, and proceed there. Most of the Brahmanical temples, that is, temples where there is some involvement by Brahmin priests in the performance of ritual worship, are dedicated to manifestations of Devi/ Parvati, Vishnu, or Shiva and to their consorts, devotees, and/or families. Footwear is always left outside the temple precincts; and with it, one leaves the dust and grime of worldly thoughts and passions. Sometimes, the worshipper may buy flowers, camphor, coconuts, or fruits from the dozens of shops and stalls outside the temple. The simplest act of worship in a temple is for the worshipper to go whenever the temple is open and make an offering of camphor, fruit, flower, or coconut to the deity. In a small temple, the offering may be made directly; in most temples, the worshipper hands over the offering to a priest.

Perhaps the most popular ritual in a Hindu temple is the offering of fruits or food to the deity and then taking part of it back home. This ritual is part of *puja* (worship). After first being offered to the deity, the flower or fruit that the devotee brought as an offering is returned as "blessed" and as holding the favor of the Divine Being. Such a piece of blessed food is usually called *prasada*, a very tangible and spiritual "favor" of the deity. This act of devotion, of seeing the deity, offering food, and getting it back in a blessed state, is the simplest and most popular among votive rituals in a temple. Temple rituals are dominated by the offering of food to the deity and serving the "leftovers" of what is spiritually consumed by the deity back to devotees.

When a group of devotees pray, whether at home or in the temple, the ritual may end with an *arati*, or waving of lamps. The priest, or one of the worshippers, will light a piece of camphor in a plate and wave it clockwise in front of the deity. The camphor flame is then shown to the worshippers, who reverentially place their hands on top of the flame and touch their eyelids briefly as if to internalize the light of devotion or knowledge that showed them the Supreme deity in the temple. The main act in this ritual is to see the Deity and to be seen by this God or Goddess (*darshana*); this is as important as hearing the sacred words of Hindu scripture.

Worship in many Hindu temples is traditionally not congregational in the Judeo-Christian sense of the term with set services for the community and interactive participation. There are several shrines within the temple complex; sometimes, people go around and then sit out to talk with each other. There are, however, no pews or seats either for temporary or permanent seating. In some temples in northern India, and certainly in houses all over India, there are group songs (*bhajan*) accompanied by a percussion instrument and a keyboard, but this is not a formalized service. More of these group-worship rituals are also seen in the diaspora, where worshippers tend to congregate on the weekend.

In both the daily and seasonal routines of prayers and services, the temples in America built by immigrants from India try to remain faithful to those in the home country. The morning wake-up prayers (*suprabhatam*), the offering of food to the deity, the daily round of worship (*archana*), and the recitation of prayers at specific points of the day are all followed correctly; however, unlike temples in India, in the diaspora the participation of the community is seen primarily on the weekends. While the temples in the United States of America celebrate a few seasonal festivals, they try as far as is astrologically possible to plan big events around the holidays of the American secular calendar. Thus, the main festivals in America are celebrated during the long weekends between Memorial Day and Labor Day, and stretching out until Thanksgiving in southern states. The sacred-time orientation of the temple is made to coincide, as far as the ritual almanac will allow, with the secular calendar of the land in which it is located. While the reasons for this time orientation are obvious—unlike the Indian temple, the festivals are organized by people working in other places, and long weekends are the time many families do long-distance traveling—it is important to note the framework of the American secular calendar. These are the times when the weather and holidays cooperate to get full participation from the devotees.[12]

Thus, in addition to being a center for individual piety, temples set up by Hindus from India serve as large community halls for the local population. These temples function as institutions that have self-consciously undertaken the role of educating the younger generation of Hindus born in America. This is done through weekly language and religion classes, frequent religious discourses, study circles for adults, teaching of classical music and dances, and through summer camps. In addition to these classes, many Hindu temples also have academic tests and other preparation courses both to encourage families to come to the temple and to invest in the success of the younger generation. Since many of the founding trustees of Hindu temples are physicians, temples frequently organize blood drives and health fairs with health screenings. In all these matters, the temples in the diaspora are different from those in India and have assumed the functions found in the community at large in the home country.

While there are many differences in architecture and modes of worship, there are at least two common elements in the temples set up by many of these Hindu communities of Indian origin in the diaspora. In almost all instances, the temples focus on *devotional* practices as opposed to meditational or yogic exercises. Second, many of them teach, sponsor, or at least advertise regular classes on classical Indian dances like Bharata Natyam. This dance form has become one of the main ways of transmitting Hindu culture to the younger generation girls in the diaspora.

Performance, dances, music

Acting, music, and dance have been considered to be some of the optional ways to salvation within Hinduism. The treatise on theater and dance, the *Natya Sastra*, written by a legendary person called Bharata, is considered to be the fifth Veda or scripture. Dance is said to involve a total control of the body, a control central to the physical discipline of yoga. The *Natya Sastra* is supposed to have originated with a divine being called Brahma and passed on to the sage Bharata. Brahma is said to have taken the reading text from the Rig Veda, the earliest and one of the most sacred texts in the history of Hindu literature; music from the Sama Veda; gestures from the Yajur Veda; and *rasa* (literally, "essence" or "juice"), that is, the aesthetic element, from the Atharava Veda; and combining the essence of the four Vedas, compiled a fifth Veda that depicts dance as a way to salvation. In oral tradition, the very name Bharata is said to incorporate the main elements of Bharata Natyam: *Bha-* stands for "*bhava*," a state of mind, an attitude; *-ra-* for "raga"; and *-ta* for "tala" or rhythm. In addition to this, music and dance were known as the *Gandharva Veda*. It is also said that knowledge of music leads one to *moksha* or liberation from the cycle of life and death.[13]

While music and dance have had an exalted status, historically the performers did not always share that prestige. However, in the twentieth century, women of the so-called "upper" castes began to learn classical dances, and one dance form called *dasi attam* ("the dance of the servants") came to be called Bharata Natyam ("the dance according the [book of the sage] Bharata" or "the dance of India"). The rise of nationalism and anti-colonial sentiments, an increased consciousness of pre-modern women poets, a new pride in Indian classical performing arts, as well as the new public spaces created for expressions of devotion created a veritable boom in classical music and dance. Starting around the 1930s, classical music and dance performed in private salons and temple rituals came to be valorized as part of one's cultural heritage, "secularized," and performed in popular forums. Eventually, in a cyclical pattern, these dances have become so emblematic of Hindu—and Indian—identities in the diaspora that they are frequently taught and performed in temples in many parts of the world, especially in North America.

Learning the dance forms and performing them in public events during festival days becomes one main avenue for young girls to participate in the larger Hindu community. Popular dance forms like the Indian dance *garbha* are extraordinarily popular in Gujarat, India, and in many parts of the world where Gujarati presence has been prominent. Indian-American and Indo-Canadian students regularly perform these classical and folk dances—and, through them, "perform" their identities as part of public celebrations of Deepavali or Navaratri in college campuses.

One can get liberation either through dancing or by being overwhelmed by the joy which comes by witnessing the dance. This could be any dance; theoretically speaking, all dance is divine; thus, in classical Bharata Natyam, there are "pure" dances or dances without any particular lyrics and emotion attached to them. Many of the dances, however, are devotional in tone. At times, the dancer expresses devotion through his/her body and soul to get liberation. This is particularly seen in the Bharata Natyam style of south Indian dancing, where the dancer may express her love for the Lord in explicitly erotic terminology. The pining of a human soul for union with the Lord is expressed through passionate *longing* and a desire to *belong* to him. The audience is also granted salvation through participation in the divine joy of movement. Either by dancing or by beholding the beauty of the divine dance—whether it is that of Krishna with his cowherd friends, or Shiva, known as Nataraja or the King of the Dance—one obtains liberation.

It thus seems, in traditional forums at least, that when the focus of discussion is *moksha* (liberation), rather than *dharma* (issues of righteousness) in this world, a greater freedom is seen in women's participation in public spaces, as in dance. Androcentric norms on women's modesty or actions in public that were incumbent on some castes and classes are simply bypassed in cases where the tradition focuses on the salvation potential of all human beings.

Religious authority

The earliest holy men and women who "saw" the truth and composed the Vedas were called "seers." Although the many lineages of holy teachers in Hinduism were composed of men of the Brahmin caste, hundreds of saints and charismatic people considered to be "gurus" have come from all castes of society. In many Hindu communities, the sacred teacher is considered to be as important as the deity and adored, venerated, and even worshiped, while many others may not consider them significant. Women gurus have become very important since the twentieth century, and many are considered to be deities.

Many sectarian traditions have lineages of teachers called *acharya*s, but, in general, there are no priests/ministers with pastoral roles as in Christianity. The priests in temples know reams of mantras and prayers and are considered to be specialists who can conduct simple and elaborate rituals. The training of these priests in India is generally different from those who come to one's homes and do domestic rituals. There is yet another category of specialists— those who specialize in interpretive commentaries on sacred texts as well as what is called *harikatha* (literally, "stories of Vishnu," but referring to all religious narratives).

In addition, men and women of piety command a great deal of respect, and older members in a family—men or women—may be granted a great deal of respect and seen as keepers and interpreters of the tradition.

Hinduism: Current approaches

As in every religion, there are multiple approaches to the study of Hindu traditions. There is learned, in-depth study of texts by traditional scholars/religious leaders within the Hindu tradition who then disseminate the interpretations, frequently with an emphasis on the particular sectarian viewpoints of their community. These are then brought to the attention of the larger public by oral and written commentaries. While the scholarship by traditional *acharya*s, or even new gurus, has been vibrant for many centuries, the media have changed. Many of them give commentaries on radio or television channels, and there is a huge appetite for such programs, not just India but in the diaspora as well—Bali, for instance, has regular programs on Hindu *dharma*.

In Indian universities, where the academic field of religion is not prominent, the study of the Hindu religion is done through diverse fields including Sanskrit, regional languages, philosophy, and ancient Indian culture. Some universities such as Madras University also have departments of Vaishnavism and Saiva Siddhanta. The approach in all of these is largely textual and involves a close reading of philosophical works.

The Western study of the Hindu tradition began with the advent of European settlements in India after the seventeenth century. Some of the early studies were done with the idea of converting the local population, and this historical motivation did not, according to many Hindus even now, ever disappear. This suspicion is dominant in some of the controversies which have risen since the late twentieth century about the academic study of religion in European and American countries. The academic study of the Hindu traditions is connected both with area studies, specifically South Asian studies, in Europe and America and also with the older field of Indology in Europe. Scholars also approach the phenomena from academic disciplines such as religion, anthropology, sociology, and language studies. Over the years, such studies have fostered professional collaborations and personal friendships between cultures, but there has also been deep contestation of the territory on a number of registers. Such contestations spring from several perspectives including (a) lingering suspicions of colonial scholarship on the origins of Hinduism; (b) questioning the validity and integrity of methods through which the religious material is studied and interpreted, specifically, psychoanalysis; (c) the authority to study Hindu texts and practices by "outsiders" who may or may not have the scholarly competence to do so; (d) the use of texts and practices long connected with the Hindu traditions but without associating them with the Hindu religion today; and (e) who speaks for Hinduism and who has the right to represent it in scholarly and public fora.

Some of the loudest and most intense debates on the approaches to the study of the Hindu traditions have focused on the question of the origins of Hinduism, the privileging of some data, and the colonial predisposition to scholarship. Western academic studies had largely held, until almost the close of the twentieth century, that the Indus Valley Civilization was an indigenous culture, and that around 1500 BCE or so, the Indo-European "invaders" (a term changed to "migrations" eventually) came and settled in India, eventually composing the Vedas. This theory has been challenged from many quarters, and at stake is the notion of whether India was the original homeland of these Indo-Europeans. The debate has some political overtones; at worst, people who question Indo-European migration are sometimes accused of faulty scholarship or rightwing nationalism, and those who promote the theory that the Indo-Europeans came to India from outside may be accused of perpetuating colonial stereotypes where all good things (like the Vedic civilization) were said to have originated from Europe.

The appropriateness of using psychoanalytic approaches to the study of Hinduism has also been the subject of intense debate. Specifically, there has been some furor over studies which suggest that some texts, iconography, or practice are sexual in nature when most Hindus do not understand them to be so. The debates over whether this is another act of intellectual colonialism, reductionism, scholarship not supported by "facts," or being in denial about anything to do with sex are strident in parts of the diaspora, especially in the United States of America.

Another vociferous debate rages over what is perceived as appropriation without proper credit to Hinduism. These questions really go back to whether Hindus (and others) view practices and ideas (like yoga), which are largely connected with the Hindu tradition, as having very specific socio-historic contexts in the subcontinent or if they spring from a "universal" religion which is a common heritage of all human beings. One such battle rages over questions such as: Is yoga Hindu? Are the teachings of Vedanta or forms of meditation part of a universal knowledge which leads one to spiritual enlightenment, or are they part of the Hindu traditions? Can we consider meditation and yoga to be beneficial to one's health and nothing more? These are some of the intellectual questions and the basis of turf wars that one encounters in the study of the Hindu traditions in America. Manifestations of philosophies and practices which have roots in Hinduism, but which are presented without any reference to Hindu culture or ethos, or even considered religious, are very popular in America and globally. Hindus themselves seem divided on these issues and, in fact, one can trace the "universal" messages to early ambassadors of Hinduism to the West, such as Swami Vivekananda and Yogananda.

Hinduism thrives now—as it did almost a millennium ago—as a global religion, but in new continents and with new adaptive techniques. There are both centripetal as well as centrifugal forces within the Hindu traditions, at once tying in various groups, communities, beliefs, and practices, and at the same time making them stand out in distinctive splendor. Arenas for the practice of Hinduism keep changing; what may be domestic rituals and celebrations like Deepavali in south India may become staged in public community spaces in the diaspora, or even a secular stage in college campuses in the Americas. Gender roles are fluid; new women leaders and gurus may emerge, but as in the emergence of almost all "new" practices, precedence from one of Hinduism's hundreds of texts may be quoted to justify innovative observances.

The challenges facing Hindu traditions today are manifold. There is the constant threat of modernity as in any other religious tradition. The mix of religion and politics is seen both as necessary and as anathema by Hindus. Hindu groups are also doing a lot of soul searching as well as embarking on self-conscious social reforms with the threat of evangelical and proselytizing activities by other religions. In many areas of India, missionary activity is very strong, and some Hindus are framing the issue of aggressive conversion as an assault on human rights. There is also a perception that some of the best practices of Hinduism are being "plundered" and co-opted without credit being given for the mother tradition by forces of "universalism" and "spirituality," and being packaged as "stress-reduction" techniques.

On the other hand, there has never been a time when Hinduism has flourished in a more vibrant way—television stations in India are filled with religious commentaries, singers, and dancers rendering sacred song and text through performing arts, as well as continuous serials of narratives drawn from the epics and *Purana*s. In many parts of the world, Hindus are building prestigious temples and making their marks on the local landscapes as well as communities. Just as Islam and Christianity have become part of the Indian landscape, Hinduism has become an integral part of countries in many parts of the world. The final blessings that ring out after most rituals in Hindu temples, both in India and in other countries, proclaim the aspirations of all devotees: *sarva jana sukhino bhavantu*: "May all people be happy!"

Discussion questions

1   What would be the primary categories we can use to understand and interpret Hindu practices? Discuss examples of rituals which exemplify these categories.

2   In what ways would the food and diet regulations and recommendations in the Hindu tradition be similar to and different from the Jain tradition? Are the underlying reasons and categories for recommendations similar in nature?

3   If you have an opportunity to go to a local Hindu temple, observe and write about the deities enshrined there and the rituals you see. How are the icons of the deity treated in the temple? Using the website and fliers produced by the temple, describe how knowledge of the Hindu tradition is transmitted to the younger generation.

Key terms (in Sanskrit)

avatāra—"descent" of the Supreme Being to earth; usually a reference to one of the many incarnations of Vishnu on earth.

Bhagavad Gita—"Sacred Song" or "song of the Sacred Lord." One of the most important texts in the Hindu tradition. Eighteen chapters from the epic *Mahabharata*, it is a conversation between Lord Krishna and his cousin, Arjuna.

dharma—righteous action.

jāti—"birth group," or the community into which one is born.

karma—"action"; the results of good and bad deeds performed by a human being and which, to some extent, determines the quality of life both now and in later births.

Navarātri—"nine nights;" an autumnal festival celebrated in most parts of India.

prasāda—food that has been offered to the deity and is returned to the worshipper blessed by the deity.

pūjā—worship, usually using images of the divine, to which offerings are made.

Purāṇa—"ancient lore"; narratives of Hindu deities in Sanskrit language texts and texts in vernacular languages.

Rāmāyaṇa—"The Way (or story) of Rama." One of the two epics beloved in India and Southeast Asia.

Veda (pl. **Vedas**)—"sacred knowledge"; the oldest religious texts in India, they are composed in the Sanskrit language.

Notes

1 Edwin Bryant. *The Quest for the Origins of Vedic Culture: The Indo-Aryan Migration Debate*, New York: Oxford University Press, 2001; Edwin F. Bryant and Laurie L. Patton (eds.) *The Indo-Aryan Controversy: Evidence and Inference in Indian History*, Abingdon: Routledge, 2005.

2 *Bhagavad Gita* (4.8).

3 http://censusindia.gov.in/Census_Data_2001/India_at_glance/scst.aspx

4 Madhu Kishwar, "Manusmriti to Madhu smriti." http://www.ambedkar.org/News/hl/Manusmriti%20to.htm

5 Pandurang Vaman Kane, *History of Dharmasastra*. Vol 1/Part 1, Poona: Bhandarkar Oriental Research Institute, 1968: 7.

6 Rig Veda 10.85.44–47. The translation incorporates several interpretive concepts drawn from oral traditions.

7 *Manu Smriti* 8: 227.

8 The Rig Vedic verse (Rig III.31.1) which is rather difficult in structure has been interpreted to mean that there is a practice of declaring a daughter to be one's son (Kane, *History of Dharmasastra*, Vol 2/Part 1/435–6).

9 Tracy Pintchman, *Guests at God's Wedding: Celebrating Kartik among the Women of Benares*. Albany, NY: State University of New York Press, 2005. Anne Pearson, *"Because it Gives Me Peace of Mind:" Ritual Fasts in the Religious Lives of Hindu Women*, Albany, NY: State University of New York Press, 1996.

10 Pandurang Vaman Kane, *History of Dharmasastra*. Vol 2/Part 1 Poona: Bhandarkar Oriental Research Institute 1974: 757–800.

11 George Michell, *The Hindu Temple: An Introduction to its Meanings and Forms*, Chicago, IL: University of Chicago 1988: 69

12 Vasudha Narayanan, "Creating the South Indian 'Hindu' Experience in the United States." In Raymond Williams (ed.) *A Sacred Thread: Modern Transmissions of Hindu Traditions in India and Abroad*, Chambersburg, PA, 1992: 147–76.

13 *Yajnavalkya Smriti*, 3.115.

Recommended resources

Baird, Robert, ed. *Religion in Modern India* (2nd edition). New Delhi: Manohar, 1995.

Bryant, Edwin F. *Krishna: A Sourcebook*. Oxford: Oxford University Press, 2007.

Carman, John and Frederique Marglin. *Purity and Auspiciousness in Indian Society*. Leiden: E.J. Brill, 1985.

Gold, Ann Grodzins. *Fruitful Journeys*. Prospect Heights, IL: Waveland Press, 1988.

Hawley, John Stratton and Donna Marie Wulff, eds. *Devi: Goddesses of India*. Berkeley, CA: University of California Press, 1996.

Jackson, William J. *Tyāgarāja, Life and Lyrics*. Delhi: Oxford University Press, 1991.

Llewellyn, J. E. *Defining Hinduism: A Reader*. London: Equinox, 2005.

Miller, Barbara Stoler, trans. *The Bhagavad Gita: Krishna's Counsel in Time of War*. New York: Columbia University Press, 1986.

Nelson, Lance E., ed. *Purifying the Earthly Body of God: Religion and Ecology in Hindu India*. Albany, NY: State University of New York Press, 1998.

Patton, Laurie L., ed. *Jewels of Authority: Women and Text in the Hindu Tradition*. New York: Oxford University Press, 2001.

Pechilis, Karen, ed. *The Graceful Guru: Hindu Female Gurus in India and the United States*. New York: Oxford University Press, 2004.

Ramanujan, A. K. *Speaking of Siva*. Harmondsworth, England: Penguin Books, 1973.

Richman, Paula. *Questioning Ramayanas: A South Asian Tradition*. Berkeley, CA: University of California Press, 2001.

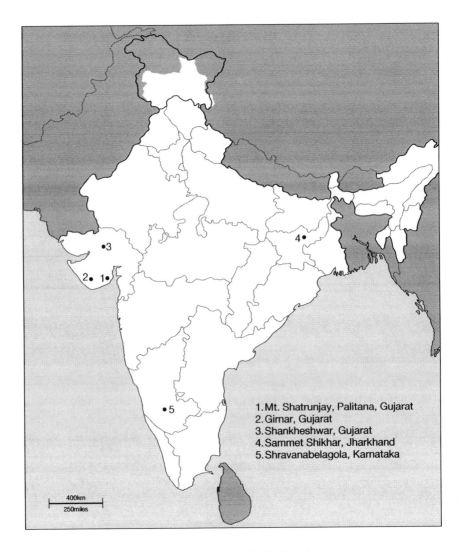

Map 3 Prominent places in Jainism as practiced in India today

1. Mt. Shatrunjay, Palitana, Gujarat
2. Girnar, Gujarat
3. Shankheshwar, Gujarat
4. Sammet Shikhar, Jharkhand
5. Shravanabelagola, Karnataka

400km
250miles

3 Jain traditions

Practicing tradition today

M. Whitney Kelting

Introduction

Jainism is an ancient tradition with its roots in the anti-Brahmanical renouncer traditions that arose in the tenth to fifth centuries BCE. Jains worship a set of enlightened teachers, Jinas, the most recent of whom is the historical figure, Mahavir. Jain teachings center on the nature of the universe, *karma* theory, monastic discipline and ethical codes derived from a commitment to non-violence. Jains believe that liberation from rebirth is best achieved through renunciation but they have also always recognized a valid and pious lay path leading to meritorious rebirth. Jains are a minority religious community clustered primarily in Western India with a smaller cluster in South India totaling approximately four and a quarter million people. The 2001 Census of India returned the figure of 4,225,053 for the population of Jains (0.4 percent of the population of India) with the highest densities in Maharashtra (1.3 percent of the state's population), Rajasthan (1.2 percent of the state's population) and Gujarat (1.0 percent of the state's population). Contemporary Jains identify themselves as an urban, middle-class, mercantile community. Scholars usually date the religious movements, which are collectively called Jainism, from the life of Mahavir who was teaching in approximately the sixth century BCE, though the historicity of the twenty-third Jina, Parshvanath, is generally accepted. Jains see Mahavir as the most recent of twenty-four Jinas who have come to revitalize the Jain faith in this era. Jains describe themselves as a four-fold community of monks, nuns, laymen, and laywomen. The mendicants (monks and nuns) follow a strict regimen of asceticism, modeled, more or less, on the accounts of the lives of the Jinas and other enlightened beings and the instructions for mendicants—attributed to Mahavir—with the goal of attaining total spiritual release from worldly bonds. Lay Jains are enjoined to support the mendicant orders and to observe a set of religious duties (*avashyaka*), which shape their religious practices. There are two distinct mendicant lineages, and lay devotees who are associated with them, in Jainism: the Shvetambar (literally, "white clad"), identified with southern Rajasthan, Gujarat, and the Bombay area of Maharashtra, and the Digambar ("sky-clad"), clustered primarily in Rajasthan, southern Maharashtra, and Karnataka. Jain sectarian identity cleaves cleanly between these two groups, their textual and historical authorities are distinct, as are their temples, temple practices, calendars, and social groupings.

Jainism: Identity

Mythic origins

Jains believe that there is no beginning of time, but rather that time is cyclical, described as a wheel, and that each cycle has a renewal and lasts for many tens of thousands of years. In each cycle of time, there will be twenty-four Jinas, "victors", who revitalize the Jain religion. The Jinas whose biographies are most fully elaborated are the first Jina, Rshabhanath or Adinath, and the twenty-fourth and most recent Jina, Mahavir. There are shorter accounts of the lives of the intermediate Jinas with the most complex tellings being the lives of the twenty-second Jina, Neminath, and the twenty-third Jina, Parshvanath.

The first of the Jinas in the present cycle, Rshabhanath, was born in the third spoke of the descending cycle of time when humans needed a teacher to guide them because the era of perfection was ending. He was born to royal parents, King Nabhi and Queen Marudevi. He had two wives, a hundred sons, and two daughters. When his children reached adulthood, he decided to renounce and installed his son Bharat as king. He achieved enlightenment and proceeded to teach his followers not only about Jainism and the nature of the universe but also all of the key components of culture: language, arts, sciences, and the skills needed to have a society. Rshabhanath attained liberation from rebirth (*nirvan*) on Mount Kailash in the Himalayas. He essentially founded both the lay and mendicant paths of Jainism, which is illustrated by the careers of his kin. His eldest son, Bharat, was a universal ruler (*cakravartin*) and ruled over India after his father renounced. His brother, Bahubali, originally fought a war with his brother over the reign of the kingdom but then saw the futility of warfare and renounced and became a monk. Bahubali has become a major figure of veneration among Digambar Jains, one of the two major sects of Jains. The other major sect, the Shvetambars, include a story in which Rshabhanath's mother, Queen Marudevi, achieves enlightenment when she sees the glory of the assembly hall that appears at her son Rshabhanath's moment of enlightenment.

The most recent Jina, Mahavir, was born in the city of Kundagram (probably a site near modern Patna in Bihar) to a royal family. According to the Shvetambar *Kalpa Sutra*, Mahavir was first conceived in the womb of a Brahmin (priestly caste) woman, Devananda, because of bad *karma* from an earlier life, but the gods decided he should not be born to a Brahmin but to a Kshatriya (royal) lineage. So the gods transferred Mahavir's embryo into the womb of the Queen Trishala. After his transfer the kingdom of King Siddharath and Queen Trishala experienced incredible good luck. Because of the auspiciousness of his conception and birth, they named their baby Vardhamana "The Increaser." Shvetambars believe that Vardhamana married and had a daughter, while Digambars reject the account of Mahavir's marriage. Both groups believe that at the age of thirty, Vardhamana renounced worldly life pulling out his hair in five handfuls. After twelve years of fasting and other intense asceticism during which he earned the name Mahavir or "great hero," he attained enlightenment (*kaivalya*). His omniscience caused a special assembly hall to appear for him to give his first sermon.

After this Mahavir initiated a group of eleven Brahmins as his chief disciples and named Indrabhuti Gautama (also known as Gautam Swami—he attained enlightenment when Mahavir attained *nirvan*) and Sudharman the leaders of the monks since an omniscient being no longer involves itself in earthly concerns, however religious. Mahavir preached sermons to his disciples, which they recorded, producing the central sacred texts of the tradition. Mahavir's followers increased, developing a large community of monks and, according to Shvetambar texts, an even larger community of nuns. Mahavir attained liberation from rebirth at his death at the age of 72 in the town of Pavapuri.

Digambar and Shvetambar Jain tellings of the life of Mahavir differ on a few points. Digambars reject two stories: the embryo transfer and Mahavir's marriage (and therefore also the birth of his daughter). The two traditions also disagree on whether or not Mahavir renounced clothing specifically (the Digambar position) or having lost his clothing simply did not seek new clothing (the Shvetambar position). This difference of account is directly linked to debates over monastic rules regarding clothing and the suitability of women renouncers who cannot renounce clothing.

After the death of Mahavir and Indrabhuti's omniscience, Sudharman was the only one of the chief disciples who had not attained enlightenment and was therefore the sole leader of the Jain monastic community. All Jain lineages (except for one sublineage of Shvetambars, Upakesha Gaccha) derive from the authority of Sudharman. Sudharman taught the sacred texts to the first of the Jain elders, Jambu. Jambu was the last person to attain liberation in this cycle of time. The seventh elder, Bhadrabahu, was the last person to have knowledge of the entire Jain canon.

Historical origins

While the earlier Jinas (also called *tirthankars* or "ford-makers") cannot be placed historically, the two most recent can be accepted as historical personages.[1] Jains traditionally date the life of Parshvanath to the tenth to ninth century BCE and Mahavir to the sixth century BCE. Though Jains see Jainism as eternal, the earliest concrete historical evidence for Jainism is accounts of the teacher Mahavir (an early contemporary of Gautama Buddha) who lived in eastern India probably in the fourth century BCE. Traditional dating puts Mahavir's life a century or two earlier but Mahavir's lifetime dating is linked to that of Gautama Buddha's, which is now believed to be the fourth century BCE.[2] Mahavir is referenced in the teachings of Gautama Siddhartha, the founder of Buddhism. Jains also trace the direct lineage of the first teachers after Mahavir as lasting between one hundred fifty and two hundred years. The end of this direct lineage is believed to also mark the end of complete and correct knowledge of Mahavir's teaching.

After the death of Mahavir, the Jain histories trace the lineage of descent through Sudharman to Jambu, the first of the elders, and onward through the rest of the eight elders including Bhadrabahu and then the eighth elder, Sthulabhadra. Sthulabhadra established a council at Pataliputra for the recitation of the sacred texts to codify and stabilize the canon 160 years after the death of Mahavir.

Digambar Jains reject the authenticity of this recitation and from that point forward, the Digambar and Shvetambar communities crystallized their separate sectarian identities. Digambar lineages split from the Shvetambar lineages; Digambars believe that the sacred texts were all lost and they trace their text tradition to Dharasena, a second century mendicant leader, who taught the last scriptures to his disciples Puspadanta and Bhutabali. Digambar histories claim that Bhadrabahu traveled south with part of the community, establishing their lineage of monks and practices.

During the medieval period in both Digambar and Shvetambar sects, temple-dwelling monks became common. Digambars created the office of the *bhattaraka* who is a head of a monastery with authority over libraries as well. Eventually these *bhattaraka*s became important ritual specialists, but ceased to be seen as true monks. To this day, however, the *bhattaraka*s still control important centers of Digambar scholarship. In the Shvetambar tradition, the temple-dwelling monks, later called *yati*s, arose to perform rituals, astrology, and medicine for lay Jains and, like *bhattaraka*s, they managed Jain libraries and temples. However, unlike the *bhattaraka*s, the *yati*s have since died out with a few minor exceptions and the institutions they controlled are under the control of lay Jain temple and institutional trusts. At the same time, some Jain monks became discontented with the trend towards these temple-dwelling monks and formed lineages that proposed a return to mendicancy and a stricter rule for monks. Ultimately these reformed monks gained prestige and authority over the temple-dwelling monks. Lineages following strict mendicancy arose in both Digambar and Shvetambar sects and it is these lineages which dominate contemporary Jainism.

Jain reform movements developed out of both the Digambar and Shvetambar lineages. The primary concerns of these reform movements were the worship of images and the building of temples. A second concern that surfaces several times is the issue of perceived monastic laxity and the role of lay Jains. In the fifteenth century, a Jain layman named Lonka Shah proposed an iconoclastic and anti-temple form of Jainism. The lineage that derived directly from Lonka has all but disappeared now. However, a seventeenth century follower of Lonka by the name of Lavaji broke off from the Lonka Gaccha because of its laxity and with other reformers from the Lonka Gaccha formed an ascetic lineage, the Sthanakavasis. The Sthanakavasi tradition is iconoclast and anti-temple. Their canon, though Shvetambar, rejects any of the texts that condone temple building and image worship. Sthanakavasis also adopted the practice of wearing the small face cloth (*muhpatti*) at all times; this visual marker of their lineage can be traced back to their founder, Lavaji.

The iconoclast tradition of the Shvetambar Terapanth was formed in the eighteenth century by a reformer monk, Acarya Bhiksu. Bhiksu was drawn to the Sthanakavasi lineage at first, but over time rejected many of the Sthanakavasi practices and apparent monastic laxity. After eight years Bhiksu left the Sthanakavasis are formed his own group of monks, the Terapanth. They share with the Sthanakavasis in iconoclasm, the abbreviated Shvetambar canon, and the wearing of the face cloth. The Terapanthis perform intense austerities and have a text centered, legalistic form of Jainism. Over time, Terapanthis developed a strong focus on guru veneration around the charismatic authority of the Terapanthi leaders. Under their fourth leader, Tulsi, the Terapanthis developed a focus on religious ethics that leads them to work ecumenically with other Jain groups but also to encourage ethical proselytizing. In recent years, Terapanthis have created a stage in the initiation process when the initiate has only partial authority but can still travel abroad. This has allowed Terapanthi teachers to give sermons to and attend to the ritual needs of Jains abroad.

The Digambar tradition, too, has had reform movement lineages. The fifteenth century scholar monk Taran Swami preached a form of Digambar Jainism that rejected any image worship, the authority of the *bhattarakas*, and mysticism. The followers of Taran Swami worship books containing the teachings of Taran Swami and other Digambar mystics such as Kundakunda and symbols of Jainism instead of Jina images. The Digambar Terapanth formed in the mid-to-late seventeenth century as a rejection of the practices and authority of the *bhattarakas*, the worship of guardian and tutelary deities, and the use of substances in worship that might attract insects. Digambar Terapanthi institutions were controlled by Digambar laymen. The Digambar Terapanth is found mostly in central southern India. Some Digambar Terapanthis have been influenced by the Jain thinker, Kanji Swami. In the twentieth century, the Sthanakavasi monk, Kanji Swami, having read the metaphysical writings of the Digambar scholar, Kundakunda, became convinced of the truth of Digambar teachings.[3] After some years of struggle, Kanji left the Sthanakavasi monkhood and became a Digambar layman. The Kanji Swami movement has remained an influential lay movement focused on esoteric interpretations of Jain texts. Most successfully, the Kanji Swami movement has led to a devotional movement centered on Simandhar Swami, a Jina preaching in another cosmic continent.

Jain claims to universality and uniqueness

Jain *karma* theory asserts that the workings of *karma* apply to all souls whether Jain or not. The principles of *karma* are understood to be universal. Thus while being a Jain is the best way to prevent or reduce the binding of *karma*, it is possible for non-Jains to decrease the binding of *karma* by avoiding the sorts of acts which bind *karma*. Likewise, most souls are capable of suddenly realizing the correctness of Jain *karma* theory. And yet, this universality of *karma* theory is tempered by the idea that Jainism is the most effective path to liberation.

While Jain theorists are unwavering in their notion that Jainism is correct, they also present a form of philosophical relativism called *anekantavada*, or many-pointedness. For example, Jains believe that other religions may hold views containing partial truth. The seventh and eighth century monk, Haribhadra, argued that anyone who follows the correct actions will benefit karmically but at the same time makes it clear that other pathways, however much they may hold elements of truth, are ultimately going to mislead the believer.[4] The position of many-pointedness is most significant in its suggestion that a person can perceive knowledge from a variety of sources, decentering Jain ideas of authority.

Location of Jains

Jainism is a relatively small, minority religion in India and most of its adherents live in the western Indian states of Maharashtra, Gujarat, and Rajasthan. The 2001 Census of India returned the figure of 4,225,053 for the population of Jains (0.4 percent of the population of India) with the highest densities in Maharashtra (1.3 percent of the state's population), Rajasthan (1.2 percent of the state's population) and Gujarat (1.0 percent of the state's population). There are substantial Jain communities in Karnataka, Madhya Pradesh, and Tamilnadu. In addition, Jains have a real presence in the major cities of Delhi and Kolkata. Jain sectarian communities are clustered, with Shvetambar Jains primarily in western India and Digambar communities in two groups—one cluster in Rajasthan and around New Delhi and another in central and south India.

Because Jains have long been a mercantile community, business interests have led groups of Jains to leave the areas of their ethnic heritage to move to other parts of India and abroad. Hence one finds large communities of Marwari (Rajasthani) Jains living in Kolkata and of Gujarati Jains living in East Africa. There are large Jain communities in the UK, USA, Canada, Kenya, South Africa, and the UAE. There are longstanding small Jain communities in Japan as well.

Jainism as a South Asian tradition

In common with many South Asian traditions, Jainism concerns itself with notions of *karma* and rebirth as well as with the ritual practices of ritualized viewing or *darshan*, and worship with offerings or *puja*. Jains share in the pan-Indic concepts of *karma* and the transmigration of souls, but understand the workings of *karma* in a unique way. Jain *karma* theory is among the oldest philosophical traditions in India. Jains believe that *karma* is a material substance, which binds to the soul whenever the soul becomes sticky with passion or other strong emotions or attachments. *Karma* bound to the soul determines certain aspects of one's present and future life conditions. This karmic matter also prevents the soul from reaching liberation—from rising to the top of the universe from which it cannot return to be reborn. Much of the Jain philosophical tradition is concerned with the workings of *karma*: ways to avoid its accrual and ways to destroy that *karma* which has already bound with one's soul. The removal of all *karma* is necessary for a soul to reach liberation.

Jain philosophy has put forth an ideology based on the goal of liberation from the cycle of rebirth and posits this as the primary goal. At the same time, Jains (including the same monks who wrote liberation ideological texts) also see well-being and auspiciousness as central values and as the karmic result of well-practiced Jainism. In the present era of spiritual decline in which Jains believe liberation is not possible, lay Jains work towards maximizing their merit while decreasing their sin, in hopes of both gaining a good rebirth to enjoy and facilitating the gradual progression of one's soul towards liberation.

Jains also participate fully in the *bhakti* devotional traditions of South Asia. Jain literature includes literally thousands of devotional hymns written of a time period spanning nearly the entirety of Jainism's history. Most Jain devotional hymns have been written by Jain monks, suggesting that devotionalism is well situated within orthodox Jainism and that Jain devotionalism is not a movement challenging traditional authority. These hymns praise the twenty-four Jinas or describe and praise particular Jina images or temples. Some hymns are addressed to the Jain guardian deities or praise the virtues of Jain saints. However, Jain devotionalism fully shares in the broader devotional practice of invoking emotional sentiments to increase the feelings of devotion in those singing and hearing the hymns.[5] Different from most South Asian devotionalism, Jain devotional hymns do not call on the gods to respond. Jinas, as enlightened beings who have transcended all emotion, do not respond to devotion. It is the Jain devotee who benefits from devotional prayer and song. In spite of Jainism's goal of equanimity and the transcendence of emotion for liberation, Jains recognize the utility of harnessing emotions to achieve the first stages of right thinking. For example, Jain texts often cite compassion as a key emotion for right thinking while simultaneously reminding readers that compassion must ultimately be replaced by equanimity. Jain authors have written in all of the prevailing devotional genres of their given language traditions.

The lives of Mahavir and Gautama Buddha share some key similarities. The two teachers were contemporaries living in the same region of India. In particular, the two lives share the importance of the teacher being from a royal lineage and a universal ruler (*cakravartin*), the renunciation of the world, and the basic structure of the five great vows. The overwhelming concern about non-violence is shared between the two traditions but manifests itself in different practices. In general, Jain texts have presented Buddhists as misguided because of the relative laxity of their monastic codes.[6] The similarities in the philosophical texts and origin narratives lead to superficial similarities in monastic practices and iconography.

Jainism: Practice

Jain worship includes much that is shared with other South Asian traditions: temple worship, festivals linked to the lunar calendar, ordination of Jain mendicants, pilgrimages, dietary rules and fasting, and rites of passage.

Temple worship

Within Jainism there are both iconoclast and image worshipping sects. The majority of Jains worship with images and they have a long history of temple patronage and liturgical texts. Jains have built some of the most ornate temples in India, particularly those at Mount Abu and Ranakpur in Rajasthan. Jain temples center on an image of one of the twenty-four Jinas of this era but they often include additional Jina images along with images of the guardian deities associated with the central Jina image and other tutelary deities. The guardian deities and intercessionary deities are drawn from regional deities shared with Hindus (such as Kshetrapals, Bhairavs, Viras, Matas, Nagas, and Bhumiyas). In some groups, most notably the Kharatara Gaccha of the Shvetambar, there are images of deceased monks who are believed to act as intercessionary forces on behalf of Jain devotees. These monks (Dadagurus) are powerful agents of protection for lay Jains.[7] Increasingly one also sees shrines built to house the relics of charismatic monks and nuns.[8] Digambar Jains in northern India usually also have a representation of the five Merus (the holy mountains on which the gods bathe the infant Jinas).

Jain temple worship involves making offerings to the consecrated images, and the performance of devotional prayers and hymns. Jains also perform liturgical worship (*puja*s and *mahapuja*s), reenacting key narratives as worship; many of these are linked to the five auspicious dates in the lives of each of the twenty-four Jinas. Image worshipping Jains perform worship (*puja*) in ways that often appear similar to worship (*puja*) performed in Hindu temples with some significant differences. Daily temple worship includes ritual viewing of the images (*darshan*) followed by a series of offerings on the image including bathing the image with water and other liquids, placing flowers on the images, and, for Shvetambars, dressing the image in special decorative coverings. Jains also make offerings in front of the image like rice, sweets, and coconuts and other fruits or, in some reform groups, only dry fruits and rice. Lamps and incense are always offered in front of the image as well. These offerings are similar to or identical to offerings made in Hindu temples of the region from which these Jains come.

In Shvetambar temples, the lay Jains will enter the inner sanctum of the temple and make the offerings onto the image themselves. In southern Digambar temples, ritual priests make the offerings on the image on behalf of the lay Jains. In addition, the Digambar worship centers on the ritual bathing of the images while the Shvetambar ritual, though it includes a ritual bath, centers on the anointing and decorating of the image. Some of the differences between forms of Jain worship are manifestations of regional difference rather than sectarian ones. For example, Shvetambar Jains and northern Digambar Jains perform the rituals of worship without the intercession of priests while south Indian Digambars employ a class of Brahmin-like Jain priests to perform the rituals that are in contact with the images themselves. This difference reflects regional differences in temple practices far more than Jain sectarian values.

Jains participate in the ritual culture of South Asia in the centrality of the practice of performing ritual viewing (*darshan*) and making offerings on and in front of the image (*puja*). But because the Jinas are enlightened and not subject to attachment, they are understood to be unresponsive to worship. Unlike Hindu deities, the Jinas do not respond to prayers nor do they consume or respond to offerings. The offerings made are not acknowledged or blessed by the Jinas because as enlightened souls the Jinas do not participate in worldly matters. Strikingly different from Hindus, Jains do not consume any of the offerings

Figure 3.1 Jain worship (*puja*) in Shvetambar Temple. Photo taken by M. Whitney Kelting.

made to the Jinas. The absence of the Jinas is often the first difference that Jains name between their worship and that of Hindus. And yet, Jains worship images of the absent Jinas, but do so as a form of meditation and renunciation (of offerings) rather than with the expectation of particular results.[9] Jain temples include unenlightened beings such as guardian deities who are routinely petitioned for assistance in worldly matters and whose worship includes the same set of offerings. Though there are a few exceptions, such as the temple at Mahudi, Gujarat, where the powerful non-liberated deity Ghantakaran Mahavir is worshipped and blessed leftovers (*prasad*) are consumed, for the most part Jains do not consume blessed leftovers from their worship of their guardian deities either.

Jain monks and nuns do not make offerings to the Jina images in temples but instead do worship mentally through hymn singing, recitations, and meditation. Monks and nuns own no possessions and therefore are incapable of making offerings in Jain temples but this does not mean that Jain mendicants are opposed to temple worship. In the image worshipping sects, Jain monks encourage patrons to build or renovate Jain temples and to install new images. These same monks regularly remind lay Jains to do *puja* and go on pilgrimage. Jain mendicants play a key role in the installation of new images and will attend large-scale ceremonies sponsored by lay Jains to recite certain powerful mantras only available to monks. Monks and nuns themselves visit Jain temples for ritual viewing (*darshan*) and to offer devotional hymns and prayers.

Members of the Shvetambar iconoclast sects of the Sthanakavasi and Terapanthi and the Digambar iconoclast lineage of Taran Swami participate in devotionalism through the singing and reciting of hymns but do not participate in temple building or image worship. In some cases, iconoclast Jain lineages permit the veneration of living monks or Jain sacred texts.[10]

Festivals

Jains participate in both festivals celebrated exclusively by Jains and pan-Indian festivals. Jain festivals are usually marked by large-scale temple ceremonies, processions, and fasting. Some Jain festivals are similar between the two major sects, such as Paryusan and Das Lakshan, but have different timings and practices associated with them. Other festivals such as the Shvetambar Ayambil Oli Festival and the Digambar Mahamastakabhishekh are exclusive to their lineages. With only one exception, Jain festivals are specific to sectarian groups. The one festival shared by all Jain sects is a fairly minor celebration of the birth of Mahavir on his actual birthday. This is usually marked by a procession by which the inclusion of Digambar and Shvetambar as well as image worshipping and iconoclast lineages serves to join the entire Jain community for the day. This is the day that the Indian government has chosen as a national holiday to represent Jainism. It is, however, not a particularly important festival for any of the Jain groups; for example, the significant celebration of Mahavir's birthday for Shvetambar Jains occurs during their festival of Paryushan. Both Shvetambar and Digambar Jains celebrate the worship of Jain knowledge (for Shvetambars Jnan Pancami, "Knowledge Fifth," and for Digambars Shruta

Pancami, "Scripture Fifth") during which Jains worship knowledge in the form of religious books. This holiday is linked to the overall veneration of the canon in the Jain tradition and the books offered veneration are central ancient texts for which the sectarian communities offer the worship. For Digambars the date of Shruta Pancami is linked to the day that the Digambar scriptures were codified and written down. For Shvetambars, Jnan Pancami is linked to the worship of Saraswati as well as Jain sacred books.

The most important annual festival for both Shvetambar and Digambar Jains culminates in the annual rite of confession and expiation on the Samvatsari. For Shvetambars it is an eight-day festival called Paryusan and for Digambars it is a ten-day festival called Das Lakshan. These festivals take place in the early autumn but at adjacent times. Both communities observe these festivals with increased dietary restrictions or fasting, with daily sermons or lessons, and ultimately the annual rite of confession.

The Shvetambar festival of Paryusan also has daily sermons, which focus on the ritual and moral obligations of the festival and on the reading of a key Shvetambar canonical text, the *Kalpa Sutra*. The recitation of the *Kalpa Sutra* climaxes in the spectacle of Mahavir's birthday (Mahavir Janam Divas) while the final day of Paryusan is marked by the congregational confession and expiation on Samvatsari. The *Kalpa Sutra* recitation includes a substantial telling of the story of Mahavir and the recitation of this narrative is linked to the most public and elaborate ritual during the Shvetambar Paryusan. On the fifth day, the *Kalpa Sutra* recitation reaches the section during which the conception and birth of Mahavir are told. The recitation breaks for lunch and the entire congregation gathers in the afternoon in their finest clothing for the celebration of Mahavir's birthday. In practice, most congregations will have an auction for the privilege to be the person to display and worship each of the fourteen dreams that Mahavir's mother had when Mahavir was conceived in her womb. These dreams presage the birth of a universal teacher and are the mark of the specialness of Mahavir even before he was born. All of the mothers of the Jinas have these dreams at the conception of a Jina. Each dream is displayed and garlanded in turn by the family who win the bid for that privilege. The largest bids are usually made for the dreams associated with the goddess Lakshmi, though in gem merchant Jain communities, the dream of the pile of gems is unsurprisingly sometimes the most popular bid.

After the dream veneration is complete, the story of Mahavir's birth is recited and the congregation will mark this celebration with the breaking open of coconuts and sharing of the coconut pieces with each other. A cradle in the front of the room is rocked first by the family whose bid won this privilege and then by most of the community in attendance. Mahavir's cradle is then processed to a specially prepared location where it will be venerated for the remaining three days of the festival. This celebration marks the halfway point of the festival and serves as the emotionally charged celebration of Mahavir's birth for Shvetambar Jains. On the last day of the Samvatsari festival, Shvetambar Jains perform a communal confession and expiation (*pratikraman*) for all of the harm intentionally or unintentionally performed in the past year. This ritual is a key marker of Shvetambar

Jain identity and all Jains in good standing will attend this confession. After the ritual confession, Jains will make particular and individual statements of apology to friends, relatives, and acquaintances.

For Digambars the focus in Das Lakshan is on ten virtues that Digambars cultivate as part of the ideal life. Daily sermons focus on one of the ten virtues and the festival ends with the rite of confession on the tenth day. There are few Digambar monks and Digambars believe the entire Agama corpus was lost (and therefore reject the *Kalpa Sutra*) so the focus of this festival differs considerably from the practices of the Shvetambar Paryusan. The central text for this festival is the *Tattvartha Sutra* and the sermons are given by educated laymen. The festival ends similarly to Paryusan with a confession and requests for forgiveness.

Sectarian festivals

The nine-day biannual Shvetambar festival of the Ayambil Oli centers round the worship of the *siddhacakra yantra*. The *siddhacakra yantra* is the visual representation of the key Jain mantra, the Navkar Mantra.

> I bow to the Teachers (*arhat*).
> I bow to the Liberated Ones (*siddha*).
> I bow to the leaders of the monks (*acarya*).
> I bow to the monk-teachers (*upadhyaya*).
> I bow to all the living mendicants (*sadhu*).
> This five-fold mantra, which destroys all sin,
> Is the most auspicious of all the auspicious things.

The Navkar Mantra is used by Shvetambar Jains as the fundamental *mantra* for creating auspiciousness, blessing beginnings, and protection. It can be recited in place of other *mantra*s if one does not know the other *mantra* and so serves as the core Jain *mantra*. Digambar Jains also recite a similar *mantra*, the Panca-Namaskara Mantra, which is comprised of the first five lines of the Navkar Mantra above. Digambar Jains have a similar visual depiction or *yantra* for the Navkar Mantra but have not developed a festival around the *yantra*. The Ayambil Oli is organized such that each of the nine days is associated with one of the nine positions on the *yantra*. Many women will perform a series of nine days of single-sitting fast of bland food for the nine-day festival in imitation of the story of Maynasundari and King Sripal. In that story, Maynasundari performs this fast and cures her husband, King Sripal, of leprosy. This fast is widely believed to bless a woman with a happy and long marriage.[11] The Ayambil Oli integrates Jain orthodox worship of the Navkar Mantra with the worldly concerns of lay Jains, making it the most popular festival after Paryusan.

For Digambars the most significant and spectacular festival is the Mahamastakabhishekh, which occurs on a twelve-year cycle (the next will be in 2018) and is celebrated in Shravan Belgola, Karnataka. This festival marks the heroic asceticism of Bahubali, the great monk and son of Rshabhanath. Bahubali's veneration is the focus of much of Digambar devotionalism, particularly in southern India.

The colossal statue of Bahubali in Shravan Belgola is bathed by 1008 substances by a series of lay Jains who have been granted the privilege to do so. At the same time, across a small valley, tens of thousands of Jains watch as the image changes colors with each offering. The presence of a number of the relatively few Digambar monks offers an opportunity for these monks to venerate this great monk ascetic and for lay Digambars to have the auspicious site of these living ideals as well.

Lay Jains also participate in some holidays more broadly associated with South Asia. The most popular of these pan-Indian festivals among Jains are Divali, Kartik Punam, and Raksha Bandhan. Some holidays are celebrated in ways that

Figure 3.2 Ritual diagram of expanded *Siddhachakra yantra*. Photo taken by M. Whitney Kelting.

are identical to their Hindu counterparts in their region, ethnic group, and class. For example, Raksha Bandhan—during which a sister ties a bracelet on her brother as a rite of protection—is indistinguishable from the Hindu celebration of this holiday. On the other hand, some Jain performances of festivals share in pan-Indian practices while including particular Jain practices. For example, in western India, Jains celebrate Divali with great enthusiasm. For Jains, Divali is the day that Mahavir attained death and liberation and this is marked by special temple decorations and recitation. But Divali is celebrated by Jains in western India primarily as the coming of the New Year and is dominated by the worship of Lakshmi, the goddess of wealth and prosperity. In addition, Jains also worship family account books and the instruments of trade (such as scales), and celebrate with special delicacies and gifting. The multi-day festival is capped for Jains by the worship of knowledge (in the forms of the goddess Saraswati and Jain religious books) on the fifth day after New Year's Day. So while Jains participate in the worship of Lakshmi, special sweets, visiting, gift giving, fireworks, and lamp lighting associated with Divali shared with other groups, they also invest this major festival with Jain significance. On the other hand, Jains reject certain festivals on the grounds that they conflict with Jain principles; for example, Jains do not participate in the festival of Holi in part because the Holi bonfire would incur violence to insects and other beings.

Ordination

For Jains, the most powerful ritual assertion of Jain religious values is the ordination (or *diksha*) of a Jain monk or nun. Ordinations provide a public restatement of Jain renunciatory values and an opportunity for the communities to gather around the model of the ideal life. The requirements for renunciation are determined by the sectarian tradition as well as by lineage. For example, Shvetambar sects ordain women while Digambar sects do not permit full initiation to women. However, Digambar Jains have a form of partial initiation for women modifying the requirement for the abandonment of clothing.

Each of the sectarian lineages performs its own ordination rituals in the presence of both mendicants and laity, but at the core of all ordinations are the formal vows. The key moment of the ordination is the taking of the five vows and the subsequent actions required by those vows. In particular, the vow of non-possession, which requires the initiate to renounce all unnecessary possessions, often visually signifies renunciation. In the Shvetambar tradition this is signified by changing into the white clothing of a monk or nun and the acceptance of the marks of initiation (the broom, staff, and begging bowls) while for Digambars renunciation of possessions is marked by the initiate removing his clothing. Unique to Jainism, initiates are required to remove their hair in five handfuls as a reenactment of Mahavir's renunciation. In the rite of "pulling out hair" (or *keshalocha*), the initiate plucks out the last clump of his or her hair completing the full transformation into a monk or nun. In fact, the pulling out of the hair of a Jain mendicant is often cited as evidence of the determination and intense austerity of their renouncers.

Figure 3.3 Ordination of a Jain nun. Photo taken by M. Whitney Kelting.

For Shvetambars, the story of Mahavir's renunciation has a key episode that is reenacted as part of the ordination ritual. First, before Mahavir formally renounces, he is believed to have spent a year giving away all of his worldly possessions. In Shvetambar ordinations, this is imitated in processions during which the initiate throws handfuls of rice and coins to the onlookers. Some initiates will perform this "year-long giving" on multiple occasions but at a minimum there is a procession on the day before the formal renunciation. The models for ordination derive from the renunciation narratives of the Jinas, most particularly that of Mahavir, while for Shvetambar nuns, the model can be derived from the renunciation of the saintly nun, Rajimati.[12]

Pilgrimage

Jains have a long history of temple patronage and built monumental temples in pilgrimage sites from the twelfth century onwards. Jain pilgrimage has centered on sites associated with the five auspicious moments in the life of each Jina: conception, birth, renunciation, enlightenment and first sermon, and death and liberation; with the most attention to the locations of their birth, enlightenment, and death. These sites, called *tirtha*s ("fords"), are shared by Digambar and Shvetambar communities, though not without some contestation. The two most elaborate *tirtha*s are Mount Shatrunjay in Gujarat and Sammetshikar in Jharkhand. Sammetshikar is the site where Parshvanath and 19 other Jinas died and reached liberation. The sites of the deaths and liberations of Rshabhanath (Mount Kailash), Vasupujya (Campapuri, Bihar), Neminath (Girnar, Gujarat), and Mahavir (Pavapuri, Bihar) are also very important pilgrimage sites for all Jains. Though few Jains live in the region where Sammetshikar is, Jains try to make a pilgrimage to this temple (along with other sites associated with the lives of the last two Jinas, Mahavir and Parshvanath, who lived and preached in the region) once in their lifetimes.

Mount Shatrunjay is believed to be the site of the first sermon of the first Jina, Rshabhanath, and the central temple houses an image of the first teaching assembly. It is also the site of the death and liberation of thousands of Jain monks. Because of a combination of its significance and the fact that it is located centrally for the majority of Jains, Shatrunjaya is the most visited of Jain pilgrimage sites. In addition to a large temple to Rshabhanath, there are literally hundreds of temples and shrines on the top of the mountain and many pilgrims' hostels at the base of the mountain. Many Jains make regular visits to Shatrunjaya but the most important day for this pilgrimage is Kartik Punam when the rainy season officially ends and Jains are permitted to go on pilgrimage again. On this day thousands of Jains will climb the mountain for worship. For those Jains who cannot make the pilgrimage, paintings and three-dimensional models of Mount Shatrunjay are venerated in their home temples.[13]

Other key pilgrimage sites center round sites associated with the death (and, in some cases, liberation) of significant Jain monks. The Digambar pilgrimage site of Shravan Belgola, Karnataka is marked with a monumental image of the monk Bahubali who was the son of the Jina Rshabhanath. This enormous stone image is the site of a major festival held every twelve or so years but it is a popular pilgrimage site for Digambars even when the festival is not happening. Shravan Belgola is also the site of the auspicious deaths of many other famous Jain monks associated with Digambar lineages and the sites of the death monuments for these monks receive veneration by Digambar pilgrims. The death sites of the founders of various Shvetambar and Digambar lineages are also pilgrimage sites.

Finally, Jains also go on pilgrimage to images believed to have magical properties or to have particularly powerful guardian deities. These temples are more commonly associated with particular communities. For example, Shankheshvar Parshvanath in Shankheshvar, Gujarat, is a key pilgrimage amongst Gujarati Shvetambars while in Hombuja, Karnataka, the image of Padmavati is extremely popular with Digambar pilgrims from southern Maharashtra and Karnataka.

Dietary rules and fasting

There are several practices which mark a home as a Jain home, but arguably the most significant domestic practices associated with Jainism are dietary rules. Because of Jain injunctions against harming beings, Jains have long been the strictest of vegetarians. In addition, some plant products are restricted because they either have life in them (for example, root vegetables like potatoes), vegetables with many seeds that cannot be removed easily (like eggplant), they are known to harbor insects (like figs), or are difficult to ensure that bugs are not in them (like cauliflower). Because Jains extend the possibility of violence to include violence against plants, on particular days and during festivals Jains often abstain from eating any vegetables, making their meals exclusively from grains and pulses. Jain food rules enjoin Jain laywomen to be particularly conscientious about checking all foods for insects, taking care in the grinding of flour and spices, and not wasting food. The attention to non-violence in Jain eating necessitates a corpus of texts on Jain cuisine, and the concern that food made by non-Jains may not uphold a high enough standard of non-violence makes eating in one's own home a moral virtue. Pious Jains often perform complex fasts that further restrict their diet and require special preparation and serving. Elderly Jains may take life-long vows that require that all of their water be boiled and that particular items or preparations be excluded from their food. In pious homes, strict dietary rules are upheld ensuring that not only will family members be protected from the worst of karmic excesses, but also that the family will be able to feed Jain monks and nuns garnering their valuable and auspicious blessings. Jain food rules, though a domestic practice, are deeply embedded in institutional practices (such as alms collecting by monks) and authoritative texts in which Jain *karma* theory and food restrictions are delineated and enumerated.

Jain fasting provides a number of contexts in which Jains enmesh their religious and domestic lives. Jains recognize several degrees of fasting, ranging from a full fast with no water to partial fasts of one or two sittings per day. These days of fasting are strung together into a series of continuous days (*oli*, or line) of fasting. The most popular line fast is that of the Shvetambar Ayambil Oli. Some fasts are performed calendrically with a fast falling on a particular astrological or lunar date. The most popular of these is the Rohini Fast performed by both Shvetambar and Digambar women to prevent widowhood. A third category of fast are those fasts, like the Updhan Fast, which require the fasting person to live with Jain mendicants while performing the fast in a modified version of the mendicant's life (these fasters never collect alms or give sermons or blessings).

In addition to the preparation and particular methods of serving food to people performing extended fasts, the completion of these longer and more elaborate fasts is usually marked with a fast-breaking celebration. These celebrations often include performances of fast-breaking songs and other devotional songs for the benefit of the person fasting, substantial donations to temples or Jain organizations in commemoration of the completion of a fast, and the procession of those Jains who complete long fasts as models of Jain idealized virtue displayed to both the wider Jain community and non-Jains. These three activities serve to link the virtue of the person fasting to the virtue of their family, their congregation, and the community of Jains. So while these fasts may, on the one hand, be seen as domestic practices, on the other, the ritual and social requirements that surround a fast make Jain fasting a public assertion of Jain values.

Jain rites of passage

Although attempts have been made to delineate a set of Jain rites of passage, in fact Jains use Hindu rites of passage drawn from Hindus in their linguistic, ethnic, and caste groups. Hindu rites are changed in minor ways to accommodate Jain values and identity. For example, the auspicious *mantra*s recited to begin the ceremony are changed to ones associated with Jainism. Conversely, Jains do not perform certain Hindu rites of passage because they conflict with Jain teachings; for example, Jains believe that upon death souls are immediately reborn in new bodies (unless they achieve enlightenment) and therefore they do not perform the *shraddha* rites that Hindus perform as part of their funerary rituals to ensure a peaceful and successful passage of a soul into its next life.

There are only two Jain rites of passage: ordination (discussed earlier) and a ritualized death called *sallekhana* or *samadhi marana*. Ordination transforms a lay Jain into a monk or nun. *Sallekhana* is a uniquely Jain rite of death that involves taking a vow to fast until death. The goal of this ritualized death is to prepare the soul for death by decreasing karmic bounds through the renunciation of food, water, and actions. The vow is only undertaken in cases where the person taking the vow is already terminally ill or dying of old age (with a rare exception for blindness as an acceptable rationale among some communities of monks). The vow can only be taken under the guidance of a Jain monk and with the consent of the person's family unless they are a mendicant. For Jains, this kind of controlled death is seen as a good death; a death, which decreases *karma* and promotes a good rebirth.

Religious authority in Jainism: Texts and canon

Shvetambar and Digambar Jains have almost entirely different textual traditions.[14] In fact, the central schism in the Jain tradition crystallizes around the question of canon authority and the legitimacy or lack of legitimacy of the fifth century CE Council of Vallabhi at which the Shvetambar Canon was codified. This council was convened in order to codify the canon but only Shvetambar monks were in attendance. The council's editorial authority and the resulting canon of scripture are rejected by the Digambar community and the division between these sectarian groups was solidified. The canon of the Jain tradition, the *Agamas*, is understood to be the absolute and correct truths about the universe as presented to Jains by their enlightened teachers and disciples. Digambars believe that the *Agamas* have been lost while the Shvetambars maintain that the council recorded the remaining teachings of Mahavir as the most recent iteration of these truths.

There are only a few extant texts shared by both Digambar and Shvetambar Jains: (1) the second century *Tattvartha Sutra* of Umasvati, which outlines the basics of Jain metaphysics; (2) the fifth century *Nyayavatara* and *Sanmatisutra* of Siddhasena Divakara outlining Jain logic and other philosophical principles; and (3) the *Bhaktamar Stotra* of Manatunga, a sixth century devotional hymn dedicated to the first Jina, Rsabhanath. Though Digambar and Shvetambar Jain canonical and textual histories diverge, the basic doctrines and philosophies of the two sects remain remarkably similar and stable.

Shvetambar canon and texts

The Shvetambar Canon has a high degree of authority but Shvetambar Murtipujak thinkers have long argued that the key authority is grounded in the lineage of teachers and their commentarial tradition rather than exclusively in texts. Shvetambars have developed a notion of a fixed canon of texts: 45 for the image worshipping sects and 32 for the iconoclast sects. At the core of these lists are three shared groups: (1) *Purvas* ("the old texts"), now extinct; (2) *Angas* ("limbs"), a set of twelve texts covering the conduct of monks, basic cosmology and metaphysics, and narratives of Jain exemplars including Jinas, model monks, and exceptional laymen; and (3) *Upangas* ("subsidiary to the *Angas*"), which expand on particular doctrines and narratives found in the *Angas* with additional explanatory narratives. The next two subsidiary genres are included in the canons of all of the Shvetambar sects though the contents of these collections differ between them. These two collections focus on monastic discipline (*Chedasutras*) and basic duties and doctrines studied by new monks including instructions for collecting alms and giving confession (*Mulasutras*). Finally, the Murtipujak Shvetambars have a further collection of miscellaneous texts with particular emphasis on death and deathbed rites. The Sthanakavasi Jains are Shvetambar, insofar as they maintain the authority of the Shvetambar Canon, but they reject those texts that encourage or even accept image worship or temple building; thus the Sthanakavasi canon has only 32 texts (as opposed to the Murtipujak canon of 45 texts). In recent years, a new form of temple has appeared called an Agam temple. These temples have the entire 45 *Agama* canon inscribed on tablets that cover the walls. These tablets then are venerated as a form of knowledge worship.

Shvetambar Jains also have a collection of nine devotional texts called the *Navasmaran* or "Nine Remembrances," which function as both devotional texts and magical mantric texts with particular and predictable effects. The recitation of these texts is a key practice for many pious Shvetambar Jains. The first of the nine remembrances is the Navkar Mantra and this key *mantra* is shared with Digambar Jains. The Navkar Mantra praises the five worthy beings and claims the efficacy of the *mantra* to remove inauspiciousness and bad *karma*. The recitation of the Navkar Mantra is a daily practice for pious (and even not very pious) Jains. It is believed to have protective powers and many Jain narratives tell of how the recitation of the Navkar Mantra was instrumental in saving the lives of pious Jains. Its significance is such that many Jains will substitute multiple recitations of the Navkar Mantra for prayers they are incapable of reciting. (Jains are "incapable" of reciting some prayers because (1) the other prayers are too long and complicated, or (2) less commonly the other prayers can only said by monks and nuns.) It serves as an encompassing *mahamantra*. For contemporary Shvetambar Jains the Nine Remembrances are seen as authoritative and powerfully effective.

Digambar canon and texts

Digambars accept the same fourteen *Purva* texts and twelve *Anga* texts and the category of the subsidiary texts but insist that these texts were completely lost well before the Council of Vallabhi. They believe that a significant portion of the *Purva* texts were passed down through the monastic lineages and were collected into a text called "Scripture in Six Parts." For Digambars most of the key texts are collected into a series of post-canonical works called the *Anuyoga*s or "Expositions" focusing on (1) the lives of the Jinas and other moral exemplars; (2) *karma* theory and cosmology; (3) the conduct of monks (and laypeople); and (4) Jain metaphysics and logic.

For North Indian Digambars the most popular devotional texts are the *Darshan Path*s written by Digambar laymen Bhudhardas, Budhjan, and Daulatram in the eighteenth and nineteenth centuries. These texts are memorized and recited daily by pious Digambar Jains and are part of daily temple worship. Though they are not authoritative in the sense that the *Anuyoga* texts are, these are by far the best-known texts. The ninth century *Adipurana* of Jinasena is a marker of Digambar identity and the focus of their veneration. This book tells the story of Rshabhanath (also known as Adinath) and his sons, Bharat and Bahubali. Bahubali becomes the focus of Digambar veneration and many statues of Bahubali have been erected, with the most famous at Shravan Belgola. This text itself is venerated in domestic shrines in Digambar homes. Among Taran Swami Digambar Jains, several sacred texts including the works of Taran Swami and Kundakunda are venerated in their temples instead of Jina images.

Monks

Jainism has its roots in the renunciation of its enlightened teachers. The stories of these Jinas center on their renunciation, attainment of omniscience, and subsequent teaching. Jainism has always maintained that the Jain renouncer is the ideal for Jains, providing a model for most effectively striving towards *karma* reduction and eventual liberation from rebirth.

According to Jain 1996 figures (and Digambar figures from 2001) there were 11,271 Jain mendicants:[15]

1450 Shvetambar Murtipujak Monks
4923 Shvetambar Murtipujak Nuns
508 Digambar Monks
394 Digambar Aryikas
553 Sthanakavasi Monks
2690 Sthanakavasi Nuns
169 Shvetambar Terapanthi Monks
584 Shvetambar Terapanthi Nuns

Shvetambar and Digambar Jains disagree on the presence and role of women mendicants. Shvetambar Jains claim not only the presence of nuns since the earliest times but the preponderance of nuns (usually about three times as many nuns as monks) at every era in the history of Jainism. However, Digambars only permit a community of women mendicants who are not fully ordained nuns. In addition, the role of nuns varies from being seen as pious partial nuns to the very influential nuns of the Kharatara Gacch.

The daily routine of a Jain mendicant is shaped by the five great vows taken by all Jain monks and nuns. The five vows are (1) non-violence; (2) not lying; (3) non-stealing or using what is not his; (4) celibacy; and (5) non-attachment. The first of these vows involves particular care in eating, sleeping, gathering alms, and moving from place to place. In order to promote their *karma* reduction, Jain monks are required to change residences every three days except during the rainy season when travel would involve injury to the many life forms that arise in that time. The daily life of a mendicant centers on the six daily obligations: equanimity, praise of the Jinas, veneration of the teachers, confession, still meditation, and abandonment of the body.[16] At the center of these obligations are the rites of the enumeration of errors for which expiation is required and the confession and expiation of those faults. This ritual focuses the mind of the mendicant on the degree of attention needed to correctly uphold the five great vows.

Jain monks and nuns interact with the laity in several ways. Perhaps most significantly for mendicants, their vows require that they themselves cannot prepare or cook their own food and therefore Jain mendicants must collect all of their food from lay Jains. In order to ensure that no violence is done on behalf of a Jain mendicant, alms gathering is constructed as arbitrary and non-transactional.[17] The Jain mendicants are supposed to gather alms in such a way that lay Jains are not preparing food intentionally for them and that no one in the household should be asked to go without because the food was given away. The rituals of feeding monks and nuns, especially the rituals of feeding Digambar monks, are highly elaborate exchanges in which the lay Jains attempt to get the monks or nuns to accept food from them. To feed a Jain mendicant brings merit to the donors, but only if the exchange upholds the Jain mendicant's dietary restrictions and alms-giving protocols. Shvetambar mendicants send representatives of their groups to collect alms twice a day. The food is collected in alms bowls and shared among the group. Digambar monks collect alms only once a day in the morning and collect the alms in their cupped hands. Monks and nuns must be sure that the families presenting them with alms are of a high moral standing. In both cases, the lay Jains receive merit and prestige from feeding Jain mendicants. To be rejected as a donor is to have one's moral virtue called into question. Because of the relative scarcity of Digambar monks, the merit and prestige earned by feeding one, and inevitable concern over being a worthy donor are multiplied. Although there is no reciprocity expected in the giving of alms, Jain mendicants will usually give a family a blessing or, if there is time and inclination, a brief sermon after accepting alms.

In addition to the interactions surrounding the gathering of alms, Jain mendicants are invited to spend the rainy season in a single congregation each year. During the rainy season retreat, monks (and in some lineages, nuns) give daily sermons for the lay community, perform ritual recitations and blessings for individual Jains, and give advice and instruction informally to those Jains who approach them with questions. During the rest of the year, Jain mendicants will often perform the same services for whichever community they are in for their short stays. On a grander scale, Jain monks perform the ordinations of both monks and nuns and, in image worshipping sects, perform a key ritual in the installation of Jina images.

Lay movements

The Shvetambar Jain tradition has always described itself as a four-fold community with monks, nuns, laymen, and laywomen. The earliest texts instructing monks on the collection of alms tells these monks to collect from those householders who participate in the Jain moral universe.[18] This model of the complete Jain society grants Jain laity an uncontestable status in the religion. While all Jains recognize that to be a monk or nun increases the likelihood of attaining liberation from rebirth, they also see the lay path as one with spiritual value. Institutionally lay Jains are responsible for the building and maintaining of Jain temples and pilgrimage sites. Because Jainism has only rarely had state sponsorship, wealthy Jain merchants have paid for the construction of most Jain temples. The role of grand patron (*sanghpati*) is a central ideal for Jain laymen. Jains do not see a strong separation between institutional religion and domestic religion in part because for Jains laymen and laywomen are part of the institutional structures of the tradition. The symbiosis between Jain mendicants and laity facilitate significant interplay between the two groups and the injunctions against monks' or nuns' involvement with certain social institutions leaves the control of Jain temples, publications, and other institutions exclusively in the hands of lay Jains.

Jainism: Current approaches

Concerns within the tradition

In the global communities of Jains, one of the chief concerns is the absence of Jain mendicants outside India. Because fully ordained Jain mendicants are not permitted to travel in motorized vehicles, Jains living outside India have developed strategies for institution building and ritual performances without the presence of monks. For example, Shvetambar Jain mendicants are required for the installation of new Jina images and therefore Jains abroad were confronted with the problem of how to install images in Jain temples. Shvetambar Jains have developed a system of having a monk perform his part of the Jina installation while the image is still in India and then moving the image (in much the same way that images are processed) to the temple abroad. Once there, the image is then reinstalled into the temple in the same way that an image that has been brought out of a temple for procession is reinstalled.

Lay Jains in India rely on Jain mendicants for religious instruction and advice on how to live a Jain life. In order to accommodate the needs of overseas Jains, the Terapanthi lineage has introduced a level of partially initiated mendicants (*saman* and *samani*) capable of travelling to Jain communities outside India in order to give sermons and instruct lay Jains in Jain philosophy and practices.[19] These *saman* and *samani* are highly influential among Jains abroad and are spreading the Terapanthi doctrines among these Jains.

Although Jains in India are a religious minority, interreligious dialogue is not of great concern. Outside India, Jains are deeply engaged with discussions with other traditions and with new epistemes. The two new epistemes with which Jains have engaged are animal rights and environmentalism.[20] Jain moral requirements to be vegetarian, to not harm animals and other living beings, and the extension of protection to non-animals like plants, water, earth, and fire have provided the groundwork for Jain thinking about the environment.

Jains in India are often seen as a sub-group or sub-caste of Hindu. While many Jains participate or accept this widely held view, some Jains have attempted to distinguish Jainism from Hinduism in a number of ways. There have been movements to get Jainism acknowledged as a minority religion in India, which provides the community with some governmental recognition and privileges.[21] With the rise of Hindu claims on sites Jains have long seen as key pilgrimage sites, Jains struggle to protect their claims to these important sites using legal channels.[22] In North America, Jains have worked towards forming pan-Jain organizations with an emphasis on shared philosophical and ethical doctrines and an engagement with broader interreligious dialogue and concerns while at the same time struggling with issues of ethnic and sectarian identities.[23]

Academic approaches

Historically Jain studies has been a branch of the philologically driven Indology. Nineteenth and early twentieth century Sanskrit and Prakrit scholars were drawn to the corpus of Jain literature in part because of its chronological relationship with Buddhism.[24] In fact, some of the earliest scholars believed Jainism was a strand of Buddhism. Indological scholarship on Jainism then moved into examinations of Jain philosophical works and Jain narrative traditions.[25] More recently Jain studies has moved into new areas of inquiry such as ethnographic studies,[26] history,[27] and art history.[28] Increasingly, scholars of Jainism are examining minority communities within the Jain tradition[29] and communities of Jains in migration within India and within the global communities outside of India.[30] Recent years have also brought the first sustained studies of Jain nuns[31] and laywomen.[32]

Discussion questions

1   How have Jains articulated a unique Jain identity as a minority religion? How is this identity challenged by regional and sectarian differences?
2   How has the four-fold community of monks, nuns, laymen, and laywomen shaped the development of Jainism?

Key terms

Dādāgurus—The deceased and venerated miraculous monks of the Khattara Gacch (a lineage within the image worshipping Svetambars) who are credited with powers in this world.

Digambar—The smaller of the two major sects of Jainism, named "sky clad" because their monks do not wear robes.

dīkṣā—The ordination ceremony of a Jain monk or nun.

Mahāvīr—The last of the most recent set of twenty-four tirthankars, a contemporary of Gautama Buddha.

Mūrtipūjak—Image worshippers, the largest of the Svetambar sub-sects.

Nāvkar—The most important of Jain mantras shared by all sects and sub-sects with minor variations.

Sallekhanā—The ritual of fasting to death at the end of one's life in order to decrease *karma*, the ideal death for Jains.

Sthānakavāsī—The second largest of the Svetambar sub-sects, significant enough to often be seen as a third major sect, called "those who dwell in the halls" referring to this sub-sect's rejection of image worship and temples.

Śvetāmbar—The larger of the two major sects of Jainism, named "wearers of white" because their monks (and nuns) wear white robes.

Terāpanthī—The path of the twelve, a sub-sect of Svetambar Jains who reject image worship and center their veneration on the charismatic authority of their founder, Tulsi. There is also a Digambar Terapanth, which is not directly connected to the Svetambar one.

Tīrthaṅkar—Literally "a ford-maker," one of the twenty-four enlightened teachers of Jainism, also called Jina.

Notes

1 P. Dundas, *The Jains*, London: Routledge, 2002, p. 20.
2 Dundas, *The Jains*, pp. 24–5.
3 Dundas, *The Jains*, pp. 265–71.
4 Dundas, *The Jains*, pp. 229–30.
5 M. W. Kelting, *Singing to the Jinas*, New York: Oxford University Press, 2001, pp. 87–9, 130–7, 152–61.
6 Dundas, *The Jains*, pp. 240–4.
7 Scholarship on these figures includes: Lawrence A. Babb, *Absent Lord*, Berkeley, CA: University of California Press, 1996, pp. 102–36; James Laidlaw, *Riches and Renunciation*, Oxford: Oxford University Press, 1995, pp. 50–1, 259–61; and Caroline Humphrey and James Laidlaw, *The Archetypal Actions of Ritual*, Oxford: Clarendon Press, 1994, pp. 172–3, 206–8.
8 Peter Flugel, "The Jaina Cult of Relic Stupas," *Numen* 57 (2010): 389–504.
9 Babb, *Absent Lord*, 93–101.
10 For veneration of living monks, see Babb, *Absent Lord*, 61–2 and A. Vallely, *Guardians of the Transcendent: An Ethnography of a Jain Ascetic Community*, Toronto: University of Toronto Press, 2002.
11 M. W. Kelting, *Heroic Wives: Rituals, Stories, and the Virtues of Jain Wifehood*, New York: Oxford University Press, 2009, pp. 79–105.
12 Kelting, *Heroic Wives*, pp. 112–14.
13 J. E. Cort, *Jains in the World*, New York: Oxford University Press, 2001, pp. 176–9.
14 An excellent brief overview of the Shvetambar and Digambar Canons can be found in Kristi Wiley, *Historical Dictionary of Jainism*, Lanham, MD: Scarecrow Press, 2004, pp. xix–xxvi; for longer discussions, see Dundas, *The Jains*, pp. 60–82 and P. Jaini, *The Jaina Path of Purification*, Berkeley, CA: University of California Press, 1979, pp. 47–88. For a discussion of questions of canon formation see Kendall Folkert, *Scripture and Community*, Atlanta, GA: Scholars Press, 1993, pp. 53–84, 85–94.
15 Peter Flugel, "Demographic Trends in Jaina Monasticism," in Peter Flugel (ed.) *Studies in Jaina History and Culture*, London: Routledge, 2006, pp. 312–98.
16 Cort, *Jains in the World*, pp. 100–6.
17 Cort, *Jains in the World*, pp. 106–11; Laidlaw, *Riches and Renunciation*, pp. 296–301, 316–17.
18 Dundas, *The Jains*, pp. 174–6.
19 Vallely, *Guardians of the Transcendent*, pp. 72, 101, 108–9.
20 C. Chapple (ed.), *Jainism and Ecology: Nonviolence in the Web of Life*, Cambridge, MA: Harvard University Press, 2002.
21 http://docs.google.com/View?id=dcrgdpv8_112cwwhqngf
22 http://www.digambarjainonline.com/
23 http://www.jaina.org/
24 John E. Cort, "Models of and Models for the Study of Jains: Methods and Theory," *The Study of Religion* 2.1 (1990), pp. 42–71.; Folkert, *Scripture and Community*, pp. 23–33, 95–112; P. S. Jaini, "The Jainas and the Western Scholar," in P. S. Jaini (ed.) *Collected Papers on Jaina Studies*, Delhi: Motilal Banarsidass, 2000, pp. 23–36.
25 Nalini Balbir, "The Micro-Genre of Dana-Stories in Jaina Literature: Problems of Interrelation and Diffusion," *Indologica Taurinensia* XI (1983): 145–61; Ralph Strohl, "Of Kings and Sages," in Phyllis Granoff (ed.) *The Clever Adulteress and Other Stories: A Treasury of Jain Literature*, New York: Mosaic Press, 1990, pp. 208–44.
26 Babb, *Absent Lord*; Lawrence Babb, *Alchemies of Violence: Myths of Identity and the Life of Trade in Western India*, New Delhi: Sage Publications, 2004; Marcus Banks, "Competing to Give, Competing to Get," in Pnina Werbner and Muhamed Anwar (eds.) *Black and Ethnic Leaderships in Britain: Ethnicity, Economy, and Gender Relations*, London: Routledge, 1991, pp. 226–50; Michael Carrithers, "Passions of

Nation and Community in the Bahubali Affair," *Modern Asian Studies* 22 (1988): 815–44; Cort, *Jains in the World*; Kelting, *Singing to the Jinas* and *Heroic Wives*; Laidlaw, *Riches and Renunciation*; Humphrey and Laidlaw *The Archetypal Actions of Ritual*; Vallely, *Guardians of the Transcendent*.

27 Dundas, *The Jains* and Paul Dundas, *History, Scripture and Controversy in a Medieval Jain Sect*, London: Routledge, 2007.

28 Phyllis Granoff, *Victorious Ones*, Ahmedabad: Mapin, 2010; Julia A. B. Hegewald, *Jaina Temple Architecture in India*, Hochschulschrift, Zugl: Aachen, Techn. Hochsch., Habil.-Schr., 2008; Peter Flugel, "The Jaina Cult of Relic Stupas," *Numen* 57 (2010): 389–504.

29 On Taran Swami Panth: John E. Cort, "A Fifteenth-Century Digambar Jain Mystic and His Followers: Taran Taran Swami and the Taran Swami Panth," in Peter Flugel (ed.) *Studies in Jaina History and Culture*, London: Routledge, 2006, pp. 263–310. On Terapanthis: Peter Flugel "Demographic Trends in Jaina Monasticism," in Peter Flugel (ed.) *Studies in Jaina History and Culture*, London: Routledge, 2006, pp. 312–98; Vallely, *Guardians of the Transcendent*.

30 Banks, "Competing to Give, Competing to Get," pp. 226–50; Marcus Banks, *Organizing Jainism in India and England*, Oxford: Clarendon Press, 1992; Marcus Banks, "Why Move?: Regional and Long Distance Migrations of Gujarati Jains," in J. Brown and R. Foot (eds.) *Migration: The Asian Experience*, New York: St. Martin's Press, 1994, pp. 131–48.

31 Vallely, *Guardians of the Transcendent*; Anne Vallely, "These Hands are Not for Henna," in Meena Khandelwal, Sondra L. Hausner, and Ann Grodzins Gold (eds.) *Women's Renunciation in South Asia: Nuns, Yoginis, Saints and Singers*, New York: Palgrave, 2006, pp. 223–46; Sherry Fohr, "Gender and Chastity: Female Jain Renouncers," Ph.D. Dissertation, University of Virginia, 2001—her thesis includes research with nuns in a variety of lineages, both Shvetambar and Digambar.

32 Kelting, *Singing to the Jinas* and *Heroic Wives*; Josephine Reynell, "Women and the Reproduction of the Jain Community," in Michael Carrithers and Christine Humphrey (eds.) *The Assembly of Listeners*, Cambridge: Cambridge University Press, 1991, pp. 41–65; Josephine Reynell, "Religious Practice and the Creation of Personhood among Svetambar Murtipujak Jain Women in Jaipur," in Peter Flugel (ed.) *Studies in Jaina History and Culture*, London: Routledge, 2006, pp. 157–80.

Recommended resources

Chapple, Christopher, ed. *Jainism and Ecology: Nonviolence in the Web of Life.* Cambridge, MA: Harvard University Press, 2002.

Cort, John E. *Jains in the World.* New York: Oxford University Press, 2001.

Dundas, Paul. *The Jains.* London: Routledge, 2002.

Flugel, Peter, ed. *Studies in Jaina History and Culture.* London: Routledge, 2006.

Jaini, Padmanabh. *The Jaina Path of Purification.* Berkeley, CA: University of California Press, 1979.

Jaini, Padmanabh. *Gender and Salvation.* Berkeley, CA: University of California Press, 1991.

Kalpa Sutra. In *Jaina Sutras*, Part I, ed. and trans. by Hermann Jacobi, 217–311. Sacred Books of the East Series, series editor F. Max Müller. Delhi: Motilal Banarsidass, 1989.

Kelting, M. Whitney. *Singing to the Jinas.* New York: Oxford University Press, 2001.

Kelting, M. Whitney. *Heroic Wives: Rituals, Stories, and the Virtues of Jain Wifehood.* New York: Oxford University Press, 2009.

Vallely, Anne. *Guardians of the Transcendent: An Ethnography of a Jain Ascetic Community.* Toronto: University of Toronto Press, 2002.

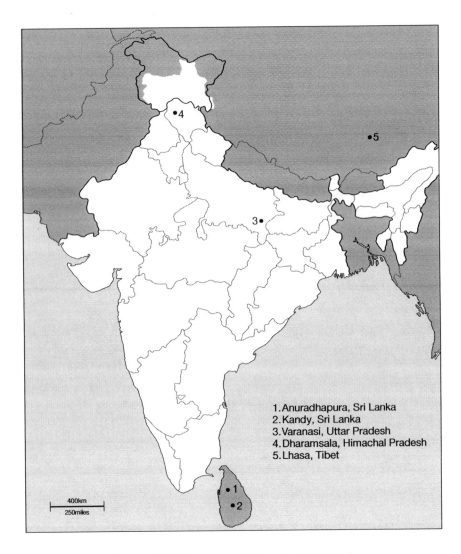

1. Anuradhapura, Sri Lanka
2. Kandy, Sri Lanka
3. Varanasi, Uttar Pradesh
4. Dharamsala, Himachal Pradesh
5. Lhasa, Tibet

400km
250miles

Map 4 Prominent places in Buddhism as practiced in South Asia today

4 Buddhism in South Asia

Practicing tradition today

Sunil Goonasekera

Introduction

What are the basic identity markers of the Buddhist tradition? First and foremost, people who hold the beliefs and engage in practices founded on the doctrines of Siddhartha Gautama, the Buddha, identify themselves as *bauddhas*. They know the South Asian region, following the traditional cultural nomenclature found in the classical Buddhist texts, as the *Jambudvipa*. All *bauddhas* view the *Jambudvipa* with a certain filial affection as a point of origin. All agree that their faith is indigenous to this region.

Features of the Buddha's career are described in the early Buddhist literature such as the Jatakanidhanakatha and the Tipitaka and are held by Buddhists to be "historical," although they include what would be considered legends and myths by historians today. The language of these texts is Pali, and in this essay I use Pali terms.

The Buddha was born in the sixth century before the Common Era, as a prince of the Sakya tribe that inhabited the southwestern slopes of the Himalayan range. His given name was Siddhartha. His family belonged to the Sakya clan named Gautama. Thus his social name was Siddhartha Gautama. His father was a king named Suddhodhana and his mother Mahamaya. He was born in a village named Kapilavastu, located in present-day southern Nepal. Siddharta Gautama abandoned his household and became a *samana*, a wandering ascetic, when he was 29 years old. He achieved his enlightenment or *sambodhi* under the bodhi tree when he was 35 years old, at Buddha Gaya (Bodh Gaya), in what is today the Indian state of Bihar. He wandered in the regions along the Ganges River, preaching his doctrines that contradicted other religious and philosophical doctrines. At that time, there were many religious systems in this region. Among them were other *samana* doctrines such as those of the Ajivakas and Jains, the materialistic ideas of the Carvakas or Lokayatas, and the Vedic beliefs of Brahmanism. He rejected the Brahmanical theories of society founded upon the caste hierarchy of inherent purity, as outlined in the Brahmanical Dharmasutras and Dharmasastras.[1]

Buddhists believe that the Buddha's words or the *Buddhavacana* are recorded in the Tipitaka or "three baskets" of doctrines. One *pitaka* or "basket" is called the Sutta pitaka or the basket containing the basic doctrines. The second basket is called the

Vinaya pitaka. It contains rules of conduct for Buddhist monks (*bhikkhus*) and nuns (*bhikkhunis*). The third basket is called the Abhidhamma pitaka, containing theories of Buddhist microanalyses of doctrines in the Sutta pitaka. The believers and practitioners of the doctrines and rules of conduct at varying degrees of complexity and commitment constitute the Buddhasasana or the Buddhist community. It has four limbs: *bhikkhus*, *bhikkhunis* (the monastic component), and *upasakas* and *upasikas* (the lay component). Together they sustain the Buddhasasana.

Sociologically, Buddhism exists in South Asia as two great schools of thought that converge with regard to certain basic doctrinal, behavioral, and social organizational features but diverge regarding other doctrinal, behavioral, and organizational details. The older school that claims descent from the Buddha's monastic organization is known as the Theravada (the Elders' tradition). The younger school that emerged perhaps five centuries after the Buddha's demise and became a well organized school of thought a millennium after the Buddha's death is known as the Mahayana school. The Mahayana (the Great Vehicle) uses the pejorative term Hinayana (the Lesser Vehicle) to designate the Elders' tradition that takes an orthodox stance regarding doctrinal matters.

Present-day Buddhists live in all the nations of the region in varying population densities. In Bhutan practically all indigenous people are Buddhists and their Bhutanese identities are inextricably fused with their identity as Buddhists.[2] In Tibet until 1959, and in the Tibetan diaspora, more than 80 percent of the population is Buddhist. In Sri Lanka nearly 70 percent of the population—roughly 14 million—is Buddhist. In India, Nepal, and Bangladesh relatively negligibly small populations identify themselves as Buddhists although until Hindu revivalism and the Islamic invasions in medieval times they were much larger demographic entities.

In this essay I outline some basic features of Buddhism in South Asia. As students of Buddhism in this region already know, this is a vast subject involving many nations, cultures, and social systems; both main schools of Buddhism; and their historical trajectories spanning over twenty-five centuries or so. The doctrines of and variations between these two branches of Buddhism form a substantial library, and understanding the cultural differences between the northern Himalayan societies and the southern societies has involved complex scholarly endeavors. As such only an introductory approach, focusing more on religious practices and historical processes, and less on doctrinal matters, is adopted here with the hope that the reader would be encouraged to explore this subject in greater depth.

Buddhist tradition: Identity

Buddhism in South Asian and universal context

The Buddhist tradition distinguishes itself from other South Asian belief systems on account of its very specific sense of the world. Accordingly, the Buddha observed that all phenomena of existence are unstable and impermanent (*anicca*), there is no such thing as a permanent soul or a stable self with an independent existence (*anatta*), and that all existence is characterized by suffering (*dukkha*).

Based on these observations he developed a doctrine known as the Four Noble Truths (*cattaroariyasacca*). The First Noble Truth is that existence is characterized by suffering. It is called the Noble Truth of suffering (*dukkha-ariyasacca*).

The Second Noble Truth is that there are causes for the arising of suffering (*dukkhasamudaya-ariyasacca*). These causes are mental dispositions of attachment to (*lobha*) and craving for (*tanha*) things, beings, and existence in the world; anger and hatred (*dosa*); and delusion and ignorance (*moha*).

These mental dispositions depend on one another and support each other. For example attachment and craving lead to anger and hatred which, in turn, produce delusion. Or, ignorance and delusion lead to attachment and craving that produce anger and hatred. The end result of all these is the emergence of suffering. This theory of the origin of suffering finds its logical premises from the theory of dependent origination and is a pivotal point in the Buddhist doctrines of existence and ethics. The theory of dependent origination is concerned with two basic objectives: to establish the concept *anatta* or absence of a permanent independent self (soul), and to establish the concept of *dukkha*—suffering. Let us examine this core doctrine briefly.

The theory holds that ignorance and delusion (*moha*) conditions action (*kamma*) which, in turn, conditions consciousness (*vinnana*). This conditioned consciousness then conditions the arising of physical and mental phenomena or *namarupa*; that is, the attribution of meanings to the physical world and construction of notions and mental images. They in turn condition the six organs of perception—five bodily organs and the mind which condition perception—which are the sensory and mental contacts with the world. The conditioned perception then conditions sensation or reception of physical and mental stimulation through sensory contacts. Sensation then conditions the arising of *tanha* or thirst (craving and desire) that then conditions the arising of *upadana* or clinging to the desired phenomenon. Such clinging then conditions the nature of the world to be or becoming. Becoming then conditions birth and the arising of a sense of self. This conditioned arising of self then conditions the arising of senility, sickness, death, and suffering—*dukkha*.

Any conditioned phenomenon has no independent eternal identity or existence. Hence, the impossibility of an independent and permanent self or "I-ness" and hence *anatta*. As everything in existence is being conditioned by other things which themselves are conditioned, impermanent or transitory, so is suffering. Thus suffering can be eliminated, and the final release from suffering is *nibbana* (extinction of suffering). This is *dukkhanirodha-ariyasacca*, the Third Noble Truth in Buddhism.

The Fourth Noble Truth, *dukkhanirodhagaminipatipada-ariyasacca*, is that there is a way to eliminate suffering. This is known as the Noble Eightfold Path, which advocates living on a middle path between total immersion in bodily and mental pleasures—a feature of the household life of materialists—and the extreme self-mortification or mortification of the body practiced particularly by the Jains and certain Hindu sects.

These Four Noble Truths are held as the axiomatic premises in Buddhism. The Noble Eightfold Path begins with correct understanding, correct intention, correct speech, correct conduct, correct livelihood, correct effort, correct mindfulness, and correct concentration.

Another important doctrinal feature that distinguishes the Buddhist tradition from other South Asian traditions is its refusal to outline a definite cosmology. This arises from the premise that all phenomena are mental constructs; not that a material world does not exist, but that our perceptions of it are clouded by transitory and delusional states of the mind and are hence unreliable; and that its origins are unknowable and analyses of its material constitution are useless speculative exercises as they do not contribute to addressing the fundamental issues in hand—those outlined in the Four Noble Truths.

All this is commonly held by all Buddhists as the theoretical foundation of their tradition. Adherence to these concepts constitutes the fundamental markers of being *bauddha*. They lead to the ideals of Buddhist thought and practice. Primarily, they provide the foundation for the next set of features that constitute Buddhist identity. One is taking refuge in the Triple-Gem (Sinhala: *teruvan*; Pali: *raranatta*; Sanskrit: *triratna*). This is known as establishing *tisarana* (ti—three; sarana—refuge). The other is observing the five behavioral restraints (*pancasila*). Buddhism has three sacred categories known as the Triple-Gem: the Buddha, the truths that he preached (*dhamma*), and the monastic community (*sangha*). *Tisarana* involves every Buddhist seeking the refuge of the Triple-Gem although doctrinally one must seek only one's own refuge. As a practical component of the *dhamma*, Buddhists observe, at least nominally, the five (*panca*) behavioral restraints (*sila*) commonly known as the five precepts: refraining (1) from taking

Figure 4.1 Birth of Prince Siddhartha, Samudragiri Viharaya at Mirissa (late nineteenth century). Photo taken by Sunil Goonasekera.

life; (2) speaking falsehoods; (3) taking whatever that does not belong to or is not given to one; (4) inappropriate sexual behavior; and (5) indulgence in intoxication. These constitute the ethical foundations of the tradition.

Yet another identifying characteristic of the Buddhist tradition is the faith in the non-canonical Jataka stories that outline the Buddha's previous births exemplifying his ethical conduct that guided him towards his enlightenment in his final birth. Traditionally, these stories are considered actual events that occurred in the past and examples for guiding conduct at present.

These conceptual and behavioral maxims have a universal appeal. The rapid early spreading of Buddhist doctrines throughout eastern and southeastern Asia attests to their universal appeal. This is corroborated by the popularity of Buddhism even in the Western world—Europe, Americas, and Australia—from the late nineteenth century. Its appeal has been such that many distinguished Buddhist monastics such as Nanaponika Thera and Bhikkhu Bodhi arose in Western civilization and numerous Western scholars explored Buddhist texts and doctrines. Lay scholars such as T. W. Rhys Davids, F. L. Woodward, I. B. Horner, F. Max Mueller, and many others established the Pali Text Society to translate the Buddhist canon in Pali into English, and other European scholars made Buddhist doctrines available in German and French. Many later scholars such as W. Y. Evans-Wentz, E. B. Cowell, E. H. Johnston, J. Blofeld, E. Conze, D. T. Suzuki, D. Kalupahana, H. V. Guenther, R. Thurman, and others translated into English the Sanskrit and Tibetan works on the South Asian Buddhist tradition. Today, many Sri Lankan and Tibetan *bhikkhu*s (monks) living in exile have made Buddhist thought widely available internationally.

Undoubtedly, the transportability of the basic Buddhist doctrines such as the Four Noble Truths and the Noble Eightfold Path across cultures gave Buddhism its universalistic appeal. Both of the above could be used to interpret everyday experiences and organize everyday conduct irrespective of other differences between these traditions and the Buddhist tradition. Shorter works such as the Dhammapada that distill Buddhist ideals and notions into simpler but no lesser terms without any other cultural encumbrances, such as necessities to believe in various supernatural beings in order to engage in Buddhist discoursing, have contributed to this popularity of the Buddhist tradition in societies west of South Asia.

However, not all the conceptual structures of Buddhism are of universal appeal. This is particularly the case with the materials outside the Tipitaka. While the basic features of the Buddhist doctrines—the Four Noble Truths and the Noble Eightfold Path—could be explored and appreciated without reference to other concepts of the pan-South Asian culture, some later accretions could not be understood without ideas and practices of other non-Buddhist South Asian traditions that do not seem to cohere with the cut and dried logic of the early Buddhist theories. A short introduction to these specifically South Asian accretions is necessary.

The Buddhist tradition, it must be stressed, did not arise in a social and cultural vacuum: many belief systems existed in the region prior to its emergence. These included the Vedic, Jain, Ajivaka, Lokayata and many other faiths such as the

Bon tradition in the Himalayan region as well as tribal belief systems. Early Buddhists, including Siddhartha Gautama, believed in a wide variety of notions about the world. Buddhist tradition was just one among many others, and the early Buddhists who converted to Buddhist faith did not abandon all of their pre-Buddhist beliefs. They embraced the basic tenets of the tradition, sought the refuge of the Triple-Gem, and adopted the behavioral restraints of the *pancasila* (five precepts), but continued to uphold many ideas in their former faiths, thus constructing a worldview that included them by adjusting those pre-Buddhist notions to fit into the Buddhist notions and modifying Buddhist notions to accommodate the pre-Buddhist and non-Buddhist ones. This syncretic process had gone on in other traditions as well and continues today.

To put it briefly, in pre-Buddhist South Asia at least three major strands of beliefs had existed. These were the Vedic tradition that emerged nearly four thousand years ago, an indigenous tradition of *samanas* or wandering ascetics, and tribal traditions involving deity worship, each with highly localized patterns of beliefs and behavioral ideals. The latter two traditions had existed even before the formation of the Vedic tradition which later absorbed elements of those traditions by tweaking various cultural elements to produce the mythological tradition of grand narratives such as the *Mahabharata, Ramayana*, and the various *Puranas* or what may be called theogonies of gods and goddesses and their heroic careers. The deity cults blended with the Vedic religion to produce sensibilities of pantheistic beliefs in the impersonal all-pervading divinity named Brahman as in the *Upanishads*.

One of the most enduring amalgams that this grand syncretic process produced was the cosmology involving a vast spiral flow of time cycles called the *kalpas*, within which the world as known comes into being and becomes extinct only to reemerge. This idea of cycles includes the human lifespan. Human beings experience birth, death, and rebirth within these cycles of time in a manner that is influenced by the results of their personal conduct in the world (*karma*). Existence in the world as characterized by cycles of birth and rebirth is called *sansara*. If the *karma* produced during a given birth is bad then an unfavorable rebirth follows as a matter of cosmic retribution. This is the nature of *sansara* and is universally feared. All South Asian religious traditions accept this notion of *sansara* and all prescribe ways to escape from it. The Buddhist notion of *nibbana* or freedom from suffering is one way.

The Vedic and Puranic traditions known today as Hinduism developed the notion of a creator in the Vedic deity Prajapati, now identified with Brahman and gods Shiva and Vishnu. However, non-Vedic traditions such as Buddhist, Ajivaka, and Jain traditions refused to accept the notion of a creator. The Jains produced a mathematically defined agnostic cosmology wherein the uncreated and eternal cosmos has a definite shape and an internal structure.

The Buddhist tradition rejects the Brahmanical developments in the *Vedas, Puranas*, and *Upanishads* as well as the Jain contemplations about the nature of the cosmos as mere speculations about something unknowable and irrelevant to the resolution of the problem of suffering. But Buddhism's popular beliefs accommodate the *kalpa* theory of cosmic time cycles, *karma, sansara,* and rebirth theories, albeit in their own way. Buddhists theoretically reject the Brahmanical theory of *karma* as it involves beliefs in an immortal soul. The Buddhist notion of *kamma* refers to action only whereas the Hindu and Jain theories of *karma* refer to results of action. Buddhists disagree with the Jain theory of *karma* also because it postulates that *karma* is constituted of subtle particles similar to time, space, motion, and stability conceived as subtle matter. However, popular Buddhist beliefs accommodate the Hindu theory of *karma* as result of action and are deeply involved in accumulating "good *karma*" and avoiding accumulating "bad *karma*" in relation to their accommodation of the Hindu theory of rebirth. In terms of soteriological conduct, Buddhists theoretically disagree with Hindus by their rejection of deity worship and ritual practices as means to achieve freedom from suffering. They reject the Jain soteriology as the Jains prescribe severe mortification of the body as an important technique for soul purification and reaching *moksa*, their permanent resting place.

Buddhists accommodate many deity cults such as those of Vishnu, Skanda, Pattini, Avalokiteshvara, Tara, and others such as rock, tree, river, and mountain deities as well as other Puranic deities such as Sakra and demigods, demons and various lowly beings. The gods are propitiated for benefits in mundane affairs and not for soteriological purposes. The demonic and other malevolent lowly beings are feared as they are believed to destructively interfere with domestic life, prosperity, and health. To address these issues Buddhists have absorbed from other traditions or invented ritual procedures, liturgies, and iconographies that have little to do with basic principles of the Buddhist tradition. Buddhists have also absorbed the astrological traditions to predict and ritually prepare for future events. Additionally, Buddhists share with other South Asian traditions the institution of what is roughly known in the European traditions as magic and miracles.

These non-Buddhist elements of the South Asian cultures, posited in the popular Buddhist tradition, appear to be intellectually unattractive to cultural traditions west of South Asia. While the popular Buddhist tradition has no doubts about the existential reality of these beings, cosmic cycles, and rebirth according to *kamma* generated during one's lifetime, as well as the supernatural capabilities of some religious virtuosi, modern traditions west of South Asia can understand these events, processes, and entities only as symbolic forms that signify social, political, and psychological realities and not on their face value as these have no place and cannot be accommodated in their monotheistic Judeo-Christian and modern scientifically oriented cultural traditions.

Further, total immersion for laypeople in the Noble Eightfold Path, and even in some aspects of the five precepts, tends to be incongruous with the traditions where farming and animal husbandry constitute foundational elements of their economic realities. It is difficult to put into practice some Buddhist behavioral restraints unless one completely renounces these economic practices. And if all Buddhists renounced these economic practices then societal existence appears to be jeopardized. The South Asian popular Buddhist tradition has diluted these concerns for lay practitioners in South Asia by developing internal conceptual loops that allow a certain degree of violence in life at the cost of prolonged suffering in *sansara* (cycle of birth and rebirth), since such violence produces unfavorable karmic effects. In the Sri Lankan Theravada Buddhist tradition this modification also involves the belief that at present it is impossible for anyone to achieve *nibbana* (freedom from suffering) as a matter of cosmic law and, given the declining moral quality of the cosmic conditions, it is impossible to refrain from violating the precepts in order to survive. These modifications have rendered the Buddhist tradition inconsistent and apologetic as laymen as well as monastics use these notions to justify their nonconformity to and violations of the precepts. Anyone from any other tradition interested in the basic Buddhist concepts and who expects Buddhists to follow them to the letter might find practical Buddhism in South Asia rather disconcerting and even disappointing.

Internal identities within the Buddhist tradition

Although the Buddhist tradition is united with regard to the basic doctrines of Buddhism, the Buddhist community of South Asia has been internally segmented. This segmentation is based on sect formation. This situation arose early in the Buddhist monastic community over differential interpretations of the Vinaya (disciplinary) rules and certain premises in the Abhidhamma or further elaborations of the basic concepts. However, these early sects were confined to schisms in the sangha and not in the lay community. The issues that arose in these contexts were resolved through the second, third, and fourth Councils of the Sangha (*Sangiti*).

Nonetheless, certain doctrinal differences arose from about the first century BCE and continued to grow, producing a great schism that persists to this day. The schism produced the Theravada and Mahayana sects. In the South Asian region the Theravada sect exists primarily in Sri Lanka with traces in India, Bangladesh, and Nepal. The Mahayana sect exists in Tibet, Bhutan, Nepal, and Ladakh and Sikkim territories of India and, since the Chinese intervention in Tibet in 1959, in Dharamsala, India, and in the Tibetan diaspora scattered in various parts of the world.

According to Buddhist lore, the Buddha had permitted the worship of three kinds of *caityas*—reliquaries, and objects and figures that would represent him. These are *saririka*, *uddesika*, and *paribhogika caityas*. The *saririka caityas* contain physical remains of the Buddha. The *uddesika caityas* are symbols and objects that represent the idea and likeness of the Buddha such as the bodhi tree and Buddha images. The *paribhogika caityas* are objects that the Buddha had used. The *saririka caityas* and *parobhogika caityas* were built in the form of stupas shortly after the Buddha's demise. So the pious worshipped the things he used and places he stayed in. Later, the emergence of specifically Buddhist art (in the Buddhist kingdoms of the northwestern regions such as the Gandhara in today's eastern Afghanistan and northern Pakistan, where the first Buddha image was sculpted; in present-day Madhya Pradesh where the famous shrines of Bharhut and Sanchi existed, and in the north at Mathura in contemporary Uttar Pradesh) signifying the growing cultural power of Buddhists in India might have led to further development of Buddhist and rival identities. In Sri Lanka, too,

Buddhism is established in Sri Lanka

In Sri Lanka, Theravada Buddhism was first established around the third century BCE. It is probable that Buddhists lived on the island together with adherents of various other religions in the region prior to the formal establishment of the Buddhist community (Buddhasasana). However, at the inception, there was no such identity as Theravada Buddhist as all Buddhists had a common identity. By the second century BCE a specifically militant Buddhist identity may have come to the forefront as there were frequent attacks on Buddhist establishments by south Indian invaders who were of Brahmanical and other non-Buddhist faiths. According to the sixth century monastic chronicle Mahavamsa (Chapter 25), the well known first major war between the Buddhists and the non-Buddhist Damila invaders occurred to the latter's detriment when the Sinhala king Dutthagamani led armies accompanied by *bhikkhus* against them. The chronicle states that the king had proclaimed that he waged the war for the sake of the Buddhasasana—the Buddhist community—thus indicating the formation and strengthening of a specifically Sinhala Buddhist identity among the inhabitants of Sri Lanka, at least of the sixth century. It is also important to note that the conflict of identities might have accompanied the concomitant development of specifically Buddhist material culture, particularly around the third century BCE but could have been so even before that. According to the Buddhist sources in Sri Lanka, the Indian Buddhists had begun to worship the *bodhi* tree, the *Ficus religiosa*, under which the Buddha had sat down to meditate and defeated Mara, the arch enemy in Buddhist lore who is responsible for continuation of suffering in *sansara*, and achieved his *sambodhi*. Buddhists had begun to consider this tree sacred. An identity conflict might have developed as the *Ficus religiosa* has been venerated by people of South Asia from much earlier times, as far back as the Indus Valley era and during the Vedic era. Whose claims to a particular site of a tree were more significant—Buddhist, Vedic, or pre-Vedic—might have been a point of contention. In Sri Lanka, both the Buddhists and those of Brahmanical faith might have competed for ownership of *Ficus religiosa* shrines leading to identity formations and conflict.[3]

the construction of early stupas such as the Mahiyangana and Thuparama stupas might have exacerbated the Buddhist and anti-Buddhist identity formations.

This state of affairs changed around the first century before the Common Era when a proto-Mahayana belief system called *puggalavada* developed within the Buddhist sangha in India. It held, contrary to the Tipitaka's *anicca* or impermanence and *anatta* or no-soul doctrines, that individuals had a *puggala*, an eternal essence comparable to the soul doctrines of the Vedic and Puranic religions and Jainism. This produced a monastic sect known as the Vajjiputtakas who were also called Puggalavadins. An Indian *bhikkhu* named Dhammaruci attempted to introduce this doctrine to Sri Lankan monks but was unsuccessful. Thus the Buddhist monastic identity remained intact.

In the third century CE a new proto-Mahayana doctrine known as *vaitulya-vada* that held that the Tipitaka did not contain all the doctrines preached by the Buddha, that the Buddha was not actually born in the world but lived in the Tusita *divyaloka* (world of gods) and sent only a phantom, more like an avatar, and that he did not preach the *dhamma* but only bhikkhu Ananda[4] delivered the *dhamma*, and many other doctrines that contradicted the Theravada positions spread to Sri Lanka. We shall return to these topics a little later.

In Sri Lanka those who followed the *vaitulyavada,* or the Vaitulyavadins, had some success in monastically suppressing the orthodox Theravada tradition, although they were unsuccessful in creating a major social division leading to the splitting of the Sri Lankan Buddhist identity. The Theravada tradition regrouped and caused the expulsion of the Vaitulya tradition from the island thus precipitating an established opposition to any school of thought within the Buddhist community that opposed the completeness of the Tipitaka as the sole authority on the Buddha's words.

The schools of thought that constructed extensions of the Tipitaka coalesced to form a new sect in India. This sect called itself the Mahayana (the Great Vehicle) and the tradition that limited itself to the Tipitaka, the Hinayana (the Lesser Vehicle). Thus a fundamental division in Buddhist identity emerged in South Asia.

It must be stressed that the division of the Buddhist community into Theravada and Mahayana was not merely a monastic matter similar to the early schisms. The new identity formation occurred in both conceptual and practical spheres thus separating the Theravadins from the Mahayanists. Nonetheless, the two communities commonly held a strong *bauddha* identity vis-à-vis other indigenous faiths and held the essential validity of the Tipitaka as a collection of foundational doctrines. The common devotion to the Sakya Muni Buddha, as the Mahayana Buddhists call him, and the acceptance of the authority of the Tipitaka, led to the common identity, but the Mayayana doctrines concerning the nature of Buddhahood and incompleteness of the Tipitaka split this identity in monastic and social organizational formations.

This state of affairs was thoroughly disturbed from the sixth century onwards because of three historical currents. First, there was a revival of Brahmanical religion that drew support from the ruling classes as new ideas generated within that tradition became attractive to them. These had to do with the notion of divine kingship. Kings began to be identified as incarnations of divinities such as Shiva and Vishnu. This identity blended with *bhakti* or devotion. The two functioned together to strengthen the ruling elite who, in turn, withdrew support for not only the Buddhist community but also from all other non-Brahmanical traditions including the Jains. This resulted in two trends. The non-Buddhist traditions accommodated Brahmanical deity cults and thereby supported the notions of divine kingship. On the other hand, those who refused to concede to the Brahmanical theory of kingship as well as to the social theory based on caste (the *varna* system of the Dharmasutras) were persecuted and expelled as heretics.

By the fifteenth century these trends caused the virtual extinction of Buddhist communities in the southern regions of South Asia except in Sri Lanka, which became the destination for the many Buddhist communities that escaped from persecution.[5]

Second, the Islamic invasions caused the total destruction of Buddhist establishments in the northern and northeastern regions. Those Buddhists escaped to the Himalayan regions where Buddhist communities existed. These two processes caused the concentration of the Buddhist tradition in the geographical margins of the South Asian region.

The Theravada tradition

Over the millennia, Theravada Buddhists have developed a complex ritual life involving specifically Buddhist as well as assimilated non-Buddhist practices. These may be examined as strictly monastic and non-monastic rituals but such a division can be misleading as there is interplay between monastic and lay communities. Similarly, there is only a thin line between strictly Buddhist rituals and non-Buddhist rituals as Buddhism has open boundaries that allow non-Buddhist ideas and practices to seep through as long as they do not contradict Buddhist concepts and values. Also, while some monastic rituals are restricted to the monks, others are open to the nuns and to the general public. On the other hand, the members of the sangha participate in many lay Buddhist and even some non-Buddhist rituals. This being the case, perhaps, it is best to begin with a brief introduction to the nature of the world that the Theravada Buddhists inhabit.

The sacred hierarchy

Buddhists in South Asia consider Siddhartha Gautama the Buddha as the ultimate being who is, however, no more. He is unavailable for help.[6] But his *dhamma* remains supreme. Next to the Buddha are the *pasebuduns*[7] who have achieved *sambodhi* but are unable to preach the *dhamma*. In the third rank of the hierarchy are the *arhats*, the monks who have achieved *nibbana*. Beneath them are four categories of sacred personages. In the order of sacredness, the closest to *arhats* are the *anagamis* or those who have entered the Buddhist path and will never return to the *sansara* for they will become *arhats* in this life itself. Next are the *sakadagamis*, individuals who are on the path but will return to the cycle of *sansara* once more before they become *anagamis*. Third are the *sotapannas*: those who have entered the path but return to *sansara* again and again. Some monks and nuns may belong to these categories.

This hierarchy of sacred personages, particularly the first four or five ranks, is of no use in everyday life as they have renounced the world and are not concerned with it. The average Buddhist is an *upasaka* or *upasika* (pious man or woman). Depending on their *karma*, which accumulated in their past lives and in this life, they face various circumstances that are beyond their control. Thus they seek help from the supernatural beings in their world.

The pantheon

Theravada Buddhists believe that there are thirty-three billion gods and goddesses existing in a hierarchy of heavens (*divyalokas*). These include powerful gods such as Vishnu, believed to be the protector of the island of Lanka and the Buddhasasana; Natha or Maitreya, the next Buddha to be; Skanda or the god of Kataragama village shrine; Saman or the god of the mount Sri Pada; goddesses Pattini and Brahmanical Saraswati; and demigods Dadimunda and Suniyam. All these deities are believed to protect Buddhists and the Buddhasasana. Vishnu, Kataragama, Natha, and Pattini are also the guardian deities of the Sinhala Buddhist nation. The world of humans exists in between auspicious upper realms (*brahmalokas* and *divyalokas*) and horrible lower realms (*apayas* or hells). The formal belief is that it is best to be reborn as a human for even the bodhisattvas, the future Buddhas currently residing in the upper realms, must be reborn as humans as only humans can achieve *nibbana*. Thus, ideally, humans should hear the *dhamma*, live by it, and hope to be reborn as a human in an appropriate place at an appropriate time when the *Buddhavacana* (sayings of the Buddha) still exist so that they can hear and follow them. In reality, most Buddhists wish to be reborn as a god or a *brahma* to enjoy heavenly comforts.

Beneath them is the world of *yakshas* or demons. There are 18 well known demons who roam about frightening, attacking, and sickening people. The Mahasona or the great cemetery demon, Riri yaka or the blood demon, Huniyam yaka or the demon of sorcery, and Kalukumaraya or the black prince demon are the most feared as they cause unspeakable horrors in the lives of Buddhists. Luckily, they fear the *Buddhavacana* or the Buddha's words and obey commands from great gods. Then there are the fearsome but more disgusting varieties of spirits called *pretas*—deceased relatives who continue to linger among the living causing sickness and misfortune, *pisacas*—angry and hateful beings that cause misfortune, *kumbhandas*—hateful beings with scrota as big as large pots and so massive that they are unable to move about but are condemned to sit on these massive organs hating the world, and a host of other such unfortunate unseen beings that cause misery.

The Theravada Buddhist belief is that rebirth in any one of these realms is conditioned by the moral quality of life lived in the world. One can expect a rebirth in a higher plane of existence when the quality is high, meaning there is good *karma*. Poverty, sickness, and unluckiness are seen as results of bad *karma*. When the moral quality is very low the result is rebirth in a lower realm such as those of demons or other lowly spirits. These are generally considered as hells. Other hells include the realm of animals, and subterranean hells where demonic hell hounds torture the morally condemned in various horrendous ways and the hell-bound beings suffer these agonies for extraordinary lengths of time. The lowest hell is called the Avici where those who committed the most heinous sins such as causing bodily injury to a Buddha, murdering one's parents, etc. suffer interminable agonies.

In order to ward off influences from the malevolent beings and from the varieties of black magic known as *huniam* or *kodivina* Buddhists have various ritual procedures mixed with some Buddhist content that are supposed to nullify these influences if all else fails. Some of these are calendrical while others are occasional.

Before we begin an exploration of the practices in the Theravada tradition let us turn to the other branch of Buddhism in South Asia—the Mahayana (Great Vehicle) tradition.

The Great Vehicle (Mahayana)

The demographic distribution of the Mahayana Buddhist community in South Asia is complex and a product of political vicissitudes of the various regions. The vast majority of Mahayana Buddhists live in the Himalayan regions, primarily in Nepal (six million), Tibet (two million), and Bhutan (half a million), but also in Indian territories Himachal Pradesh, Sikkhim, and Ladakh (less than half a million).[8] The community in Himachal Pradesh is of Tibetan origin as is the Tibetan diaspora, coming into existence from the 1950s, as China annexed Tibet as a Chinese territory. The headquarters of the Dalai Lama, the spiritual head of the Tibetan Buddhist community, is in Dharamsala, the spiritual center of Tibetan Buddhists world-over. Their issues with China and their situation as a diaspora form an internationally known political conflict involving powerful international supporters.

In addition to these ethnic, demographic, and geopolitical features—the external markers of South Asian Mahayana Buddhist identity—there are also internal identity markers. Their monastic tradition exists in four fraternities: Nyingma pa (*rNyng ma pa*), Kargyu pa (*bka' brgyud pa*), Sakya pa (*Sa skya pa*), and Gelug pa (*dGe lugs pa*). They all agree on the basic principles of Mahayana Buddhism but differ on details. These differences appear to be inconsequential in everyday social life among the laypeople. They formally identify themselves as supporters of a particular fraternity and appear to be endogamous. The differences are based on the relevance and efficacy of various practices. Despite these differences there is strong unity among these four sects with regard to the doctrines of the Mahayana and the Dalai Lama's leadership in the Buddhist community.

The Mahayana tradition arose in India, slowly and from uncertain origins, but grew with increasing vigor from about the second or the first centuries BCE. It accepts the foundational character of the Tipitaka, the refuges in the *triratna* (Triple-Gem)—same as the Theravada *tisarana*—the five precepts for the laity (the *pancasila*), the Vinaya proceedings for the monastics, and many calendrical rituals of the Theravada monastic tradition. The recruitment to monastic orders also follows a similar path although it varies in details in different regions where Mahayana exists today.

Differences between Theravada and Mahayana

Several features distinguish the Mahayana from the Theravada tradition. As there are numerous treatises that expound the doctrinal elements in great detail, I shall present only a simple outline. Primarily, the official language of Mahayana in South Asia is Sanskrit, and now also Tibetan, whereas that of the Theravada tradition is Pali. The Mahayana has a very large corpus in Sanskrit and Tibetan. The Tibetans constitute the principal community that sustains the tradition in South Asia. This is comparable to the Theravada, which has a large corpus in Pali and Sinhala, the language of the Sinhala community in Sri Lanka, the ethnic center of the Theravada tradition in South Asia.

The Buddhist monastic order underwent many schisms even during the Buddha's lifetime. Within a century or so after his demise various schools of thought that clashed with one another emerged among the sangha (monastic community). Many of these conflicts were over the interpretation of the Vinaya (monastic disciplinary) rules. Some had doctrinal divergences as well. The first major separation of the monastic community into two different sects each with its own set of disciplinary rules was the development of the Theravada (School of the Elders) that proposed extension of the original rules to render the monastic discipline more strict, and the Mahasanghikas (the Great Monastic Community) who opposed such a reform of the rules.

As mentioned above, the Mahayana has uncertain origins but the scholarly opinion is that it may have emerged from the Mahasanghikas. Around the first century BCE several doctrines emerged within the early Buddhist tradition. One was that while the Tipitaka contains the essential doctrines of the Buddha it does not contain everything that the Buddha preached and that the Buddha's word or the *Buddhavacana* exists concealed in various places—in lakes, rocks, mountains and so on. Great Buddhist meditators discovered these doctrines. The earliest such discoveries known to the proto-Mahayanists were the Prajnaparamita sutras (the virtue of wisdom) and the Lankavatara sutra. They also readjusted various premises of the Tipitaka according to newly discovered aspects of the *dhamma*. In this process several theoretical positions emerged that challenged certain features of the Theravada.

Central doctrines

A doctrine known as Puggalavada emerged in the first century BCE and was widely known in South India. This doctrine involved the premise that individuals have a *puggala*, a self, an essence that survived death. This notion, according to Theravada, is inconsistent with the paradigmatic notion of *anatta* or non-existence of a permanent self or soul or *atman* as in the Vedas and Jainism. What is known as a person is merely a combination of five aggregates or *khandas*: material form, sensation (receiving phenomena through the five sense organs and the mind), perception (classifying or synthesizing the phenomena), mental formation (responding to the phenomena), and consciousness (arising through the volitional interactions with the phenomena).

What we call person, personality, or self is made of these *khandas* functioning in tandem. These *khandas* cause attachment to the phenomena thus invented. But the *khandas* are constantly in a state of flux and are thus impermanent. Therefore personhood or *puggala* is inconsistent with both the *anatta* (no permanent self) and the *anicca* (doctrine of impermanence) notions that are foundational concepts in Buddhist thought. Hence, the Theravada rejection of the doctrine of *puggala*.

The Theravada also rejected the Mahayana view that the Tipitaka is foundational but incomplete. As mentioned above, the Mahayana postulated that it does not contain all of the *dhamma* and therefore new discoveries of the *dhamma* through deep meditation should be included in the canon. This doctrine is found in the Mahayana sutra *Saddharmapundarika*. As it holds, the Buddha found that some aspects of the *dhamma* were too complex for those who aspired to be only *arhats* and not Buddhas. The Buddha preached the more advanced views to others who were capable of grasping the truths contained therein and retaining them for future discovery. The great yogis of the Mahayana have discovered some of these and more are continually being discovered. The views contained in the sutras such as the Prajnaparamita, Vajracchedika, Lankavatara, Sandhinirmocana, etc. contain such higher doctrines not found in the Tipitaka. These views were unacceptable to the Theravada. Sri Lankan sources indicate that this doctrine was prevalent in the third century CE and it was known as Vaitulyavada. The doctrine was banned in Sri Lankan Theravada Buddhism. It recurred a century later but was suppressed again.

The Mahayana pantheon

The Mahayana also developed the notion that the Buddha has supernatural qualities. There are numerous universes and each of them has its own Buddhas who have achieved *nibbana*. These Buddhas are of divine character. As beings who have achieved *sambodhi* they are uninvolved in the worlds they live in and take no part in guiding the people in those worlds. They exist as models of perfect compassion and detachment.

The Mahayana developed a Buddha pantheon presided over by a primordial Buddha called the Adi Buddha (primordial Buddha). The structure of this pantheon is hierarchical and concentric with authority at the top or converging at the center, a reflection of the earthly regimes of the lands where the belief system was gradually constructed. The Adi Buddha is the embodiment of universal *sambodhi* and is not directly concerned with the world. Instead he projects five Buddhas who reside at the next level. These are Amitabhaya, Amoghasiddhi, Akshobhaya, Ratnasambhava, and Vairocana. They appear in the form of a *mandala* or organized formation with Vairocana at the center, Amitabhaya to the west, Amoghasiddhi to the north, Akshobhaya to the east, and Ratnasambhava to the south. The position of Vairocana at the center indicates that he is the principal Buddha who is also sometimes considered as the Adi Buddha. These five are called the Dhyani Buddhas, the Buddhas in meditation, and are also called the Jinas—the victors. They are all celestial Buddhas and live in their own *divyalokas*—abodes of gods.

They project other celestial as well as corporeal human Buddhas and bodhisattvas, which constitute the third level. They are considered as spiritual sons of the Dhyani Buddhas. For example, Siddhartha Gautama is such a human Buddha, the son of Amitabhaya. Among the well known celestial bodhisattvas are Maitreya, the next Buddha to be, Avalokiteshvara, Manjusri, Vajrapani, and goddesses Tara and Marici. Their human bodhisattva projections include the apotheosized great patron kings and Lamas of the past. The Dalai Lamas are considered as reincarnations of Avalokiteshvara. All celestial Buddhas and bodhisattvas are believed to be immortal.

Below them in importance are the guardians and protectors of Buddhists. All the celestial Buddhas except the Adi Buddha and the bodhisattvas play the roles of such protectors and guardian deities of pious Buddhists. At the fifth level, they are assisted by various Indian demonic and other spirit beings. These lower spirits carry out orders from the higher levels in the hierarchy. They appear to be easily accessible to the ordinary mortals and therefore are most frequently invoked and propitiated. Then there are the defenders of the Buddhasasana. They carry out commands from the guardians and their demonic assistants mentioned above. In the seventh rank are the ferocious demon lords.

Additionally, the Mahayana pantheon includes supernatural beings, such as *deva* (gods), *naga* (serpents), *yaksha* (demons), *gandharva* (musician deities), *asura* (demigods of evil nature), *garuda* (serpent-eating supernatural bird), *kimnaras* (musicians associated with Kubera, the deity who protects possessions), *mahoraga* (great reptiles), Indra, Varuna, Yama, and Agni, as well as other lower supernatural beings such as *pretas, kumbhandas, pisacas, putanas* etc. All these supernatural beings are shared by the Theravada as well as other indigenous religious traditions of South Asia.

Madhyamaka and Sunyata

Around the second century CE the South Indian Buddhist monk Nagarjuna, in his work *Mulamadhyamakarika*, presented the view of *anatta* or absence of a permanent self in persons, based on the notion of *sunyata* or emptiness that held that what is considered as self or *atman*, as in Brahmanism, is in fact empty of any attributes. This position, known as the Madhyamaka, became a major contribution to the development of the Mahayana as an established school within South Asian Buddhism. Although the Theravada tradition in Sri Lanka rejected the notion of *sunyata* during the period referred to earlier as it was held by their rival theorists whom they called the Vaitulyavadins, the Tipitaka doctrines do involve a notion of emptiness as a central thesis associated with the notion of *nibbana*. The Madhyamaka position, as developed by Nagarjuna, was that *sunyata* or emptiness is based on the *paticcasamuppada*, a primary concept in the Tipitaka that holds that the sense of reality of any perceived "object" is conditioned by antecedent conditions of perception and cognition and that the world in its pre-perception and pre-cognition state of existence has no inherent qualities, properties, or meanings apart from such cogitations; in short, the world is devoid of any inherent meanings unless we impose meanings on it. It is through such conditioned imposition of meanings that a sense of a stable and permanent self arises. But if the meanings of the world so imposed have no inherent and independent meanings then whatever they condition including the arising of the self cannot have an independent and stable existence. Nagarjuna considered his thesis as

The Bodhisattva: Difference between Theravada and Mahayana

Related to the above, the Mahayana holds that the soteriological duty of those who have entered the path should be helping others achieve *nibbana* while postponing their own *sambodhi*. Such individuals are bodhisattvas. Just as everyone is a potential Buddha everyone also can be a bodhisattva. Thus, a householder can be as much a spiritual leader without abandoning the household as a monk or nun (*bhikkhu/bhikkhuni*) who has physically renounced the household. When a bodhisattva achieves his/her *sambodhi* his/her wisdom carries all the knowledge accrued from helping others to ameliorate their suffering and enter the path. In contrast, according to the Mahayana, a monk or nun is concerned only with his/her own *sambodhi* and refuses to socially engage in the liberation of others. An innumerable number of bodhisattvas of various levels of enlightenment exist in the world; the chief one among them is Maitreya who would be the next Buddha. The Theravada dismisses this idea as it goes against the grain of their notion that the path towards liberation directs one away from the household mentally and physically and that those who have set forth are soteriologically superior (that is, superior in matters of achieving *nibbana*) to the householders who are still mired in the world.

The notion of bodhisattva exists in the Theravada to denote the previous lives of the Buddha as in the *Jataka*s—the compendium of stories that describe how Siddhartha Gautama perfected himself by perfecting and performing ethical deeds (*paramitas*) during five hundred and fifty previous lives in various forms of existence leading up to his *sambodhi*. However, this notion is analytically different from the Mahayana concept because it describes only the Buddha's deeds, whereas the Mahayana concept can apply potentially to everyone. Eventually, the Mahayana idea of bodhisattva entered the practical aspects of the Theravada as evidenced by the presence of bodhisattva figures in image houses in Sri Lanka from the eighth century onwards.

the Madhyamaka, the middle way between the *asthikavada* of Brahmanism that postulated the existence of an ultimate reality, that is, inherent independent meanings and qualities in the world, and the *nasthikavada* of the Carvakas who held that there was no such thing as the ultimate reality.

Yogacara Buddhism

Around the fourth century CE a proto-Theravada Sthaviravada *bhikkhu* named Asanga and his brother Vasubandhu theorized that in addition to providing guidance to others, engaging in conceptual analysis and other such scholastic activity, meditation (*dhyana*) should be given emphasis, as an aspect of the bodhisattva path. The way of the bodhisattva is practicing yoga and this involves meditation on consciousness. This line of thinking and acting came to be known as the Yogacara.

To put very complex ideas in a nutshell, Asanga postulated that there are six modes of perception: *rupa* (form), *sabda* (sound), *gandha* (smell), *rasa* (taste), *sparsa* (touch), and *mano* (mind). Each of these produces a specific type of *citta* or thought based on information perceived about the world. Together they constitute a consciousness substratum that he called the *manas*. *Manas* is the mental activity that organizes these perceptions and separate thoughts (*citta*) into notions. We might use a modern psychological concept to approximate Asanga's idea of *manas*: cognition. The *manas* may or may not produce correct notions about the world as perception itself is conditioned by the perceiver's circumstances. The *manas* and the six kinds of thoughts (*citta*) that are produced through six organs of perception constitute the readily knowable aspects of consciousness, the *vinnana*. It is aware of and is directed towards the world of phenomena mistaken as inherently meaningful objects.

There is another level of consciousness deeper than this superficial *vinnana*. Asanga calls this the *alaya vinnana* which is indifferent to the world of phenomena and is not directed towards them. Rather, it exists quietly, inert, as a repository of memories of past actions; and of potentialities for making wrong judgments about the world leading to wrong actions that produce unfavorable results, prolonging the erratic perceptions, thoughts, and cognitions, as well as potentialities for correct judgments leading to correct action which is conducive to achievement of *nibbana*. This potential for correct mental action he calls *paramalaya* or the universal consciousness that exists in all beings, and it is the potential for achieving *nibbana*. The whole function of the Yogacara is to meditate on these processes, grasp the *paramalaya*, and achieve *nibbana*.

Tantra, mantra, and vajra

While the Yogacara was being conceptualized another cultural movement that was taking shape in India influenced it. This was the *tantra* tradition within the post-Vedic Hinduism. Tantra was a form of meditational practice based on using imagination and autosuggestion to produce a frame of mind that would grasp the nature of and union with Brahman in the Hindu belief system. Yogacara Buddhists found many aspects of *tantra* useful in their quest for understanding the *paramalaya* (universal consciousness) that arises from the *sunyata* or emptiness that the Madhyamaka Buddhism conceptualized. The Yogacara held that the realization of *nibbana* took many births over eons of patient *paramitas* or perfections of wisdom. The tantric system, however, promised that perfection could be achieved in this birth itself through the practice of its ritualized meditation techniques. Yogacara Buddhists conceptualized that the Buddha himself had disclosed these *tantras*, unknown to the Tipitaka tradition but later discovered by the Mahayana practitioners. Yogacara Buddhism assimilated the basic conceptual and ritual frameworks of the tantric tradition and called these Buddhist tantric practices the "Tantrayana," the vehicle of the *tantras*.

The tantra used, in addition to ritualized meditation, incantations of verbal formulae that functioned as mnemonic devices to bring to mind complex conceptual schemes. These were already in existence in the Vedic tradition where the syllable Om had achieved the status of being the summation of Brahman itself. Many other such vocalizations were invented to summarize doctrinal materials and to invoke deities who signified these doctrines. Such formulae were, and still are, known as *mantra*s. Popular Buddhism already had a tradition of using verbal incantations called *parittas*, or *pirit*, as a part of its technology for manipulating the forces of the world to bring about protection and beneficial effects in everyday life. The Yogacara adopted the mantras as an inalienable aspect of their Tantrayana and called the proper construction and use of Buddhist mantras the "Mantrayana." The best known mantra in this tradition is the mantra of Avalokiteshvara: *Om Mani Padme Hum!*[9]

They also inherited from the Vedic and post-Vedic traditions the concept of Vajra—diamond. The Vedic god Indra or Sakra, the head of the pantheon, had a *vajra* as his weapon. The *vajra* or diamond is the hardest known substance capable of cutting through anything. In Mahayana Buddhism it became a signifier of sharpness of the mind that cuts through the veils of ignorance to discover truth. Tantric meditation using mantras as an instrument to dispel illusions and delusions to discover *paramalaya* became known as the Vajrayana.

Mahayana Buddhism thrived in India, particularly in the eastern, southern, and northwestern regions. But it was not to last for too long. Muslim invasions from the eighth century onwards intervened with its developments as Islamic ideals clashed directly with the Buddhist institutional system—monasteries, image houses, agnostic beliefs, and, in Mayahana enclaves, tantric practices. The result was the obliteration of Buddhism in northern India. Buddhist establishments survived in southern Indian principalities until waves of Hindu revivals pushed them out. Fortunately, Sri Lanka and Myanmar were receptive to the plight of Indian Buddhists as many migrated to these lands. Tibetan Buddhism began, perhaps just before or just as these trends started unfolding in the rest of South Asia, absorbing Mahayana Buddhists fleeing from persecution.

Padmasambhava's contributions to Tibetan Buddhism

As Tibetan sources hold, Buddhism arrived in Tibet in the seventh century during the reign of King Songsten Gampo (618–650). The king had two queens, one Nepali and the other Chinese. Both were Buddhists and they converted Songsten Gampo. The two queens had several temples built for the veneration of Avalokiteshvara and Sakya Muni Buddha. Tibetan sources state that the king did much to spread Buddhism in Tibet. However, the king's death interrupted the continued growth of Buddhism on Tibetan soil.

A century later, King Tri Songdetsen (740–798) attempted to establish the first Buddhist monastery in Tibet. Tibetans already had a deep culture, which went back to times immemorial, and myths. This is the culture of Bon, a religion that involved beliefs in a polytheistic world populated by a very large hierarchical pantheon of sacred beings that inhabited all natural features of the landscape and possessed various ritualistic technologies to harness the power of the divine types among these beings and dispel the influences of the malevolent types.[10]

According to the Tibetan tradition the Bon deities obstructed the king's endeavor by creating various disasters. An Indian monk named Santarakshita was invited to quell the anger of the supernatural beings and establish monastic Buddhism, but to no avail. Under his advice the king invited Padmasambhava, from a place called Oddiyana located between Kashmir and Afghanistan, just as the first Muslim invasions of these regions began. Padmasambhava carried with him a powerful combination of ideas and skills including Vajrayana Mahayana doctrines, Tantrayana, which was growing throughout the Indian subcontinent, as well as its appendage Mantrayana, and the classical Indian institution of *pratiharya* (performance of miracles that modern scholars define as magic). He defeated the supernatural powers, converted some of them to be guardians of Buddhism in Tibet, established the Buddhasasana under royal patronage, and became the most venerated historical figure in Tibetan culture as Guru Rinpoche. Buddhism became the state religion of Tibet in 719 CE. After Tri Songdetsen, King Relbachen (815–836) did much to propagate Buddhism and is regarded as one of the three great Buddhist kings alongside Songsten Gampa and Tri Songdetsen.

Tibetan Buddhism thus began as an imported system of beliefs and practices within an existing cultural milieu to develop into a unique institution that included elements of both Buddhist and Bon traditions. This is to say that Bon adherents became Buddhists for soteriological purposes while remaining Bon practitioners (Bonpas) for domestic purposes—in much the same way their Indian, Sri Lankan, Burmese, Thai, and Chinese counterparts adopted Buddhism, while remaining adherents of native beliefs and practices in mundane non-soteriological contexts. The impact of Buddhism on Bon is also evident in the Bon adoption of various popular Buddhist concepts such as *kamma*, rebirth, and other doctrinal elements as well as monastic institutions, and the creation of legends to show that what the Buddhists believe had already been available long before the Buddha was born, through the teachings of a grand imperial monarch named Tonpa Senrap.

Thus, Tibetan Buddhism inherited a vast pantheon of supernatural beings who found Buddhist expression. Songsten Gampo began to be regarded as a manifestation of Bodhisattva Avalokiteshvara. His queens were apotheosized as incarnations of the goddess Tara, born of Avalokiteshvara's tears, as his consorts. The Nepali and Chinese queens are called green and white Tara, respectively. Tri Songdetsen is apotheosized as an incarnation of the Bodhisattva Manjusri. King Relbachen is regarded as an incarnation of the Buddha Vajrapani. These, together with the supernaturalized Buddhas, Bodhisattvas, and Vedic and Puranic deities populate the Tibetan Buddhist world.

Buddhist practice: The practice of Theravada Buddhism in Sri Lanka

I limit this discussion of Buddhist practice to those in Sri Lanka as the space available does not permit a discussion of the Mahayana practices.

Occasional household rituals

Among the occasional Buddhist rituals that Theravada Buddhist householders perform are protection ceremonies (*pirit*), almsgiving (*dana*), and mortuary rituals. Members of the sangha participate in these rituals.

Pirit

Pirit (Pali: *Paritta*) means protection. This is an ancient institution with its roots going back to, according to traditional beliefs, the times of the Buddha. The rites consist of selections of *suttas* and other non-canonical compositions in the Pali language that are chanted by a group of *bhikkhus* or laymen. When chanted by laymen it is known as *gihi pirit*.

The purpose of chanting *pirit* is to ward off evil influences to give protection and bring about good fortune and merit. There are four types of *pirit* ceremonies: *set pirit* (*pirit* for blessing), *maha pirit* (the great *pirit*), *varu pirit* (*pirit* for half-day), and *sati pirit* (*pirit* chanted over a week). *Set pirit* is the shortest form and the most frequently performed ritual prior to commencement or termination of any activity. The Sri Lanka Broadcasting Corporation, the national radio service, begins the day by broadcasting *set pirit*. The Sri Lankan government and various departments, and private institutions as well as many households inaugurate all activities with *set pirit*. Even the national cricket team has a few monks chant *set pirit* before a cricket match, sometimes at the airport before they go abroad for tournaments.

Set pirit consists of one of the three main *suttas*—Mangala (the auspicious), Ratana (the Jewel), and Metta (compassion), which together are called *maha pirit* (the great *pirit*), extracted from the Tipitaka—and a few other non-canonical Pali language incantations. On specific occasions after chanting *set pirit* the participant laymen are blessed with *pirit nul*. These consist of three strands of cotton thread intertwined and held in the hands of the chanting monks to imbue them with the power of the *pirit* and also in the hands of the laymen who organize the event. After the chant pieces of the thread are tied around the wrists or arms of the laymen as talismans or charms that will protect and support the laymen for a few days. *Set pirit* are meant for the quick delivery of blessings.

Maha pirit includes all three *suttas* mentioned above together with other non-canonical materials and are meant for more elaborate domestic or larger social occasions. Unlike the *set pirit*, these take more time. The chanting of the same set of *suttas* for a half day—in the morning or evening—is known as *varu* or *vel pirit* (*varua* or *vela* in Sinhala means half-day). *Varu pirit* may be chanted on any occasion. The difference between *set pirit* and *varu pirit* is a matter of availability of time.

More complex and extended *pirit* ceremonies are held prior to major life cycle events such as marriage, prior to housewarming ceremonies, inauguration of business activities, three months after a funeral, etc. These rituals begin in the early evening and continue through the night and sometimes over a week (*sati pirit*). In these rituals the entire set of protective verses meant for these ceremonies, contained in a compendium called the *pirit pota*, is chanted. These are elaborate ceremonies performed inside specially constructed decorated chambers. Chanting ceremonies through the night are more usual for domestic purposes whereas week long ceremonies are meant for public purposes such as blessing the nation at times of inauspicious astrological conditions.

Dana—almsgiving

Dana in Pali and Sinhala means alms as well as giving or charity. One may perform *dana* anytime or anywhere but almsgiving (*dana*) rituals are usually performed to offer alms to the members of the monastic order (*bhikkhus* or monks in general and, since the establishment of the *bhikkhuni* or nuns' order, to nuns as well) following *pirit* ceremonies, during commemorations of the death of relatives, and during mortuary rituals. There are several ways to offer alms. Laypersons may carry alms to the monastery or invite *bhikkhus* to residences. The latter occurs when the donor has a residence spacious enough to accommodate a large group of monks. In general donors prefer to render their almsgiving a *sanghika dana* where at least four fully ordained *bhikkhus* are present representing all the sangha in four directions. This form is believed to be more meritorious than alms given to a lesser number. A senior *bhikkhu* administers *tisarana* (taking refuge in the Triple-Gem) and *pancasila* (the five precepts) which the gathering of laymen repeat after him, and the head of the household is asked to repeat after the monk a stanza in Pali that declares that he is making the offering to the whole of the sangha.

All *dana* rituals commence with offering a *buddha puja*—offerings to the Buddha. This involves placing separate portions of all that is offered at the *dana* on a plate that is placed before a picture or a statue of the Buddha, usually found in any Buddhist household.

A *dana* may involve the offering of non-alcoholic beverages, usually tea, fruit juice, or coconut water. This is more usual in the afternoon. But the *dana* proper involves offering breakfast—usually after an evening or all night *pirit* ceremony, and/or lunch, and includes solid food as well as beverages. Solid food must be offered before noon as the Vinaya code of discipline prohibits consumption of solid food in the afternoon. After the *bhikkhus* finish partaking of the meal another offering is made. This, in an affluent household, may include the eight items that a *bhikkhu* needs, including such items as an alms bowl, three robes, a belt, a razor, a water-strainer, and a sewing needle. However, most households cannot afford to provide these items for all of the monks, so customarily only one is offered to the most senior *bhikkhu* and others are offered robes, towels, books, umbrellas etc. that are more affordable. Thereafter the almsgiving ritual ends with a transference of merit obtained from the act of giving to all in the gathering as well as to the gods and the deceased kindred who are awaiting rebirth or are in inauspicious rebirths.

Mortuary rituals

Death causes much lamentation by the relatives although, formally, death is taken as a part of life that leads from one birth to the next and a reminder of *anicca*—impermanence. Once the death of an individual is confirmed the relatives, neighbors, and the *bhikkhu*s of the nearby monastery are informed. The corpse is kept in the house for three days unless the deceased has requested a same day funeral. Since colonial encounters it has become normal to embalm the body and place it in a coffin even when a *bhikkhu* passes away and to place coconut oil lamps at the head and feet of the corpse, which is oriented in the east–west direction with feet towards the east.

Mortuary rituals begin three days after death occurs. *Bhikkhu*s arrive shortly before the corpse is taken out of the house. It is usual to invite at least four ordained *bhikkhu*s, as in the almsgiving under other circumstances, in order to render the alms given at the funeral a *sanghika* offering. Once the corpse is taken out, in the yard of the deceased's residence or at the burial/cremation ground, *bhikkhu*s are seated for mortuary rituals that normally occur in the afternoon. They are seated by the corpse in a semi-circle. As usual in all Theravada Buddhist activities, the monks administer *tisarana* and the five precepts and commence mortuary rituals. This consists of the collective chanting of the well known stanza in Pali that brings to the attention of the gathering the impermanence of life:

Anicca vata sankhara, uppadavayadhammino.
Uppajjitva nirujjhanti tesam vupasamo sukho.
Impermanent alas are formations, subject to rise and fall.
Having arisen, they cease; their subsiding is bliss.

Thereafter an offering known as *mataka vastra puja* occurs. Here a piece of white cloth to be cut up and made into a monastic robe is offered to the *bhikkhu*s. Having performed this, the relatives of the deceased sit on a mat, around a cup and a pitcher of water. A senior member of the immediate family holds the pitcher, while others lay their hands on it to signify collective participation, and pours water into the cup and lets it overflow while the *bhikkhu*s chant the concluding Pali stanzas:

Unname udakam vattam yatha ninnam pavattati
evameva ito dinnam petanam upakappati.
Yatha varivaha pura paripurenti sagaram
evameva ito dinnam petanam upakappati.
Just as the water fallen on high ground flows to a lower level,
Even so what is given from here accrues to the departed.
Just as the full flowing rivers fill the ocean,
Even so what is given from here accrues to the departed.

The function of this ritual is to transfer to the departed the merit accrued during the act of *dana* to the sangha so that he/she may find an auspicious rebirth. The belief here is that the departed is now in a state of in-between existence after the death and before a rebirth. This concludes the first stage of the mortuary rituals.

On the third day or within a week of the funeral another important mortuary rite called *mataka bana* occurs. A monk is invited to the house of the deceased in the evening and invited to deliver a sermon. After following the usual initial procedures the *bhikkhu* delivers the sermon for about an hour. The *bhikkhu* is then presented with alms such as a towel or a book etc. and he transfers merit to the departed and to all present in the house. In some families an almsgiving ritual is held seven days after the funeral, but this is optional. It is mandatory that three months from the date of death a major almsgiving is performed, which usually consists of offering the monastic community lunch before noon. How many *bhikkhu*s participate in this ritual depends on how many the family can afford to invite. The minimum number is four fully ordained *bhikkhu*s in order to render the almsgiving a *sanghika dane*. This usually concludes the mortuary rituals. The more affluent families may commemorate the death annually with a *sanghika dane*.

Calendrical rituals: Poya

Traditional Theravada Buddhism functions on the basis of the lunar calendar mixed with the astrological solar calendar. The solar year begins on April 14 when the Sun transits from Pisces (Meena *rashi*) to Aries (Mesha *rashi*). Thus the first lunar month falls between mid-April and mid-May and is called Bak. Calculating this way, the second month is Vesak, followed by Poson, Asala, Nikini, Binara, Vap, Il, Unduvap, Durutu, Navam, and Madin, which falls between mid-March and mid-April. In every lunar month there are four sacred days: the full moon, waning half moon, new moon, and waxing half moon. These occur at one week intervals and are called *poya* days and are auspicious for religious observances. The full moon and new moon are called *uposata* days, which are particularly important days for both the sangha and the laity. I shall discuss the significance to the sangha later. For now, let me focus on the lay conduct on the *uposatha* or full moon and new moon days.

Of the two *uposatha* days the full moon day is the more important. The tradition has it that the moon has fifteen (*pasalos*) curves (*vaka*) and when full it has all the fifteen curves. Therefore the full moon days are called *pasalosvak poya* days. The half moon on either side contains eight (*ata*) curves. The new moon is known as *amavaka*. The full moon and waxing moon are seen as more auspicious than the new moon and waning moon.

The Theravada Buddhists in South Asia have aligned all the major Buddhist events on full moon days except for the full moon in April when the new moon *uposata* is celebrated. They believe that the Buddha was born, achieved his *sambodhi*, and passed away on the Vesak full moon day. Also, it was on a Vesak *poya* day that the Buddha visited Kelaniya on the southwestern coast of Sri Lanka to preach the *dhamma* and settle a dispute between two Naga princes. Thus it is the most sacred day and, wherever Theravada Buddhists live, they celebrate it with many rituals. During the day the *upasakas* (pious males) and *upasikas* (pious females) observe the *atthanga sila* or *atasil* (eight precepts that include the regular *panca sila* and three more restraints: refraining from indulging in amusements and using adornments, refraining from using high seats, and refraining from consuming solid foods from noon until the following morning). They observe these precepts either at home or, more communally, at a preferred temple (*pansala*) where a *bhikkhu* establishes them on the eight precepts by having the pious repeat after him as he chants the relevant verses in Pali language.

Poya days are public holidays on which the pious people observe the precepts. On these days they have the opportunity to stay away from domestic and professional chores and accompanied aggravations, and look inwards. They spend the day reading, discussing, and listening to deliveries of the *dhamma*, and meditating on compassion, disgust, consciousness and the like. These are the most popular varieties of meditation. They meditate on compassion in an attempt to eliminate feelings of aggression and hatred and to spread kindness towards those who have wronged them. They meditate on disgust in an attempt to distance themselves from their bodies that are analyzed as constituted of disgusting elements, the locus of their immediate sense of self, and bodily cravings. The meditation on consciousness is the most elaborate, encompassing the other two forms of meditation, in an examination of one's own mind to detect hatred, cravings, and other such mental impurities in order to eliminate them and establish the right mindfulness and awareness of one's consciousness as prescribed in the Noble Eightfold Path.

Their family members attend to all their needs throughout the day. At the temples and monasteries monks deliver sermons in the evening. Those *upasakas* (laymen) and *upasikas* (laywomen) who opt to stay the night at the temple and their kindred, friends, and other pious individuals constitute the audience.

Figure 4.2 Worshipping the Buddha at Degaldoruwa Royal Cave. Photo taken by Sunil Goonasekera.

These activities are not specific to the Vesak *poya* day but to all full moon *poya* days. The difference is that on the Vesak day they perform these rituals in larger numbers and with even more *sraddha* (piety) as the converging events in the Buddha's life are of such emotional significance to the Buddhists.

The Vesak *poya* is also a celebration of these events with a grand lamp offering. Every family lights several coconut oil lamps—as many as they can afford—to celebrate the Buddha. In urban areas various Buddhist organizations establish a "gifting place" (*dansal*; Pali: *dana sala*) where vegetarian food and non-alcoholic beverages are donated to those who go to or return from religious rituals at the temples and to others who spend the night on the roads enjoying the sight of the light offerings in households. In urban centers there are extravagant displays called *torana* (pandals). Some of these are as tall as fifty feet and as wide. They are flat erect structures containing many large cutouts of the Buddha in his four traditional poses (seated, standing, and lying down as in sleep or as on deathbed, as well as the baby Bodhisattva walking on the seven lotuses immediately after his birth) with massive halos each studded with hundreds of electric bulbs of the five colors of the Buddha's halo (blue, yellow, red, white, and orange) which blink in set patterns; and pictorial presentations of Jataka stories or events in the Buddha's life, some static, others with mobile cutouts to depict action. These are immensely popular entertainments on the Vesak day.

The next most important full moon day falls in the following month, Poson. It is believed, as is also mentioned in the Buddhist chronicles, that *bhikkhu* Mahinda converted the Lankan king Devanampiyatissa together with many of his subjects on this day in the third century BCE, at Mihintale, near Anuradhapura in the north-central part of the island. From that day, except during the colonial period from 1815 up to 1947 and thereafter until 1972, Theravada Buddhism has been held as the state religion of Sri Lanka. Most of the Vesak activities occur on this day as well, although with less extravagant displays of piety.

The third most important full moon follows the Poson. This is the Asala month's full moon. The Asala *poya* is important as this is believed to be the day on which the Buddha delivered his first sermon, the *Dhammacakkappavattanasutta* or the *sutta* by which the wheel of the *dhamma* was established. However, this day is significant for seven more events in the story of Buddhism and in the story of Buddhism in Sri Lanka. Buddhists believe that the Buddha's mother, queen Mahamaya, conceived the Bodhisattva; the Bodhisattva renounced the household; the Buddha performed the Great Yamaka Miracle; the Buddha preached the Abhidhamma in the Tusita heaven; the first Sri Lankan was ordained as a bhikkhu in Sri Lanka; king Dutthagamani laid the foundation for the Great Ruvanveli stupa in Anuradhapura; and the same king deposited the Buddha's relics (*sarvagna dhatu*) in that stupa on this *poya* day in different years. This multivocal symbolism of the day is celebrated with the grand procession of the Temple of the Tooth Relic in Kandy in which the Tooth Relic (the *danta dhatu*) of the Buddha is taken on a grand elephant around the ancient city of Kandy. The Asala *poya* is also monastically important as the annual *vassa* or rain retreat commences on the day after the *poya* day.

Other *poya* days, though important, are of lesser significance when compared to the Vesak, Poson, and Asala *poyas*. The monks who could not begin their *vassa* retreat on the day following the Asala full moon are allowed to begin their retreat on the Nikini *poya* day (mid-August) that follows the Asala. The following Binara *poya* (mid-September) is sacred as it was on such a *poya* day that the Buddha established the ordination of *bhikkhunis* with the ordination of his stepmother, queen Maha Pajapati Gotami, and her retinue. The Vap *poya* follows in mid-October and the monastic *vassa* retreat is concluded, leading to the commencement of the *kathina* rituals whereby the monks are offered new robes. The *kathina* rituals proceed until mid-November, the Il *poya*. This *poya* also celebrates the commencement of the missionary activities by the sangha as the Buddha sent sixty *bhikkhus* for this purpose. The mid-December Unduvap *poya* is highly significant for two main events: the arrival of *bhikkhuni* Sanghamitta with the bodhi sapling and her establishment of the Sri Lankan order of nuns (*bhikkhuni sasana*) by ordaining queen Anula and her retinue of five hundred courtly ladies. The next, Durutu *poya*, which falls in mid-January is a very significant day for Lankan Buddhists as it was on this day that the Buddha visited the island for the first time. He arrived in Mahiyangana where he preached the *dhamma* to the Yakkhas—believed to be demons but, more ethnologically, a group of indigenous people on the island. The event led to the construction of the first stupa on the island to commemorate the event. After the Buddha's demise his hair relic and a collarbone relic were deposited in the stupa. This stupa is also the beginning of stupa worship in Sri Lanka.

The following Navam *poya* in mid-February is bittersweet for on that day the Buddha announced his *parinibbana* (death) after two more moons, in the following Vesak. On that day the Buddha appointed arhats Sariputta and Moggallana as his chief disciples. The Medin *poya* follows, announcing the Buddha's visit to his parental house and his ordination of princes Rahula, the son born before his renunciation, and Nanda, his cousin. We come to the end of the *poya* ritual cycle with the Bak *poya* that falls in mid-April. This *poya* is different from others as it is celebrated on the new moon day. Tradition has it that the Buddha visited Nagadipa Island on the northeast coast of Lanka to preach the *dhamma* and quell disputes among the Nagas who inhabited the island. This was his second visit to Lanka. With that we complete the *poya* ritual cycle and it will be Vesak once again, when another year of celebration of grand events of the faith, observances of precepts, and contemplation of the *dhamma* is begun.

Monastic occasional rituals

Recruitment—pabbaja

The Buddhist monastic order is open to anyone irrespective of ethnicity, caste, class, or gender, although the minimum age is seven years. There are no formal public rituals for recruitment to the order.[11] When an individual develops the motivation to leave the household and enter the monastic order s/he communicates this decision to the immediate family, and with them communicates it to an ordained monk. It is likely that such individuals already have close contacts with one or more monks in a chosen monastery and have been observing the various precepts that are beyond the *pancasila* or five precepts.

The senior monk then considers several preliminary requirements for recruitment. If the aspirant is a child the Vinaya rules demand that the aspirant has the consent of his/her family. Every aspirant must declare that s/he is a human being, is not suffering from a serious illness, not burdened with debt, not a slave, and not a soldier. Once these conditions are satisfied the aspirant's head is shaven and s/he is given monastic clothes—the yellow or orange robe—and is asked to observe the ten precepts. Ordinarily, this formal recruitment rite is a simple ceremony performed before the members of the aspirant's family and is called the lower ordination.

All those who enter the order as novices must begin by observing the ten precepts (*dasasil*). The novices are required to extend the eight precepts (*atasil*) by observing two more: abstention from accepting gold or silver—meaning money—and, by extending the seventh precept, abstention from adornments of any kind. The tenth rule is followed by wearing yellow or orange robes as the ordained monastics do. Some laypersons also observe the ten precepts and permanently leave the household without joining the sangha. As a way of abstaining from adornments they wear white clothes only and live around religious establishments, reading Buddhist texts, meditating, and engaging in religious discourses. Interestingly, the *upasaka* (male) ten precept holders are not organized into a community comparable to the sangha while the *dasasil upasikas* (females), as we shall discuss later, are organized into groups. The *upasakas* are more or less lonely wanderers and each takes the responsibility to supervise his/her own adherence to the precepts. Further, the lay community, while not organized in a supervisory capacity, notices their conduct. Any unsatisfactory behavior that is not in accordance with the precepts that the *upasaka/upasika* claims to hold causes loss of credibility and social recognition as a ten precept holder.

From the moment a layperson enters the monastic order as a novice, that individual is bound by the Vinaya rules appropriate to his/her standing within the order. There are several layers in the monastic hierarchy. Males (*bhikkhus*) are always superior to the females (*bhikkhunis*). Those who are fully ordained (or received higher ordination known as *upasampada*) are superior to the non-ordained. However, this does not apply to the *bhikkunis*, who are inferior to *bhikkus* irrespective of the date of ordination, which is the same in Jain monastic orders. Also among the fully ordained, seniors, determined by the date of ordination, are superior to juniors irrespective of the chronological age. The ordained males are preceptors to the nuns and novices. The seniors train the juniors. The education of the novices takes place in monastic schools known as *pirivenas* (*parivena*).

Calendrical rituals

In contrast to the novices, the ordained members of the sangha are bound by the complete set of Vinaya rules and monastic authority structure. The Vinaya rules are composed of two parts, namely, the *suttavibhanga* and the *khandaka*.

The *suttavibhanga* primarily consists of three sections: the *parajikas* (core rules), *sanghadhiseshas* (other rules), and the *patimokkha* (a non-canonical commentary of core significance). The *parajika* or core rules refer to the most serious violations of monastic conduct leading to the condemnation amounting to expulsion from the order and reduction in monastic status to that of a mere ten precept holder wearing white clothes signifying loss of monastic membership.

There are four *parajika* rules for *bhikkhus* and eight for *bhikkhunis*. These include violation of celibacy, taking what is not given, intentionally killing a human being or encouraging others to do so, and claiming supernatural powers. The additional four *parajikas* for *bhikkhunis* are making physical contact with a man between his shoulders and knees, allowing males to make physical contact, approving or concealing violations by other nuns, and continually supporting a monk expelled for violating the norms.

There are thirteen *sanghadisesa* or other rules. Five of these have to do with relations with the opposite sex. Two rules deal with a *bhikkhu's*/*bhikkhuni's* conduct with regard to building monastic residences and monuments. Six rules deal with the use of speech to insult or defame, create schism, and to quarrel.

The *khandaka* section involves rules governing monastic etiquette—how monks and nuns should behave towards each other taking into consideration one's position in the organization. This section has possibly influenced the general sense of etiquette and everyday culture in the Buddhist community as a whole. They include what may be called "table manners," general deportment in communal situations, how to behave towards elders, how to perform ablutions, and so on.

The patimokkha

The *patimokkha* is one of the most important institutions in Buddhist monasticism. It involves monastic recitation of the *patimokkha* rules of the Vinaya in order to facilitate confession of violation of the Vinaya by a *bhikkhu* or *bhikkhuni*. In a given monastic establishment, the monks who reside within the boundaries of the institution must meet fortnightly on *uposatha* (full and new moon) days to perform this confessional rite. In order to establish a quorum there must be at least five monks in attendance. During the recitation, the most senior among them asks each of the others whether his/her conduct during the preceding fortnight violated any rules. If such a violation occurred, however minor it might be, it must be disclosed in order to discipline the offender in accordance with the rules. Silence is accepted as absence of violations. Here the disciplining for violations of *parajika* and *sanghadisesa* are governed by the rules. To define and discipline such violations, the monastic establishment applies the *parajika* (core rules) and *sanghadisesa* (other rules).

This is an exclusive ritual. When *bhikkhus* perform the *patimokkha* there should not be present any *bhikkhunis*, novices, criminals, individuals expelled for *parakija* offences, individuals whose conduct has been on further scrutiny, eunuchs, or hermaphrodites. And the *patimokkha* should not be performed on any day other than an *uposatha* day.

Over the centuries, the *patimokkha* has undergone certain modifications. If a monk has violated a rule he can privately confess to another monk of senior standing and the matter can be addressed thereafter prior to the formal rite so that during the rite silence can be maintained indicating absence of violations. This modification is, of course, a face saving strategy. However, if the violation comes under a *parajika* or core rule, it must be disclosed during the rite.

The vassa

Another important monastic ritual is called *vassa* (the rainy-season retreat). Early Buddhist monasticism, similar to its Jain counterpart, involved continuous wandering. The wandering monks would create a temporary residence to stay in during the night. However, this was not practicable during the monsoons in late summer and early fall months from late August to November as the roads would be flooded and construction of temporary residences difficult. Pious layper-sons constructed permanent buildings for the convenience of the wanderers. In time Buddhist monastic wandering gave rise to sedentary monasticism in these permanent buildings which later became monasteries (*viharas*). In a given monastic residence there would be a community of monks or nuns and their conduct needed to be regulated in order to sustain communal harmony. Thus arose many of the rules in the Vinaya *pitaka*. Many aspects of the *suttavibhanga* and *khandaka* are responses to these needs of the sedentary monastic community.

The kathina

Another important monastic ritual is called *kathina*, held towards the end of the *vassa* or the rain retreat. The term refers to a rough, coarse stained cloth. Symbolically, this signifies the attire prescribed for a *bhikkhu*. Theoretically, this should be a cloth discarded by laypersons and found in cemeteries and so on, and soiled, as signified by the stains. Over the centuries, the soiled, stained, and discarded cloth of no value, became a piously donated robe which has been purposely stained to signify if not emulate the ideal soiled cloth. Monks are offered these cloths ceremonially during the *kathina* ritual.

The dhutanga

The Vinaya allows a certain degree of individual freedom to make personal commitments to observing restraints as long as they do not clash with the basic rules. Such allowances are called *dhutangas*. For example, nothing in the Vinaya compels a *bhikkhu/bhikkhuni* to restrict his or her diet to vegetarian foods but a monk or nun may practice vegetarianism.

Another set of *dhutangas* allows *bhikkhus/bhikkhunis* to choose between scholarship and meditation as his/her focus. Monastics with fine memories and aptitude for retaining large texts opt to be scholars. These were the individuals who carried the Tipitaka in their memories until it was committed to writing. Classic examples are *bhikkhus* Ananda and Upali who, as the tradition has it, retained in their memories the Sutta and Vinaya *pitakas*, respectively. Some of them write commentaries on various aspects of the *dhamma*. These tend to be younger, energetic monks. Traditionally, one moved from scholarly activities to meditational (*vipassanadhura*) activities as one aged. *Vipassana* meditation is also known as insight meditation and is popular even among elderly laymen and laywomen (*upasakas* and *upasikas*).

Similar *dhutangas* relate to where a *bhikkhu* can reside. A monk or nun can opt to reside in a monastery in a village or in a forest hermitage. The village *bhikkhus* tend to be the more scholarly types playing scholarly roles that involve memorizing the Tipitaka, although there is no such necessity according to Vinaya. At present, memorizing the *dhamma* is not necessary as it is preserved in printed word, even in the digital domain. Present-day scholarly *bhikkhus* tend to be well educated teachers and physicians of traditional medicine (*Ayurveda*), and render social service by participating in appropriate domestic rituals of laymen such as *pirit* chanting, almsgiving, and mortuary rituals. They even practice astrology and exorcisms and some are well known mantra specialists, despite the belief that such were condemned by the Buddha, although they are not specifically prohibited by the Vinaya rules. As such they also receive a certain degree of public opprobrium as well.

On the other hand, the forest *bhikkhus* tend to focus on meditation as the isolation of forest living is conducive to such activity. Again, this is a *dhutanga* or allowance rather than a disciplinary demand. The forest living and separation from social activities, dependence on public charity, and renown for meditation have brought them much public adoration and honor. This attention can transform the meditation monks into village monks: pious laypersons who appreciate the conduct of these monks attempt to make "improvements" in the forest dwellings and bring them alms including items that are more suitable for village monks and thus draw them into village existence.

Monastic mortuary rituals

There are no specific rituals prescribed for monastic funerals. The model for monastic funerals is found in the story of the Buddha where, after several days of adoration of his physical remains, it was cremated. Presently, in Sri Lanka, this has grown into a very elaborate and expensive affair, called *adahanostsava*. It is apparent that certain European cultural elements have also seeped into the monastic practice. A good example is the use of an expensive coffin and public announcements.

Historical vicissitudes

Monastic landlordism

While the above ritual practices continue, over the millennia, various modifications have been made for a variety of reasons, many of which have been politically initiated. At the very inception of Buddhism in Sri Lanka a strong connection was established between the state and the sangha, thereby rendering Buddhism the state religion of Sri Lanka. From then onwards, the kings had to consult the sangha, centered at the Maha Vihara, the Great Monastery in Anuradhapura, whenever a legal issue conflicted with the tenets of Buddhism. Much has already been written about the extent to which Buddhist sangha and the state were involved in warfare against foreign aggressors during the reign of king Dutthagamani just two centuries or so after the establishment of Buddhism in Sri Lanka. Further, three other norms entered the state of Sri Lanka: the state must protect the Buddhasasana (Buddhist community); must construct monuments to sustain religious fervor; and must maintain the sangha.

One of the most significant outcomes of this relationship was the growth of monastic landlordism. As a way of maintaining the sangha, kings donated large tracts of land, entire villages with inhabitants therein, for the maintenance of the sangha, monasteries, and temples. Thus the monasteries became great landowners with rights to buy real property for monastic purposes. However, monastic lands could never be sold for any purpose. As the lands were granted under the *brahmadeya* theory, by which they were given as supreme gifts, they were beyond the jurisdiction of the state officials and the sangha had absolute ownership of the lands and judicial authority over the inhabitants in those lands. Only the chief incumbent and his deputies had authority over lands owned by the monastery. The land was not given to individual *bhikkhus* or the sangha as a whole but to particular monasteries. This relationship continues to this day.

However, by the tenth century kings began to gift lands to individual *bhikkhus*, in violation of the Vinaya rule prohibiting *bhikkhus* to own property, with far reaching effects. Hitherto, monastic inheritance was based on the theory of lineage from student to student, whereby the title passed from the chief incumbent to his senior-most pupil. Now, as the lands belonged to individual monks as their private property, they could do as they wished and the principles of inheritance underwent a radical change. A new principle of "lineage of kindred students" came into being whereby the landowning *bhikkhu* could give the land to a kindred *bhikkhu*, thus altering the norms of monastic recruitment. Rather than restricting recruitment to individuals with the motivation for monastic life, kinship would be given primacy for the sole purpose of inheriting land. By the time King Kirti Sri Rajasinghe reorganized the monastic order in the mid-eighteenth century, the sangha could not find four fully ordained *bhikkhus* as monasteries had become havens for unordained property-owning individuals. The king had to import ordained monks from Thailand to reestablish the Theravada sangha in Sri Lanka.

The bhikkhunis

Although the *bhikkhunisasana* or the order of *bhikkhunis* was established by the *bhikkhuni* named Sanghamitta in the third century BCE, it disappeared from about the eleventh century as the Anuradhapura and Polonnaruva kingdoms collapsed, and the Buddhist community virtually abandoned these regions and migrated towards southwestern and central regions. For nearly nine centuries there was no

Caste and monasticism

One of the consequences of Kirti Sri Rajasinghe's intervention in Buddhist affairs in the eighteenth century was the entry of caste as a criterion for monastic recruitment. As the king, a Shaivite Hindu, and the nobility could not bow down to low caste individuals, recruitment was restricted to the highest caste, the Goigamas, among the Sinhala people. This prevented highly motivated non-Goigama individuals from entering the sangha.

This led to the development of the Amarapura *nikaya* (monastic order) in the late eighteenth century. This new fraternity also was restricted to Karava, Durava, and Salagama castes. Around the mid-nineteenth century a third fraternity called the Ramanna *nikaya* was formed to accommodate anyone motivated to become a monk irrespective of his caste. Both these fraternities obtained higher ordination at their inception from Burmese *bhikkhu*s. The reformed monastic order after the establishment of higher ordination by Thai monks became known as the Siyam *nikaya*, with headquarters in Kandy at the Asgiriya and Malwatta monasteries, and in Kelaniya at the Kalaniya monastery. The three fraternities do not have any doctrinal disputes and thus are not sects. However, they observe higher ordination, confession, and rain retreat ceremonies independently, and have a few outward markers of fraternity identity which are, at present, disappearing. Laymen do not appear to be sensitive to these distinctions as all *bhikkhu*s are highly respected. This, however, does not mean that the lay community is uncritical of the *bhikkhu*s.

ordination of *bhikkhuni*s. Female renunciation had the limited scope of *dasasil-mata*s or "mothers with ten precepts," who were more like unordained laypeople, without even the possibility of becoming a novice.

Towards the end of the twentieth century there were several *silmata* (disciplined mothers) organizations and attempts were made to introduce ordination of *bhikkhuni*s, with the support of several Sri Lankan Theravada *bhikkhu*s and Taiwanese and Korean *bhikkhuni*s, but they received no support from the established *nikaya*s (monks' orders). In 1989 in Los Angeles, USA, a *bhikkhuni* ordination was performed by Taiwanese *bhikkhuni*s, and again in Varanasi, India, in 1996 with the help of Korean *bhikkhuni*s. The three Sinhala *nikaya*s and several *silmata* organizations rejected these as invalid ordinations as the Taiwanese and Korean *bhikkhuni*s belonged to the Mahayana tradition and the ordinations were performed according to the Mahayana rites. In 1997, in order to conform to the Theravada tradition, a Sri Lanka *bhikkhuni* training center was formed and 32 *silmata*s were recruited after establishing them in the discipline as novices. In February 1998 in Buddha Gaya (Bodh Gaya), India, Taiwanese *bhikkhuni*s performed ordination of ten of these novices, this time following the Theravada rites. Thereafter they received ordination from Sri Lankan Theravada *bhikkhu*s at Saranath, India. In the following month 22 more novices were ordained at Dambulla, Sri Lanka. By June 2000, the number of ordained *bhikkhunis* exceeded 160. More recently, in July 2010, 31 novices, including a professor and a university lecturer, received ordination at Dambulla. To this day the established *nikayas* have kept silent about these significant events in the South Asian Theravada tradition.

Further changes

During the last two centuries or so monasteries have become owners of various material possessions not allowed by the Vinaya rules. Gone are the days when *bhikkhus* wore robes made of cloth thrown away by people. Silk robes, fine furniture, luxury cars, televisions and so on were donated to monasteries by wealthy patrons as well as politicians seeking monastic support for political purposes. Recently, a *bhikkhu* even attempted to obtain legal rights to acquire a driving license which a court rejected.

There are many other current practices that appear to go against the grain of the Vinaya rules. From the mid-1950s some *bhikkhus* who received a level of education incommensurate with the secular education have been appointed as school teachers. These *bhikkhu* teachers have been teaching subjects such as Buddhism, Buddhist culture, Sinhala language, and Sinhala literature, which constitute aspects of curricula in primary and secondary schools, and have received remuneration in the same way lay teachers do. They have been receiving salaries and owning personal bank accounts. Although the Vinaya prohibits acceptance of money—not directly but through the injunctions in the ten precepts—unless it is donated to acquire basic amenities specified in the Vinaya rules, *bhikkhus* accept money for various services rendered—from delivering sermons to providing astrological, demonological, and medical assistance. They justify this violation by declaring that the money is received as contributions to develop the monasteries or the community in general. This practice has gone on for a long time. The pre-colonial institution called *kappiya karaka*, where a lay attendant is appointed to receive money on behalf of the monks, is a good example of an invention to justify receiving money. The letter of the rule is upheld but its spirit is violated.

Another feature of present-day monastic practices, again shared by the Theravada traditions elsewhere, is the use of the monastic system as an avenue for socioeconomic advancement. Individuals from poorer families enter the monastic system for the purpose of receiving an education at the expense of monasteries, and disrobe once they complete their secular education and return to lay society.

It is well known that throughout the history of Buddhism in Sri Lanka religion was closely associated with politics and affairs of the state. As mentioned above this relationship was threatened and ignored during the colonial period from the sixteenth to the mid-twentieth centuries. However, the political activism of Buddhist monks took a new turn from the late nineteenth century and has entered a particularly violent phase since independence in 1948. In 1958 several *bhikkhus* were involved in a coup to overthrow the government and a *bhikkhu* assassinated the then Prime Minister and was later subjected to capital punishment. In 1971, during the rebellion organized by the revolutionary Marxist Janata Vimukti Peramuna (People's Liberation Front or the JVP), many young monks were involved in violent activities and were among the thousands of rebels killed by the state security forces. They were involved in even larger numbers during the reign of terror created by the same political group in the late 1980s and were once again victims of the brutal suppression by the state. This researcher has seen the bodies of young monks, still in their robes, floating in the rivers. One of the events that attracted international attention was the participation of some politically motivated *bhikkhu*s or monastic imposters of revolutionary yet ethno-nationalist political parties in the horrendous pogrom of ethnic Tamils in Colombo. In these contexts, lay Buddhists as well as real or fake *bhikkhu*s forgot the precepts completely and instead subsumed them under ethnic politics, and even justified their involvement in committing so much violence by citing monastic chronicles. In response the Liberation Tigers of Tamil Elam, the Tamil separatist guerrilla group, massacred many novices and *bhikkhu*s.

During my field inquiries it was brought to my attention that certain elite monasteries selectively accept invitations to almsgivings only from elite families. I was also informed that instead of accepting whatever is given *bhikkhu*s now demand that meat and sausages be included in the menu. Informants stated that the items necessary for monks that are donated as alms are being sold to merchants for resale instead of sending them to poorer monasteries in the countryside. In addition some monks are found to indulge in sexual relations with women, alcohol consumption, and even watching pornographic films. Perhaps transgressions of the Vinaya have always occurred and the Vinaya rules were established precisely to redirect the wayward monastics towards proper monastic conduct. The issue here is not the fact of violations of Vinaya but its frequency.

It is also important to consider the fact that present-day *bhikkhu*s do not live in an environment comparable to that during which the Vinaya rules were promulgated. The rural and relatively sedate sociocultural environment of the pre-colonial period does not exist any longer. Not only is the monastic role in the society seriously truncated for reasons discussed above, the *bhikkhu*s encounter numerous circumstances where they are drawn into indiscipline. Political parties exploit their prestige among the laymen. *Bhikkhu*s also notice glaring social inequalities that modern politico-economic regimes have engendered. This was particularly the case during the colonial era when the practice of Buddhism was prohibited in colonially occupied areas, Buddhist monks driven away, and Buddhists were discriminated against and compelled to convert to Christianity. In contemporary Sri Lanka some aspects of the impact of colonialism still prevail to the detriment of the Buddhists. Coming from the economically oppressed and socially humiliated rural communities it is hardly surprising that these monks are easily attracted to revolutionary politics, particularly when exposed to revolutionary philosophies at the universities. Further, most *bhikkhu*s start their careers as children and grow up largely ignorant of the ways of the world at large. Many of these individuals are not renouncers, so to say, but children donated to the monasteries because of astrological and or socioeconomic reasons. Reluctant young novices grow up wanting to run away but are unable to do so. They are easily tempted by the world around them. A bus trip to another monastery or a school, even to a Buddhist ceremony, exposes them to lurid and soft porn movie billboards and corny love songs. In educational institutions as well as at temples, women are attracted to young male *bhikkhu*s.

All these and more provide encouragement to forget the Vinaya and indulge in what the world has to offer. Thus it is necessary to consider both sides of the equation: *Bhikkhu*s violating the Vinaya and the world prompting them to do so, however unintentionally.

Buddhist tradition: Current approaches

Until the mid-twentieth century, studies of South Asian Buddhism were dominated by translation and analysis of texts. This "textualist" tradition continues to this day. Some scholars such as Rhys Davids constructed highly romantic accounts of the past of Buddhism focusing on India of the days of the Buddha. By the mid-twentieth century, perhaps influenced by the German sociologist Max Weber's study of religion of India and the growth of the social sciences, Buddhist studies also took a social scientific turn emphasizing studying Buddhism as a social institution from anthropological, sociological, psychological, and historiographical perspectives which contributed to one another. Current approaches to South Asian Buddhist studies thus consist of both of these traditions and many contemporary scholars combine both to develop composite perspectives—reading texts from social science angles and viewing institutions from doctrinal standpoints.

More recent developments include the use of what anthropologist Clifford Geertz called "the native perspective." This approach is in response to the criticism that South Asian Buddhism—and non-Western religions and cultures in general—are studied only from a Western perspective by reducing them to a few variables that only reaffirm the Western worldview, and that from such studies one does not understand what these religions consciously mean to the practitioners. Hence, the thrust for the native perspective. The methodological stance adopted here, borrowed from the phenomenological philosophical tradition, is suspension of disbelief as well as the Western intellectual categories and immersion in the native culture in all its complexity in order to grasp the meanings of, say Tibetan Buddhism, to the believers and practitioners.

The issue that arises here is how to render these native meanings intelligible to non-natives. The response is to adopt an interpretive stance. While employing the native perspective researchers also "translate" their understandings into the researcher's own intellectual categories so that the intellectual community can grasp what these meanings are. This approach is generally known as the hermeneutical approach.

But this too was found to be unsatisfactory as suspicions arose regarding intellectual politics involved in the interpretive activity. The hermeneutical stance initially developed in Europe to translate Judeo-Christian religious categories into the categories of modern secular philosophy in order to facilitate communication between European religion and modern European thought. In anthropological and comparative religion studies, however, this translation was found to be unsatisfactory because the modern European philosophical concepts and methods are upheld as universal concepts and methods thereby rendering them the dominant mode of discoursing on religion and culture at the expense of the inherent independence and conceptual self-sufficiency of non-Western religions and cultures.

These issues became particularly significant for the scholars who were also non-Western and natives of the non-Western cultures under study. Why should they translate their native concepts into Western concepts in order to make sense out of them when they already know, as natives, what these notions mean? Thus arose the approach of the subaltern studies that question the hegemonic nature of Western interpretations of non-Western cultures and religions.

These are some of the philosophical, theoretical, and methodological issues involved in the contemporary studies of Buddhism in South Asia. The discussion above attempts to be sensitive to all these stances. The account is incomplete as the theme is vast and complex involving information covering twenty-five centuries or so. But a feature that stands out of this mist of time is that both schools of Buddhism have been dynamic institutions changing in time both doctrinally and behaviorally. While the Tipitaka stands as an unchanging body of ideas, prescriptions, and proscriptions, its meanings have undergone transformations to accommodate the historical and sociocultural vicissitudes of communities that uphold it. Thus, to be fair by the believers and practitioners of Buddhism in South Asia, the present-day Buddhism in South Asia must be viewed with minds wide open to grasp the Buddhist concept *anicca* in the contexts of social and historical existence of Buddhism as well. Things change all the time and so does Buddhism in South Asia.

Discussion questions

1   Although early Buddhism attempted to break away from the pan-South Asian beliefs and practices, subsequent developments pulled it back towards them. Comment.

2   *Anicca* and *anatta* are complementary concepts that support the concept of *dukkha*. Discuss the relationships among these concepts as they illustrate the nature of existence. How does Buddhism use these concepts both to define what is problematic about existence and to define a solution to the problem of existence?

3   Buddhist monasticism theoretically eschews all entanglements with politics but in practice it finds itself firmly connected to the political processes of society. Discuss.

Key terms

anatta (Sanskrit *anātman*)—The impossibility of a permanent self (soul).
bhikkhu—Monk; *bhikkhuni*—nun.
Buddhasāsana—The Buddhist community.

caitya—Reliquary and objects and figures that would represent the Buddha. Reliquary structures usually take the shape of a dome and are known as stupas; in Tibetan tradition these are known as *chortens*.

dukkha—Suffering.

kamma—Action in canonical Buddhism.

karma (Sanskrit and in Hinduism, Jainism, and popular Theravada Buddhism in Sri Lanka)—Results of action.

nibbāna (Sanskrit *nirvāṇa*)—Freedom from suffering.

pañcasīla—Observing the five precepts of behavior restraint (not killing, not stealing, not engaging in sexual misconduct, not lying, not engaging in intoxication).

sambodhi—Enlightenment.

sansāra (Sanskrit *saṃsāra*)—The cycles of birth, death, and rebirth.

Tipitaka (Sanskrit *Tripitika*)—"Three Baskets"; teachings of the Buddha preserved in a canon of texts divided into the three sections of discourses of the Buddha, code of discipline, and philosophical reflections.

tisarana (Sinhala)—Establishing refuge in the Triple-Gem. In Pāli: saranāgamana—coming to the refuge.

Triple-Gem (Pāli: *ratanatta*; Sanskrit: *triratna*; Sinhala: *teruvan*) Buddha (teacher), dhamma (teachings), sangha (monastic community that preserves the teachings).

Notes

1   The Vedic society consisted of four hierarchically organized segments called the varna. They exist even today. They are known, from the highest purity to lowest, as Brahman (priests), Kshatriya (royalty), Vaishya (agriculturists and merchants), and Sudra (menial laborers). The first three segments constituted the Arya community. Those who did not belong to this society were (and still are) known as the Mleccha or barbarian untouchables (also currently called Dalits).

2   The Bhutanese are mainly of Tibetan origins and are located mostly in the northern regions where Buddhism is the predominant religion. Southern Bhutan, bordering India and Nepal, is populated by Nepalese immigrants who are Hindus.

3   Such conflicts across faiths occurred even in recent times. At an unknown date, perhaps after the twelfth century but it could have been even earlier, Brahmins had claimed the bodhi tree in Buddha Gaya (Bodh Gaya), India. The late nineteenth and early twentieth century Sinhala Buddhist culture-hero of Sri Lanka, Anagarika Dharmapala, contested the brahminical claims and reestablished Buddhist claims to the tree. Since then, the bodhi tree in Buddha Gaya became a gathering place for all Buddhists in the world irrespective of doctrinal and sectarian differences (Richard Gombrich, *Theravada Buddhism: A Social History from Ancient Benares to Modern Colombo*, London and New York: Routledge, 1988). In Sri Lanka, Hindus, Buddhists, and Muslims claimed the same tree shrine in Colombo, Sri Lanka. See A. C. Dep, *History of Ceylon Police Force*, Vol. II, 1866–1913, Colombo: Times of Ceylon Press, 1969.

4   Bhikku Ananda is believed to be the Buddha's personal attendant who heard all the sermons the Buddha delivered. Thus the *suttas* or sermons in the Sutta pitaka begin with the statement "Thus I heard." The *vaitulyavadi* contention seems to have arisen from this statement.

5   It is important to note that the Buddhists of both sects responded to the *bhakti* religiosity and apotheosis of kingship by developing their own forms of *bhakti* and methods

to apotheosize political leadership while achieving political power as rulers of the supernatural world. Thus feudal and hierarchized monastic organizations and other religious institutions emerged. I have examined elsewhere how the bodhi tree, a most sacred institution in the Buddhist world, has been feudalized by arranging bodhi trees in a concentric system of significance or, to put it in another idiom, arranged them in a hierarchy of significance, with the great bodhi tree either at the center or on top of the organization as a "king." In the same way religious practitioners became hierarchized within the overall hierarchy of sacred beings headed by the Buddha. In the Mahayana this produced the notion of Mahasiddhas. In the Sri Lankan Theravada it found expression in the formation of central monastic authorities as in the Mahavihara during the Anuradhapura period and, at present, in the Malwatta and Asgiriya chapters of the Siyam *nikaya*, as well as the identification of the Tooth Relic of the Buddha with political sovereignty. And this occurred in a political environment in which kings were identified as Bodhisattvas in a dramatic confluence of sacred and secular power. A classic example of this symbiosis appears in the history of Tibetan Buddhism where, in the eighth century, Mahasiddha Padmasambhava conquered the world of Bon spirits and religious virtuosi at the invitation of king Trhisong and was apotheosized as a Bodhisattva, while the first Buddhist king of Tibet, king Songsten Gampa, became apotheosized as Bodhisattva Avalokiteshvara, and his queens as manifestations of the goddess Tara. For an incisive examination of these processes in medieval India between the 7th and 12th centuries see Ronald M. Davidson, *Indian Esoteric Buddhism: A Social History of the Tantric Movement*, New York: Columbia University Press, 2002.

6 However, Buddhists in Sri Lanka believe that although the Buddha died his power and authority, known as *buddhanubhava*, remain as a cosmic force that can be invoked to threaten, tame, frighten, and expel malevolent beings and neutralize the effects of forms of black magic known as *kodivina* and *huniyam*. For details see Dandris de Silva Gooneratne, *On Demonology and Witchcraft in Ceylon*, New Delhi and Madras: Asian Educational Services, 1998 [1865]; Gananath Obeyesekere, "The Ritual Drama of Sanni Demons: Collective Representations of Disease in Ceylon," *Comparative Studies in Society and History* 11:2 (1966): 174–216; Gananath Obeyesekere, "The Idiom of Demonic Possession: A Case Study," *Social Science and Medicine* 14 (1975): 97–111; Bruce Kapferer, *A Celebration of Demons*, Bloomington, IN: Indiana University Press, 1983; Bruce Kapferer, *The Feast of the Sorcerer: Practices of Consciousness and Power*, Chicago, IL: Chicago University Press, 1997; David Scott, *Formations of Ritual: Colonial and Anthropological Discourses on Sinhala Yaktovil*, Minneapolis, MN: University of Minnesota Press, 1994.

7 Pali: *paccekabuddha*; Sanskrit: *pratyekabuddha*.

8 Statistics are hard to obtain as most nations no longer classify populations by religion, perhaps because of political reasons. I obtained this figure from Peter Harvey, *An Introduction to Buddhism: Teachings, History and Practices*, Cambridge: Cambridge University Press, 1990, p. 5.

9 The meaning of this mantra is a matter of debate. The traditional translation into English reads as "Oh! Jewel in the Lotus!" But current scholarship finds this translation erroneous. Lopez translates it as "O you who hold the jeweled [rosary] and the lotus [have mercy on us]," Donald S. Lopez, Jr., "Introduction," in Donald S. Lopez, Jr. (ed.) *Religions of Tibet in Practice*, Princeton, NJ: Princeton University Press, 1997, p. 14.

10 Bon is the national religious tradition of pre-Buddhist imperial Tibet. This tradition is often looked down upon by those who highlight Buddhist achievements in the Himalayan regions. For example see L. Austin Waddell, *Tibetan Buddhism with its Mystic Cults, Symbolism and Mythology*, New York: Dover Publications, Inc., 1972 [1895]. However, these prejudices appear to be misplaced. Bon is a religion that includes a philosophy and a monastic system akin to Buddhism that also accepts shamanism, animistic beliefs, and sacred technologies to manipulate nature. For

details see David L. Snellgrove (ed. and trans), "The Nine Ways of Bon: Excerpts from gZi-brjid," *London Oriental Series* 18, London: Oxford University Press, 1967; David L. Snellgrove, *Buddhist Himalaya*, Oxford: Oxford University Press, 1975 [1957]; David L. Snellgrove, *Indo-Tibetan Buddhism: Indian Buddhists and Their Tibetan Successors*, 2 vols., Boston, CA, and London: Shambhala Publications Inc., 1987; David L. Snellgrove and Hugh E. Richardson, *A Cultural History of Tibet*, Boulder, CO: Prajna Press, 1980 [1968]; and Per Kvaerne, *Tibetan Bon Religion: A Death Ritual of the Tibetan Bonpos*, Iconography of Religions 12–13, Leiden: E. J. Brill, 1985; Per Kvaerne, *The Bon Religion of Tibet*, Boston, MA: Shambhala Publications Inc., 1995; Per Kvaerne, "Bon Rescues Dharma," in Donald J. Lopez, Jr. (ed.) *Religions of Tibet in Practice*, pp. 98–102, Princeton, NJ: Princeton University Press, 1997; Per Kvaerne, "Cards for the Dead," in Donald J. Lopez, Jr., *Religions of Tibet in Practice*, pp. 494–8. Princeton, NJ: Princeton University Press, 1997.

11 Lately, elaborate public rituals have been organized by various organizations with state support to celebrate the recruitment of large groups. These public expressions are to energize the Buddhist community and encourage individuals to enter the monastic orders. There is a general disappointment that fewer than usual numbers are entering the system while more than usual numbers are disrobing for various reasons.

Recommended resources

Carrithers, Michael. *The Buddha*. Oxford: Oxford University Press, 1983.

Collins, Steven. *Selfless Persons: Imagery and Thought in Theravada Buddhism*. Cambridge: Cambridge University Press, 1999 [1982].

Gombrich, Richard. *Theravada Buddhism: A Social History from Ancient Benares to Modern Colombo*. London and New York: Routledge, 1988.

Gombrich, Richard and Gananath Obeyesekere. *Buddhism Transformed*. Princeton, NJ: Princeton University Press, 1988.

Harvey, Peter. *An Introduction to Buddhism: Teachings, History and Practices*. Cambridge: Cambridge University Press, 1990.

Kariyawasam, A. G. S. "Buddhist Ceremonies and Rituals in Sri Lanka." *Access to Insight: Readings in Theravada Buddhism*, http://www.accesstoinsight.org/lib/authors/kariyawasam/wheel402.html. Accessed May 6, 2010.

Lopez Jr., Donald, ed. *Religions of Tibet in Practice*. Princeton, NJ: Princeton University Press, 1997.

Olivelle, Patrick. "The Renouncer Tradition." In Gavin Flood (ed.) *The Blackwell Companion to Hinduism*, Maldon and Oxford: Blackwell Publishing Ltd., 2005 [2003]: 271–87.

Powers, John. *Introduction to Tibetan Buddhism*. Ithaca, NY: Snow Lion Publications, 2007.

Rahula, Rev. Walpola. *What the Buddha Taught*. New York: Grove Press Inc., 1974 [1959].

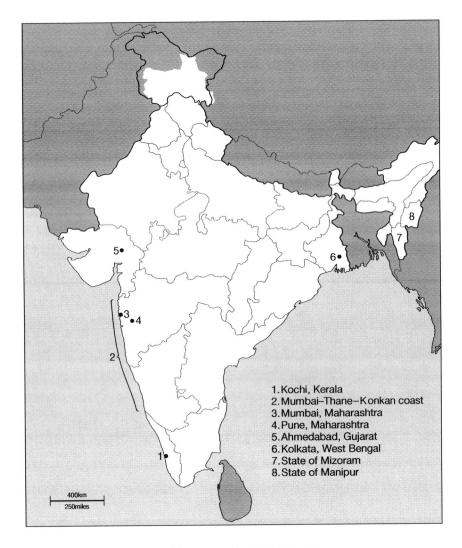

1. Kochi, Kerala
2. Mumbai–Thane–Konkan coast
3. Mumbai, Maharashtra
4. Pune, Maharashtra
5. Ahmedabad, Gujarat
6. Kolkata, West Bengal
7. State of Mizoram
8. State of Manipur

400km
250miles

Map 5 Prominent places in Judaism as practiced in India today

5 South Asian Judaisms

Practicing tradition today

Nathan Katz

Introduction

Judaism is the religion of the Jewish people, traditionally dated from the time of Abraham around 1800 BCE. Conventional wisdom has it that Judaism is a "Western" religion, and views it largely in a European cultural context. Some more informed observers include its permutations in North Africa and the Middle East. Indeed, the two largest groups of Jews, the Ashkenazim and the Sephardim, trace their traditions back to Eastern Europe and Spain and thence the Middle East, respectively.

But there is another group of Jews, the Mizrachi or "eastern" Jews, whose traditions developed more or less independently from both the Ashkenazim and Sephardim. Among the best-known Jewish cultures of the Mizrach are to be found in Ethiopia, Yemen, Persian-speaking domains (Iran, Afghanistan, Uzbekistan, etc.), India, and China. These lesser-known Judaisms belie the conventional view of Judaism as "Western" or European; indeed, the traditional understanding of Jews as an *am-olam*, a global people, turns out to be more accurate.

The Torah, the central text of Judaism, describes the meanderings of Abraham and his descendants from Babylonia, to what is now Israel, to slavery in Egypt, to liberation from slavery and years of wandering in the Sinai Peninsula where the Torah was revealed, and ultimately to the conquest and settlement of the Land of Israel that God had promised to Abraham and his descendants in the Torah narrative.

In Israel, Judaism focused on the sacrificial rites performed by hereditary priests, known as *kohanim*, at the Holy Temple in Jerusalem. So important was the Temple that all Jews were required to make pilgrimage there three times each year to perform/observe their sacred work (*avodah*).

Jerusalem was conquered twice, and each time the Temple was destroyed by powerful conquerors—first the Babylonians during the seventh century BCE, and finally by the Romans in the year 70 CE. With the entire focus of the religion, the Temple, destroyed, Jewish leaders reconfigured the religion from a Temple-centric system based on the priestly performance of sacrifice to a more portable, textually centered global faith, led by scholars (known as *rabbis* in Ashkenazi tradition and *hachamim* among the Sephardim).

At the same time, the destruction of the Temple and the expulsion of Jews from Jerusalem led to the "Great Exile" (*Galut*) of Jews to "the four corners of the earth," including India. Indeed, the Jews of Kochi trace their origin to these events nearly two thousand years ago.

Eventually, the fifteenth-century expulsion of Jews from Spain, the pinnacle of Jewish culture of the time, led to the migration of Sephardim to India, among many other places, where these newcomers interacted uneasily with local Mizrachi Jews, resulting in unique patterns of Judaic culture and observance.

South Asian Judaisms: Identity

India's several distinct Jewish communities have, over the centuries, each developed a unique identity, established and reinforced through distinctive systems of religious practice. The patterns of acculturation into regional Indian cultures reflect creative interactions between Judaic and Indic civilizations, and are best approached with newly refined approaches and methods.[1]

Perhaps for as long as two millennia, there have been Jewish communities throughout much of South Asia. Most have been in such port cities as Surat, Kochi (formerly Cochin), Mumbai (formerly Bombay), and Kolkata (formerly Calcutta).

Some of these communities are very old, dating at least from the early medieval period if not ancient times, having enjoyed centuries of harmonious relationships with neighboring Hindu, Muslim, Christian, and Zoroastrian (called Parsi in India) neighbors. One Jewish community was more or less co-terminous with the British raj. Others have emerged as recently as the past several decades, Judaizing movements that have, on occasion, been blended into the worldwide fabric of the Jewish people. Some have been fleeting, such as Ashkenazi refugees from European Nazism. Another is the ephemeral quasi-Jewish life among Israeli backpackers who have made Goa and other resorts a home of sorts, which has, in turn, impacted secular Israeli culture.

Many Asian Diaspora communities have been in decline for the past half-century due to emigration, mostly to Israel.[2] Those who remain seek to maintain Jewish life in India while developing complex relations with family and community members in Israel and elsewhere. And for some of those who have emigrated, or wish to, the "Who is a Jew?" question is never far beneath the surface.

Three communities, plus

For centuries, India has been home to three very distinct Jewish communities. The oldest has lived in and around the southwestern port of Kochi (formerly Cochin) for at least a thousand years and perhaps twice that. The largest is known as the Bene Israel, originally from the rural Konkan coastal region of Maharashtra but almost all of whom in India are found in Mumbai (formerly Bombay) and nearby Thane. During the British era, Arabic-speaking immigrants flourished mostly in Mumbai, Kolakata, Yangon (formerly Rangoon), and became known in India as "Baghdadis."

These three communities are well known, but there are others, too. Especially during the Mughal period, Jews from Afghanistan and countries to the west

Figure 5.1 Beth El Synagogue, Kolkata. Photo taken by Ellen S. Goldberg.

flourished along the trade routes that linked Delhi with Kabul (the origin of the Mughals) and elsewhere to the west. There were communities with synagogues in Peshawar and Quetta, and their influence was felt at the Mughal courts in Agra and Delhi.[3] Later, India became a refuge for Ashkenazi Jews (Jews with an eastern European background) fleeing Nazism. Sometimes they enjoyed protection from kindly maharajahs, and some filled a medical niche in Indian society.[4]

During the past half-century, some tribal people along the Indo-Burmese border "discovered" their lost Jewish identity. Their Judaizing movement was met with sympathy and support from some American and Israeli Jews, and a leading Israeli rabbi confirmed them as of "the seed of Jacob."[5] They have become something of a political football in contemporary Israel: they often settled "across the green line" and are supported by nationalist groups in Israel, but center-left parties often try to bar them from immigrating. And another Israeli presence in India is found in such tourist haunts as Goa and Manali, where Hebrew posters and falafel stands proliferate. It has become a custom for many young Israelis to spend some months in India and Nepal to "blow off some steam" after completing compulsory military service. Some of these intrepid travelers have built cottages and started small businesses, resulting in enduring quasi-Jewish quasi-communities. And in their wake, emissaries from Chabad-Lubavitch, the best known sect among the populist eighteenth-century European movement known as Hasidism ("pietism"), as well as some other Hasidic sects, have set up shop in an effort to bring these meandering young Israelis back into the Jewish fold.[6]

The three older and more substantial communities have each evolved unique identities reflective of their social, cultural, and economic environment. Each of these identities is established and maintained by unique styles of Judaic rituals and customs, known in Hebrew as *minhagim* (singular: *minhag*). So intricate are these systems of observance, that new methods of analysis have been developed—all to help understand the unique observances of the festival of Simhat Torah in Kochi, or the role of the prophet Elijah (Eliyahoo Hanabi) among the Bene Israel, or patterns of discrimination that the Baghdadis imposed on other Bene Israel, or that the Kochini Paradesi sub-caste imposed on the Malabari sub-caste.[7] It is precisely at this juncture of identity and *minhagim* (religious practices) that the study of Indian Judaisms is the most challenging and rewarding.

South Asian Judaisms: Practice

Kochi

The Jewish community of Kochi[8] is the oldest and most highly positioned among India's Jews. Over a thousand (perhaps two thousand) years, they developed elegant mechanisms for acculturation into their milieu. They came to articulate historical traditions that resonated well in both Hindu and Jewish worlds. Their *minhagim* evidenced borrowings from local Hinduisms while maintaining fidelity to Judaic norms, known as *Halakhah*. And their patterns of social organization reflected the hierarchies of Kerala.

According to local traditions, Jews first settled on India's southwest coast when the Second Temple was destroyed and the Romans exiled all Jews from Jerusalem in the year 70 CE. They fled along maritime trade routes that had been in use since King Solomon's time and which had recently been speeded by the discovery of the monsoon winds by Greek navigators early in the first century. They settled at Cranganore, among other towns, where they were granted political autonomy by local monarchs and flourished as agriculturists, international spice merchants, petty traders, shipbuilders, and in government service and the military. During the fourteenth century they migrated to Kochi. Their numbers in the Malabar rose as high as 3,000 at the time of independence, but fewer than 50 remain today. Where there were once nine flourishing synagogues, Jewish schools, scribes, scholars, mystics, and poets, today the Cochin Synagogue, built in 1568, fails to obtain a prayer quorum of ten adult males unless there are Jewish visitors from elsewhere in India or abroad.

The Kochi Jews, always part of the Jewish mainstream both commercially and culturally, were knowledgeable about their religion and savvy about affairs of state, as well as currency fluctuations even in far-off Europe, not to mention among the plethora of princely states of South India. Knowing the languages of the subcontinent, the Middle East, and Europe, they played invaluable roles in both commerce and diplomacy.

Their religious practices evidence a high degree of acculturation into their Indian context, but not assimilation. For example, during their autumn holy days and at weddings, many Nayar (the local dominant caste) customs and symbols of royalty were adopted. At a wedding, as another example, the Jews would borrow an elephant from a neighboring Hindu temple to convey the bridegroom to the synagogue for nuptials. During the festival of Rejoicing in the Torah (Simhat Torah), Kochi's Jews added three elements to their celebrations found nowhere else in the Jewish world: they displayed their Torah scrolls on a temporary Ark on the days just prior to the festival; during the afternoon prayers, they made outdoor circumambulations of the synagogue with their Torah scrolls; and at the conclusion of the festival, they ritually demolished their temporary Ark to the accompaniment of unique Hebrew songs. All of these behaviors reflect Hindu temple festivals, when the deity (*murti*) of the temple is first displayed, then taken on procession, and then (often) disposed of. None of these practices violate Judaic law (*Halakhah*), so these borrowings from the local Hindu culture were judicious, reflecting their firm Jewish identity, based on Judaic learning. They were acculturated, which is to say they were culturally at home in their Hindu environment, without becoming assimilated, which involves a surrender of identity.

Kochi Jewish women also created local observances, in particular songs in the Malayalam language that were performed chiefly at life cycle, as opposed to synagogal, rituals. Musically, their songs closely resemble those of local Christian and Hindu women, but the Jewish songs interweave biblical themes with images from the culture of Kerala.[9]

For example, a wedding song called "Dressed in Gold" refers to the luxurious, Indian-style costume of a groom at his wedding. The bride and groom

Figure 5.2 Kochini woman cleaning wheat for Passover. Photo taken by Ellen S. Goldberg.

are bedecked with symbols of royalty that characterize both Jewish and Hindu wedding rituals. The song describes a lavish, Kerala-style wedding:

> All dressed up in gold and riding in a palanquin
> He comes to see the wedding. *Nalla!*
> Wearing a golden chain upon his breast,
> And shaped in golden silk, *Nalla!*
> Behold the kind, the ruler—he arrives
> All clothed in golden silk, *Nallah!*
> Out in front, four rows of advance guards
> Carry peacock-feathered fans. *Nalla!* ...
> Oh are they not the soldiers there,
> The ones who sing and dance. *Nalla!*
> Thundering mighty blasts, the army band
> Plays trumpets, drums and flutes. *Nalla!*
> All of those who push and rush inside
> Honor him with gifts of rings. *Nalla!*
> Here come many other people too,
> Riding in palanquins. *Nalla!* ...
> There stands the ceremonial oil lamp
> And the special tray with betel nuts. *Nalla!*[10]

And in another song, the arrival of the Jews—represented by a bird—is embellished with rich local color:

> Nearby the seashore of Palur,—*Aiyaya*
> The bird saw the short palm trees there.—*Aiyaya*
> Nearby the seashore of Palur,—*Aiyaya*
> There the bird went and bathed.—*Aiyaya* ...
> A splendid green mansion then it found,—*Aiyaya*
> An umbrella made of precious gems.—*Aiyaya*
> This was the choicest place of all;—*Aiyaya*
> This was the place it settled down.—*Aiyaya*.[11]

In the social structure of Kerala, Jews organized themselves as a caste and were recognized as such. Internally, they proliferated into endogamous sub-castes, maintaining dining and ritual divisions until the mid-twentieth century, by which time their number had become so attenuated as to make their traditional patterns untenable. While the historical narrations and ritual embellishments posed no Halakhic difficulties, in discriminating against fellow Jews they defied *Halakhah*, as foreign rabbis had admonished repeatedly since the early sixteenth century.

Bene Israel

The largest group of Indian Jews is known as Bene Israel[12] and is found chiefly in and around Mumbai, with active communities in Pune, also in Maharashtra state, in Ahmedabad in Gujarat State, and in New Delhi. All told, there are 4–5,000 Bene Israel in India and 40–50,000 in Israel, where they make up a significant ethnic group (*edah* in Hebrew).

While Mumbai is home to most of India's Bene Israel, the nearby Konkan coast is their spiritual home. Like the Jews of Kochi, the Bene Israel articulated historical traditions that could be traced back to seven couples from ancient Israel who survived a shipwreck off Navgaon, in the unknown, distant past. Their story is often sung in the popular North Indian ballad form known as *kirtan*.

Somehow they clung to vestigial Judaic observances despite centuries of isolation. Their tenacity in maintaining the Sabbath, ritual circumcision, Jewish dietary codes, and the Hebrew *Shema*—the affirmation "Hear O Israel! The Lord is our God, the Lord is One"—set the stage for their unlikely transformation from an anonymous oil-pressing caste in the remote Konkan into modern, urban members of the world Jewish community. This evolution occurred over two hundred years, beginning in the middle of the eighteenth century.

An eighteenth century Kochi merchant (alternately, a twelfth century Egyptian), David Rahabi, heard rumors of a Konkani caste that rested on Saturday and circumcised their sons on the eighth day, so he visited them. After spending some time with the community, examining their dietary habits as well as eccentric (by Hindu standards) religious observances, he concluded that they were lost Jews. He took three of them back to Kochi where he educated them in Hebrew and the rudiments of Judaism and sent them back with the title of *kazi*, religious leader. This began a longstanding relationship between Bene Israel and Kochi Jews; as Bene Israel prospered, they hired Kochi Jews to be their cantors, teachers, ritual slaughterers, and scribes. Bene Israel recall these events as their "first awakening."

Subsequent encounters with British and American missionaries and with the nascent Baghdadi community (more about the Baghdadis in the next section) of Mumbai built upon their sense of Jewishness. This period is known as their "second awakening." They learned Bible stories from the missionaries, and they shared their synagogues (they built their first one in Mumbai in 1796) and cemeteries with the Baghdadis. Both the British and the Baghdadis offered opportunities in Mumbai, whether in the military, for the railway in the civil service, or in the mills and docks of the illustrious Sassoons, and Bene Israel migrated to the new, glamorous city in search of their fortunes. It did not take long until there were more Bene Israel Jews in Mumbai than in the Konkan.

Gradually the Baghdadis, in an effort to become accepted by the British as "European" rather than "Indian"—a label with tangible economic benefits as well as social snobbery—came to adopt British condescension toward all things Indian, including the Bene Israel Jews, who were unmistakably Indian in both appearance and culture. This condescension became all the uglier when the Baghdadis came to cast aspersions upon the very Jewishness of the Bene Israel. The heart and soul of their newly found and hard-earned identity was under attack. After a thorough inquiry, Israel's Chief Sephardic Rabbi affirmed their Jewishness, but doubts lingered.[13]

In Mumbai the Bene Israel encountered both the Zionist and Swaraj (Self-Rule) movements for independence from Britain in Palestine and India respectively, and they were rent by the competing nationalisms. On the one hand, as Jews they had internalized the longing to return to Jerusalem and rebuild Zion. On the other hand, their unhappy experiences with the Baghdadis led them to mistrust foreign Jews, and as Indians they yearned for independence from the British. On yet a third hand, they were also fond of the British, their employers and often patrons, and wanted to support them as well. Mahatma Gandhi appreciated their ambivalence. Leaders of the Ahmedabad Jewish community (where Gandhi had headquarters at his Sabarmati Ashram) asked the Mahatma what should be the stance of India's Jews vis-à-vis the independence movement. He is said to have replied that the Jews should "stand aside" because as a microscopically small community, they would be crushed between the competing and overwhelming forces of the British Empire, Indian nationalism, and Muslim separatism. As a community, they did stand apart, although many Bene Israel became involved as individuals. The bottom line, however, is that the great majority of Bene Israel emigrated to Israel.

The biblical prophet Elijah, or Eliyahoo Hanabi, assumed a major role in the religious life among the Bene Israel. He is said to have visited India, alighting at the very spot where the original seven couples landed after being shipwrecked, in a town called Khandala. Local Jews attributed some scratches on a large boulder there to the wheels of Eliyahoo's chariot, and local Hindus and local Muslims venerated their saints at just the same spot. Paralleling other religions of the Konkan area, pilgrimage to Khandala at auspicious times culminated in an offering of parched rice and fruits accompanied by prayers in a rite known as *malida*. In the Jewish *malida*, Eliyahoo is the focus of the rite, which is known by either *malida* or Eliyahoo, and it became a core expression of Bene Israel identity.

As most Bene Israel migrated to Israel, today the *malida* rite is performed at a cave associated with Eliyahoo, near Haifa, and has become an identity marker for their community, who are known in Israel simply as "Hodi'im," or "Indians." Their narrations and ritual enactments establish their new identity as "Indians in Israel," just as they had celebrated their previous identity as "Jews in India."

The Bene Israel community today has stabilized. Those who intended to emigrate have done so, and most of those who remain intend to stay. Most are in Mumbai, where they work in the professions—education, industry, the military, and commerce. Most are educated and in the middle class. Twenty-five years or so ago, the Organization for Rehabilitation and Training (ORT) established two schools in Mumbai, one for boys and one for girls, to provide vocational training. The ORT schools became very popular among Jews and Gentiles alike. Soon services expanded to include classes in religion, Hebrew, and Israel studies. More recently, the Joint Distribution Committee (JDC) has become active in Mumbai, sending rabbis from America to help meet the community's religious and educational needs. The Israeli Consulate, too, serves as a community focus. Several of the synagogues in Mumbai have a full range of programs, from prayer services to singles groups to computer classes. Summer camps at a rural retreat center have provided an intense infusion of Jewish spirit to many of Mumbai's younger Jews. Kosher meat and wine, ritual objects, books, Indian–Jewish calendars, and

Figure 5.3 Maghen Abraham Synagogue, Ahmedabad. Photo taken by Ellen S. Goldberg.

the accoutrements of Judaic religious life are available, and India's generally tolerant approach to religions and religious pluralism bode well for the future of the Jewish community in Mumbai.

Smaller organized communities in Ahmedabad and Pune face more difficult challenges, but their synagogues are lively, and social and educational programs are well subscribed. In New Delhi there are only a handful of Bene Israel families, but Israeli and American diplomats and businesspeople augment them. Regular prayers are held at the synagogue, and the Israeli Embassy helps out with the community's Passover Seder.

Baghdadis

The most recently arrived group are known in India as Baghdadis, Middle Eastern Jews, Arabic speakers mostly, who migrated to India in the late eighteenth century, about the same time as the British arrived, and who settled in India's port cities, especially Mumbai and Kolakata. Numbering about 5,000 at their peak, they have declined to a few hundred, almost all of whom are elderly.

The Baghdadis played a significant role in the development of British India's ports. Beginning as jewelers and in the opium trade, Baghdadi entrepreneurs soon moved into textiles, shipping, and the film industry in Mumbai, and real estate, jute, manufacturing and tobacco in Calcutta.

The Baghdadis counted some of Mumbai's and Kolkata's leading families among their number. Numerous schools, hospitals, libraries, monuments, and wharfs even today bear Baghdadi names.

History transformed Baghdadi identity in four stages: early history, the "1857 Mutiny" period (which Indians rightfully call their "first war for independence"), post-World War I, and post-Indian and Israeli independence. During the early period, the Judeo-Arabic identity subtly shifted, and they became "Arabian Jews of India and the Far East," referring to their interactions with the cultures they encountered in India and beyond as their businesses expanded to Singapore, Yangon, Japan, and China. After the "Mutiny of 1857" and the deterioration of relations between the British and their Indian subjects, they began to distance themselves from things Indian (sadly, including the Bene Israel) and to identify with the British instead. Following World War I, the breakup of the Ottoman Empire, and the demise of their spiritual leaders, the great hakhamim (rabbis) of Baghdad, they wanted to be identified as "European." This was due in part to the economic benefits that came with such an identity. Thereafter, they were torn by the powerful forces of competing nationalisms: the Indian independence movement, or Swaraj, and Zionism. During the 1930s, the Baghdadis received thousands of Ashkenazim who were seeking refuge from Nazism. This rescue effort strengthened their ties to Zionism as well as to Britain, which was seen (with no sense of irony) as a savior for the Jewish people. After Britain was compelled to grant independence to India in 1947 and to Israel in 1948, most Baghdadis left India. Highly Anglicized Baghdadis moved to London or elsewhere in the English-speaking world; those more influenced by Zionism moved to Israel. Paradoxically, those who remained in India developed an Indian-Jewish identity, something that had not been done before. But by then, the community was inexorably moving toward extinction.

Baghdadi identity was never bounded by India. From the community's early times, they simultaneously looked westward for its spiritual moorings in Iraq and Israel (then Palestine) and eastward to the opportunities enjoyed by satellite communities in Southeast Asia, Japan, and China. Their identity was transnational; a microcosm of Jewish identity in general, with strong cultural, religious, familial, and economic bonds that eventually came to span the globe.

In their religious life, Baghdadis proudly followed Syrian and Iraqi traditions. Synagogues in Kolkata, for example, chanted prayers and read the Torah with melodies from Aleppo and Baghdad; they spoke Arabic and for a time wore turbans and caftans. But they adopted British snobberies about their Bene Israel co-religionists, as they sought a high-status niche in the complex colonial social order.

They were also very charitable. They dispensed their largesse not only locally to support Jewish and non-Jewish causes, but also to maintain synagogues and shrines in Iraq, especially to their "patron," the Scribe Ezra, and for religious schools and shrines in the Land of Israel, in Hebron, Tiberias, and Jerusalem.

Bene Menashe and Bene Ephraim

About sixty years ago, several shamans and leaders of tribal people in extreme eastern India (the states of Mizoram, Manipur, and Tripura) and western Myanmar (formerly Burma) began having dreams and visions which told them of their lost, true identity: that they were Jews of the Tribe of Menashe who had meandered from ancient Israel along the Silk Route to Kaifeng, China, then through Southeast Asia, finally settling in their current mountainous, remote homes. Their religious enthusiasm spread, such that today there are untold thousands of Kuki tribals on both sides of the border who are living as Jews. Some have gone to Israel, where they learned Hebrew, studied and ultimately converted to Judaism, and have returned home as religious leaders. A number of synagogues have sprouted up, and now there are regular visits from Israeli and American co-religionists. Called the "children of Menashe" or Bene Menashe, some now live in Israel, but most wait for their redemption.

About two decades ago, a similar story emerged from Andhra Pradesh, a state on the Bay of Bengal on India's southeast coast. A group of Dalits (people who occupy a low rung on India's social hierarchy) started to call themselves Bene Ephraim. Some formally and some informally, at least several hundred have built their synagogues and live a Jewish life under the leadership of their rabbi, who studied and was ordained in New York.

Most demographics of Indian Jewry do not include these tribals, and there are no reliable estimates of their numbers, but it is incontestable that some of them have undergone conversion and are therefore Jewish. It is also the case that the vast majority are sincere in their beliefs and aspirations. Israeli immigration officials generally take an unsympathetic, skeptical approach, believing them to be opportunists who seek only a higher standard of living. Their passionate yearning for Israel has provoked controversy in Israel. Some accuse immigration authorities of racism, pointing out that many Russians who are not Jewish but who are white have been welcomed, but that these tribals who have at least some claim to Jewishness but who are not white, receive only scorn.

Nevertheless, the Chief Rabbi has affirmed their status as being "the seed of Jacob," much as his predecessor had defended the Jewishness of the Bene Israel fifty years before. This ruling meant that their conversions to normative Judaism should be expedited. These twin Judaizing movements mirror a contemporary global trend of "lost tribes" emerging and claiming a place within the Jewish world.

Hasidim, tourists, and businessmen in India

The terrorist attack on Mumbai on November 26, 2008, brought another manifestation of Jewish life in India to the world's attention. The slaughter at the Chabad House in Mumbai highlighted the presence of Israelis, businessmen, and other transient Jewish groups in India.

In Jewishly remote parts of the world, the Chabad-Lubavitch movement, a Hasidic sect, has provided the requisites of Jewish life to indigenous and foreign Jewish residents and travelers. These Chabad Houses provide synagogues, kosher foods, a place for a friendly meal of familiar foods, and occasionally emergency support wherever Jews wander—in South America, Africa, India, and Southeast Asia. Their fascinating and compelling story has not been told.

As is better known, after completing military service many young Israelis take a year off to travel the world, many opting for the familiar South Asian tourist route—the beaches of Goa, the temples of Kathmandu, the culture of Varanasi, the hills of Manali, the fairs of Pushkar, the ashrams of Pune, or the Tibetan life of Dharamsala. Hebrew posters are ubiquitous and Israeli style restaurants and cyber cafes cater to the trekkers' needs. Some of the young Israelis stay on, exporting cheap Indian clothes or selling pancakes and falafels in inexpensive restaurants. Theirs is a mobile community, linked by Hebrew travel guides and word of mouth, cemented by Hebrew and shared experiences. There are so many Israelis traveling in India that the merchants assume that Israel must be as populous as Britain or Germany, an assumption based on their customers' languages.

The waning indigenous Jewish communities as well as Jewish IT specialists and diamond merchants are joined by the backpackers for prayers at a Chabad synagogue or a Shabbat meal from Mumbai to Bangkok to Hanoi, a pattern also found across Africa and South America.

The India-trekkers bring something back when they return to Israel: a cultural fusion of music and mysticism that is now beginning to be noticed in Israel. And once noticed, anthropologists will not be far behind!

South Asian Judaisms: Current approaches

The study of South Asian Jewish communities uproots several of our stereotypes. For example, the adage that "east is east and west is west" becomes transparent as a "colonizing myth" once a Jewish perspective is adopted.

Their study also reconfigures our common understanding of Judaism and the Jewish people. It is commonly held that Judaism is one of the sources of Western civilization, and that Judaism is a Western religion. Such a view blinds us to Jewish experience in Asia; it silences the millennia-old rich cultural interactions between Judaic, Indic, and Sinitic cultures. On the other hand, Jews have traditionally spoken of themselves as an *am-olam*, a "universal people," a cultural and mercantile bridge in a world bifurcated in relatively recent times into an East and a West. The study of Asian Jewish experience debunks the Jews-as-Westerners view and confirms the traditional self-understanding as a truly universal people.

For the study of the relationship between identity and rituals, case studies of Indian-Jewish communities are especially suggestive. Precisely how the ritual life of the Kochi Jews was infused with Hindu symbols and behaviors, all while maintaining fidelity to Judaic halakhic norms, is especially noteworthy and instructive. How both the Kochi Jews and the Bene Israel evolved status-generating historical traditions that skillfully interweave Indian and Jewish motifs, suggests new approaches to origin tales and underscores the role of narration in the generation of identity. The Bene Israel *malida* ceremony served to mark them off as Jews in India, and later served to distinguish them from among modern Israel's many *edot*, or ethnic groups, indicates the malleability and transportability of ritual behaviors. And finally, the Baghdadis' transnational identity linked their attenuated diaspora to their twin homes in Iraq and Israel, a striking early model of maintaining communal identity while simultaneously participating in globalization. This feat was achieved not only through cultural forms of language, diet, and dress, but also through patronage of shrines and schools.

The study of Indian-Jewish communities reveals new metaphors and models for understanding the relationship between religious life and diasporized identity, as well as their mediation of complex "host" and "guest" cultures. As such, they are an excellent starting point for the exploration of identity in an increasingly globalized world.

Discussion questions

1   What were the three identity-generating strategies that evolved in the Kochi Jewish community?
2   What were the steps in the transformation of the Bene Israel from a rural Konkan community of sesame seed pressers into a modern Jewish community in Mumbai and environs and in Israel?
3   The Baghdadi Jews evolved an identity that was transnational. How did they establish an identity that was rooted in their ancestral home of Israel, their cultural home in Iraq, and their scattered residences across southern and eastern Asia?

Key terms

edah, plural *edot* (Hebrew)—Ethnic group in modern Israel.

Eliyahoo Hanabi (Hebrew)—Elijah the Prophet.

Hakham (Hebrew)—A Sephardic rabbi.

Halakhah (adj. halakhic) (Hebrew)—Judaic law, both ethical and ritual.

kazi (Hebrew-Arabic)—A ritual leader of the Bene Israel community during the period of their "first awakening."

kirtan (Hindi)—A north Indian ballad with religious themes.

malida (Marathi)—A platter of parched rice, fruits, and other items offered to a deity.

minhag (pl. *minhagim*) (Hebrew)—Local custom of religious observance.

Simhat Torah (Hebrew)—A festival of "rejoicing in the Torah" that falls at the conclusion of the autumn holiday cycle.

Notes

1   The methodological issues and innovations applicable in the case of Kochi are explored in N. Katz, "Understanding Religion in Diaspora: The Case of the Jews of Cochin," *Religious Studies and Theology* 15:1 (1996): 5–17. This method of analyzing these deep cultural interactions is applied to India's three major Jewish communities in N. Katz, *Who Are the Jews of India?* Berkeley, CA: University of California Press, 2000.

2   N. Katz and E. Goldberg, "Leaving Mother India: Reasons for the Cochin Jews' Migration to Israel," *Population Review* 39:1–2 (1995): 35–53.

3   N. Katz, "The Identity of a Mystic: The Case of Sa'id Sarmad, a Jewish-Yogi-Sufi Courtier of the Mughals," *Numen: International Review for the History of Religions* 47 (2000): 142–60.

4   Anil Bhatt and Johannes H. Voigt (eds.), *Jewish Exile in India 1933–1945,* New Delhi: Manohar, 1999. See also His Highness Shatrushalyasinji, "Holocaust Refugees and the Maharaja of Jamnagar," *Journal of Indo-Judaic Studies* 3 (2000): 137–9.

5   T. Parfitt, "Tribal Jews," in Nathan Katz, Ranabir Chakravarti, Braj M. Sinha, and Shalva Weil (eds.), *Indo-Judaic Studies in the Twenty-First Century: A View from the Margin*, New York: Palgrave, 2007, pp. 181–93. Israeli journalist Halkin's book (*Across the Sabbath River: In Search of a Lost Tribe of Israel*, Boston, MA: Houghton Mifflin Co., 2002) brought the Bene Menashe question to a wide audience.

6   D. Narkovich and K. Alon, "The Sterilized Otherness: India in Israel, Israel in India," *Journal of Indo-Judaic Studies* 10 (2009): 61–7. The role of Chabad in India has yet to be studied.

7   N. Katz and E. Goldberg, "Jewish Apartheid and a Jewish Gandhi," *Jewish Social Studies* 50:3–4 (1988/1993): 147–76.

8   The definitive work on this community is N. Katz and E. Goldberg, *The Last Jews of Cochin: Jewish Identity in Hindu India*, Columbia, SC: University of South Carolina Press, 1993.

9   Albert Frenz and Scaria Zacharia, *In meinem Land leben verschiedene Völker: Baustein zu einem Dialog der Kulturen und Religionen, Texte alter jüdischer Lieder aus Kerala, Südindien*, Germany: Schwabenverlag, 2002.

10   B. Johnson and S. Zacharia, *Oh, Lovely Parrot! Jewish Women's Songs from Kerala,* Jerusalem: The Jewish Music Research Centre, The Hebrew University of Jerusalem, 2004, pp. 23–5.

11   Johnson and Zacharia, *Oh, Lovely Parrot!* p. 22.

12 There are a number of solid studies of the Bene Israel. The most wide-ranging one is S. B. Isenberg, *India's Bene Israel: A Comprehensive Inquiry and Sourcebook*, Bombay: Popular Prakashan, 1988.
13 Joan G. Roland, *Jews in British India: Identity in a Colonial Era*, Hanover, NH: University Press of New England, 1989.

Recommended recources

Halkin, Hillel. *Across the Sabbath River: In Search of a Lost Tribe of Israel*. Boston, MA: Houghton Mifflin Co., 2002.

Isenberg, Shirley Berry. *India's Bene Israel: A Comprehensive Inquiry and Sourcebook*. Bombay: Popular Prakashan, 1988.

Johnson, Barbara C., and Scaria Zacharia. *Oh, Lovely Parrot! Jewish Women's Songs from Kerala*. Jerusalem: The Jewish Music Research Centre, The Hebrew University of Jerusalem, 2004.

Katz, Nathan. "Understanding Religion in Diaspora: The Case of the Jews of Cochin." *Religious Studies and Theology* 15:1 (1996): 5–17.

Katz, Nathan. *Who Are the Jews of India?* Berkeley, CA: University of California Press, 2000.

Katz, Nathan. "The Identity of a Mystic: The Case of Sa'id Sarmad, a Jewish-Yogi-Sufi Courtier of the Mughals." *Numen: International Review for the History of Religions* 47 (2000): 142–160.

Katz, Nathan, and Ellen S. Goldberg. *The Last Jews of Cochin: Jewish Identity in Hindu India*. Columbia, SC: University of South Carolina Press, 1993.

Katz, Nathan, and Ellen S. Goldberg. "Leaving Mother India: Reasons for the Cochin Jews' Migration to Israel." *Population Review* 39:1–2 (1995): 35–53.

Narkovich, Dalya, and Ktzia Alon. "The Sterilized Otherness: India in Israel, Israel in India." *Journal of Indo-Judaic Studies* 10 (2009): 61–7.

Parfitt, Tudor. "Tribal Jews." In Nathan Katz, Ranabir Chakravarti, Braj M. Sinha, and Shalva Weil (eds.) *Indo-Judaic Studies in the Twenty-First Century: A View from the Margin*. New York: Palgrave, 2007, pp. 181–93.

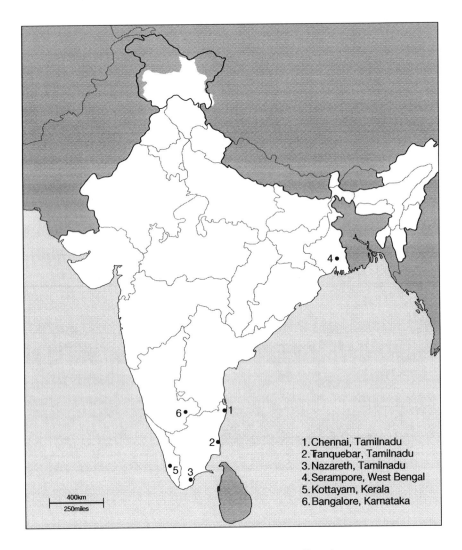

1. Chennai, Tamilnadu
2. Tranquebar, Tamilnadu
3. Nazareth, Tamilnadu
4. Serampore, West Bengal
5. Kottayam, Kerala
6. Bangalore, Karnataka

Map 6 Prominent places in Christianity as practiced in India today

6 South Asian Christianity

Practicing tradition today

M. Thomas Thangaraj

Introduction

Christianity began as a religious movement that ascribed the status of Christ (or Messiah—the anointed and anticipated one) to Jesus, a young Rabbi from Nazareth in the first century CE in the Middle East. This movement's main source of inspiration was the life, ministry, and teachings of Jesus of Nazareth. Since his teachings angered the religious and political leaders of his day, Jesus was condemned as a criminal and was crucified. His disciples claimed that he was resurrected from the dead on the third day and had shown himself to several of them. They began to proclaim his resurrection as a vindication of his Messiahship, and he became the good news to be preached about in and around Jerusalem. Soon his disciples traveled from Jerusalem to different parts of the Greco-Roman world of their day, and established Christian communities that included both Jews and Gentiles. Since they proclaimed Jesus as the Christ, they were named as "Christians" by people around.

South Asian Christianity: Identity

It is believed that St. Thomas, one of the disciples of Jesus, traveled to India and established churches there soon after the emergence of the new Christian communities in the Middle East. Even though some historians question the veracity of this claim, there is indeed a contemporary Christian tradition in India that traces its beginnings to the arrival of St. Thomas in South India. It is, however, an established historical fact that Christianity was a part of the religious landscape of South Asia from the fourth century onwards, if not before. There are evidences to assert the presence of Eastern Orthodox Christianity in Pakistan by the fifth century CE. As far as Sri Lanka is concerned, there is "evidence for the presence of Christianity from at least the 5th century, with traditions for a much earlier presence."[1] Sinhalese kings had employed in their service Christian officers during the period from 473 to 508 CE. In today's post-colonial setting, Christians in South Asia consider it important to claim that the earliest arrival of Christianity in their region is not due to the expansionist policies of Western colonialism, even though colonialism had a major influence in the extension of South Asian Christianity in a much later period.

South Asia consists of India, Pakistan, Bangladesh, Sri Lanka, Bhutan, the Maldives, and Nepal. Since all these separate nations were part of a single Indian subcontinent, I am using most of the materials from the Republic of India to present the history, beliefs, and practices of South Asian Christianity. Moreover, even within India, I am focusing more on the Protestants than on the Roman Catholics and Eastern Orthodox.[2] Most of the beliefs and practices mentioned here can be found in more or less similar forms in Sri Lanka, Pakistan, and Bangladesh. Of course, the dominant religious and cultural context within which Christianity finds itself is markedly different in each of these countries. Islamic religion and culture is dominant in both Pakistan and Bangladesh, while Hindu ethos dominates the religious landscape of India and Nepal. Sri Lankan Christianity is set in the context of both Hinduism and Buddhism. What is common to all these nations is the fact of British colonialism and its profound influence on the history of Christianity in these countries.

Syrian Christians

As noted earlier, St. Thomas, the disciple of Jesus, came to India during the first century and established churches. Most historians of Christianity in India support this view and A. M. Mundadan maintains that "the age-old consciousness of the community of St. Thomas Christians – that their origin as Christians is from the mission of St. Thomas the Apostle in India – stands sufficiently justified."[3] The early Christian community that claims St. Thomas as its founder had a lively connection with the East Syrian, or Persian Christians. Both in its liturgy and in its administration it was a Syrian Orthodox Church. Its membership included both Persians and local inhabitants.

The early Christian community was accommodated well within the Indian religious and cultural setting. It took on an indigenous character by adapting itself to the caste-based arrangement of Indian social reality. The word "Syrian" came to denote both Eastern Orthodox Christianity and a sub-caste (*jati*) within the larger caste system (*varna dharma*). There existed a harmonious relationship between the Syrian Christians and the local Hindus. They participated in one another's religious festivals and assisted one another with their resources. The fundamentalist Hindus of recent times quote the Syrian Christians as the best example of accommodating oneself to the dominant Hindu ethos in contrast to some Roman Catholics and most Protestant Christians who tended to take a negative view of local culture.

Roman Catholicism

Vasco da Gama's discovery in 1498 CE of a shipping route to India via the Cape of Good Hope in Africa offered more possibilities for a flourishing trade between India and Portugal. The arrival of the Portuguese in India is a fresh new page in the history of Christianity in India. The kings of Portugal saw this as an opportunity, in addition to trade, to spread Christianity in India. As one historian notes,

Figure 6.1 San Thome Church, Chennai, India. Front of church with brass flagstaff traditionally found in front of Hindu temples, here topped with a cross. Photo taken by Karen Pechilis.

In consideration of the king of Portugal's zeal for the spread of the Faith, Pope Leo X in 1514 granted to him and his successors the right of ecclesiastical patronage in the lands conquered or to be conquered in Africa and Asia.[4]

Thus the Portuguese "padroado" or the right of patronage came into effect. By 1536, the Portuguese merchants had reached Chittagong in Bangladesh and the actual establishment of churches happened thanks to efforts of Jesuit missionaries.

Goa, a town on the western coast of India, was made an Episcopal seat, and Franciscans and Dominicans carried on the mission. Soon the Portuguese had established their churches and bishoprics firmly on this coast. It was at this time that King John III of Portugal appealed to the Pope to send missionaries to India. So Francis Xavier (1506–52), a Jesuit priest, was sent. Xavier was able to convert to Christianity a large number of people belonging to the fisher caste, primarily on the eastern coast of India. He was able to build the Roman Church in India on firm grounds with an increasing membership.

The Roman Catholic missions flourished in the centuries that followed. Most of the converts to Christianity came from the lower rungs of the caste ladder. Since the coastal towns on the western and eastern shorelines of India were populated by fisher folks, large numbers of Roman Catholics were of lower caste. It was a notable Jesuit missionary, Robert de Nobili, who attempted to broaden the membership of the Church and thus to attract upper caste Hindus to embrace Christianity. In 1606 de Nobili began his work among the higher caste groups in and around Madurai, South India. He separated himself from the existing Catholic mission, adopted the lifestyle of a Hindu monk, mastered Sanskrit and Tamil, and was able to attract several high caste Hindus to the Christian faith. De Nobili had a vision of generating a Christian faith that was rooted in the local Hindu cultural ethos and practices, including the caste system. He published several works in Tamil and wrote hymns both in Tamil and in Telugu. Although de Nobili's work was successful in the initial stages, he came into conflict with the Roman authorities with regard to his views of inculturation and his evangelistic methods. Yet, today, de Nobili is viewed as a pioneer in the indigenization of Christian faith in India. Another notable Jesuit missionary was Father Constant Joseph Beschi who published both poetic and prose works in Tamil during the period 1711–42. These were several such missionaries who attempted to free Christianity in India from what was then commonly referred to as the "reproach of foreignness."

Protestant Christianity

The Protestant mission in India began with the arrival of two German missionaries, Bartholomew Ziegenbalg and Henry Pluetschau, who were sent by King Frederick IV of Denmark. In Sri Lanka, however, the Dutch came to occupy the island in 1659 and had planted a Dutch Reformed Church. Ziegenbalg and Pluetschau arrived in the coastal town of Tranquebar (Tharangampadi), south of Madras (Chennai) on July 9, 1706. They proceeded to learn Portuguese and

Syrian and Catholic Christianities

The initial friendly relations between Syrian Christianity and Western Catholicism were to be marred by differences in beliefs, practices, and especially ecclesial governance. While Syrian Christians continued to recognize the Patriarch of the East, Portuguese Catholics demanded allegiance to the Pope in Rome. There were also differences among them with regard to the number of sacraments, the manner of giving communion, and priestly celibacy. These differences led to hostility and finally at the Synod of Diamper by Roman Catholics, held in 1599, a permanent divide between Syrian Christians and Western Catholics was created. The struggle between these two groups of Christians went on until 1653, when the majority of Syrians rebelled unsuccessfully against the Roman authority and Portuguese hierarchy. Some of those who revolted resumed Roman obedience, while a minority persisted as an Eastern Orthodox tradition.

Tamil, since these were the two languages that were dominant at that time in South India. Ziegenbalg had a keen mind to grasp the languages of India and began translating the Bible into Tamil. He was able to establish congregations in and around Tranquebar and thus began the Protestant expansion in India.

He was to be followed by several missionaries from the West, representing the various denominational and national missionary societies in the West. The establishment of various Protestant mission societies in the West, such as the Society for the Propagation of the Gospel and the Church Missionary Society (both belonging to the Church of England), the Baptist Missionary Society, the London Missionary Society, and others led to the arrival of many more Western Protestant missionaries in India. Thus, Protestant Christianity grew in India, with several denominational and national linkages with the West. One of the leading figures in the Protestant missionary activity of the nineteenth century was William Carey, sent by the Baptist Missionary Society of England, who established the Serampore Mission near Calcutta and promoted the cause of Christianity in many ways. It was through his work that Protestant Christianity was first planted in Bangladesh. He was involved in translating the Bible into several Indian languages, founding the first institution of higher learning in India (Serampore College), and working with the Hindu reformers and British rulers to ban the practice of *sati* (the burning alive of widows on the funeral pyres of their husbands).

Further developments: Syrian, Catholic, Protestant

The origin of Protestant Christianity in Pakistan was due to the work of American Presbyterians who began their work in Lahore in 1849. They were followed by missionaries from various Protestant denominations, including American Methodists. While the Protestant expansion was taking place in India, the Roman Catholic tradition experienced its own parallel expansion. In addition to establishing parishes and dioceses in India, the Roman Catholic Church was heavily involved in founding and maintaining educational institutions around the country. Various religious orders were involved in medical, technical, and other differing forms of service.

The further history of Syrian Christianity in India is marked by the development of a schism that led to the formation in 1887 of the Mar Thoma Church. The Church Missionary Society's missionaries were invited by Mar Dionysios II to teach in their seminaries and bring about a revival in the Syrian Church. Their involvement in the life of the Syrian Church led to the formation of a reformed party by a group of Syrian Christians under the leadership of Abraham Malpan. Ultimately they left the Syrian Church and formed the Mar Thoma Church.

One of the remarkable features in the history of Christianity in South Asia is the movement toward unity among mainline Protestants in the twentieth century. In 1919 a set of church leaders, both clergy and laity, drawn from different denominations met in the town of Tranquebar in India and issued what is now called the Tranquebar Manifesto. This Manifesto bemoaned the divisions among Protestants and called for coming together as a unified church. Conversations toward unity continued from then on between the Anglican, Methodist, Presbyterian, and Congregationalist churches in South India for several years. Finally it led to the formation of the Church of South India, an organic union of all four denominational traditions, on September 27, 1947. Similar conversations took place between Protestant churches in North India, which led to the formation of the Church of North India in 1970.

There are continuing conversations even today among the three churches— Church of South India, Church of North India, and Mar Thoma Church—toward a conciliar formation of a Church of India. The Lutherans, Baptists, American Methodists, and others remain as churches in their own right. The attempts to broaden the unity among Protestants have not led to further mergers, though there is a spirit of ecumenical collaboration. Ecumenical cooperation is seen clearly in the work of the National Christian Council of India, which came into being in 1912 under the name National Missionary Council of India. The goals of the National Christian Council are to assist the various churches in their missionary vocation, to coordinate the activities of the regional councils, and to help form Christian opinion on matters of national and social interest through consultation among churches. Most of the theological schools and seminaries in South Asia function as ecumenical institutions as well.

Since Vatican II, the Roman Catholic churches in India have been working together with Protestant churches in matters of common concern. When the Eastern Orthodox churches joined the World Council of Churches in 1961 during its Assembly at New Delhi, an intentional collaboration between Protestants and Eastern Orthodox Christians in India gained importance.

According to the census of 2001, 2.3 percent of the population of India is Christian, while 80.5 percent are Hindu and 13.4 percent are Muslim. In Pakistan,

Christians form only 1.6 percent of the total population, in Bangladesh 0.3 percent, in Sri Lanka 7.5 percent, and in Nepal 0.5 percent. Among the 1.2 billion people in India, Christians number 24 million. Some statisticians include those Indians who are called "crypto-Christians" due to their secret admiration and devotion to Christ without membership in a Christian denomination, and thus put the number of Christians closer to 5 percent of the population. Christians in India belong to all the three major ecclesial traditions, namely, Eastern Orthodox, Roman Catholic, and Protestant. The Indian Orthodox Church, Orthodox Syrian Church of the East, Armenian Apostolic Church, Chaldean Syrian Church, and a few other smaller Orthodox groups carry on the Eastern Orthodox tradition. These churches are mostly based in the southern state of Kerala. Roman Catholics, who are spread throughout India, comprise nearly half of the Christian population in India. Protestants are split into nearly a thousand denominations. Some of these denominations had their beginnings in Europe or North America, while others are indigenous churches established either by individual charismatic leaders or by groups of local Christians. The Church of South India, a union of former Anglicans, Presbyterians, Methodists, and Congregationalists, has a membership of around three million. The Church of North India, a similar union of major Protestant churches, is one and a half million strong.

Christians are not evenly distributed in the Indian landscape. The Christian population in the states of Kerala, Tamilnadu, and Andhra Pradesh together account for more than 60 percent of the total number of Indian Christians.[5] There is also a concentration of Christians in the north-eastern part of India—in the states of Nagaland (87.5 percent), Meghalaya (64.6 percent), and Mizoram (85.7 percent). The Christian population is significantly smaller in the north-central and north-western regions of India.

Indian Christianity derives its multiplicity and variety not only from its denominational differences, but also from regional and linguistic particularities. Christianity as it is practiced in Nagaland in the north-east is significantly different from that in Tamilnadu in the south, because of the differences in local culture and language. These differences are manifested in worship patterns, liturgical practices, church architecture, and in the observation of individual rituals, rites of passage, and family ceremonies, such as weddings and funerals. We will discuss some of these practices in the next section. Thus, any discussion of Indian Christian identity will be dependent on the region, language, denomination, and social groupings. So is the issue of how Christians in India negotiate their identity as Christians.

Constructing Christian identity in South Asia

The question of Christian identity is a complex issue as far as South Asia is concerned. One can see a variety of ways in which South Asian Christians had negotiated their identity. The first thing to note with regard to the emergence and history of the formation of Christian identity in India is the striking difference between the way Eastern Orthodox Christians and other Christians (Roman Catholics and Protestants) engaged themselves in this negotiation. For several centuries in its history, the Eastern Orthodox tradition in India had remained as Syrian Orthodox tradition under the patronage of the Patriarch of Damascus. This meant that the Eastern Orthodox Christians saw themselves as Syrian Orthodox Christians located in India. As mentioned earlier, the term "Syrian" became a word that marked them both as Christians and as a particular sub-caste within the Indian caste system. As Corinne Dempsey notes, the early Christians were "highly integrated into Hindu society." She writes, "Through their practice of local customs, including a variety of ritual observances for upholding 'caste' purity, it seems that early Christians enjoyed a high social status similar to that of the well-to-do Hindu Nair caste."[6] Therefore, the early Eastern Orthodox Christians were able to construct their Christian identity without placing themselves over against Hindus, whereas the Roman Catholics and Protestants tended to define their Christian identity in contrast to their former Hindu identity. The Indian Orthodox Church of today is one which is intentionally committed to functioning as an *Indian* church.

When the Portuguese arrived in India during the sixteenth century, the Eastern Orthodox Christians encountered a crisis of identity. They were brought under the care of Rome and thus were incorporated into the Roman Catholic Church during the historic Synod of Diamper in 1599 CE. As an Indian Church historian writes,

> In a way, the synod of Diamper achieved one of the aims of Portuguese policy in Kerala, viz., to separate the Syrian Christians of Malabar from the Chaldean Patriarch and to extend the influence of his Catholic Majesty over those parts.[7]

This particular crisis of Eastern Orthodox identity came to an end during another historic moment in 1653 CE, called the Coonen Cross, when the Eastern Orthodox Christians freed themselves from the rule of Rome and returned to their earlier ecclesial tradition. From then on until today, the Eastern Orthodox churches maintain their distinctive identity with the Christian population of India. Yet one cannot ignore the emergence of Mar Thoma Church in the latter part of the nineteenth century, due to the influence of missionaries belonging to the Church Missionary Society of the Church of England. Mar Thoma Christian identity is a creative combination of Eastern Orthodox liturgical tradition with Protestant evangelical piety.

As far as the Roman Catholics and the Protestants in India are concerned, the negotiation of Christian identity has been multifaceted and varied. As we noted earlier, it is dependent on where one's denominational loyalties lie, what language one speaks, what region one lives in, and what sub-caste one belongs to. It is also shaped by the theological outlook of the missionaries who initiated the early converts into the life of the church. Due to this complexity, what is feasible is to look at some general trends that promote and maintain the identity of Christians. Two historical factors are significant for this discussion. First, a vast majority of Roman Catholics and Protestants in India belong to the lower rungs of the caste ladder. Most of them come from the lowest sub-castes, formerly known as

Untouchables and now referred to as Dalits. Position within the caste hierarchy has tremendous influence of one's negotiation of Christian identity. The number of persons who converted from Islam to Christianity is negligibly small and thus the issue of Christian identity has not played a major role.

Second, people converted to Christian faith both as individuals and as large groups (most often belonging to a single sub-caste or as villages). To cite an example, there is a town called Nazareth in south India, which came into existence when the whole village of Chanpatthu converted to Christianity and renamed their village as Nazareth. The process of converting to Christianity, either as a lone individual cutting of one's ties with family, caste, and community or as a member of large group, had a profound influence on constructing one's Christian identity. This process is guided by what one may call a dynamics of difference. What difference does it make to become a Christian in India? Who are Christians different from? How does one express and exhibit this difference in tangible ways? What are the ways in which a Christian in India may maintain an identity that celebrates the difference? These are some of the questions that guided the early converts in forging their Christian identity. For convenience and clarity, we will use the case of Tamil Christians, especially those in the village of Nazareth, to expound this, with the proviso that this is not true of every Roman Catholic and Protestant group in India. The writings of Selva Raj deal with some of the ways in which Roman Catholics in India have constructed their identity via culture-specific practices.

It is clear that the early converts went through a tension between their identity as Indians on the one hand and their identity as Christians on the other. The way they dealt with these two loyalties was through a clear commitment to maintaining matters of their distinctiveness and difference. On the one hand, the early converts to Protestant Christianity in south Tamilnadu needed to define their new identity as *different* from their Hindu neighbors. Even though there was a sizable population of Muslims in that area, the converts were all from the Hindu tradition. Why was this difference important for the new converts? First, the new converts were keen on a distinct Christian identity because of Hinduism's history of co-opting every new religious tradition into its fold, thus blurring its own distinctiveness. Second, the Protestant missionaries were committed to preventing the new converts from reverting back to their former religion and also to protecting them from sporadic acts of persecution, though few, by their Hindu neighbors.

While this particular difference mattered most, the early converts defined their own Christian identity rather than take on the Western Christian identity of European missionaries. They were not passively receiving a form of Christian identity that the missionaries offered them. They constructed for themselves a Christian identity that had clear differences from that of the Western missionaries, at times to the utter dismay of the missionaries themselves.

Different from Hindu identity

In simpler terms, "we are NOT Hindus but Christians instead." Such a difference was maintained by organizing some of the elements and practices of the

Christian faith as markers of Christian identity. First of all, taking on biblical and Western names or the names of Christian saints is seen among many Christians as a clear marker of Christian identity. This was done as an important element in the baptismal rite both of adult converts and infants in Christian families. All Christians including those belonging to the Eastern Orthodox tradition take on biblical and Western names. Some of the Christian theologians in India have names that clearly mark them as Christians, such as, M. M. Thomas, Felix Wilfred, Henry Wilson, and others. Some of the leading Indian Christian artists include Alfred Thomas and Frank Wesley. Of course, this is not true of all parts of India, and in areas where people operate with surnames there is a tendency to have biblical and Western names as first names. Name as a marker of identity is not limited to individuals alone. For example, Christian institutions have names such as St. John's or St. Xavier's College, Sarah Tucker College, and so on. When people converted to Christianity en masse as villages, they renamed the villages as Nazareth, Jerusalem, Megnanapuram (Town of True Wisdom), Jebagnanapuram (Town of Prayerful Wisdom), Sawyerpuram (named after a missionary called Sawyer—Town of Sawyer), and so on.

There are several more areas where Christian identity is worked out in contrast to Hindu identity. Hindu festivals are totally given up and only Christian festivals are celebrated by Indian Christians, even though there are particular areas where the distinction is not strictly maintained. For example, no Christian in

Architecture as a symbol of difference

Another symbol of difference is church architecture. Most churches in India are built in either Gothic or Roman styles. St. John's Cathedral in the town of Nazareth stands at the center of town and looks like any other Anglican church building in England. It has a tall steeple with clocks on all four sides announcing every hour of the day with the chiming of bells. As one enters the main sanctuary, one is impressed by the high altar with crosses and candles, adorned in appropriate liturgical colors with three stained-glass windows with biblical themes at the back of the altar. The cross is the major marker of a Christian place of worship. Even though there have been attempts to build churches in the Hindu/Indian architectural style such as those one finds in Christian ashrams, seminaries, and such specialized places, Christians over all have tended to see the traditional Western church architecture as a marker of their Christian identity.[8] Similarly, Western church music continues to be seen as a marker of the distinctive identity of Protestants, while the Roman Catholics have adopted local musical traditions in their liturgy and worship after Vatican II. Today, however, due to the processes of globalization Western music has so widely pervaded and influenced the Indian musical community that it no longer functions as a marker of Christian identity.

Nazareth or neighboring villages celebrates the Hindu festivals of Deepavali (Diwali—festival of lights), Pongal (harvest festival), and Ayudha Puja (festival venerating the tools of one's trade). But Christmas, New Year (according to the Common Era), Easter, and saints' days are celebrated. Another important marker for Christians in certain parts of India is the prohibition of the wearing of *tilak* (a dot on the forehead, traditionally signifying the third eye of intuition). Roman Catholics and some Protestant groups have favored wearing the *tilak* as an Indian cultural (not religious) practice, whereas others see it as explicit marker of Hindu religiosity. Some Protestant missionaries specifically banned that practice.

The method of differentiation elaborated so far exemplifies the converts' way of negotiating their Christian identity in relation to their being different from Hindus. This method helped bring clarity to their newly formed Christian identity. More importantly, it gave them a new sense of selfhood and dignity. For example, the use of Western music gave them a sense of pride, given the fact that as rural Hindus they did not have access to the classical music tradition of South India. It also provided a clear sense of loyalty to the Christian tradition as transmitted through the work of Western missionaries.

The dynamics of difference that we have highlighted is mostly true in the life of those new converts to Christianity who belonged to the lower groups within the caste system. It has not been so for those belonging to the upper castes that had not experienced their former religious tradition as either socially or economically oppressive. Therefore, such converts claimed their Hindu identity along with their newly found Christian identity. This is very true, for example, in the life of Brahmabandhab Upadhyay (1861–1907), a Brahmin from West Bengal who converted to Christianity and became a leading figure in the Roman Catholic Church in India. He answers the question—Are we Hindus?—with these words.

> By birth we are Hindus and shall remain Hindu till death. But as *dvija* (twice born) by virtue of our sacramental rebirth, we are Catholic ... In short, we are Hindus so far as our physical and mental constitution is concerned, but in regard to our immortal souls we are Catholic. We are *Hindu* Catholic.[9]

Different from Western Christian identity

Indian Christian identity was also marked by its difference from the Christian identity of European and American missionaries. While the new converts saw the missionaries as models in very many ways, they were equally keen to mark their difference from the missionaries in negotiating their Christian identity. In simpler terms, "We are NOT Western Christians but Indian Christians instead." One can see this very clearly in the manner with which Indian Christians dealt with the issue of caste. Most of the Protestant missionaries desired, though only some of them demanded, that the early converts denounce caste and construct their Christian identity transcending their caste identity. Bishop Wilson's instruction to fellow missionaries in 1833 clearly indicates this. He wrote:

The distinction of castes then must be abandoned, decidedly, immediately, finally; and those who profess to belong to Christ, must give proof of their having really put off concerning the former conversation the old, and having put on the new man in Christ Jesus.[10]

Christians in the northern parts of India did not cling on to their caste identity as much as south Indian Christians did because the south Indian Christians converted to Christianity in large groups belonging to the same sub-castes. Some of the south Indian Christians effectively argued against the missionaries' call to denounce caste.[11]

In the matter of caste, Christians did not distinguish their identity from the identity of their Hindu neighbors. Hindu social order has historically been dominated by the concept of *dharma*, meaning justice, order, duty, and religion. *Dharma* entails two aspects, namely, *varnadharma* and *ashramadharma*. The former is the recognition of one's duty in light of one's position in caste hierarchy, and the latter is the discovery of one's duty in relation to one's stage in life. Indian Christians, even though they experienced a sense of liberation from the oppressive character of the caste system, did not opt out of the system itself. The Eastern Orthodox Church in India accommodated itself easily into the caste structure of Hindu society.

> Syrian Christians have been for centuries encapsulated within caste society, regarded by Hindus as a caste, occupying a recognized [and high] place within the caste hierarchy, ... and (seem) to have been quite content to accept and operate the caste system without any egalitarian protest.[12]

This comfortable positioning of Syrian Christians within the caste hierarchy was jolted by the joining of low-caste groups to the Syrian church in the nineteenth century. Syrian Christians have since encountered great difficulty in accepting the low-caste Christians as their equals within the church.[13]

The Roman Catholic Church has its own share in the problem of the practice of caste within the church. A Roman Catholic missionary success was the conversion of fisherfolk on the southern tip of India. The fisherfolk belonged on the lower rungs of the caste ladder and thus the Roman Catholic Church was a church of the low caste. Missionaries like Robert de Nobili, on the other hand, attempted to win converts from the upper caste by the adoption of Hindu rituals and practices. He believed that one need not renounce caste by becoming a Christian. In the midst of all these missionary experiments, the Roman Catholic tradition in India regarded caste as a civil institution and adopted a policy of accommodation. Even though the caste system is verbally condemned as contrary to Christian faith, there is an accommodation of it in the organization of the church and in the individual lives of Roman Catholics.

Protestant missions did not have a unified view of the role of caste distinctions within a Christian community. For example, the Lutherans were more accommodative than Anglican missionaries. The only success in the Protestant missionary battle against caste is the practice of eucharistic participation without caste considerations. Ecclesial governance, family relations, and individual Christian behavior are still governed by caste considerations in most Protestant churches. Since a majority of Christians practice endogamy, caste distinctions continue to be perpetuated within the churches.

There are other practices that differentiate Indian Christians from Western missionaries. Even today, there are Christians who follow the astrological calendar with regard to auspicious times and auspicious days. To give a concrete example, no Christian family in South Tamilnadu will hold a wedding on a Tuesday since it is not an auspicious day for weddings. In some South Tamilnadu towns, the ceremonial planting of the first pole for the *pandal* (a temporary extension to the house to accommodate guests) for a wedding is done in a typically Hindu ritualistic manner though with a Christian minister marking the sign of the cross on the pole. Just like the newly married Hindu couples who celebrate their first Diwali festival with the bride's family, Christian couples do so during their first Christmas. In most of the villages in South India, men sit on the floor on one side of the aisle in the church while women sit on the other. Children and young adults sit in the front and older folks at the back. Indian Christians in non-urban areas are very particular about removing their shoes before they enter the church. These practices are prevalent in many parts of India. Even though the early converts sang Western hymns translated into their own languages, soon their own poets composed hymns and lyrics set to Indian music and that gave them a clear sense of *Indian* Christian identity.

During the twentieth century there have been intentional efforts by churches—Roman Catholic and Protestant—to express Indian Christian identity in Indian and non-Western terms. For example, the most recent Eucharistic liturgy of the Church of South India is organized with a sympathetic attention to Hindu liturgical practices. Paintings by a contemporary Roman Catholic artist, Jyoti Sahi, an internationally known artist who runs an ashram near Bangalore, also exemplify this movement, which is generally referred to as inculturation of Christian faith in India. He was preceded by artists such as Frank Wesley, Alfred Thomas, and others.[14] The church union movement among the Protestants, which began in 1919 and resulted in the emergence of Church of South India (1947) and Church of North India (1970), is also an attempt to negotiate a distinctively Indian Christian identity rather than take on a Western identity.

Relations with other religions

The relations between South Asian Christianity and other religious traditions within South Asia take different forms depending on the denomination, region, and caste. For example, Christians in Sri Lanka have lively relations with Hindus, Muslims, and Buddhists, whereas the situation in Pakistan and Bangladesh is limited largely to Christians' relation with Muslims. Even though there is a sizeable population of Muslims in India (nearly 13 percent of the total population), Indian Christians' major concern is their relation with Hindus. The Henry Martin Institute at Hyderabad, India, is devoted to dialogue between Christians and Muslims and to bringing reconciliation among people of various religions,

Caste and Christian identity

There is also a dynamics of difference among Christians themselves. Even after some bold experiments in ecumenism, Christians in South Asia cling to their denominational loyalties. More particularly, especially in South India, Christians define their Christian identity in relation to their particular sub-caste as well. Shudra Christians have tended to intentionally differentiate themselves from their Dalit brothers and sisters within the Christian community and there has been a history of oppressing and exploiting Dalit Christians. Even though one may not see this difference at work during worship or other related spiritual activities of the church, it does play a significant role in the matter of Church governance, social relationships, and arranging of marriages. South Indian Christians use the story of Abraham finding a bride for his son, Isaac, from his own kindred in Genesis 24 as a warrant for their caste-based wedding arrangement.

Even though the setting up of caste-based congregations is condemned and avoided, there have been instances of churches organizing their congregations on a sub-caste basis. For example, a multi-caste congregation may experience the dominance of one particular sub-caste, and the least dominant eventually separate to form a congregation solely for their own sub-caste. In certain parts of India, particular Protestant denominations are known as particular caste-based denominations.

especially Hindus and Muslims, even though it began as a place to equip oneself for evangelism among Muslims. The more recent incidents in India of church burnings, attacks on Christians from tribal areas, and the rhetoric of the Hindu-only movement may appear as if there is real hostility between Christians and others. It is not the case, even though there have been sporadic cases of persecution of Christians. On the whole, Christians and others have lived together in peace and harmony. As mentioned earlier, the Eastern Orthodox tradition in India accommodated itself into the prevailing Hindu social ethos such that it did not experience any major conflict with the religious communities around them. Such friendly relations were extended not only to Hindus and Muslims, but also to a small Jewish community in the State of Kerala. During the pre-colonial period, the relation between Syrian Christians and Hindus was one of mutual appreciation and help. For example, "at least one Hindu temple regularly lent out its temple elephants to Syrian worshippers for use in their festival processions."[15]

The Roman Catholics and Protestants have maintained, over all, mutual respect and friendship with Hindus over the last five centuries. During the Moghul period an interesting phenomenon took place. The great Moghul emperor Akbar (1556–1605) was very open to religious pluralism and invited scholars of various religions to serve at his court in Lahore. He became interested in Christianity and welcomed Jesuits in his court. This offered an opportunity to Roman Catholics to interact with the Hindus and Muslims in India. Akbar also hoped that a new religion, called *Din Ilahi*, combining elements from the three existing religions—Hinduism, Islam, and Christianity—could be formed. Jesuits did not view this move with favor and so found it difficult to continue in Akbar's court and withdrew from it.

In the field of social reforms and changes, Hindus and Christians have worked together. For example, the work of Hindu reformers like Raja Ram Mohan Roy and Mahatma Gandhi has drawn on Christian resources and support. Hindus and Muslims have generally been appreciative of the humanitarian service of Christians throughout India. In religious attitudes, a majority of Protestants in India have maintained an attitude of condescension and condemnation toward their neighbors of other religions. They have been informed by a certain missionary view that looked upon Hindus and Muslims simply as people to be converted to Christianity. Such a view is accompanied by considering Hindu religion as idolatrous, superstitious, and even demonic. Such religious attitudes have not fully isolated Indian Christians from their neighbors. One can find, here and there, in the history of Christianity in India, instances of either Hindus or Muslims persecuting Christian converts. But these were rare and sporadic. The Hindu view of the multiplicity of paths to God had a built-in tolerance that accommodated the new religion within its own worldview. As Grafe puts it,

> The relation between the two religions during the 20th century is characterized by a breaking apart of the religious-communal and the purely religious aspects: On the one hand communal clashes between Hindu and Christian groups, on the other hand a spirit of disdainful or benevolent toleration or cautious dialogue.[16]

After Independence, the provisions of the Constitution of India have guided the relation between Christianity and other religions. The followers of every religion in India are guaranteed the right to practice, profess, and propagate their religion. It is the Indian Christians who have made the most use of the provision given in the Constitution to engage in evangelistic activity. Such an engagement is looked upon with suspicion by a minority of Hindus. It is often represented as Christians' attempt to "proselytize" through fraudulent and coercive means. Recent years have seen a few cases of attacks on individual Christians, their communities, and their churches, especially in the northern part of India. Certain states within the nation had earlier attempted to pass regulations and laws to control the proselytizing activity of Christians. For example, in 1967 and 1968, State "Freedom of Religion" Bills were passed in the states of Orissa and Madhya Pradesh, which were later annulled by the Supreme Court of India. Thus the question of "conversion" has become a bone of contention between Hindus and Christians.

There are also intentional attempts by South Asian Christians to promote dialogue between Christianity and other religions. South Asian Christianity can boast of its leadership in the matter of inter-religious dialogue in the world church: P. D. Devanandan was one of the early proponents of inter-religious dialogue in India. South Asia has produced leaders such as Stanley J. Samartha

(India), Wesley Ariarajah (Sri Lanka), and Shanta Premawardhana (Sri Lanka), who served as Directors of the program on inter-religious dialogue of the World Council of Churches. Several Roman Catholic theologians have been in the forefront of inter-religious dialogue. Aloysius Pieris and Tissa Balasuriya of Sri Lanka, Raimundo Panikkar, Swami Abhishiktananda, and Jacques Dupuis from India have also played a significant role in the matter of inter-religious dialogue. The Christian ashrams often function as places of dialogue at the level of mystical religious experience. There are many dialogue centers in South Asia established and promoted by Protestant and Roman Catholic churches. The Roman Catholic and Protestant seminaries in India have been pioneers in the promotion of dialogical relations between Christians and others. The future of South Asian Christians' relationship with Hindus, Buddhists, Sikhs, and Muslims rests upon how South Asian Christians succeed in maintaining freedom of religion and the possibilities for dialogue and mutual enrichment.

South Asian Christianity: Practice

Worship

Visitors to South Asia today will not fail to notice at least the following things that announce the presence of Christianity or function as its markers. First of all, one can see tall steeples attached to church buildings. One can notice roadside shrines for saints in the Eastern Orthodox and Roman Catholic traditions. The tradition of building steeples or towers comes from the period of Roman Catholic and Protestant missionary expansion. As we noted earlier, these steeples became markers of Christian identity. But today, most Christians see the steeples as "evangelistic" since these are referred to as "witness" to Christ. Publicly exhibiting the presence of Christians in a town or village was and is even today understood as a form of witnessing to Christ. Invariably, one can find a neon cross on top of the tower, which is lit up during nights. The cross on top of the steeple is understood as an invitation to the good news available in Christ. The steeples in the coastal towns of South India, however, have an additional character to them. They function as lighthouses and symbols of divine protection to those Christian fishermen who go out into the sea to fish during the night. Most Christians take pride in the grandeur and beauty of their churches and feel emotionally attached to the building, to the extent of believing in the miraculous character of the building itself. In remote villages, the dust in the church was seen as having such healing power that if one fell sick, one would be given water mixed with the dust from the church to drink as a medicine.

Such attachment to the church building may be attributed to two possible factors. First of all, since most Christians belonged to the lowest sub-castes in the caste ladder, in their earlier religious life they were denied access to most of the big Hindu temples. They could only have some small local shrines dedicated to lesser gods in the Hindu pantheon. Therefore, when these lower caste groups converted to Christianity, their possessing a big church of their own with a tall steeple became a matter of pride and honor. There are Christian villages in South Tirunelveli where the Protestant congregations sing songs that are composed in honor of their church building and those are sung with gusto in general gatherings of the congregation.

More importantly, the attachment to the church building is due to the centrality of corporate worship, in contrast to the Hindu tradition where corporate worship occupies a marginal status limited to modern expressions of Hindu faith. Worship, especially on Sundays, has become a central feature of South Asian Christianity. An attachment to corporate worship brought along with it a love for liturgy and hymns. Here again, a variety of expressions abound. The Eastern Orthodox churches formed their liturgical practices in the Syrian tradition, with Syriac as their liturgical language. This was to be followed later by the use of Latin rites among some Syrian Christians and the use of the local language Malayalam. The Divine Liturgy (Liturgy used during the celebration of the Eucharist) takes precedence in the life of Orthodox Christians in India.

The Roman Catholic churches initially adopted the Latin liturgical traditions and in their contacts with the Syrian Christians developed Syrian rites as well. However, Vatican II brought a significant change in the worship life of the Roman Catholic churches in India. These changes included the use of vernacular languages for liturgy, the employment of local musical traditions, and the adoption of Indian architectural patterns in the building of churches. There have been genuine attempts to present Christian worship through local cultural idiom.

Protestants brought the worship patterns of the varying Western Protestant denominations. These were adapted to the local settings through a limited incorporation of local language, cultural practices, and music. However, there remained a domination of Western liturgical elements in Protestant worship. Over the centuries, the Protestants themselves have gone through a liturgical renewal, and now adopt local religo-cultural practices for Christian worship. The formation of the Church of South India in 1947 led to a process of forming Christian worship in an ecumenical mode that is inclusive of the various Protestant traditions. *The Book of Common Worship*, published in 1963, is the outcome of such an attempt. The most recent attempt at a truly Indian liturgy is exemplified in the alternate version of Eucharist Liturgy published in 1985. In its own words, it "attempts to express an understanding of worship that is more Indian than our traditional Christian worship forms," and encourages people to conduct the service in as authentic an Indian style as possible. The liturgy is organized around five stages: Entry (*pravesa*), Awakening (*prabodha*), Recalling and Offering (*smarana-samarpana*), Sharing in the Body and Blood of Christ (*darsana*), and Blessing (*preshana*). The language of the liturgy is guided by concerns of both inculturation and the liberation of the oppressed.

Apart from the Eastern Orthodox, Roman Catholic, and mainline Protestant churches, Pentecostal and non-denominational churches have had their own modes and methods of inculturation of Christian worship. For example, Pentecostal churches were among the first to exploit the emerging light music tradition of India (a mixture of Western and Indian musical traditions) for their worship and piety. What is common to all these Christian churches is the conscious and intentional attempt to develop and practice the worship of the Christian community in local linguistic and cultural forms. The more difficult question that these churches face is to define what the local, linguistic, and cultural forms are. The processes of globalization have brought a certain amount of cultural hybridity in which local forms are shot through with global cultural expressions. For example, the so-called "praise songs" of popular TV evangelists in the United States of America are gaining great popularity among Christians in India.

However, the religious practices of South Asian Christians are not limited to what happens within the four walls of the church. There are several home-based religious practices as well. Indian Christians have adapted several Hindu rites of passage into their own religious life. These practices vary according to region and denominational affiliation. Christian weddings take on several local cultural practices which are Hindu in origin. Indigenous elements are more conspicuously present in worship settings outside the church building. The prayer meetings held in people's homes, lyrical or musical preaching performed during festive occasions, prayer services at homes related to rites of passage such as puberty, marriages, and funerals and other such home-based worship services bear clear marks of indigenous elements and influence.

In addition to Christmas and Easter, most Christian congregations celebrate festivals such as the Church Anniversary Festival that commemorates the building of the church in that place, and the Harvest Festival in which people bring their farm products to offer to the church as a mark of their gratitude and thanksgiving to God. These are occasions for much more celebrative worship services. The form and nature of these worship services differ from region to region and according to earlier denominational links. Although there have been attempts, especially in theological seminaries, to celebrate the Hindu festivals, such as Diwali, Pongal, Onam, and others, most Christians tend to see these as

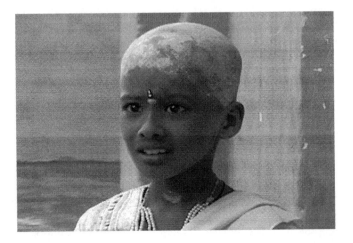

Figure 6.2 Young Christian girl who has had her head shaved at the festival of St. John de Britto in Oriyur, Tamilnadu. Photo taken by Selva J. Raj.

beyond the appropriate boundaries of Christian life and witness. In the Roman Catholic tradition, too, there are several festivals linked to the local shrines. For example, the Roman Catholic church at Velankanni in Tamilnadu is considered as a pilgrimage center by people belonging to all religions in the area.

There are several major community events that shape the sacred life of Indian Christians. The Mar Thoma Church has conducted an annual revival meeting since 1895, called the Maramon Convention, in which thousands of Mar Thoma Christians and others gather for several days of preaching, prayer, and celebration. The Syrian Orthodox churches have their own celebrations and events. The celebration of the sainthood of St. George is one such. The Roman Catholic churches have adapted the Hindu festival processions for their own festivals. The Hindu practice of pulling the temple chariot along the streets of the town on festive occasions has been adapted by Roman Catholic churches for festivals connected with local Roman Catholic shrines. Protestants, on the other hand, have tended to avoid any appearance of close similarities to Hindu festivals but rather have celebrated the church anniversaries, Christmas, and Easter with a few elements that have Hindu cultural roots, for example, the wearing of new clothes for Christmas. Hindus, generally, wear new clothes during Diwali festival.

The Bible

The second marker of Christian presence in India is the display of Biblical verses on walls, billboards, and on vehicles such as motorbikes and cars. There is great amount of power attached to Biblical verses that the very display of them will move the hearts of those who read them to repent and believe in the Christian gospel. Most churches have special billboards erected to display biblical verses. Where does this fascination and almost obsession with biblical verses come from? How is the authority of the Bible understood in South Asia?

The Bible has occupied a central place in the religious life of South Asian Christians since the arrival of Protestant missionaries from the West. The Eastern Orthodox traditions within India did not pay attention to the translation of the Bible into local languages. Therefore, the sacred text for the Orthodox is the liturgical practices rather a written document such as the Bible. A Malayalam translation of the Bible was available to the Eastern Orthodox Christians only through the work of the Protestant missionaries in the nineteenth century. The Roman Catholic missions in India were slow to engage in the translation of the Bible into local languages, yet they produced other Christian literature in local languages right from the beginning of their mission. As early as 1616, Father Thomas Stephens, a Roman Catholic missionary who worked among the Konkani people, published a magnificent Marathi poem of 10,962 verses on Biblical history to take the place of Hindu *Puranas*.[17] Other Roman Catholic missionaries wrote extensively in local languages in both poetry and prose, yet were hesitant to translate the Bible into local languages. Some even actively opposed the Protestant translations of the Bible. For example, Abbe J. A. Dubois objected that the translations offered by the Protestant missionary societies were of a very low literary quality and that the Bible was not easily comprehensible or appealing to Hindus if it was simply translated and given to them.[18]

The translation of the Bible into the local languages of India had a high priority in the activities of the Protestant missionaries. The first Protestant missionary, Ziegenbalg, translated the New Testament into Tamil within five years of his arrival in India. A major turnout of translations happened with the work of William Carey at Serampore. As Robin Boyd writes, "He [Carey] and his colleagues eventually set up at Serampore what might almost be called a Bible factory with different linguistic departments, and succeeded in translating the Bible, in whole or part, into more than thirty languages."[19]

The relationship between the Bible and the Hindu scriptures has been a matter of debate throughout the history of Christianity in India. The early Protestant missionaries, while translating the Bible, named it the Veda, or *Vedagama* (a combination of *veda* and *agama*, the two major scriptural corpuses in Hinduism). Robert de Nobili referred to it as the fifth Veda, relating the Bible to the legend that the fifth Veda of the Hindus was lost in antiquity. In most Indian languages the Bible is referred to as Veda, a name ascribed to the four ancient scriptures of Hinduism. Such naming of the Bible has its own implications for understanding the authority of and for interpreting the Bible as well. One of the more creative attempts at relating the Hindu scriptures with the Bible was made by Chenchiah, a twentieth century Christian lay theologian, when he suggested that Indian Christians might accept the Hindu scriptures as their Old Testament instead of the Hebrew Bible. He argued that one could read the Hindu scriptures in the light of Christ, in the same way that Jesus' early Jewish disciples read their own Hebrew scriptures.[20] Most Christians in India do not accept this view, though many see the Hindu scriptures as a preparation for the arrival of the Bible in India.

The centrality of the Bible in the lives of Christians in India can be attributed to another sociological factor as well: an overwhelming majority belong to the lowest sub-caste. This meant that as Hindus they did not have access to the highly developed Sanskritic scriptures of the Hindu faith. Therefore, owning their own scriptures and reading them in their own mother tongues became a matter of pride and dignity to early Christians. As soon as a child learns to read, he or she receives the Bible as the first gift and children begin reading the Bible from a very young age. Therefore, displaying biblical verses on walls and billboards becomes an important marker of the presence of Christians in India. Of course, such attachment to the Bible did not stop Christians from producing other religious literature.

Religious literature other than the Bible abounds in the history of Christianity in India. Indian Christians have been prolific in the writing of hymns, epic poems, apologetic writings, and theological treatises, both in English and in vernacular languages. These writings were heavily influenced by Hindu ways of thinking, imaging, and articulating. Some of the well-known hymn writers in India are H. A. Krishna Pillai, Narayan Vaman Tilak, Vedanayagam Sastri, Subba Rao, and Brahmabandhav Upadhyaya. These poets reflected *bhakti* (devotion) sentiments similar to those found in Hindu *bhakti* literature. A significant body of Christian literature, theological and devotional, also exists in the English language. These were produced primarily in the late nineteenth, and the twentieth and twenty-first centuries. The list of such writers includes Brahmabandhav Upadhyaya, A. J. Appasamy, P. Chenchiah, V. Chakkarai, Raymond Panikkar, M. M. Thomas, Manilal C. Parekh, K. M. Banerjea, and Swami Abhishiktananda from India; D.T. Niles, Wesley Ariarajah, Lynn de Silva, Tissa Balasurya, Aloysius Pieris, and Preman Niles from Sri Lanka; and Charles Amjad-Ali from Pakistan. While such treatises are available, the religious life of South Asian Christians, especially in rural settings, is shaped primarily by worship in the church, reading the Bible, and home-based religious practices.

Institutional identity

The third marker of Christian presence in South Asia is the various institutions attached to the church and also the very institutional structure of the church. Christianity came to South Asia with its already developed institutional character. The Syrian Orthodox Church inherited the ecclesial structure of the Eastern churches with its Patriarch in Syria. The Roman Catholic Church carried with it the Roman and papal structures into South Asian church life. Although there were conflicts between the Syrian Christians and Roman Catholics over understandings of ecclesial and institutional governance, Roman Catholics maintained their linkage with the Roman institutional structure. The Protestants, in their denominational multiplicity, also imposed their modes of institutional structure and governance on their own denominational churches in South Asia. One can see within India, for example, a variety of forms of governance and institutionalization. While some of the major Protestant churches, such as the Church of South India, the Church of North India, the Methodist Church in India, and most Indian Lutheran churches, operate with the tradition of having bishops as the presiding officers of their churches, others function with the autonomy of congregations over issues of governance. The institutional character of the Christian churches in India, especially the functioning of the church as a voluntary association with membership, has been a contrast and a challenge to the ordering of Hindu religious life, which is independent of clearly defined institutional structure.

Much more noticeable are the institutions that are linked to the work of the churches in South Asia. These are schools, colleges, hospitals, and social service agencies organized and maintained by Christian churches. Let us look at the case of India. The early part of the nineteenth century saw the founding of several colleges throughout India due to the work of missionaries, chief of which were Alexander Duff in Calcutta, John Wilson in Bombay (Mumbai), whose work led to the establishment of Wilson College, John Anderson in Madras (Chennai) who founded the Madras Christian College, and Stephen Hyslop in Nagpur. While these colleges were admitting only male students, there were separate colleges founded for women as well, notable among them being Women's Christian College in Madras, Isabella Thoburn College in Lucknow, and Lady Doak College in Madurai. Roman Catholic missions were also involved in the founding of several colleges and schools throughout India. Notable among them are Loyola College in Madras, St. Xavier's College in Bombay, and St. Xavier's College in Calcutta. It should be noted that hundreds of elementary, middle, and high schools were founded throughout India by the Christian churches in India. There were varying perceptions about the relationship between these educational institutions and the evangelistic task of the churches. Some missionaries, like Alexander Duff, saw the educational project as a potential way to convert Hindus to the Christian faith although, in reality, Hindus who were educated in Christian schools and colleges did not necessarily abandon the Hindu religion to turn to the Christian faith.[21] Others saw the educational mission simply as a duty of love and care. Even today, Christian communities in India are heavily invested in this form of educational service. In addition, there is an increasing interest in offering non-formal education to the poor in hopes of raising their sociopolitical consciousness to initiate change and liberation.

Organized medical missions are a phenomenon of the nineteenth and twentieth century missionary activity in India. The American Board of Commissioners for Foreign Missions sent John Scudder, the first of many medical missionaries, to Madras in 1836. More medical missionaries followed and hospitals and medical and nursing schools began to appear throughout India. Some of the well-known schools are the Christian Medical College in Vellore, and the North India School of Medicine for Christian Women in Ludhiana, Punjab. The Christian Medical Association of India is currently an organization that functions as a clearing house for all Christian medical institutions and Christian medical personnel.

One of the unique features of South Asian Christianity is the establishment of ashrams—both in India and Sri Lanka—patterned after the Hindu ascetic and monastic traditions. Ashrams were places where the residents practiced regular and intense spiritual discipline, followed a simple lifestyle, and adopted Hindu cultural and religious patterns in worship, prayer, and architecture. The twentieth century saw the emergence of several ashrams, both Protestant and Roman Catholic. Two doctors in South India, Dr. Jesudason and Dr. Forrester-Paton, founded the *Christukula Ashram* in Tamilnadu in 1921. In the same year, Anglican missionary J. C. Winslow established an ashram at Pune that was later renamed as Christa Prema Seva Sangh in 1934. There were other ashrams associated with the work of people such as Stanley Jones, an American Methodist missionary and Bishop Peckenham Walsh of the Anglican Church in India. The Roman Catholics had their own share of ashrams as well. Notable among Roman Catholic ashrams is the Saccidananda Ashram, near Trichy in Tamilnadu, established by the work of Father Jules Monchanin in 1950. He was succeeded by Father Bede Griffiths. Bold experiments in Hindu-Christian spirituality were then, and continue to be, attempted and maintained even today.

Christian programming

The fourth marker of Christian presence in South Asia today is the increasing number of Christian programs telecast through cable TV. Any visitor to India who switches on the TV and surfs through the channels cannot miss Christian channels such as Angel TV, God TV, Jesus the King TV, Asirvatham TV, and so on. In addition to these are programs telecast on other commercial channels. Christian programs can be heard over the radio stations as well.

Most of these programs, while offering teaching to the Christian public, aim mostly at presenting the good news in Jesus the Christ to the viewers and inviting them to join the Christian faith. Using local resources to spread Christian faith has been there since the arrival of Protestant missionaries. Most of the villages in South Tirunelveli area, for example, were first approached by Christians from other parts of Tamilnadu even before a foreign missionary arrived to consolidate congregations and churches.

During the twentieth century, there has been intentional founding of missionary societies following the pattern of the missionary societies that engaged in evangelistic outreach in India, as far as the structure is concerned, while maintaining a clear commitment to use only resources—money and personnel—from within India. In 1903, the Indian Missionary Society of Tinnevelly was started by V. S. Azariah and it sent missionaries to Andhra Pradesh to work in the Dornakal area. Azariah, who went as a missionary himself to Dornakal, later became the first Indian bishop to be ordained by the Church of England. In 1905, a pan-Indian missionary society, the National Missionary Society (Bharat Christya Sevak Samaj), was started as well. Both of these missionary societies are very active even today. Since the founding of these missionary societies, many more such societies have come into operation, working within India using Indian resources alone. The Indian Evangelical Mission, Friends Missionary Prayer Band, and Church Growth Movement are some of those new societies.

While the developments in media and information technology have helped Christians to launch into TV and the Internet, the eighteenth and nineteenth century missionary methods for the expansion of Christianity are still alive in local settings. Preaching at street corners, distributing religious literature, such as tracts and booklets, and visiting homes, hospitals, and institutions for a one-to-one sharing of Christian faith are still employed as methods for spreading Christian faith. All these traditional and modern methods of missionary work have come under great suspicion as coercive and questionable. This came to a big crisis when Christian evangelists engaged in proselytism in Sri Lanka among people who were affected by the tsunami in 2004. As mentioned earlier, most attempts to curb unethical conversions are generated precisely by such missionary activities during times of calamity, illness, and loss.

South Asian Christianity: Current approaches

The status of Dalits

Current concerns in South Asian Christianity revolve around two movements. The first movement is an attempt to redefine or recover the Christian faith as that which aims at and works for the liberation of those who are exploited and oppressed by the larger society. The movement to uplift the political, economic, and social situation of Christian Dalits in India is a supreme example of such a movement. Similarly, the Christian Workers' Fellowship which began in 1958 in

Sri Lanka is liberation oriented. The Dalit movement in India has grown over the last thirty years. As noted earlier, the majority of Christians belong to the lowest castes in the caste system. Among them a significantly large proportion of persons belong to the so-called "untouchables," who were named by Mahatma Gandhi as *harijans*, meaning "people of God." In the Constitution of India, they are referred to as "Scheduled Castes," for the purposes of affirmative action. In recent times, the scheduled castes have claimed the name Dalit for themselves. The word "Dalit" means "oppressed" or "crushed."

Dalit Christians have faced two major challenges. First, despite converting to Christianity, their status within the Christian churches had not changed significantly. Ecclesial power remained largely in the hands of the non-Dalits among the Christians. Today, Dalit Christians have made noticeable progress in the sharing of power within the churches' hierarchies. Moreover, theological thinking and ecclesial practice within churches had been historically controlled and shaped by the ethos of Christians other than Dalits. Therefore, a concerted effort is afoot within churches to develop Dalit theologies and Dalit ecclesial practices. In their theological task, Dalit Christians have discovered an agenda that "includes interacting theologically with the little theological traditions of Dalit Christians, with other theological traditions within the Indian Church, and with Dalits who do not share their Christian convictions."[22] Some of the leading figures in the development of Dalit theology are Arvind Nirmal, M. E. Prabhakar, James Massey, Sathianathan Clarke, and V. Devasahayam. There have been musician–theologians, such as Theophilus Appavoo of Tamilnadu Theological Seminary at Madurai, who promoted the distinctive musical traditions of Dalit Christians.[23] The second challenge for Dalit Christians is the claiming of the compensatory discrimination available to Dalits within the Indian Constitution. The Constitution of India, while affirming the equality of all citizens before law irrespective of caste, class, race, religion, or place of birth, offers states the right to make special provisions for the upliftment of scheduled castes and scheduled tribes. Dalits who became Christian were not included in this provision, on the grounds that Dalits no longer belonged to the caste system once they accepted Christianity as their religion. Currently, Dalit Christians, with the support of other Christians, are asking the Government to redress this particular disparity.

In meeting these two challenges, Dalits have made considerable progress. As Webster notes,

> The most significant development during this period of Dalit Christian history has not been the emergence of a new Dalit Christian elite ... Instead this period has witnessed the emergence of Dalit Christians from the obscurity in both Church and society ... Even without political reservations, Dalit Christians have become increasingly active both in the wider Dalit movement and in their own movement for equal justice. In this process some of the barriers dividing Christians from other Dalits have been removed and there are signs of the two coming closer together in a shared struggle for equality.[24]

Indigenous churches in India

The second movement within modern Indian Christianity is the rise of indigenous churches in India. Of course, the Eastern Orthodox churches are indigenous churches in that they were dependent right from the beginning on Indian financial resources. The Mar Thoma Church, too, is truly indigenous without any links to traditions outside of India. Protestant churches, however, depended heavily on Western Christian churches and their support. The founding of indigenous churches began as early as the nineteenth century among Protestants. "One remarkable Hindu believer in Christ at Madras was O. Kandaswamy Chetti, founder of the Fellowship of the Followers of Jesus, who openly confessed his faith in Christ as the only Saviour but declined baptism."[25] Arumainayagam Sattampillai of South Tamilnadu founded the Indian Church of the Only Savior (popularly known as the Hindu-Christian community) in 1857 in protest against Western missionary domination. K. E. Abraham founded the Indian Pentecostal Church of God, around 1930. Some of the contemporary examples of indigenous churches include the Apostolic Christian Assembly, founded by Pastor G. Sundaram, the movement around K. Subba Rao in Andhra Pradesh, the New Life Fellowship in Bombay, Agape Fellowship churches in the state of Punjab, and the Isupanthi movement in North Gujarat.[26]

Much more prominent today are churches and denominations (often known or claimed as non-denominational) started and maintained by individual charismatic preachers. Some of these preachers literally ape the charismatic TV evangelists of the United States of America. Some among them have lively connections with those evangelists in the West. One can see billboards announcing "Revival Meetings," "Evangelistic Crusades," or "Faith-Healing Campaigns" in which pictures of Indian and American preachers appear together. Most often, these independent churches are peopled by those who once were members of mainline churches and those who while keeping their membership with the mainline churches attend worship services at these independent churches.

South Asian Christianity and gender relations

Most South Asian communities are gender-segregated. This means men and women congregate separately and avoid any physical contact with the other gender outside marriage. The Christian missionaries understood this ethos of South Asia, respected it, and channeled their work accordingly. When the early Christians gathered in the church for worship, men sat on one side of the aisle and the women on the other. Even today in most rural churches and in some urban ones, too, men and women sit separately. When schools and colleges were started by the missionaries, except at the elementary school level, students of all other levels studied separately in separate institutions such Boys' High School, Girls' High School, Men's College, and Women's College. Such gender segregation was accepted as normal by all Christian institutions, even though there were a few exceptions. The patriarchal arrangement of family life was kept intact even after people embraced the Christian faith.

Yet the very business of educating boys and girls without any difference brought a significant change in the gender relations within South Asian Christian settings. Women took advantage of their educational opportunities and brought a new level of acceptance of their worth as persons in a subtle way. Eliza Kent's study of the conversion of women to the Christian faith in South India shows both the radical freedom and dignity that Christian women enjoyed on the one side and the sliding back to new forms of patriarchal arrangement on the other. Christianity did bring with it a fresh acceptance of and respect for widows within the church. For example, in India widowhood was seen as the worst that could happen to a woman to the extent that in some communities widows were expected to jump into the fire where their husband's corpse was being cremated. This practice is called *sati* or *suttee*. In such a setting, widows in the churches enjoyed a high level of dignity and respect. It is interesting to note that the first convert to Christian faith from the Tirunelveli area was a young Brahmin widow who was rescued from the possibility of *sati*.[27] She is celebrated as the mother of the church and the little chapel she built for herself has become a shrine and a pilgrimage center.

Women's leadership in the life of the churches in South Asia has come a long way even though it has not risen to the level of gender equality at all levels. Only in recent decades have the mainline churches decided to ordain women to the ministry of the church. Yet a number of Indian Christian women, both lay and clergy, have offered theological leadership in India, including Panditha Ramabai, Vandana Mathaji, Aruna Gnanadason, Gabrielle Dietrich, Leelamma Athyal, Lalrinawmi Ralte, Evangeline Rajkumar and others. Mukti Barton, a theologian from Bangladesh, is worthy of note here. In Pakistan the list includes Ann Mary Clement, Christine Amjad-Ali, Jennifer Jag Jivan, and several others. Shanti Abeyasingha, Ranjini Rebera, Damayanthi Niles, and Chitra Fernando are some of the women theologians in Sri Lanka.

South Asian Christians in the diaspora

South Asian Christians who migrated to other nations, especially the Arabian Peninsula, Europe, and North America have established their own Christian congregations wherever they went. Let us look at the case of Indian Christians. Since Indian Christians speak a wide variety of languages, the diaspora communities have gathered as language-based Christian congregations outside India. Few studies have yet been undertaken to describe and understand the nature of Indian Christianity within the diaspora communities. A major work on this subject is *Christian Pluralism in the United States: The Indian Immigrant Experience* by Raymond Williams (Cambridge: Cambridge University Press, 1996). There are Indian Christian congregations in most of the major cities in the United States of America, such as New York, Boston, Houston, and Atlanta. These cities have several Indian Christian congregations, each of which is organized around either a common language or a common ecclesial tradition. For example, an India Catholic Association of America was informally organized in 1979 and then incorporated in 1980. The single organization served Indians of all three rites (Syro-Malabar, Syro-Malankara, and Latin) until 1982, when the Malankara Catholic Church was founded and the other groups began to meet separately.[28]

All the three traditions have established parishes throughout the United States of America. Protestants from India have their own churches according to their particular ecclesial traditions. The Church of South India bishops authorized extra-territorial parishes in 1975, and have at times supported those parishes with ministerial personnel. Other church groups from India such as Brethren, Pentecostals and others, have established their own parishes in the United States of America. Similar patterns of Indian Christian parishes occur in Britain, Canada, and several of the Arab nations, as well.

Eastern Orthodox Christians from India are much more organized in the United States of America than Roman Catholics and Protestants from India. In 1979, the Malankara Orthodox Diocese of North America and Europe was established. In 1988, the Mar Thoma Diocese of North America was established. Other Orthodox churches in India have organized missions and dioceses for their members who have emigrated to other countries in the West.

One of the problems that immigrant Indian Christians face outside India is the practice of their peculiarly Indian Christian faith in a culture other than that which has sustained their own Christian existence. Therefore, Indian Christians face the double challenge of keeping their Christian faith and their Indian cultural ethos together in a foreign land. New immigrants play an important role in maintaining the Indian and Christian sides together in the life of Indian Christians abroad. This is true of other South Asian Christian groups, too.

Academic approaches

South Asian Christianity has been the subject of study almost exclusively among Church historians and missiologists for a long time in the West. Although South Asian Christianity has contributed greatly to the study of religions through the work of several missionary scholars, historians of religion have not paid much attention to the phenomenon of South Asian Christianity. For example, Ziegenbalg, the first Protestant missionary to India, studied the Hindu tradition with care and published an important work, titled *The Genealogy of the South Indian Gods*. Other missionary scholars engaged in the translation of Hindu scriptures and other Indian literature to enable Western scholars of religion to understand the religious traditions of India. G. U. Pope's translation of *Tiruvacagam*, a Tamil Shaivite devotional poem, illustrates this as well.

European missionaries began the tradition of studying Indian Christianity as a separate religious phenomenon in India. Bror Tiliander's *Christian and Hindu Terminology: A Study in Their Mutual Relations with Special Reference to the Tamil Area* (Uppsala, 1974), C. G. Diehl's work, titled *Church and Shrine: Intermingling Patterns of Culture in the Life of Some Christian Groups in South India* (Uppsala, 1965), and the research on village Christians in Andhra Pradesh conducted by P. Y. Luke and John B. Carman, titled *Village Christians and Hindu Culture: Study of a Rural Church in Andhra Pradesh, South India* (London: Lutterworth Press, 1968) are supreme examples of such work by missionaries.

In recent times, there has been a growing interest among historians of religions in engaging Indian Christianity as a religious phenomenon in its own right and not just an extension of the Western missionary enterprise. The Church History Association of India has been influenced by the discipline of history of religions in such a way that extensive discussions were held on the importance of choosing the phrase "History of Christianity in India" rather than "Indian Church History." More and more scholars in the West, in India, and elsewhere are turning their attention to Indian Christianity. In the last ten years several books have been published studying Indian Christianity from historical, ethnographic, and sociological angles. These works include: Susan Bayly, *Saints, Goddesses, and Kings: Muslims and Christians in South Indian Society, 1700–1900* (Cambridge: Cambridge University Press, 1989), Susan B. Harper, *In the Shadow of the Mahatma: Bishop V. S. Azariah and the Travails of Christianity in British India* (Grand Rapids, MI: W. B. Eerdmans Publishing Company, 2000), Dennis Hudson, *Protestant Origins in India: Tamil Evangelical Christians in India, 1706–1835* (Grand Rapids, MI: W. B. Eerdmans, 2000), Corinne G. Dempsey, *Kerala Christian Sainthood: Collisions of Culture and Worldview in South India* (Oxford: Oxford University Press, 2001), Robert E. Frykenberg, *Christians and Missionaries in India: Cross-Cultural Communication since 1500 with Special Reference to Caste, Conversion, and Colonialism* (Grand Rapids, MI: W. B. Eerdmans, 2003), and Eliza F. Kent, *Converting Women: Gender and Protestant Christianity in Colonial South India* (Oxford: Oxford University Press, 2004).

Discussion questions

1   In all the countries in South Asia, Christianity is the religion of a negligible minority. In what ways does Christianity situate itself with ease and comfort in such a setting? What kind of negotiation is required in its beliefs and practices?
2   What are the effects of the processes of globalization on South Asian Christianity? Are there indicators of these processes supporting and reinforcing a theology that measures religiosity with prosperity?

Key terms

Apostle—Each of the twelve disciples of Jesus, or an important early Christian teacher, such as St. Thomas the Apostle
Dalit—"Oppressed"; the name by which those on the lower rungs of the Hindu caste system identify themselves

ecumenical—Promoting unity among the world's Christian churches

Indian Eucharist Liturgy—A 1985 attempt to conduct the Christian worship service in an authentic Indian style, including: Entry (*pravesa*), Awakening (*prabodha*), Recalling and Offering (*smarana-samarpana*), Sharing in the Body and Blood of Christ (*darsana*), and Blessing (*preshana*)

Jesuit—A member of the Society of Jesus, a Roman Catholic monastic order founded by St. Ignatius Loyola, St. Francis Xavier and others in the mid-sixteenth century. St. Francis Xavier (1506–52), a Jesuit priest, missionized in India.

Messiah—Christ, the anointed and anticipated one

Syrian Christians—Christians in India who trace their heritage to St. Thomas the Apostle. This community took on an indigenous character by adapting itself to the caste-based arrangement of Indian social reality; the word "Syrian" came to denote both Eastern Orthodox Christianity and a sub-caste (*jati*) within the larger caste system (*varna dharma*).

Vedagama—A combination of *veda* and *agama*, the two major scriptural corpuses in Hinduism; the name was used by early Protestant missionaries to describe the Christian Bible to converts. The Bible has also been called the "fifth Veda," relating the Bible to the legend that the fifth Veda of the Hindus was lost in antiquity.

Notes

1 John C. England, Jose Kuttianimattathil, John M. Prior, Lily A. Quintos, David Suh Kwang Sun, and Janice Wickeri (eds). *Asian Christian Theologies: A Research Guide to Authors, Movements, Sources,* Vol. I Asia Region, South Asia, Austral Asia. Maryknoll, NY: Orbis Books, 2002, p. 461.

2 The beliefs and practices among Roman Catholics in India are treated extensively by authors such as Selva J. Raj and Corinne Dempsey, for example Selva J. Raj and Corinne G. Dempsey, *Popular Christianity in India: Riting Between the Lines.* Albany, NY: SUNY Press, 2002.

3 A. M. Mundadan, *History of Christianity in India: From the Beginning Up to the Middle of the Sixteenth Century,* Vol. I, Bangalore: Church History Association of India, 1984, p. 64.

4 Cyril Bruce Firth, *An Introduction to Indian Church History,* Revised edition, Madras: The Christian Literature Society, 1998 [1976], p. 51.

5 David Barrett, George T. Kurian and Todd M. Johnson (eds.), *World Christian Encyclopedia,* Vol. I, Oxford: Oxford University Press, 2001, p. 363.

6 Corinne G. Dempsey, *Kerala Christian Sainthood: Collisions of Culture and Worldview in South India,* Oxford: Oxford University Press, 2001, pp. 5–6.

7 Joseph Thekkedath, *History of Christianity in India: From the Middle of the Sixteenth Century to the End of the Seventeenth Century,* Vol. II, Bangalore: Church History Association of India, 1982, p. 75.

8 Jyoti Sahi, *Holy Ground, A New Approach to the Mission of the Church in India,* Christian Conference of Asia and Asian Christian Art Association, 1998.

9 Julius Lipner and George Gispert-Sauch (eds.). *The Writings of Brahmabandhab Upadhyay,* Vol. I, Bangalore: United Theological College, 1991, pp. 24–5.

10 M. K. Kuriakose, *A History of Christianity in India: Source Materials,* Delhi, India: Indian Society for Promoting Christian Knowledge, 1999, p. 118.

11 D. Dennis Hudson, *Protestant Origins in India: Tamil Evangelical Christians, 1706–1835,* Grand Rapids, MI: W. B. Eerdmans, 2000, pp. 182ff.

12 Duncan B. Forrester, *Caste and Christianity: Attitudes and Policies on Caste of Anglo-Saxon Protestant Missions in India*, London: Curzon Press, 1980, p. 14.
13 Forrester, *Caste and Christianity*, pp. 110–14.
14 For a detailed discussion of the painting of Jesus by Indian artists, see Richard W. Taylor, *Jesus in Indian Paintings*, Madras: Christian Literature Society, 1975.
15 Susan Bayly, *Saints, Goddesses, and Kings: Muslims and Christians in South India, 1700–1900*, Cambridge: Cambridge University Press, 1989, p. 253.
16 Hugald Grafe, *History of Christianity in India, Vol. IV, Part 2: Tamil Nadu in the Nineteenth and Twentieth Centuries*, Bangalore: Church History Association of India, 1990, pp. 165–6.
17 Stephen Neill, *A History of Christianity in India, The Beginning to AD 1707*, Cambridge: Cambridge University Press, 1984, p. 241.
18 Abbe J. A. Dubois, *Letters on the State of Christianity in India, etc.*, ed. Sharda Paul, New Delhi: Associated Publishing Press, 1977, pp. 65–8.
19 Robin H. S. Boyd, *An Introduction to Indian Christian Theology*, Revised edition, Delhi: Indian Society for Promoting Christian Knowledge, 1989 [1975], pp. 15–16.
20 R. H. S. Boyd, *An Introduction to Indian Christian Theology*, p. 158.
21 C. B. Firth, *An Introduction to Indian Church History*, pp. 182–5.
22 John C. B. Webster, *A History of the Dalit Christians in India*, San Francisco, CA: Mellen Research University Press, 1992, p. 218.
23 Zoe C. Sherinian, *The Indigenization of Tamil Christian Music: Folk Music as a Liberative Transmission System*, Ann Arbor, MI: UMI Dissertation Series, 2006.
24 J. C. B. Webster, *A History of the Dalit Christians in India*, pp. 176–7.
25 Roger E. Hedlund, "Indian Instituted Churches: Indigenous Christianity Indian Style," *Mission Studies* 16:1 (1999): 16–42, quote from p. 31.
26 R. E. Hedlund, "Indian Instituted Churches," pp. 33–6.
27 Eliza Kent, *Converting Women: Gender and Protestant Christianity in Colonial South India*, Oxford: Oxford University Press, 2004, pp. 31ff.
28 Raymond B. Williams, *Christian Pluralism in the United States: The Indian Immigrant Experience*, Cambridge: Cambridge University Press, 1996, p. 144.

Recommended resources

Barrett, David, George T. Kurian, and Todd M. Johnson, (eds). *World Christian Encyclopedia, Vol. I*. Oxford: Oxford University Press, 2001.
Dempsey, Corinne G. *Kerala Christian Sainthood: Collisions of Culture and Worldview in South India*. Oxford: Oxford University Press, 2001.
England, John C., Jose Kuttianimattathil, John M. Prior, Lily A. Quintos, David Suh Kwang Sun, and Janice Wickeri (eds). *Asian Christian Theologies: A Research Guide to Authors, Movements, Sources,* Vol. I Asia Region, South Asia, Austral Asia. Maryknoll, NY: Orbis Books, 2002.
Hudson, D. Dennis. *Protestant Origins in India: Tamil Evangelical Christians, 1706–1835*. Grand Rapids, MI: W. B. Eerdmans, 2000.
Neill, Stephen. *Story of the Christian Church in India and Pakistan*. Grand Rapids, MI: W. B. Eerdmans, 1970.
Neill, Stephen. *A History of Christianity in India: The Beginning to AD 1707*. Cambridge: Cambridge University Press, 1984.
Raj, Selva J., and Corinne Dempsey. *Popular Christianity in India: Riting Between the Lines*. Albany, NY: SUNY Press, 2002.
Thangaraj, M. Thomas. "The History and Teaching of the Hindu Christian Community Commonly Called Nattu Sabai in Tirunelveli." *Indian Church History Review* 5:1 (1971): 43–68.

Thangaraj, M. Thomas. "Religious Pluralism, Dialogue and Asian Christian Responses." In Sebastian C. H. Kim (ed.) *Christian Theology in Asia.* Cambridge: Cambridge University Press, 2008, pp. 157–78.

Webster, John C. B. *A History of the Dalit Christians in India.* San Francisco, CA: Mellen Research University Press, 1992.

Williams, Raymond Brady. *Christian Pluralism in the United States: The Indian Immigrant Experience.* Cambridge: Cambridge University Press, 1996.

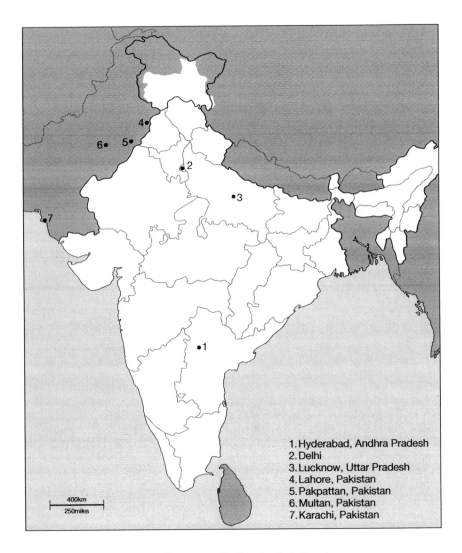

1. Hyderabad, Andhra Pradesh
2. Delhi
3. Lucknow, Uttar Pradesh
4. Lahore, Pakistan
5. Pakpattan, Pakistan
6. Multan, Pakistan
7. Karachi, Pakistan

400km
250miles

Map 7 Prominent places in Islam as practiced in South Asia today

7 Islam in South Asia

Practicing tradition today

Karen G. Ruffle

Introduction

In the eighteenth century, the poet Ghulam 'Ali of Bilgram, also known by his pen name "Azad," extolled India as a "sacred Islamic land," where Adam descended from Heaven, and the religious sciences have flourished.[1] Within less than a century of the Prophet Muhammad's death in 632 CE, the Indian subcontinent absorbed Islam as Arab Muslims spread their religion through military expansion, trade, and mysticism. Islamic doctrine and practice stress a commitment to social justice, and belief in God's uniqueness as Creator and Lord of the Day of Judgment. Particular emphasis is placed on following the "straight path" (*sirat al-mustaqim*) exemplified by the lived example of the Prophet Muhammad. The global Muslim population is 1.57 billion, of which more than 480 million Muslims live in the South Asian countries of Pakistan, India, and Bangladesh. Approximately 15 percent of India's population is Muslim (160 million) making it the third most populous Muslim nation in the world. Almost half of India's Muslims are found in the North Indian states of Uttar Pradesh, Bihar, and West Bengal, although Jammu and Kashmir, Lakshadweep, and Assam are notable for their significant Muslim populations. Significant South Asian Muslim emigrant communities can be found throughout the world, particularly in the United Kingdom, the United States of America, Canada, and the Persian Gulf, where most are economic migrants who spend a number of years working while their families remain behind at home. Labor migration to the Gulf has transformed the architectural, sartorial, and religious landscape in South Asian Muslim communities, as new homes and consumer goods (particularly electronics) proliferate, and religious beliefs and identities have been influenced by Wahhabi and other reformist ideologies.

Islam in South Asia: Identity

Beginnings of Islam

"There is no god but God, and Muhammad is the Messenger of God." Five times each day the call to prayer (*adhan*) resonates through Muslim localities throughout South Asia, calling the faithful to prayer. Five times daily Muslims

are reminded that there is only one God, that the Muhammad was the final recipient of the prophetic message, and that the Qur'an is the final book of law received by humanity. Islamic doctrine centers on God's uniqueness and incomparability to any other divine figure (*tawhid*), which is affirmed by the absolute prohibition of associating any being or attribute to God (*shirk*). The Qur'an's incessant affirmations of God's uniqueness and warnings against worshipping other deities, the daily rituals structuring Muslim life, and the lived tradition (Sunnah) of the Prophet Muhammad emphatically affirm the notion of *tawhid* in God's role as Creator (al-Khaliq) and Judge (al-Hakam) of humanity. The opening chapter of the Qur'an, *surat al-fatiha*, encapsulates the fundamental aspects of Islamic theology and doctrine:

> In the name of Allah, Most Gracious, Most Merciful.
> Praise be to Allah, the Cherisher and Sustainer of the Worlds;
> Most Gracious, Most Merciful;
> Master of the Day of Judgment.
> You do we worship, and Your aid do we seek.
> Show us the straight way.
> The way of those on whom You have bestowed Your Grace, those whose (portion) is not wrath, and who do not go astray.
>
> Qur'an 1:1–7[2]

Although not the first revelation that Muhammad received, the opening chapter of the Qur'an succinctly outlines the fundamentals of Islam: God is unique; the Creator of the universe and humanity; the Lord of the Day of Judgment; and the Merciful source of guidance for living a good life that is centered on God-consciousness (*taqwa*).

God's first revelation was disclosed in 610 CE to a middle-aged man named Muhammad ibn 'Abdallah. A contemplative man, Muhammad ascended the stony mountains surrounding his hometown of Mecca several times each year to meditate and retreat from the world. A trader by profession, Muhammad traveled throughout the Middle East where he met a diversity of Christians, Jews, and Zoroastrians; oftentimes their conversations focused on spiritual matters, especially the notion of monotheism. These conversations piqued Muhammad's curiosity and as the years passed, he grew increasingly contemplative about the meaning of the universe and the nature of creation.

Muhammad was also deeply troubled by the precarious existence that confronted the most vulnerable people of Mecca, particularly widows, orphans, and the poor. In the century before Muhammad's birth in 570 CE, Mecca emerged as an important pilgrimage and trading center in the Arabian Peninsula. Mecca was situated along north–south and east–west trade routes connecting Europe, the Near East, Africa, and South Asia. The city of Mecca grew as tribes, most notably the Quraysh, settled and abandoned their nomadic lifestyle. As a result of the Quraysh becoming sedentary, the social fabric of Mecca became stratified along clan and socioeconomic lines. Widows, orphans, and those from less prestigious tribes and clans of the Quraysh lost the protection of their chiefs and experienced increasing vulnerability. Although born into the Quraysh, Muhammad was a member of the less wealthy Banu (clan) Hashem, which possessed high spiritual prestige for their role as the caretakers of the Ka`ba, where 360 of the tribes' icons were housed. Before his birth in 570 Muhammad's father `Abdallah died, and when he was five or six years old, his mother Amina fell ill and passed away. Orphaned, Muhammad was placed in the care of his grandfather for a few years before ultimately settling with his uncle Abu Talib, one of the custodians of the icons in the Ka`ba.

Before Muhammad's first revelation marking the advent of Islam and God's final message of monotheism, the Arab tribes were predominantly pagan. Warfare was endemic among the Arabs, who fought over water, pasturage, and to protect tribal honor. Despite constant warfare, a quarterly safe zone (*haram*) was set up in Mecca so that the tribes could come and propitiate their icons. Allah (the God) was the presiding deity overseeing all other tribal icons installed in the precinct of the black stone of the Ka`ba. Just as the Ka`ba was the focal point of worship for the Arab pagans so, too, it is in its direction that all Muslims pray five times daily and perform the *hajj* (pilgrimage). From revenue generated by pilgrims during the quarterly cessation of warfare, the Quraysh became increasingly wealthy and progressively less concerned for the welfare of Mecca's vulnerable.

When Muhammad retreated to the cave on Mount Hira around 21 Ramadan in 610 CE, he had no idea that what he was about to experience would produce the second largest religion in the world. While in the cave Muhammad meditated on the situation in Mecca and the meaning of his life, which was interrupted by a pressure that was exerted on his chest so intense that he felt he could not breathe. As this weight bore down on Muhammad's body, a booming voice cried out, "*Iqra!*" (Recite!). Terrified, Muhammad declared that he could not recite. Again this supernatural being cried out, "*Iqra!*" This happened three times, and then Muhammad received his first revelation from Allah through the Angel Gabriel:

> Proclaim! in the name of your Lord and Cherisher, Who created—
> Created man, out of a (mere) clot of congealed blood:
> Proclaim! And your Lord is Most Bountiful,
> He Who taught (the use of) the Pen,
> Taught man that which he did not know.
>
> Qur'an 96:1–5

Terrified, Muhammad left the mountain and returned home to his wife Khadijah in Mecca. Hearing her husband's message, Khadijah became the first convert to Islam.

Muhammad was no longer an ordinary man, concerned with the trade caravans he led for his wife Khadijah, a shrewd and well-respected businesswoman. With this first revelation he became a Messenger (*rasul*) and a prophet (*nabi*). Muhammad was a Messenger because he was given the Qur'an, which is not only a book of revelation, but of law as well. Muhammad was also a prophet, a special individual chosen by God to explain the revelation and to serve as a living model of the ethics, laws, and doctrine set forth in the Qur'an.

With this revelation received by Muhammad, a new religion was brought forth, which focused on absolute submission to God: Islam. A Muslim is one who submits to the will of God. Word slowly spread about this new message that Muhammad was receiving from God and a community of Muslims emerged in Mecca. The Islamic message of belief in God's singular uniqueness (*tawhid*), and the role of Divine Will in the creation and judgment of humanity appealed to many of Mecca's most vulnerable inhabitants including women and the poor. The social message of the Qur'an spoke to the rapid changes that had taken place in Mecca with the breakdown of the traditional network of welfare and support that the tribes provided their members:

> Your Guardian-Lord has not forsaken you, nor is He displeased.
> And verily the Hereafter will be better for you than the present.
> And soon will your Guardian-Lord give you (that wherewith) you shall be well-pleased.
> Did He not find you an orphan and give you shelter (and care)?
> And He found you wandering, and He gave you guidance.
> And He found you in need, and made you independent.
> Therefore, do not treat the orphan with harshness,
> Nor repulse the petitioner (unheard);
> But the Bounty of your Lord—rehearse and proclaim!
>
> Qur'an 93:3–11

In these verses from one of the early Meccan revelations received by Muhammad, God reminds the Prophet of his own precarious existence as an orphan, who attained a degree of financial success through his wife Khadija's business. These verses affirm God's mercy and generosity for all of his creation.

The Quraysh of Mecca heard Muhammad's message of one God and they regarded it as, at the least, the imagination of a man in the middle of an existential crisis, and eventually as the ravings of a madman or soothsayer (*kahin*), which the Qur'an clearly refutes: "Therefore you proclaim the praises (of your Lord): for by the Grace of your Lord, you are no (vulgar) soothsayer, nor you are one possessed" (52:29). In the preceding century the Quraysh had amassed considerable wealth and power as Mecca was established as a center of trade and pilgrimage. Muhammad's new message of God's singularity threatened the Quraysh's security, and as more Meccans converted to Islam, their opposition grew increasingly violent.

For a twelve-year period following Muhammad's first revelation in 610, the community (*ummah*) of Muslims slowly grew, as did their persecution by the Quraysh. The year 619 is referred to in Islamic history as the "year of sorrows": Muhammad's wife and companion Khadijah died, as did his uncle Abu Talib, who never converted to Islam and remained a custodian of the icons in the Ka`ba. Two of Mecca's most highly regarded citizens were no longer alive and able to protect Muhammad from the Quraysh's persecution. From 619 until 622, the Quraysh were more public in their attacks on Muslims and more brazen in announcing their intention to kill Muhammad in order to put an end to this new religion that threatened their power, prestige, and livelihood in controlling the Ka'ba and pilgrimage trade.

In 622 the Muslim community was irrevocably changed when they migrated to Medina, a city located approximately 250 miles northwest of Mecca. This event is known as the *hijra* (migration) and it marks the beginning of Islamic history. In the three years following the year of sorrow, Muhammad searched for a safe haven for the Muslim community. The leaders of two Jewish tribes asked Muhammad to arbitrate a long-standing dispute, to which he agreed with the proviso that his Muslim community also be allowed to settle in the city and be protected. The leaders agreed and in small groups Muslims began migrating to Medina. On the night when the Quraysh planned to kill Muhammad, the Prophet escaped Mecca with his close Companion (*sahabi*; pl. *sahaba*) Abu Bakr. The Companions of the Prophet played a central role in the early history and development of Islam, for they comprised the first community of Muslims and served as primary transmitters of the *hadith* (reports about Muhammad's words and actions). The two men were tracked through the desert but were protected by God when they hid in a desert cave. In the night, a giant spider web was woven over the cave's opening and a pigeon roosted at its edge. This event is referred to in the Qur'an:

> If you help not (your Leader), (it is no matter): for God did indeed help him, when the Unbelievers drove him out: he had no more than one companion: they two were in the Cave, and he said to his companion, "Have no fear, for God is with us": then God sent down His peace upon him, and strengthened him with forces which you did not see, and humbled to the depths the word of the Unbelievers. But the word of God is exalted to the heights: for God is Exalted in might, Wise.
>
> Qur'an 9:40

The spider web covering the cave and Muhammad's successful migration to Medina affirms for Muslims the power of God's mercy for those who have submitted to Him, and for the truth of Islam.

After the *hijra*, Medina became a Muslim city and provided a safe environment for Islam to develop more fully and for the Muslim population to increase. The people of Medina came to be known as the "Helpers" (*ansar*), and the Muslims who migrated from Mecca were collectively referred to as the *muhajirun* (Emigrants). Although the Muslim community had left Mecca, the Quraysh remained determined to abolish Islam and its monotheistic message. Between 624 and 628, the Muslims and the Meccans fought a series of battles and the survival of the community was not always certain. In 628, the Muslims and Meccans fought the battle of Khaybar, which proved to be a decisive victory for Muhammad and Islam. The Treaty of Hudaybiyya was agreed to in 628 and was inspired by a revelation from God:

> Truly God did fulfill the vision of His Messenger: you shall enter the Sacred Mosque, if God wills, with minds secure, heads shaved, hair cut short, and

without fear. For He knew what you did not know, and He granted besides
this, a speedy recovery. Qur'an 48:27

Qur'an 48:27

In this revelation God instructs Muhammad and the Muslims to return on
pilgrimage to Mecca—not to worship the icons of the Ka`ba but, rather, to restore
the structure to its original form as God's house on earth by Abraham and his
son Isma`il.

In 630 Muhammad peacefully returned to Mecca and reclaimed the city for
Islam. The icons of the Ka`ba were destroyed and most of the Meccans converted
to Islam. Both sides lived up to the terms of the Treaty of Hudaybiyya and there
were no casualties. Muhammad's triumphal return to Mecca and the mass
conversion of the Meccans and other tribes throughout the Arabian Peninsula
assured the survival of the message of Islam. Muhammad lived his final two
years in Mecca, where he died in his bed following a brief illness in 632. These
last two years brought considerable numbers of Muslims into the *ummah*, or
global community of Muslims. With the rise of Islam, many of the old tribal
ways were sublimated, especially the basis of individual identity on one's clan
and tribe. The final revelation that Muhammad received in the months preceding
his death affirm the unity of Muslims as a religious community: the believers
are but a single brotherhood: "So make peace and reconciliation between your
two brothers; and fear God that you may receive mercy" (49:10). In the after-
math of Muhammad's death arose the question of succession: who would lead the
community of Muslims and what would be the nature and extent of that person's
authority?

Succeeding the Prophet Muhammad: Sunni and Shi`i origins

Muhammad was not only a prophet, he was also a family man and statesman.
Muhammad had navigated political crises, periodic tensions with the *ansar*
(Helpers) of Medina, and through his astute leadership and ability as a shrewd
negotiator, he brought tribes from the Arabian Peninsula and beyond within the
fold of Islam. When Muhammad died in 632 a debate erupted in the Muslim
community about who should be his successor. Should the next leader of the
Muslim community be an elder statesman (*shaykh*)? If so, should he be from
the *ansar* or *muhajirun* (Emigrants)? Perhaps the next leader should be one
of Muhammad's blood relations? As Muhammad's corpse was prepared for
burial, these questions dominated the conversations of the Muslims in Mecca
and beyond.

Several criteria were generally agreed upon in determining the appropriate
successor. Foremost was blood descent or tribal relationship with Muhammad;
second was the extent and depth of the individual's status as one of the
Companions (*sahaba*) of the Prophet. Finally, when one converted to Islam was
an important factor—someone who had not submitted to Islam at the beginning of Muhammad's prophetic mission was less qualified.[3] For the majority
of Muslims, these three criteria were sufficient for selecting Muhammad's

successor. Inevitably, rifts did emerge and individuals joined sides in hopes of seeing their tribal, political, and regional interests served.

One group of *ansar* elders gathered underneath the *saqifah* (portico) of the Banu Sa`idah clan to stake their claim that Sa`d ibn `Ubadah should be Muhammad's successor. They argued that without the *ansar*, the Meccans would have destroyed Muhammad and his religious community. Likewise, the *muhajirun* asserted their authority: as the first Muslims, the successor to Muhammad must therefore be a member of their community. Intervening in the dispute, Abu Bakr suggested that the *khalifah* (representative of God; political leader) come from the *muhajirun* and the *ansar* would serve in advisory and other administrative positions. Eventually, Muhammad's close Companion and father-in-law Abu Bakr was elected to be the first *khalifah* or vice-regent of the Muslim community.

The office of the *khalifah* was endowed with political and administrative power. The *khalifah* also served as the *imam* (leader) of the Friday (*jum`ah*) prayer, delivering a short lecture on a specific verse or theme from the Qur'an. The first four *khalifahs* were instrumental in establishing several important aspects of Islamic doctrine and ritual practice. During the caliphate of the first four *khalifahs,* Abu Bakr, `Umar, `Uthman, and `Ali, who are conventionally referred to by Sunni Muslims as the "Rightly Guided" (*Rashidun*), Islam grew exponentially in size as it spread from the Arabian Peninsula through North Africa and the Middle East.

For many in the community, Abu Bakr was the most appropriate choice to be Muhammad's successor. One of the earliest converts to Islam, it was Abu Bakr who had escaped with Muhammad and hid in the desert during the *hijra* in 622. Abu Bakr was an elderly man and highly respected, positive qualities in the ostensibly tribal ethos of seventh-century Mecca. Muhammad's marriage to Abu Bakr's daughter `A'isha further enhanced his status of having a blood relationship with the Prophet. Abu Bakr served as the first *khalifah* for a brief two-year period, and he died of natural causes in 634. Abu Bakr was the only of the *Rashidun khalifahs* who was not assassinated.

The caliphate of the second *khalifah*, `Umar ibn al-Khattab, ushered in a period of tremendous change for the nascent religion. `Umar was the first *khalifah* to assume the title Amir al-Mu'minin (Commander of the Faithful). It was he who consolidated and formalized such Islamic religious practices as how to perform *hajj* (pilgrimage to Mecca) and the rules for keeping and breaking the fast during the month of Ramadan, and he also established the legal permissibility and punishments for certain behaviors and crimes. Islamic history was given an official date of origin beginning in 622 with the *hijra* (migration). For this reason the Islamic calendar, which `Umar designated to be lunar, counts its first year from 622. Islamic dates are usually indicated with the suffix AH, Latin for *anno Hegirae* (in the year of the *hijra*). In 644 `Umar was stabbed by a Persian slave and he subsequently died of his wounds without having designated a successor.

`Umar's death caused a small crisis in the Muslim community, for as more people converted to Islam and the religion spread further away from Mecca and Medina, the office of the *khalifah* grew increasingly powerful. `Umar refused to appoint his successor, believing that it was the responsibility of a small governing council (*shura*) of Muslims to select the most appropriate man to become *khalifah*.

After much deliberation, `Uthman ibn `Affan, a member of the powerful Banu `Umayya clan was elected to be the third successor to Muhammad. `Uthman was Muhammad's son-in-law and, like Abu Bakr and `Umar who preceded him, was able to assert his claim to authority through blood relationship by marriage to the Prophet.

`Uthman's caliphate is portrayed in the Islamic historical record as the breaking point in which the *khalifah* served as a representative of Muhammad. Like Abu Bakr and `Umar before him, `Uthman chose an epithet to publicly proclaim his leadership mandate. `Uthman called himself *khalifat Allah* (God's envoy), and he claimed a degree of religious authority that neither of his predecessors possessed. During his twelve-year caliphate, which historians temporize as having six good and six bad years, `Uthman produced the official recension of the Qur'an. Because Muhammad received oral revelations from God over more than two decades, these qur'anic verses were not kept or ordered in a systematic fashion. Muhammad's Companions memorized the revelations that the Prophet recited to them, and they wrote these down on scraps of parchment, animal skins, and even on rocks (*suhuf*, singular *sahifa*). Each of the Companions and some of the Prophet's wives, including `A'isha, had their own collections (*mushaf*) of these loose pieces of written material. `Uthman sought to consolidate these thousands of versions of the Qur'an that were in circulation, and which could ultimately result in an Islam that would be doctrinally and dogmatically fractured. `Uthman ordered the collection of these *mushaf* and had them destroyed. Basing his official recension of the Qur'an on Abu Bakr's *mushaf*, the order and vocalization of the scripture was canonized less than two decades after Muhammad's death. This was the work of a man who believed that he was God's envoy (*khalifat Allah*).

Although Islam spread considerably to the West and especially the East during `Uthman's caliphate, not all Muslims looked favorably on his leadership. `Uthman was criticized for his nepotistic policies of installing relatives in positions of authority throughout the Islamic empire, where there was unlimited potential to amass wealth and power. Muslims grew increasingly disillusioned with `Uthman's leadership and his transgression of the caliphal boundary between religious and political power. In 656 `Uthman was besieged and assassinated in his house, again leaving the Muslim community without a clearly designated successor—a matter that would help to bring about the eventual emergence of the Sunni and Shi`i branches of Islam.

Following `Uthman's death, there was a struggle for power. During his caliphate, `Uthman appointed his cousin Mu`awiyah ibn Abi Sufyan governor of Syria. In the aftermath of `Uthman's death, Mu`awiyah declared himself *khalifah* and established his capital at Damascus. There was, however, another claimant to the title of *khalifah*: Muhammad's cousin and son-in-law. `Ali ibn Abi Talib was elected to be the fourth and final *Rashidun khalifah*, and he set up his capital in Kufa, Iraq, where he had a contingent of supporters. In addition to being the fourth *khalifah*, a small group of Muslims known as the *shi`at `Ali* (partisans of `Ali; the Shi`a) believed that `Ali was the rightful political and *spiritual* successor to Muhammad. The *shi`at `Ali* believed that there were clear signs from God and that Muhammad had explicitly designated `Ali to be his successor.

These partisans of `Ali asserted that Muhammad had appointed `Ali his successor during the Farewell Pilgrimage in 632 just before the Prophet died. Following the *hajj* Muhammad had traveled back from Mecca to Medina and stopped at Ghadir Khumm, a wellspring along the route through the desert. There, Muhammad gathered people together and declared that he was leaving behind two precious things for the Muslim community, namely the Qur'an and his progeny, that is, the people of his household (*ahl-e bait*). This event is referred to in Shi`i sources as the *hadith al-thaqalayn* (the tradition of the two weighty things). Muhammad then reaffirmed `Ali's authority, declaring "For whomever I am leader, `Ali is leader, too."

In an event known as the Incident of the Pen and the Paper, the Shi`a also asserted that upon Muhammad's deathbed he again designated `Ali to be his successor. According to Shi`i historical sources, Muhammad asked for a piece of paper and a pen so that he could put in writing his designation of `Ali to be his successor. Arguments broke out among those present, and Muhammad fell unconscious. Muhammad's Companion `Umar declared that the Prophet was unable to make clear decisions while ill and whatever he wrote down should be disregarded. Days later Muhammad died, and while `Ali and his wife (and Muhammad's daughter) Fatimah al-Zahra were preparing the Prophet's body for burial, the elders of the Muslim community appointed Abu Bakr *khalifah*. When `Ali did become *khalifah* in 657, he assumed political power during a period of instability for the Muslim community. The first civil war (*fitna*) was fought in 656 at the battle of Camel, which was instigated by `A'isha, Muhammad's wife and daughter of the first *khalifah* Abu Bakr. `A'isha was angry with `Ali for his unwillingness to avenge the death of `Uthman, with whom she was closely allied. The next year `Ali fought the battle of Siffin against Mu`awiyah, the *khalifah* of the nascent `Umayyad dynasty. On the morning of 19 Ramadan, while praying during the early hours in Kufa's main mosque, he was stabbed with a poison-tipped sword. Two days later `Ali died, marking the end of the *Rashidun* (Rightly Guided) caliphate.

For the *shi`at `Ali*, Muhammad's cousin and son-in-law was clearly designated through God's divinely inspired designation (*nass*). Aside from being *khalifah*, the Shi`a recognized `Ali as Imam, who possesses both political and spiritual power. The Imam possesses initiatic spiritual knowledge (`*ilm*) that allows him to understand the distinction between the external aspects of the Prophet's revelation and the hidden truths (*haqa'iq*) or mysteries of the Divine that are incomprehensible to average minds. The Imam leads the community and is able to instruct others regarding these deeper matters. According to the doctrine of the Imamate, one must be a blood descendant of the Prophet Muhammad through his daughter Fatimah al-Zahra and her husband `Ali. A succeeding Imam must be appointed by his predecessor through divinely inspired designation, which is based on the model of Muhammad designating `Ali to be his spiritual and political legatee.

The majority of the global Shi`i population is known as the Ithna `Ashari or "Twelvers," referring to the number of Imams who were sent to guide humanity. The twelfth Imam, al-Mahdi, has been missing in a state of occultation (*ghayba*) since the ninth century, and they believe that he will return to fight a cosmic battle of good and evil and will usher in a period of justice before the Day of Resurrection (*qiyamat*). A smaller group of Shi`a are known as the Isma`ilis (also known as the Khojas in South Asia), who believe that Ja`far al-Sadiq, the sixth Imam, appointed his son Isma`il to be his successor and not his other son Musa al-Kazim. Isma`il died before his father, and the majority of the Shi`a accepted Musa al-Kazim as the seventh Imam. The partisans of Isma`il believed that he was in hiding and would return. The Isma`ilis believe in an ongoing tradition of Imamate, and the current Aga Khan Karim Hussaini is the forty-sixth Imam to lead the community. South Asia is home to a significant portion of the world's Isma`ilis, particularly in Mumbai, Karachi, and the Hunza region of the Pakistani Himalayas. African countries such as Kenya and Tanzania, the United States of America, and Canada are also home to many Isma`ilis of South Asian descent.

Sacred literature

Qur'an

> Had We sent this as a Qur'an (in a language) other than Arabic, they would have said: "Why are not its verses explained in detail? What! (a Book) not in Arabic and (a Messenger) an Arab?" Say: "It is a guide and a healing to those who believe; and for those who do not believe, there is a deafness in their ears, and it is blindness in their (eyes): they are (as it were) being called from a place far distant!"
>
> Qur'an 41:44

The Qur'an was sent to Muhammad in the Arabic language and its message was sent to the polytheistic Arabs—the last community to receive God's revelation. Although God affirmed that his message was being sent in the Arabic language, the relevance of its message is not limited to Arabs. The fact that Islam spread so rapidly throughout North Africa, the Middle East, and into South Asia within a century of Muhammad's death indicates the universal appeal of the Qur'an's message of a unique God who created humanity as a sign of his mercy. As the Qur'an itself reveals, it is a "guide and a healing to those who believe," and the verses (*ayah*, sign) in its 114 chapters (*surah*) are a blueprint for how to live a Muslim life that will be rewarded with the pleasures of Paradise after the Day of Judgment.

As a guide for humanity, the Qur'an provides clear instructions for Muslims on how to worship God, treat one another, and to perform the ritual obligations of the religion. The Qur'an contains moral guidelines, the laws of God, and the rules of the religion. In the more than 6000 verses that comprise the Qur'an, a variety of forms of speech such as moral directives, warnings, admonitions, exhortations, and promises are used to engage with Muslims and to teach them the lessons of Islam. The Qur'an is not structured in a linear narrative fashion, rather the *surahs* are ordered by length, with the second chapter being longest and the 114th the shortest. The exception is the opening *surah*, *al-Fatiha* (The Opening), which is a hymn of praise to God.

Muslim revelatory history

Muslim revelatory history is divided into two time periods: the Meccan and Medinan periods. Between 610 and the *hijra* in 622, the Meccan revelations were typically eschatological (concerned with the end of time), warning the Arabs that there will be a resurrection of their bodies and they will be brought before God for judgment, and either rewarded with Paradise or punishment in Hell. The Meccan revelations, many of which are *surahs* that are brief in length, repetitively affirm the general message of God's uniqueness and the coming Day of Judgment. These early revelations exhort the Meccans to heed Muhammad's monotheistic message.

The Medinan revelations are different in tone and focus from the universalizing message of the Meccan period. The Medinan verses are much longer in length and more particularized. Many of these revelations came down to Muhammad in response to particular questions posed by Muslims, to explain the meaning of or to provide a lesson about the outcome of a particular event (e.g. a battle) or situation. It is in the Medinan period that the revelatory message of the Qur'an spoke specifically to the Arab community and its social, political, gender, and religious contexts.

A lineage of prophets links many of the messages and themes of the Qur'an and serves to validate Muhammad's status as God's final prophet and Messenger. The prominence of prophets such as Adam, Abraham, Moses, David, Solomon, Jacob, Joseph, Jesus, and Noah establishes continuity between Judaism, Christianity, and Islam. In the Qur'an God declares that "To every people was sent a prophet" (Qur'an 10:37). These prophets are portrayed in the Qur'an as exceptional people who have been chosen by God to deliver his message to particular communities. The prophets' responsibility is to teach God's message and to renew the book of law that has been set forth by past messengers such as Moses, David, or Jesus. Likewise, if one accepts the prophecy of Muhammad then one must accept the authority of the Qur'an and God's *tawhid* (oneness). Muslims believe that the Qur'an is God's final book of law and revelation and it completes and corrects the books of law that preceded it. Islamic doctrine accords four books as sacred, the Torah (*Taurat*) of Moses, the Psalms (*Zabur*) of David, the Gospel (*Injil*) of Jesus, and the Qur'an received by Muhammad.

Because of the non-linear ordering of the Qur'an, its variety of messages, its complexity of language, and the multiple contexts in which it was revealed, the study and interpretation of this scripture is a central part of the Islamic religious sciences (*`ulum al-din*). *Tafsir* is the act of interpreting and explaining the meaning of particular verses in the Qur'an. The science of *tafsir* aims to explain legal principles, legal rulings, and underlying meanings of the Qur'an. *Tafsir* is not focused on allegorical or mystical interpretation of the Qur'an; rather, it focuses on explaining the exoteric meaning. A *mufassar* (one who performs *tafsir*) seeks to understand how various verses and sections of the Qur'an relate to one another, the relationship between general and specific revelations, and the role of the Sunnah (lived example) of the Prophet Muhammad vis-à-vis qur'anic legislation. *Tafsir* focuses on a number of elements of the Qur'an: its vocabulary, use of rhetoric, grammar; causes of revelation (*asbab al-nuzul*); and prophetic history. Scholars performing *tafsir* approach the Qur'an by focusing their interpretation on legal or philosophical questions, Islamic history and the biography of Muhammad and his Companions, or through an analysis of the metaphorical meaning of the scripture's verses.

Related to *tafsir* is *ta'wil*, or the allegorical interpretation of the Qur'an. *Ta'wil* explains the hidden (*batin*) meanings of a particular revelation. God speaks of the hidden meaning of his revelations to Muhammad eighteen times in the Qur'an: "He it is Who has sent down to you the Book: in it are verses basic or fundamental (of established meaning); they are the foundation of the book: others are allegorical ..." (Qur'an 3:7). *Ta'wil* emphasizes a balance between scripture and reason and, like *tafsir*, only one who has mastered the religious sciences can perform it.

Hadith

Another element of the religious sciences is the *hadith*, or stories, narratives, and reports about something the Prophet said or did in a particular situation. The *hadith* also describe in great detail aspects of Muhammad's comportment, manner of dress, and interpersonal relations with a variety of people. Like *tafsir*, the *hadith* are an important field of study in the religious sciences (`ulum al-din*). From a practical perspective, the *hadith* are the written reports of Muhammad's Sunnah (lived example or tradition). Sunnah means "the trodden path," referring to the exemplary lived example that Muhammad provided for how to be a good Muslim. Muhammad was the most authoritative exponent of the Qur'an, and his life, conduct, and acquired religious authority was observed closely and emulated by the Muslim community until his death in 632.

For those Muslims who did not have the opportunity to see how Muhammad conducted his everyday and spiritual life, the *hadith* serve as a comprehensive guide to all aspects of belief, practice, and daily conduct. As one might imagine, within two centuries of Muhammad's death, more than three hundred thousand *hadith* were circulating throughout the Islamic world. In the ninth century, Imam Muhammad al-Bukhari traveled to the ends of the Islamic world to gather these *hadith*. It was common knowledge that most of these *hadith* were inauthentic, and al-Bukhari set about scientifically determining their veracity through careful analysis of their chain of transmission and the text of the report. Each *hadith* is divided into two parts, the text (*matn*), and the chain of attesters or transmitters (*isnad*). According to al-Bukhari's criteria, a *hadith* is deemed authentic and sound (*sahih*) only when the *isnad* is verified and each person in the chain of transmission was determined to be of good moral character. Moreover, based on the strength of the *isnad*, sound reasoning was engaged in order to determine whether a situation in which Muhammad was reported to have said something was historically plausible, or whether there are contradictory reports with stronger chains of transmission. Al-Bukhari found only 7,275 *hadith* to be *sahih*, including repetitions of certain reports—a considerably smaller number than the hundreds of thousands that were in circulation before al-Bukhari completed his monumental work in 846.

The *hadith* have played a central role in reformist discourse on Islam in the modern period. In South Asia, religious scholars of such reformist groups as Deoband, the Barelwis, the Ahl-e Hadith, and even the Taliban have actively engaged the *hadith* to support their vision of Islam. The Deoband in particular have placed the study of the *hadith* at the center of their reform of South Asian Islamic tradition. Reformists have used the *hadith* to regulate myriad aspects of Muslim religious practice, bodily comportment, and other aspects of everyday life. In some movements, Muslims are encouraged to grow their beard in the same style that it is reported in the *hadith* that Muhammad wore, and the *hadith* have been used to restrict customary practices such as playing music, flying kites, and visiting the shrines of Sufi saints (*dargah*).

Islamic law

"For each We have appointed a divine law and traced out way" (Qur'an 5:48). In Arabic the word *shari`a* refers to a clear path to be followed and the trodden way that leads one to a watering hole. *Shari`a* is the law of Islam as it is has been interpreted by Muslims. Islamic law is based on the legal tradition of jurisprudence (*fiqh*) and theology (*kalam*). The primary sources of authority in Islamic law are the Qur'an, and the Sunnah and *hadith* of the Prophet Muhammad. Since the Qur'an is the word of God, Muslims place primary authority with it. All qur'anic regulations were expanded and multiplied in jurisprudential books, which aim to provide answers to the widest possible range of queries that might be addressed to the legist (*faqih*).

Shari`a* regulates only the external relations of human beings to God and other people. Islamic law does not focus on aspects of one's inner consciousness, which is held to be a matter of faith and based on one's relationship with God. *Shari`a seeks to protect life (*`uqubat*) through corporal and capital punishments; property (*mu`amalat*) by regulating contracts and commercial transactions; honor (*adab*) through the control of interpersonal relationships, sexuality, morality, and etiquette; and belief (*i`tiqadat*) in God and worship (*`ibadat*) by establishing rules for fasting, prayer, paying alms, and pilgrimage. The degree of permissibility of an action exists within a spectrum that ranges from obligatory (*wajib* or *fard*) to absolutely forbidden (*haram*). Traditionally legal cases have been adjudicated informally with most issues not being presented in a court of law.

The most severe punishments meted out in Islam are for *hadd* crimes such as fornication, murder, theft, and slander. Under the *hadd* laws, one might be lashed or issued the death sentence depending on the severity of the crime. It is important to note that historically in many parts of the Islamic world, including South Asia, *hadd* crimes have not been punished with lashes or the death penalty.

For example, in her study of the relationship between illicit sexuality (*zina*) and Islamic law in Aleppo Syria, Elyse Semerdjian has observed that in examining three hundred years of court records she was unable to find a single instance of a man or woman being sentenced to stoning for prostitution or adultery.[4] In twentieth-century South Asia, punishments for *hadd* crimes were written into law in Pakistan and in Taliban-controlled Afghanistan in the 1990s, and there are cases of those guilty of *zina* and other *hadd* crimes being publicly executed.

Despite the punitive aspect of *hadd* laws, the *shari`a* is, as Semerdjian's research on illicit sexuality and the courts in Aleppo indicates, highly flexible. Prosecution for a *hadd* crime such as *zina* requires four men to witness the act of penetration, which is highly unlikely. Furthermore, within the Islamic legal tradition there is tremendous potential for interpretive difference, and there is always more than one possible answer in most cases. There are five schools of law (*madhhab*) in Islam, four Sunni and one Shi`i. Most Sunni Muslims in Pakistan and North India follow the Hanafi school of law, which was founded by Imam Abu Hanifa (d. 707). Sunni Muslims in South India are Shafi`is, named for the school of law founded by Imam Abu `Abdallah Muhammad ibn Idris al-Shafi`i (d. 820).

The Shi`a have their own school of law known as the Ja`fari, named after the sixth Imam Ja`far al-Sadiq (d. 765). The schools of law for the most part differ on matter of degree with regard to the permissibility and punishment of human acts, although there are some noticeable differences between Sunni and Shi`i law. Shi`i law accords equal authority of the *hadith* of the twelve Imams with those of the Prophet Muhammad, and Shi`i men are legally permitted to contract temporary marriages (*mut`a; sigheh*) in addition to the four permanent wives allowed by qur'anic injunction to all Muslim men. In November 2006 the All India Shia Personal Law Board (AISPLB) unanimously approved a model marriage contract (*nikahnama*) granting women and men more equitable rights in marriage and divorce. The AISPLB, which split from the All India Muslim Personal Law Board in 2005, established the model *nikahnama* in order to extend the rights of women to establish the conditions for marriage, and to broaden the grounds upon which the wife can obtain a divorce (*talaq*), which according to Islamic law (*shari`a*) is the exclusive right of the husband.

In South Asia, as in other parts of the Islamic world, *shari`a* has been engaged as a tool to order society, preserve religious tradition, and to provide guidance in order to keep Muslims on the "straight path" (*sirat al-mustaqim*) to God and the rewards of Paradise on the Day of Judgment. As long as there have been Muslims in the Indian subcontinent, *shari`a* has played a dynamic role in the creative yet theologically circumscribed space for Islam to become Indianized, and manifest itself as a distinctly South Asian religious tradition.

Islam in South Asia

Happy be Hindustan with its splendor of religion,
Where the *shari`a* enjoys perfect honour and dignity.
In learning Delhi now rivals Bukhara;

Islam has made manifest by the rulers.
From Ghazna to every shore of the ocean
You see Islam in its glory everywhere.
Muslims, here, belong to the Hanafi creed,
But sincerely respect all four schools.
They have no enmity with the Shafi'ites and no fondness for the Zaidites;
With heart and soul they are devoted to the path of the community and
the *sunna*.
It is a wonderful land, producing Muslims and favouring religion,
Where even the fish comes out of the stream as a Sunnite![5]

In 1289 Amir Khusrau, a court poet in the Delhi Sultanate and spiritual student (*murid*) of the great Sufi saint Nizamuddin Awliya (d. 1325), wrote this poem praising India as an ideal land for Sunni Islam to flourish. Amir Khusrau's India was a place where the principles of Islam as a religion could be lived to the fullest; Muslims adhere to the *shari'a* (Islamic law), and they uphold the Prophet Muhammad's lived tradition (Sunnah). In each line of Khusrau's poem, India is extolled as the site where Islam is exemplified as a religious, intellectual, and ethical tradition.

The Muslim assessment of the Indian subcontinent six centuries before is strikingly different from Amir Khusrau's endless praise. During the caliphate of 'Uthman (644–56), when Muslims spread far beyond the Arabian Peninsula in their campaign to increase wealth and dominion, the first military encounter in South Asia took place in the Makran, the arid coastal strip of Sindh and Baluchistan in what is now Pakistan. Upon seeing the barren desert of the Makran, the Muslims declared India to be a place where "Water [is] scarce; fruit inferior; robbers impudent; the army if small, likely to be lost, if numerous, likely to perish from hunger and thirst."[6] Despite this bleak appraisal of India, Muslims established garrisons on the plains of Sindh and Punjab along the far western edge of the subcontinent. In 711 the general Muhammad ibn al-Qasem conquered the fort at Daibul near present-day Karachi and moved his army up the Indus River to Multan in the Punjab. Less than one hundred years after Muhammad's death, Islam had spread to India and in the ensuing centuries the religion became an integral part of the South Asian religious landscape.

In the thirteenth century Qutbuddin Aibek, a former slave of Turkic origin, established the Delhi Sultanate in Lahore. In 1229, Delhi was established as the capital, and the beginning of a long history of Muslim rule in India commenced. For the first time Delhi was renowned as a center of religious learning and culture. During this period the Chishti Sufi order (*tariqa*) flourished in North India, and the shrine-tombs of such saints as Mu'inuddin Chishti in Ajmer, Nizamuddin Awliya in Delhi, and Baba Farid al-Din Ganj-e Shakar in Pakpattan, Pakistan, became important sites of pilgrimage for Muslims, Hindus, and Sikhs.

In the sixteenth century another dynasty of kings of Turkic origin was established. Commonly regarded as the great Muslim dynasty of North India, the Mughals hailed from Uzbekistan in Central Asia. The Mughal dynasty was

Islam comes to India

Conquest was just one way in which Islam spread to India. Muslims established garrisons outside non-Muslim cities. Many non-Muslims converted to Islam in order to avoid paying the *jizya*, a tax levied on non-Muslims for protection and religious autonomy. Marriage was another important way in which Islam was established in South Asia. As Muslims settled in South Asia as traders and denizens of the garrisons, they met and married local women, and the children born were accorded the status of Muslim by Islamic law. The maritime trade between the Middle East and South Asia brought merchants to the Coromandel and Malabar coasts long before the advent of Islam. Many Arab traders permanently settled along India's coastline and married local women.

Sufism, the mystical dimension of Islam, was most influential in introducing Islam throughout South Asia. Sufism readily integrated local and Islamic religious practices, which appealed to large numbers of non-Muslims, especially with regard to healing, meditative, and devotional practices.

established in 1526 by Babur (r. 1526–30), although it was during the reign of his grandson Akbar (r. 1556–1605) that we see the complex interrelationship between Islam and kingship in North India. Akbar was a deeply spiritual man, and he played an important role in the development of Islam as a South Asian religion. To give thanks for the birth of his eldest son Salim, Akbar traveled 225 miles on foot from his capital at Agra to the *dargah* (tomb-shrine) of Mu'inuddin Chishti in Ajmer. Akbar regularly conducted pilgrimage (*ziyarat*) to Mu'inuddin Chishti's tomb and he was a generous patron of the shrine complex in Ajmer.

In 1581 at his capital Fatehpur Sikri, located outside of Agra, Akbar established a new religion known as Din-e Ilahi (religion of God). At his court in Fatehpur Sikri, Akbar met with representatives from the various religions present in South Asia: Hindu, Parsi (Zoroastrian), Christian, and Buddhist. Akbar conceived of the Din-e Ilahi as an all-embracing religion and he combined what he considered to be the best aspects of these different religious traditions. Forbidden in the Din-e Ilahi were sensual lust, deceit, slander, and oppression. Akbar's official state policy was "peace with everyone" (*sulh-e kull*). Although he held dominion over Hindu and Muslim Indians, Akbar did not discriminate on religious grounds in appointing people to positions in the government, and he granted absolute freedom to non-Muslims to build their own places of worship. Along with these inclusive policies, Akbar abolished the *jizya* tax on non-Muslims in his kingdom. Akbar was a savvy political leader who realized the necessity of close relations with Hindus, and he made it an official state policy to understand the religion. To this end, Akbar commissioned translations of the Sanskrit epics the *Mahabharata* and *Ramayana* into Persian. Although the Din-e Ilahi was unsuccessful as a new religious movement, it reflects Akbar's ongoing efforts to fully integrate Islam into South Asia's religious fabric.

Historians of early modern India have viewed the emperor Aurangzeb's religious policies with much more ambivalence. Aurangzeb was the last of the great Mughal emperors, and he has been portrayed as stern in demeanor and as an uncompromisingly orthodox Muslim. Aurangzeb reinstituted the *jizya* tax, and he promised positions in his court to Hindus provided they convert to Islam. The Shi`a were not exempt from Aurangzeb's reformist vision of Islam: the commemoration of Imam Husain's martyrdom during Muharram was forbidden by imperial edict. Although he loved the poetry of the thirteenth century Persian Sufi Rumi, Aurangzeb was deeply suspicious of Sufism and its traditions of saint veneration, ecstatic devotional practices, and integration of Vaishnava meditative and devotional traditions.

The overall impact of the Mughal dynasty in shaping North Indian Islam is profound. Islam has always been an urban religion, and this holds true in South Asia, where the Muslim capitals were based in the cosmopolitan cities of Lahore, Delhi, Lucknow, and Hyderabad.

Muslims introduced new languages to the Indian subcontinent, including Persian, Turkish, and Arabic, deeply influencing the development of Gujarati, Urdu, Hindi, Bengali, and Punjabi vernacular languages. Indian musical

Figure 7.1 Tomb of Mughal Emperor Humayun (1508–56), the second Mughal Emperor of India, in Delhi. His tomb is considered a forerunner of the Taj Mahal. Photo taken by Karen G. Ruffle.

traditions have also been shaped by their interaction with Muslims. The thirteenth century poet Amir Khusrau is credited with developing Hindustani classical music, Sufi devotional music (*qawwali*), and the *tabla* (drum). Likewise, massive construction projects engaged the labors of Hindu and Muslim artisans, and one can observe clearly Hindu motifs and architectural elements in ostensibly Muslim monuments such as the Taj Mahal.

Many non-Muslims found Islam to be appealing for its message of fundamental equality. Because South Asian society was structured by the Vedic caste system, many low caste people converted to Islam, although they tended to keep their caste-based occupations after becoming Muslim. In South India, especially in the Deccan region where the Shi'i Qutb Shahi dynasty (1512–1687) was established at the beginning of the sixteenth century, the appeal of Muslim ritual and devotional life was palpable. Scholars have long referred to the culture of the Qutb Shahi dynasty as "composite," based on the development of a shared Hindu–Muslim religio-social culture. The appointment in 1585 of the Iranian émigré Mir Muhammad Mu'min Astarabadi as *peshwa* (Prime Minister) to the court of Muhammad Quli Qutbh Shah (r. 1580–1611) was most significant for the development of Shi'i devotionalism based on a Hindu–Muslim "composite" culture in the Deccan. According to S. A. A. Rizvi, Mir Mu'min endeavored to introduce and propagate Shi'ism in the Deccan:

> As if the construction of Hyderabad itself was not enough, Mir Muhammad Mu'min founded many villages as centers of Shi'i and Islamic life … The mosques and *'Ashur-khanas* brought the Hindu villagers into contact with the Islamic and Shi'i way of life. The *'alams* and other symbols of the tragedy of Karbala were introduced by Mir Mu'min into these villages where they aroused Hindu curiosity and helped to convert them to Shi'ism.[7]

As an Iranian, Mir Mu'min was instrumental in fusing Iranian Shi'i devotional elements with the religious traditions of everyday Indians creating a hybrid Deccani religious culture in which Hindus and Muslims, and their languages of Persian, Telugu, and Deccani-Urdu were brought into contact.[8]

Like Akbar, the Qutb Shahi kings maintained a liberal policy of religious freedom. Muhammad Quli Qutb Shah commissioned the construction of a number of religious structures throughout Hyderabad, and he often sponsored Hindu religious festivals. He was an accomplished poet who wrote in Telugu on the themes of Deccani and Shi'i religious festivals, the seasons, and the local flora and fauna. Muhammad Quli Qutb Shah commissioned the translation of Shi'i religious poems and prose narratives commemorating the battle of Karbala into Telugu and Deccani-Urdu in order to make them understandable to the non-Persian speaking elites.

In 1687, the Qutb Shahi dynasty collapsed following a long siege by the Mughal emperor Aurangzeb at Golconda Fort, located just outside of the capital city of Hyderabad. The siege of Golconda not only brought the end of the Qutb Shahi dynasty, but this was a formative event in establishing the saintly status of Yusuf and Sharif, two men from Aurangzeb's army who played a central role in the Mughal emperor's military success. Yusuf and Sharif were itinerant soldiers and religious seekers, who became disciples (*murid*) of the Chishti *pir* (holy man) Shaykh Kalim Allah Shajahanabadi while in Mecca. The two men followed their religious teacher back to Delhi, where they joined Aurangzeb's army and went south for the military campaign in the Deccan.

The historical and hagiographical record of the siege of Golconda narrates in great detail Yusuf and Sharif's miraculous intervention that brought about Aurangzeb's victory. One night there was a terrible storm of pouring rain and lashing winds in which all but one of the tents in Aurangzeb's military encampment were destroyed. In that lone tent, two candles were seen burning throughout the storm. Curiosity piqued, Aurangzeb approached the tent and saw Yusuf and Sharif calmly reading the Qur'an. Aurangzeb recognized the exceptional piety of these two men and God's protection of them during the storm. The emperor declared the two men to be saints, and he asked Yusuf and Sharif to pray for his victory. Yusuf and Sharif instructed Aurangzeb to visit a particular merchant whose shop lay outside Golconda's walls, which he did and learned the secret of the fort's weakness. Yusuf and Sharif's holy status was again proven to Aurangzeb when he was able to quickly infiltrate the fort and defeat the Qutb Shahi dynasty.

Today the Yusufain (two Yusufs) *dargah* is one of the busiest and most popular religious sites in Hyderabad. The shrine is located in the neighborhood adjacent to the Nampally Railway Station in Hyderabad's city center. People of all faiths come to the *dargah* on Thursday nights to hear *qawwali* (mystical Sufi music) and to seek the blessing (*baraka*) of the saints. The popularity of the Yusufain *dargah* speaks to the complex history of Islam in South Asia. Although Yusuf and Sharif's intercession was necessary for Aurangzeb to overtake Golconda Fort, which caused the end of Hyderabad's Qutb Shahi dynasty, these two saints are revered for their exceptional piety and steadfastness and not their political allegiance to the Mughal emperor.

Islam in South Asia: Practice

Central beliefs

"Faith is a knowledge in the heart, a voicing with the tongue, and an activity with the limbs."[9] In this *hadith*, Muhammad speaks about how faith (*iman*) is manifested by Muslims; however, these qualities are also integral to the five pillars of Islam, which structure the external religious life and belief of Muslims. The five pillars constitute the obligatory social and religious duties (`*ibadat*) of all Muslims. Muslim belief and practice is encapsulated in the five pillars, which also reflect the social, political, and religious contexts in which Islam emerged.

The first pillar is the foundation for all other aspects of Islamic belief and practice. The *shahada* is the "bearing witness" that "there is no god but God, and Muhammad is His Messenger" (*la ilaha illa'llah wa Muhammadun rasul Allah*). In order to become a Muslim one must say the *shahada* with full purity of intention (*niyya*). Each time Muslims are called to prayer, the summons ends with the reminder that "there is no god but God." When a baby is born, the father whispers the *shahada* into its ears making this statement of monotheism the first words it hears. The *shahada* serves as a constant reminder for Muslims of God's absolute uniqueness.

The second pillar is *salat* (prayer), or *namaz* as it is more commonly called in South Asia. Five times each day Muslims take a few moments to pray and focus their minds on God. From dawn until dusk, the Muslim day is punctuated by the call to prayer (*adhan*). Muslim men might go to the mosque if it is nearby, but it is equally commonplace to see someone praying behind a shop counter or seeking out a quiet space in a courtyard or park. On Fridays Muslims attend the noon congregational prayer (*jum'ah*), where a discourse on a verse from the Qur'an is provided by the prayer leader (*imam*). Women generally do not go to mosque and perform their prayers at home. While Islamic law does not prohibit Muslim women from praying in mosques, customary practice in South Asia has made this a taboo space. In the past decade, women's mosques have been established in the North East in Shillong, Meghalaya and in Pudukottai, Tamilnadu. The women's mosque in Tamilnadu has generated considerable controversy in South Asian Muslim communities, where such faith-based activism is derided as *bid'a* (innovation) and usurping men's patriarchal privilege to control access to religious institutions and education.

Reflecting the social environment in which Islam emerged, it is a ritual obligation for all Muslims to give alms (*zakat*) to the poor (the third pillar). Muslims are required to give a small percentage of their excess wealth in either cash or kind, which is used to provide food, clothing, and shelter to the poor. *Zakat* is usually given at the New Year during the month of Muharram.

The fourth pillar is fasting (Arabic *sawm*; Urdu *rowza*) during the month of Ramadan. All able-bodied men and women are obligated to fast from dawn until dusk during this month. Pregnant and menstruating women, the elderly, children, and those who are ill are exempted from performing the fast. Ramadan is an especially sacred month for Muslims. It is believed that Muhammad received his first revelation from God on *laylat al-qadr* ("the night of power"), which is celebrated around 21 Ramadan. Muslims spend the month in intense prayer and many go to the mosques to participate in reading the Qur'an. Ramadan is also a festive time, and the breaking of the fast provides a welcome opportunity for families to make special dishes that are served only during this sacred month. Life takes on a slower quality during the day, and the nighttime is alive with people visiting friends and family, sharing meals, and going to the bazaar where Muslim shopkeepers stay open late into the night. Ramadan ends with *'id al-fitr*, or the fast-breaking feast.

All Muslims are obligated to go on *hajj* (pilgrimage) to Mecca at least once in their lifetime if it is physically and financially feasible. The *hajj* reenacts events from the prophet Abraham and his concubine Hagar's sacrifice, when God commanded Abraham to sacrifice his son Isma'il, which he was willing to do because of his absolute faith. Pleased with Abraham's faithful obedience, God instructed Abraham to sacrifice a goat in place of his son. Another important ritual of the *hajj* is congregating as a community at Mount Arafat, where the

Prophet Muhammad delivered his final sermon. The focal point of the *hajj* is the Ka`ba (the former home of the pre-Islamic Arabs' idols), where Muslims circumambulate (*tawaf*) the cube-shaped structure in a flowing mass of humanity.

Muharram rituals

On the tenth day Muharram, the first month in the Islamic lunar calendar, in large cities such as Hyderabad, Lucknow, Mumbai, and Delhi, as well as countless villages throughout South Asia, the Shi`i commemoration of the martyrdom of the grandson of Prophet Muhammad and the third Imam Husain reaches its climax. Men gather in religious buildings known as `*ashurkhanas* and *imambaras* to perform bloody *matam* (self-flagellation) with knives, flails, and razor blades. Men and boys rhythmically strike their bodies with their hands and implements in time to the chanted *nauhas*, or mourning poems. Later in the day, thousands of men march through urban neighborhoods again performing bloody *matam* as a sign of their loyalty to Islam, Imam Husain, and his family.

Muharram is undoubtedly the most visible marker of Muslim, particularly Shi`i identity, in South Asia. For the Shi`a, who constitute a minority in both India and Pakistan, the rituals commemorating Imam Husain and his martyrdom at Karbala in Iraq in 680 provide a powerful opportunity to assert their identity in contexts in which they have been marginalized or subjected to sectarian chauvinism. The public nature of Muharram holds further appeal for it symbolically mirrors Imam Husain's commitment to his grandfather Muhammad's prophetic mission, and his political opposition to the tyrannical rule of the `Umayyad caliph Yazid.

The days of mourning (*ayyam-e `aza*) last for two months and eight days, and men and women gather daily in the *majlis* (mourning assembly) to listen to and weep over narratives detailing the suffering and heroic feats of Imam Husain and his family at Karbala. Many of these narratives reflect a distinctly South Asian worldview. The men and women of Karbala are portrayed as idealized Indian Muslims, who are socio-ethical and religious role models. Many Urdu poets of poetry such as *marsiya*, *salam*, and *nauha* (genres of mourning poems commemorating Imam Husain's martyrdom), describe Karbala through the flora, fauna, cultural practices, and clothing of South Asia.

During Muharram, men and women spend their days and nights visiting different religious buildings (`*ashurkhana*; *imambara*), where ritual objects symbolizing Imam Husain's family members are kept and displayed during the mourning period. In Hyderabad the `*alam*, a metal battle standard that is a non-figural representation of one of Imam Husain's family members is an important ritual object. Offerings (*mannat*) are made to the `*alam*, and people of all religious backgrounds come to ask for the saint's intercessory assistance. In North India, people go to the *imambara* where replicas of the tomb of Imam Husain and other family members are displayed. Most *ta`ziyehs*, as these mock tombs are known, are made anew each year out of colored paper covering a bamboo frame. Many *imambaras* also house more elaborate *ta`ziyehs* made of silver, which were typically commissioned by Shi`i kings or the nobility.

Figure 7.2 *Alams* in the Badshahi `ashurkhana* in Hyderabad, India. Photo taken by
Karen G. Ruffle.

On the tenth of Muharram (`ashura*), Shi`i mourning reaches its climax, for
this is the day when Imam Husain was killed and the women and children who
survived the battle were taken captive to Damascus. On the morning of the tenth,
Shi`i men gather at shrines to perform bloody *matam*, and throughout the day
they march in processions (*julus*) along with `alams* and *ta`ziyeh*, flagellating
themselves to publicly declare their loyalty to Imam Husain.

Muharram has an important role in the religious life of Hindus in many parts
of South Asia. Hindus of various castes are commonly seen in the *majlis* and
making vows before *ta`ziyehs* and `alams*. There is a small caste of Hindus known
as the Husaini Brahmins who trace their identity back to an ancestor named
Rahab, who traveled from his home in Punjab to Arabia where he entered into
the loyal service of Imam Husain. According to tradition, Rahab was at the battle
of Karbala along with his sons who were martyred. Rahab survived the battle
and returned to India as a devotee of Imam Husain charged with the mission of
keeping the memory of Karbala alive.

Revival and reform movements: The example of Deoband

In the mid-nineteenth century as the British established India as the jewel in
its imperial crown, Hindus and Muslims developed a heightened sense of religious identity and tradition, and many felt a profound need for reform in order to

revitalize Indian society and to restore their respective religions to their imagined original vitality and purity. In South Asia, Islamic reform movements such as the Tablighi Jama`at, the Barelwis, the Ahl-e Hadith, and the Deobandis, whose example I will use to assess Muslim religious discourse on tradition and identity, attempted to purify Islam of the many Hindu accretions that they believed had disempowered Muslims and caused them to become undisciplined, resulting in the British establishing colonial dominion over all Indians with the collapse of the Mughal empire. The rise of British power, growth of cities, and shifting standards for employment caused Muslims in this milieu to begin looking inward for ways to recover power and prestige.

In this environment, reform movements were established by religious scholars and ideologues of most South Asian religions (in what are now the countries of India, Pakistan, and Bangladesh), as a response to encounters with the British, the rapid spread of modern technologies, the opening of markets, and the perception of religion as being in a state of decline. The leadership of Deoband was convinced that there was something seriously wrong with the state of the world, and they sought to reform Islam, the centerpiece of their world. Through the establishment of the Dar ul-`Ulum *madrasa* (religious school) at Deoband in North India, religious scholars were educated, teaching and education became important for both men and women, and, with the rise of print culture, pamphlets were published as a way of increasing literacy and encouraging the practice of a Deobandi vision of "normative" Islam.

For religious reformers, such as the Deobandis, the crisis was embodied in the lives and activities of everyday Muslims. The Deobandis considered Indian Islam to be in a state of decline (albeit recoverable), caused by deviation from the correct path of the *shari`a* and dependence upon superstition and blind adherence to custom. They believed that people's situation would improve with the re-establishment of an ethical Islam based on adherence to the Qur'an, the *hadith*, and the *shari`a*.

In the nineteenth century, these reformers were primarily from the educated, upper classes. The `*ulama* (religious scholars), who were at the heart of the Deoband movement, were educated in the classical disciplines of jurisprudence (*fiqh*), Sufism, and qur'anic learning. Foremost, the `*ulama* of the Deoband movement were experts on the *hadith*, which serve as a model for pious and moral behavior. The goal of the `*ulama* was to inculcate in Muslims an appreciation for and dedication to embodying the good life of the Prophet. Through the *hadith*, it is possible for Muslims to cultivate positive behaviors.

By emphasizing *hadith* traditions, reformist `*ulama* were able to criticize customary practices that were considered to be in contradiction to the Qur'an and *shari`a*. Many of these customary practices were identified by the `*ulama* as women's culture. The `*ulama* wrote prolifically, with their sermons targeting the honorable classes (*ashraf*)—both men and women—as the type of Muslims who could reform Islam by setting an example for the poor and uneducated. In the Deoband movement, the primary goal of the reformers was to establish the `*ulama* as the guardians of Islam, the class of scholars to whom Muslims would look for correct guidance in behavior and learning.

Gender and religious identity

Gender in Deobandi reformist discourse

Women were considered an essential element in the reform of Islam by groups such as Deoband. Maulana Ashraf 'Ali Thanawi, who wrote a series of didactic pamphlets for Muslim women titled *Bihishti Zewar* (Heavenly Ornaments), considered women to be equal to men in their capacity to learn. *Bihishti Zewar* was published at the beginning of the twentieth century, when such didactic and moralizing literature for women's educational, religious and moral reform was proliferating throughout South Asia. The moral injunctions Thanawi set forth in *Bihishti Zewar* were equally applicable to both men and women; however, he believed that women were more culpable in the infiltration of Hindu rituals and customs in everyday Muslim practice, and therefore needed more guidance to set them on the straight path again. Thanawi believed that both men and women are responsible for their actions in the world, and both must confront the eternal struggle between intelligence (*'aql*) and the undisciplined aspects of the base self (*nafs*). Even though Thanawi accorded a fundamental equality between the sexes, women struggle more with their *nafs*. According to Thanawi, this "defect" is not genetically determined but, rather, it is a product of cultural conditioning. It is on this point that Thanawi's view of women differed from the theories being espoused in Europe and America at the same time.

In nineteenth-century Europe and America, women were considered morally and intellectually deficient in comparison to men. The education of women was ideally supposed to focus only upon the domestic sciences (for example, sewing, cooking, and so on). In the late nineteenth century in the United States of America, schools and universities often only provided education in the domestic sciences for women, as it was assumed that women's education was solely for the benefit of marrying a well-placed husband.

In this regard, Thanawi's emphasis on education for Muslim women is markedly different. Thanawi wanted women to become *maulavis* (religious teachers), and to be educated in Arabic, the Qur'an, and other religious sciences. Thanawi believed that it was necessary for women to be well educated to practice Islam according to the *shari'a*. For women to be well educated meant that they would be accorded a higher status within their marriage and within the family. Since women and girls were confined to the home according to the practice of *purdah*, they therefore had more time to devote to learning. *Bihishti Zewar*'s intended purpose was to serve as an elementary-level text by which women could learn to read, and to be educated according to a reformist vision of Islam. In the late nineteenth century, women tended to be illiterate, and women's culture was largely an oral one. It was believed that with literacy in Urdu would come a desire to study Arabic, and thus Muslim women might attain qur'anic literacy. Thanawi constantly encouraged women to read the Qur'an and to follow its teachings. *Bihishti Zewar* was written in simple Urdu prose. Its simple writing style enabled women of all statuses to benefit from its messages and teachings.

Bihishti Zewar was published at a time in South Asia when print culture was emerging as a dominant form of media. The Deobandis took full advantage of this by using it as a means of disseminating their teachings. Shortly after being published *Bihishti Zewar* became a bestseller. Even today *Bihishti Zewar* is given to young women upon marriage to serve as guides for properly gendered religious and domestic conduct.

The gendered dimension of Deobandi reformist discourse continues today in a number of Muslim movements and communities in South Asia. Women continue to be celebrated as the repository of religious tradition while simultaneously criticized for their gendered religious practices, which are often dismissed as folk religion or superstition. In understanding the complexity of how Islam as a global and South Asian tradition is contested, one must pay close attention to the role of women as agents and subjects of these discourses that represent liberal, reformist, and traditional-conservative perspectives.

God's strong women: The central role of women in Shi`i ritual practice

In the Shi`i context, the women of Imam Husain's family (*ahl-e bait*) serve as powerful feminine role models. In the realm of everyday practice, the Shi`a accept the centrality of the women of the Ahl-e Bait as spiritual exemplars and moral role models, which is demonstrated by the dependence upon female voices and experiences in the ritual performance of devotional mourning poems such as *nauha*, *salam* and *marsiya* in the *majlis*. Without the voices and dramatic articulation of the experiences of the women of the Ahl-e Bait in the *majlis*, Karbala could not be remembered. In the devotional poetry and hagiographical narratives performed in the mourning assembly, heroines such as Imam Husain's sister Zainab, his daughters Fatimah Kubra and Sakinah, and his mother Fatimah al-Zahra, are transformed into idealized South Asian women, and their model is authenticated by their exceptional spirituality and genealogy connecting them to the Prophet Muhammad.

Fatimah Zahra, the daughter of the Prophet Muhammad, wife of the first Shi`i Imam `Ali, and the mother of two martyred Imams, Hasan and Husain, is revered as one of the most holy of Muslim women. Fatimah's daughter Zainab was the sister of the third Imam Husain, who was martyred at the battle of Karbala, Iraq, in 680, when Muslim fought Muslim for political power: she was the messenger of martyrdom, spreading news of what happened. Zainab, too, is a spiritual and social exemplar, whose bravery and willingness to sacrifice all for the sake of religion and justice are admired by both Shi`i men and women, and she serves as a powerful and imitable role model. Both Fatimah and Zainab uphold the notion of justice (`adalah), a central concept in Shi`i social and religious life. Their intense engagement with religious and social matters in the public sphere compels many Shi`i women to work for the betterment of society by actively contributing to public life as politicians, teachers and professors, activists, doctors and nurses, and religious teachers.

Women take an active part in Shi`i religious life by hosting *majlis*, writing poetry commemorating Karbala, and training to speak as *majlis* orators (*zakirah*).

Women have established their own Muharram associations and have built their own `ashurkhanas` and *imambaras*. These women-only religious institutions are always busy with devotional prayers and rituals. At Yadgar Husaini, a women's `ashurkhana` in Hyderabad's Old City, women gather to perform `amal`, or the ritualized repetition of a call for the intercession of one the Imams or Ahl-e Bait (family of the Prophet Muhammad). Typically a small group of women, perhaps widowed or poor, are available to perform the `amal` at the request of a Shi`a seeking intercessory assistance for some matter. `Amals` might take the form of calling for Imam `Ali's help (*ya `Ali madad*), or the recitation of a particular verse or *surah* from the Qur'an. Women also perform another ritual of hospitality known as *dastarkhwan* (tablecloth). *Dastarkhwan* gatherings are specifically women-only; even pregnant women are not able to participate in the ritual activities, lest the expectant mother is carrying a male fetus. Women host the *dastarkhwan* for a number of reasons: to annually honor a particular member of Imam Husain's family; in fulfillment of a vow made; and as an opportunity for female guests to gather in fellowship and to spiritually engage the saint.[10]

Islam in South Asia: Current approaches

In the past two decades scholars have begun to more deeply explore the myriad ways in which Islam has acculturated and adapted itself to its South Asian context, especially focusing on issues of gender, everyday practice, religious pluralism, and religious performance. The past decade has seen an increase in the number of tenure-track positions in departments of religion for scholars focusing on South Asian Islam, and a new generation of students is obtaining doctoral degrees in this field.

These developments have resulted in a burgeoning of religious studies scholarship that transcends normative text-based, intellectual, and patriarchal Muslim traditions. A growing body of scholarship focuses on women's leadership in Sufism, particularly in their roles as custodians of the tomb (*sajjada nishin*), healers, and teachers. Scholarship on South Asian Sufism has tended to focus on famous (dead) male saints, histories of orders (*tariqa*) and lineages (*silsilah*), and mystical writings. Scholars are focusing more on the everyday dimension of the myriad devotional practices that take place at the *dargah*, and less on institutional history or biographies of exceptional individuals.

In many regards, studies of Sufism are following a pattern established by scholars of South Asian Shi`ism, which has tended to focus on the ritual activities of Muharram and its devotional literature. In the past two decades, a number of ethnographic studies of Muharram rituals, both public and domestic, have been published. These studies have tended to emphasize localized Shi`i discourse and practice, and gendered aspects of Muharram ritual have brought women to the forefront as active agents in devotional life. In many regards this scholarship mirrors the work of the Subaltern Studies Group in decentering narratives that focus on the patriarchal elite by focusing instead on the everyday lived experience of individuals and communities.

The question of Muslim identity and authority continues to be an important theme in studies of South Asian Islam. The question of what is Islam and who has the authority to define it as a "normative" religious tradition is deeply contested by Sunnis and Shi`as, liberals and traditional reformists alike. The tension between "normative" Islam and its localized, vernacular practice has emerged as an important area of study in the past two decades, especially as labor migration to the Gulf has exposed increasing numbers of South Asian men and women to religious discourse that is sharply critical of how Muslims have absorbed the cultural, religious, and sartorial influences of their South Asian homeland. At the crux of these debates about identity is how one can simultaneously be Muslim and a member of the global *ummah*, the identity of which is defined in the imagination by its Arab origins, yet is practiced and lived out through a South Asian ethos and worldview.

Discussion questions

1   How did Islam come to South Asia? What role has Islam played in the political and religious history of India, especially during the Mughal and Qutb Shahi dynasties? How did Akbar and Aurangzeb differ in their attitudes toward non-Muslims, and how did they integrate Islam into their imperial rule?

2   In what ways has Islam become a South Asian religion? How has Islam's origin as a monotheistic religion of the Near East been retained, and in what ways has South Asian Islamic practice been shaped by the local environment?

3   How have movements such as Deoband sought to reform Islam in South Asia? Why did they believe that reform was necessary? What role does gender play in this reformist discourse, that is, why were women simultaneously held up as paragons of tradition, yet also faulted for their customary practices that were considered un-Islamic and influenced by Hinduism?

Key terms

dargāh—The tomb-shrine of a Sufi saint.

ḥadīth—Reports of the sayings and actions of the Prophet Muhammad; in Shi`ism, this also includes reports of the Imams' deeds and words (*akhbār*).

Islām—Submission to the will of God. Islam is a religion based on absolute submission to God's uniqueness, the prophets and Messengers that have been sent to different communities, and belief in His creation of the universe and the coming Day of Judgment. One who practices Islām is a Muslim.

jizya—A tax paid by non-Muslims for protection and the freedom to worship.

khalīfah—Representative of God; the first four political successors of the Prophet Muhammad following his death in 632 CE, who are collectively referred to as the "Rightly Guided Caliphs" (*Rāshidūn*).

majlis—Mourning assembly for commemorating the martyrdom of Imam Husain at the battle of Karbala, Iraq in 680 CE.

sharī`a*—Islamic law. The primary sources of authority for the *sharī`a are the Qur'an and Sunnah, and it regulates the external relations of human beings to God and other people.

Sunnah—The lived tradition of the Prophet Muhammad, which is recorded in the *ḥadīth*. The Sunnah is the model of idealized Islamic belief, practice, and etiquette for all Muslims to imitate.

tawḥīd—The principle of God's uniqueness, exemplified by the first part of the *shahāda*, "there is no god but God" (*lā ilāha illa'llāh*).

`ulamā*—The *`ulamā are those who have attained knowledge and mastery of one or more of the religious sciences (*`ulūm al-dīn*). The *`ulamā*, by virtue of their mastery of the Qur'an and the *ḥadīth* are usually expert in Islamic law (*sharī`a*).

Notes

1 Carl W. Ernst, "India as a Sacred Islamic Land," in Donald S. Lopez, Jr. (ed.), *Religions of India in Practice*, Princeton, NJ: Princeton University Press, 1995, pp. 556–63.
2 All quotations from the Qur'an are from Abdullah Yusuf Ali, *The Holy Qur'an: English Translation and Commentary*, New Delhi: Goodword Books, 2006.
3 Mahmoud Ayoub, *The Crisis of Muslim History: Religion and Politics in Early Islam*, Oxford: Oneworld Publications, 2003, p. 7.
4 Elyse Semerdjian, *Off the Straight Path: Illicit Sex, Law, and Community in Ottoman Aleppo*, Syracuse: Syracuse University Press, 2008, p. xvii.
5 Amir Khusrau cited in Annemarie Schimmel, *Islam in the Indian Subcontinent*, Leiden: Brill, 1980, p. 1.
6 Schimmel, *Islam in the Indian Subcontinent*, p. 3.
7 Saiyid Athar Abbas Rizvi, *A Socio-Intellectual History of the Isna 'Ashari Shi'is in India*, Vol. 1, New Delhi: Munshiram Manoharlal Publishers Pvt. Ltd, 1986, pp. 311–12.
8 For a more detailed discussion of the development of Shi`ism in the medieval Deccan, see Karen G. Ruffle, *Gender, Sainthood, and Everyday Practice in South Asian Shi`ism*, Chapel Hill, NC: University of North Carolina Press, 2011, pp. 105–6.
9 A *hadith* of the Prophet Muhammad, quoted in Sachiko Murata and William C. Chittick, *The Vision of Islam*, New York: Paragon House, 1994, p. 37.
10 For more on Shi`i women's devotional rituals, see Diane D'Souza, "Devotional Practices among Shia Women in South India," in Imtiaz Ahmad and Helmut Reifeld (eds.) *Lived Islam in South Asia: Adaptation, Accommodation & Conflict*, New Delhi: Social Science Press, 2004, pp. 187–206.

Recommended resources

Ahmad, Imtiaz and Helmut Reifeld, eds. *Lived Islam in South Asia: Adaptation, Accommodation & Conflict*. New Delhi: Social Science Press, 2004.
Ernst, Carl W. and Bruce B. Lawrence. *Sufi Martyrs of Love: The Chishti Order in South Asia and Beyond*. New York: Palgrave Macmillan, 2002.
Flueckiger, Joyce Burkhalter. *In Amma's Healing Room: Gender and Vernacular Islam in South India*. Bloomington, IN: Indiana University Press, 2006.
Leonard, Karen Isaksen. *Locating Home: India's Hyderabadis Abroad*. Stanford, CA: Stanford University Press, 2007.

Marsden, Magnus. *Living Islam: Muslim Religious Experience in Pakistan's North-West Frontier.* Cambridge: Cambridge University Press, 2005.

Metcalf, Barbara Daly. *Islamic Revival in British India: Deoband, 1860–1900.* Princeton, NJ: Princeton University Press, 1982.

Metcalf, Barbara Daly, ed. *Islam in South Asia in Practice.* Princeton, NJ: Princeton University Press, 2009.

Pemberton, Kelly. *Women Mystics and Sufi Shrines in India.* Columbia, SC: University of South Carolina Press, 2010.

Ruffle, Karen G. *Gender, Sainthood, and Everyday Practice in South Asian Shi`ism.* Chapel Hill, NC: University of North Carolina Press, 2011.

Zaman, Muhammad Qasim. *The Ulama in Contemporary Islam: Custodians of Change.* Princeton, NJ: Princeton University Press, 2007.

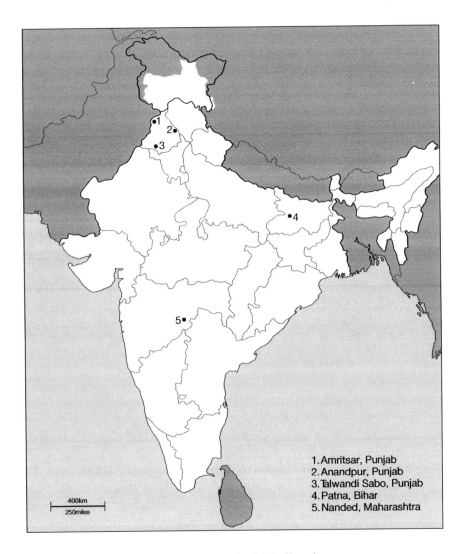

1. Amritsar, Punjab
2. Anandpur, Punjab
3. Talwandi Sabo, Punjab
4. Patna, Bihar
5. Nanded, Maharashtra

400km
250miles

Map 8 Prominent places in Sikhism as practiced in India today

8   Sikhism

Practicing tradition today

Pashaura Singh

Introduction

As the youngest of the indigenous religions of India, Sikhism originated in the northwestern region of Punjab about five centuries ago. Stressing the notion of divine unity, it quickly became demarcated from other religious traditions in its doctrines, practices, and style. Its fundamental message relates to the ideal of achieving spiritual liberation within a person's lifetime through meditation on the divine Name. It is oriented toward action, inspiring the dignity of regular labor, family life, and social responsibility. Its adherents constitute about 2 percent of India's one billion people. What makes Sikhs significant is not their numbers but their contribution in the political and economic spheres of Indian life. The global Sikh population is about 25 million, which is more than the worldwide total of the Jewish people. About 20 million Sikhs live in the state of Punjab, while 3 million have settled in other parts of India, with large concentrations in Delhi, Haryana, Himachal Pradesh, Kashmir, Uttar Pradesh, and Rajasthan, including some significant Sikh presence in the urban centers of Bombay, Calcutta, Patna, Nander, and Bhopal. Approximately 2 million Sikhs have settled in other parts of the world through successive waves of emigration in Southeast Asia, Australia, New Zealand, East Africa, the United Kingdom, and North America.[1]

Sikhism: Identity

The Sikh tradition is rooted in a particular religious experience, piety, and culture and is informed by the unique inner revelations of its founder, Guru Nanak (1469–1539). Declaring his independence from the other thought forms of his day, Nanak tried to kindle the fire of autonomy and courage in those who claimed to be his disciples or *sikhs* (learners). Notwithstanding the influences he absorbed from his contemporary religious environment, suffused with the thought and ideals of the medieval *Sants* (poet-saints such as Kabir, Ravidas, and Namdev) of North India, with whom he shared such traits as iconoclasm and mystical contemplation, Guru Nanak laid down the foundation of a new religious tradition from the standpoint of his own religious ideals. These ideals ultimately engendered the first of the three main elements on which the evolution of Sikhism depended, namely the religious and cultural innovations of Guru

Nanak and his nine successors. The second was the rural base of Punjabi society. The third significant element was the period of Punjab's history during which Sikhism evolved, in tension with the Mughals and Afghans in the seventeenth and eighteenth centuries. All these three elements combined to produce a mutual interaction between ideology and environment in the historical development of Sikhism.

Guru Nanak

Guru Nanak was born in 1469 to an upper-caste professional Khatri (merchant) family in the village of Talwandi, present-day Nankana Sahib in Pakistan. Much of the material concerning his life comes from hagiographical *janam-sakhis* (birth narratives). His life may be divided into three distinct phases: his early contemplative years, the enlightenment experience accompanied by extensive travels, and a foundational climax that resulted in the establishment of the first Sikh community in Central Punjab. In one of his own hymns he proclaimed:

> I was a minstrel out of work; the Lord assigned me the task of singing the Divine Word day and night. He summoned me to his Court and bestowed on me the robe of honor for singing his praises. On me he bestowed the Divine Nectar (*amrit*) in a cup, the nectar of his true and holy Name.[2]

This hymn is intensely autobiographical, explicitly pointing out Guru Nanak's own understanding of his divine mission, and it marked the beginning of his ministry. He was then thirty years of age, had been married to Sulakhani for more than a decade, and was the father of two young sons, Sri Chand and Lakhmi Das. He set out on a series of journeys to both Hindu and Muslim places of pilgrimage in India and abroad. During his travels he encountered the leaders of different religious persuasions and tested the veracity of his own ideas in religious dialogues.

At the end of his missionary travels Guru Nanak purchased a parcel of land on the right bank of the Ravi River in Central Punjab, where he founded the village of Kartarpur (Creator's abode) in the 1520s. There he lived for the rest of his life as the "spiritual guide" of a newly emerging religious community. His charismatic personality and teaching won him many disciples, who received the message of liberation through religious hymns of unique genius and notable beauty. They began to use these hymns in devotional singing (*kirtan*) as part of congregational worship. Indeed, the first Sikh families who gathered around Guru Nanak in the early decades of the sixteenth century at Kartarpur formed the nucleus of a rudimentary organization of the Nanak-Panth, the "Path of Nanak," referring to the community constituted by early Sikhs who followed Guru Nanak's path of liberation. In his role as what the sociologist Max Weber called an "ethical prophet," Guru Nanak called for a decisive break with existing formulations and laid the foundation of a new, rational model of normative behavior based upon divine authority. The authenticity and power of his spiritual message ultimately derived not from his relationship with the received forms of tradition but rather from his direct access to Divine Reality through personal experience. Such direct access was the ultimate source of his message and provided him with a perspective on life by which he could fully understand, interpret, and adjudicate the various elements of tradition. Throughout his writings he conceived of his work as divinely commissioned, and he demanded the obedience of his audience as an ethical duty.

As founder, Guru Nanak was the central authority for the early Sikh Panth and the definer of tradition for his age. He prescribed the daily routine, along with agricultural activity for sustenance, for the Kartarpur community. He defined the ideal person as a Gurmukh (one oriented towards the Guru) who practiced the threefold discipline of *nam dan ishnan*, "the divine Name, charity and purity."[3] Indeed, these three features, *nam* (relation to the Divine), *dan* (relation to the society), and *ishnan* (relation to self) provided a balanced approach for the development of the individual and the society. They correspond to the cognitive, the communal, and the personal aspects of the evolving Sikh identity. For Guru Nanak, the true spiritual life required that "one should live on what one has earned through hard work and share with others the fruit of one's exertion."[4] In addition, service (*seva*), self-respect (*pati*), truthful living (*sach achar*), humility, sweetness of the tongue, and taking only one's rightful share (*haq halal*) were regarded as highly prized virtues in the pursuit of liberation. As part of Sikh liturgy, Guru Nanak's *Japji* (Recitation) was recited in the early hours of the morning, and *So Dar* (That Door) and *Arti* (Adoration) were sung in the evening.

Guru Nanak's spiritual message found expression at Kartarpur through key institutions: the *sangat* (holy fellowship) where all felt that they belonged to one large spiritual fraternity; the *dharamsala*, the original form of the Sikh place of worship; and the establishment of the *langar*, the inter-dining convention which required people of all castes to sit in status-free lines (*pangat*) to share a common meal. In the partaking of food in this way, anyone could be sitting next to anyone else—female next to male, socially high next to socially low, and ritually pure next to ritually impure. This was the first reification of Guru Nanak's spiritual concern to reorganize society on egalitarian ideals. The institution of *langar* promoted the spirit of unity and mutual belonging, and struck at the divisive aspect of caste, thereby advancing the process of defining a community based upon Sikh ideals. Finally, Guru Nanak created the institution of the Guru, who became the central authority in community life. Before he passed away in 1539, Guru Nanak designated one of his disciples, Lehna, as his successor by renaming him Angad, meaning my "own limb." Thus, a lineage was established and a legitimate succession was maintained intact from the appointment of Guru Angad (1504–52) to the death of Guru Gobind Singh (1666–1708), the tenth and the last human Guru of the Sikhs.

The successors of Guru Nanak

Guru Nanak's decision to designate a successor was the most significant step in the development of early Sikh Panth. He created the "charisma of office" when he passed on his authority to his successor. Notably, Guru Nanak passed over his two sons and decided to promote his disciple, Angad, to the status of "Guru" within his own lifetime. He bowed before his own successor, highlighting the fact that it was necessary for the charismatic authority to become radically changed. In this act of humility, and his assumption of the role of "disciple," Guru Nanak was making a clear statement of the primacy of the "message" over the messenger. In so doing, he was asserting the objective independence of the power behind divine revelation, thus establishing the idea that the Guru is "one," even if its expression takes several forms.

Guru Angad consolidated the nascent Sikh Panth in the face of the challenge offered by Guru Nanak's eldest son, Sri Chand, the founder of the ascetic Udasi sect. His 62 *shaloks* (couplets or stanzas) in the Sikh scripture throw considerable light on the historical situation of the Panth during his period and mark the doctrinal boundaries of the Sikh faith in strict conformity with Guru Nanak's message. He established a new Sikh center at Khadur where the community kitchen (*langar*) was run by his wife Khivi, who used to serve a pudding of rice boiled in milk to the congregation. He refined the Gurmukhi script for recording the compilation of the Guru's hymns. The original Gurmukhi script was a systematization of business shorthand (*lande/takari*), of the kind Guru Nanak doubtless used professionally as a young man. This script certainly added an element of demarcation and self-identity to the Sikh tradition. To the Punjabis, the idea of a spiritual truth inscribed in their own native language created a sense of empowerment that had been conspicuously absent until Guru Angad popularized the Gurmukhi script among the masses.

Like his predecessor, Guru Angad passed over his two sons and appointed his elderly disciple, Amar Das (1479–1574), as his successor before his death in 1552. Notably, a major institutional development took place during the time of the third Guru, who introduced a variety of innovations to provide greater cohesion and unity to the ever-growing Sikh Panth. These included the establishment of the city of Goindval, the biannual festivals of Divali and Baisakhi that provided an opportunity for the growing community to get together and meet the Guru, a missionary system (*manjis*) for attracting new converts, and the preparation of the Goindval *pothis*, collections of the compositions of the first three Gurus and some of the medieval poet-saints. This early move towards the establishment of a more comprehensive administrative system speaks of the rapidity with which the spiritual appeal of Guru Nanak's message was gaining ground, and also of the practicality of those to whom the tradition had been entrusted in dealing with this broadening appeal.

Guru Amar Das made the decision to bequeath his spiritual leadership to his devoted son-in-law Ram Das (1534–81), passing over his own two sons. This was the first time that the office of the Guru remained within the Guru's family to avoid the possibility of a disputed succession. The fourth Guru founded the city of Ramdaspur where he constructed a large pool for the purpose of bathing. The city was renamed Amritsar, meaning "the nectar of immortality." The new building projects required considerable financial and logistical mobilization for which the appointment of "deputies" (*masands*) became necessary to deal with increasingly complex administrative demands. By now the Panth was equal to such an endeavor, confirming the point that the appeal of Guru Nanak's message had gained wider support and validation. In addition to his administrative concerns, Guru Ram Das contributed 679 hymns to the growing corpus of scriptural tradition, expanding the musical modes from nineteen to thirty. In particular, the musicality and emotional appeal of his hymns had tremendous impact on his audience. The liturgical requirements of the reciting and singing of the sacred Word became the part of the very definition of being a Sikh. The most significant development was related to the self-image of the Sikhs who perceived themselves as unique and distinct from the other religious communities of North India.

During the period of Guru Ram Das a convention was established that hereafter the succession should be limited to his direct descendants. In other words, within the Guru's family of Sodhi Khatris the most suitable person was to be chosen. Thus Guru Ram Das designated the youngest of his three sons, Arjan (1563–1606), as his successor because of his humility and devotion. It is no wonder that the very beginning of Guru Arjan's ministry was marked by the determined enmity of his eldest brother, Prithi Chand, who openly challenged his right to succeed their father. Paradoxically, this factionalism became the main impetus behind creative developments within the Sikh community. For Guru Arjan, it was the defining moment in his charting of a future course of both accommodation and competition. As fifth Guru, he inherited a vibrant religious community that had rather quickly developed around the model and tenets of Guru Nanak. His twenty-five years of reign was marked by a number of far-reaching institutional developments. First, he built the Darbar Sahib (later known as the Golden Temple) in the sacred pool of Amritsar, a shining monument to the Sikh faith that remains the central symbol to the community until this day. Second, he inherited a rich and substantial scriptural corpus that he took upon himself to systematize and organize into what became the Adi Granth, the key marker of Sikh identity for the generations to come. The Adi Granth has always served as *the* definitive statement of Sikhism's unique spiritual stance. Third, by the end of sixteenth century the Sikh Panth had developed a strong sense of independent identity, which is quite evident from Guru Arjan's assertion, "We are neither Hindu nor Muslim."[5]

Finally, the author of *Dabistan-i-Mazahib*, a mid-seventeenth-century work in Persian, testifies that the number of Sikhs had rapidly increased during Guru Arjan's period and that "there were not many cities in the inhabited countries where some Sikhs were not to be found." In fact, this growing strength of the Sikh movement attracted the unfavorable attention of the ruling authorities because of the reaction of Muslim revivalists of the Naqshbandi Order in Mughal India. To a large extent, the liberal policy of Emperor Akbar's reign provided the overall context for the peaceful evolution of the Sikh Panth. However, within eight months of Akbar's death in October 1605, Guru Arjan was executed on May 30, 1606 at Lahore by the orders of the new emperor, Jahangir, for his alleged blessings to the rebel prince Khusrau. The Sikh community perceived his death as the "first martyrdom," and it became a turning point in the history of the Sikh Panth.

A radical reshaping of the Sikh Panth took place after Guru Arjan's martyrdom. His only son and successor, Guru Hargobind (1595–1644), signaled the formal process when he traditionally donned two swords symbolizing the spiritual (*piri*) as well as temporal (*miri*) investiture. He also built the *Akal Takhat* (Throne of the Timeless Being) facing the Darbar Sahib, which represented the newly assumed role of temporal authority. Under his direct leadership the Sikh Panth took up arms in order to protect itself from Mughal hostility. From the Sikh perspective this new development was not taken at the cost of abandoning the original spiritual base. Rather, it was meant to achieve a balance between temporal and spiritual concerns. A Sikh theologian of the period, Bhai Gurdas, defended this new martial response as "hedging the orchard of the Sikh faith with the hardy and thorny *kikar* tree." After four skirmishes with Mughal troops, the sixth Guru withdrew to the Shivalik hills, and Kiratpur became the new center of the mainline Sikh tradition.

During the time of the seventh and eighth Gurus, Har Rai (1630–61) and Harkrishan (1655–64), the emphasis on armed conflict with the Mughal authorities receded, but the Gurus held court and kept a regular force of Sikh horsemen. During the period of the ninth Guru, Tegh Bahadur (1621–75), the increasing strength of the Sikh movement in the rural areas again attracted Mughal attention. Guru Tegh Bahadur's ideas of a just society inspired a spirit of fearlessness among his followers: "He who holds none in fear, nor is afraid of anyone, acknowledge him alone as a man of true wisdom, O my mind."[6] Such ideas posed a direct challenge to the increasingly restrictive policies of the Mughal Emperor, Aurangzeb (r. 1658–1707), protecting the interests of Sunni orthodoxy. The emperor had imposed Islamic laws and taxes, and ordered the replacement of Hindu temples by mosques. Guru Tegh Bahadur was summoned to Delhi by imperial orders, and on his refusal to embrace Islam he was publicly executed in Chandni Chowk on November 11, 1675. The Sikhs perceived his death as the "second martyrdom," which involved the "larger issues of human rights and freedom of conscience."

Tradition holds that the Sikhs who were present at the scene of Guru Tegh Bahadur's execution shrank from recognition, concealing their identity for fear they might suffer a similar fate. In order to respond to this new situation, the tenth Guru, Gobind Singh, resolved to impose on his followers an outward form that would make them instantly recognizable. He restructured the Sikh Panth and instituted the Khalsa (pure), an order of loyal Sikhs bound by common identity and discipline. On Baisakhi Day 1699 at Anandpur, Guru Gobind Singh initiated the first so-called "Cherished Five" (*panj piare*), who formed the nucleus of the new order of the Khalsa. These five volunteers who responded to the Guru's call for loyalty, and who came from different castes and regions of India, received the initiation through a ceremony that involved sweetened water (*amrit*) stirred with a two-edged sword and sanctified by the recitation of five liturgical prayers.

Indeed, the inauguration of the Khalsa was the culmination of the canonical period in the development of Sikhism. The most visible symbols of Sikhism known as the Five Ks—namely uncut hair (*Kes*), a comb for topknot (*Kangha*), a short sword (*Kirpan*), an iron wristlet (*Kara*), and undergarment breeches

(*Kachh*)—are mandatory to the Khalsa. Guru Gobind Singh also closed the Sikh canon by adding a collection of the works of his father, Guru Tegh Bahadur, to the original compilation of the Adi Granth. Before he passed away in 1708, he terminated the traditional line of personal Gurus, and installed the Adi Granth as the eternal Guru for Sikhs, giving another title for the Sikh scripture as "the Guru Granth Sahib." Thereafter, the authority of the Guru was invested together

Sacred literature

The Adi Granth (Original Book) is the primary scripture of the Sikhs. It includes the works of the first five Gurus and the ninth, plus material by four bards (Satta, Balvand, Sundar, and Mardana), eleven Bhatts (panegyrists associated with the Sikh court) and fifteen Bhagats (devotees such as Kabir, Namdev, Ravidas, Shaikh Farid, and other medieval poets of Sant, Sufi, and Bhakti origin), making a total of thirty-six contributors stretching historically from the twelfth to the seventeenth century. Its standard version contains a total of 1,430 pages, and all editions correspond exactly in terms of the material printed on individual pages. The text of the Adi Granth is divided into three major sections. The introductory section includes three liturgical prayers. The middle section, which contains the bulk of the material, is divided into 31 major ragas, or Indian musical patterns. The final section includes an epilogue consisting of miscellaneous works.

The second sacred collection, the Dasam Granth, is attributed to the tenth Guru, Gobind Singh, but it must have extended beyond his time to include the writings of others as well. Mani Singh compiled the collection early in the eighteenth century. Its modern standard version of 1,428 pages consists of four major types of compositions: devotional texts, autobiographical works, miscellaneous writings, and a collection of mythical narratives and popular anecdotes.

The works of two early Sikhs, Bhai Gurdas (ca. 1558–1637) and Bhai Nand Lal Goya (1633–1715), make up the third category of sacred literature. Along with the sacred compositions of the Gurus, their works are approved in the official manual of the *Sikh Rahit Maryada* (Sikh code of conduct) for singing in the *gurdwaras* (doors/houses of the Guru), the Sikh places of worship.

The last category of Sikh literature includes three distinct genres: the *janam-sakhis* (birth narratives), the *rahit-namas* (manuals of code of conduct), and the *gur-bilas* (pleasure of the Guru) literature. The *janam-sakhis* are hagiographical accounts of Guru Nanak's life, produced by the Sikh community in the seventeenth century. The *rahit-namas* provide rare insight into the evolving nature of the Khalsa code in the eighteenth and nineteenth centuries. The *gur-bilas* mainly focus on the mighty deeds of two warrior Gurus, Guru Hargobind and, particularly, Guru Gobind Singh.

in the scripture (Guru Granth) and in the corporate community (Guru Panth). The twin doctrine of Guru-Granth and Guru-Panth successfully played a cohesive role within the Sikh tradition during the eighteenth century.

Central beliefs

The primary source of central Sikh beliefs is the Adi Granth. Its preamble contains the basic statement (*Mul Mantar*, seed formula), expressing succinctly the nature of the Ultimate Reality as follows:

> There is one Supreme Being ('1' *Oankar*), the Eternal Reality, the Creator, without fear and devoid of enmity, immortal, never incarnated, self-existent, known by grace through the Guru. The Eternal One, from the beginning, through all time, present now, the Everlasting Reality.[7]

The numeral "1" at the beginning of the original Punjabi text represents the unity of Akal Purakh (the Timeless One, God), a concept that Guru Nanak interpreted in monotheistic terms. It affirms that Akal Purakh is one without a second, the source as well as the goal of all that exists. He has "no relatives, no mother, no father, no wife, no son, and no rival who may become a potential contender."[8] The Sikh Gurus were fiercely opposed to any anthropomorphic conceptions of the divine. As the creator and sustainer of the universe, Akal Purakh lovingly watches over it. As a father figure he runs the world with justice, and destroys evil and supports good. As a mother figure, the Supreme Being is the source of love and grace, and responds to the devotion of her humblest followers. By addressing the One as "Father, Mother, Friend, and Brother" simultaneously Guru Arjan stresses that God is without gender.[9] Paradoxically, he is both transcendent (*nirguna*, without attributes) and immanent (*saguna*, with attributes). Only in personal experience can he be truly known. Despite the stress laid on *nirguna* discourse within the Sikh tradition, which directs the devotee to worship a non-incarnate, universal God, in Sikh doctrine God is partially embodied in the divine Name (*nam*) and in the collective Words (*bani*) and the person of the Guru and the saints.

Guru Nanak's cosmology hymn in *Maru Raga* addresses the basic questions about the genesis of the universe:

> For endless eons, there was only darkness. Nothing except the divine order [*hukam*] existed. No day or night, no moon or sun. The Creator alone was absorbed in a primal state of contemplation … When the Creator so willed, creation came into being … The Un-manifest One revealed itself in the Creation.[10]

Guru Nanak maintained that the universe "comes into being by the divine order."[11] He further says: "From the True One came air and from air came water; from water he created the three worlds and infused in every heart his own light."[12] Guru Nanak employed the well-known Indic ideas of creation through five basic elements of air, water, ether, fire, and earth. As the creation of Akal Purakh, the physical universe is real but subject to constant change. In Sikh cosmology, the world is divinely inspired, and it is a place that provides human beings with an opportunity to perform their duty and achieve union with Akal Purakh. Thus, actions performed in earthly existence are important, for "all of us carry the fruits of our deeds."[13]

A human being is a microcosm of the macrocosm in the Sikh worldview. For Guru Nanak, human life is worth a "diamond" that might go for a "penny" if one does not realize one's true spiritual nature.[14] In his *Suhi* hymn, he proclaims:

> One is blessed with the rarest opportunity of the human birth through the grace of the Guru. One's mind and body become dyed deep red [with the love of the divine Name] if one is able to win the approval of the True Guru.[15]

For Guru Arjan, human life is the most delightful experience that one can have with the gift of a beautiful body.[16] Indeed, the human being has been called the epitome of Creation: "All other creation is subject to you, O man/woman! You reign supreme on this earth."[17] Guru Arjan further proclaimed that human life provides an individual with the opportunity to remember the divine Name and ultimately to join with Akal Purakh: "Precious this life you receive as a human, with it the chance to find the Lord."[18] But rare are the ones who seek the divine beloved while participating in worldly actions and delights.

The notions of *karma* (actions) and *sansar* (reincarnation) are fundamental to all religious traditions originating in India. Karma is popularly understood in Indian thought as the principle of cause and effect. This principle of karma is logical and inexorable, but karma is also understood as a predisposition that safeguards the notion of free choice. In Sikh doctrine, however, the notion of karma undergoes a radical change. For the Sikh Gurus, the law of karma is not inexorable. In the context of Guru Nanak's teachings, karma is subject to the higher principle of the "divine order" (*hukam*), an "all-embracing principle" which is the sum total of all divinely instituted laws in the cosmos.[19] The law of karma is replaced by Akal Purakh's *hukam*, which is no longer an impersonal causal phenomenon but falls within the sphere of Akal Purakh's omnipotence and justice. In fact, the primacy of divine grace over the law of karma is always maintained in the Sikh teachings, and divine grace even breaks the chain of adverse karma.

Guru Nanak employed the following key terms to describe the nature of divine revelation in its totality: *nam* (divine Name), *shabad* (divine Word), and *guru* (divine Preceptor). The *nam* reflects the manifestation of divine presence everywhere around us and within us, yet the people fail to perceive it due to their *haumai* or self-centeredness. The Punjabi term *haumai* (I-ness, my-ness) signifies the powerful impulse to succumb to personal gratification so that a person is separated from Akal Purakh, and thus continues to suffer within the cycle of rebirth (*sansar*). Akal Purakh, however, looks graciously upon the suffering of people. He reveals himself through the Guru by uttering the *shabad* (divine Word) that communicates a sufficient understanding of the *nam* (divine Name) to those who are able to "hear" it. The *shabad* is the actual "utterance" and in "hearing" it a person awakens to the reality of the divine Name, immanent in all that lies around and within.

The institution of the Guru carries spiritual authority in the Sikh tradition. In Indic traditions the term *guru* stands for a human teacher who communicates divine knowledge and provides his disciples with a cognitive map for liberation. In Sikhism, however, its meaning has evolved in a cluster of doctrines over a period of time. There are four focal points of spiritual authority, each acknowledged within the Sikh tradition as Guru: (1) doctrine of eternal Guru; (2) doctrine of personal Guru; (3) doctrine of Guru-Granth; and (4) doctrine of Guru-Panth. In terms of the eternal Guru, Guru Nanak uses the term Guru in three basic senses: the Guru is Akal Purakh; the Guru is the voice of Akal Purakh; and the Guru is the Word, the Truth of Akal Purakh.[20] To experience the eternal Guru is to experience divine guidance. Second, the personal Guru functions as the channel through whom the voice of Akal Purakh becomes audible. Nanak became the embodiment of the eternal Guru only when he received the divine Word and conveyed it to his disciples. The same spirit manifested itself successively in his successors. Third, the Guru Granth Sahib carries the same status and authority as did the ten personal Gurus from Guru Nanak through Guru Gobind Singh. In actual practice, it performs the role of Guru in the personal piety and corporate identity of the Sikh community. Finally, the doctrine of Guru-Panth fully developed at the inauguration of the Khalsa in 1699, when Guru Gobind Singh symbolically transferred his authority to the "Cherished Five" after receiving initiation from their hands. Thus the elite corps of the Khalsa has always claimed to speak authoritatively on behalf of the whole Sikh Panth, although at times non-Khalsa Sikhs interpret the doctrine of Guru-Panth as conferring authority on a community more broadly defined. Practically, consensus within the Sikh community is achieved by following democratic traditions.

In order to achieve a state of spiritual liberation within one's lifetime one must transcend the unregenerate condition created by the influence of *haumai* (self-centeredness). In fact, *haumai* is the source of five evil impulses traditionally known as lust, anger, covetousness, attachment to worldly things, and pride. Under the influence of *haumai* a person becomes "self-willed," one who is so attached to his passions for worldly pleasures that he forgets the divine Name and wastes his entire life in evil and suffering. This unregenerate condition can be transcended by means of the strictly interior discipline of *nam-simaran* or "remembering the divine Name." This process ranges from the repetition of a sacred word, usually *Vahiguru* (Praise to the Eternal Guru), through the devotional singing of hymns with the congregation to sophisticated meditation on the nature of Akal Purakh. On the whole the discipline of *nam-simaran* is designed to bring a person into harmony with the *hukam*, passing through different spiritual stages such as (1) the "realm of duty," (2) the "realm of knowledge," (3) the "realm of effort," and (4) the "realm of grace." The person thus gains the experience of ever-growing wonder in spiritual life, and achieves the ultimate condition of blissful "equanimity" (*sahaj*) when the spirit ascends to the "realm of Truth" (*sach khand*), the fifth and the last of the spiritual stages, in which the soul finds mystical union with Akal Purakh.[21]

The primacy of divine grace over personal effort is fundamental to Guru Nanak's theology. There is, however, neither fatalism nor any kind of passive acceptance of a predestined future in his view of life. He proclaimed, "With your own hands carve out your own destiny."[22] Indeed, personal effort in the form of good actions has a place in Guru Nanak's view of life. His idea of "divine free choice" on the one hand, and his emphasis on the "life of activism" based on human freedom, on the other, reflect his ability to hold in tension seemingly opposed elements. Guru Nanak explicitly saw this balancing of opposed tendencies, which avoids rigid predestination theories and yet enables people to see their own "free" will as a part of Akal Purakh's will, as allowing Sikhs the opportunity to create their own destinies, a feature stereotypically associated with Sikh enterprise throughout the world. Sikhism thus stresses the dignity of regular labor as an integral part of spiritual discipline. This is summed up in the following triple commandment: engage in honest labor for a living, adore the divine Name, and share the fruit of labor with others. The formula stresses both the centrality of meditative worship and the necessity of righteous living in the world.

Universality of Sikh ethics

The Adi Granth opens with Guru Nanak's *Japji* where the fundamental question of seeking the divine Truth is raised as follows: "How is Truth to be attained, how the veil of falsehood torn aside?" The Guru then responds: "Nanak, thus it is written: Submit to the divine Order (*hukam*), walk in its way."[23] Truth obviously is not obtained by intellectual effort or cunning but only by personal commitment. To know truth one must live in it. The seeker of the divine Truth must live an ethical life. Any dichotomy between spiritual development and moral conduct is not approved in Sikh ethics. In this context Guru Nanak explicitly says: "Truth is the highest virtue, but higher still is truthful living."[24] Indeed, truthful conduct is at the heart of Guru Nanak's message. The central focus in his moral scheme involves the cultivation of virtues such as wisdom, contentment, justice, humility, truthfulness, temperance, love, forgiveness, charity, purity, and fear of Akal Purakh. These virtues not only enrich the personal lives of individuals, but they also promote socially responsible living. Living by alms or begging is strongly rejected. Through hard work and sharing, Sikh ethics forbids withdrawal from social participation.

The key element of religious living is to render service (*seva*) to others in the form of mutual help and voluntary work. It must be rendered without the desire for self-glorification or setting oneself up as a judge of other people. The Sikh Prayer (*Ardas*) holds in high esteem the quality of "seeing but not judging." Social bonds are often damaged beyond redemption when people unconscionably judge others. The Sikh Gurus stressed the need to destroy this root of social strife through service. The Gurus offered their own vision of egalitarian ideals based on the principle of social equality, gender equality, and human brotherhood. Thus, any kind of discrimination based on caste or gender is expressly rejected in Sikh ethics. The Gurus placed great emphasis on the spirit of optimism in the face of adverse circumstances. They stressed the ideals of moderate living and disciplined worldliness in contrast to the ideals of asceticism and self-mortification.

Guru Nanak advocated the virtue of justice in its legal sense and made it the principal characteristic of the ruler and the administrator. Thus, he severely condemned the contemporary Muslim jurist (*qazi*), who had become morally corrupt by selling justice and who had no concern for truth: "The *qazi* tells lies and eats filth."[25] In those days the *qazi* took "bribes" in order to deprive people of justice and in Punjabi culture the phrase "to eat filth" came to refer to "unlawfully earned food." Guru Nanak further proclaimed, "To deprive others of their rights must be avoided as scrupulously as Muslims avoid the pork and the Hindus consider beef as a taboo."[26] Here one can see how, on religious grounds, Guru Nanak regarded the violation of human rights as a serious moral offense. The Sikh view of justice is, in fact, based on two principles: first, respect for the rights of others; and, second, the non-exploitation of others. To treat everyone's right as sacred is a necessary constituent of justice. A just person will not exploit others even if he has the means and opportunity for doing so.

Guru Gobind Singh advocated the doctrine that, in the pursuit of justice, a person must try all peaceful means of negotiations. Only when all such methods of redress have failed does it become legitimate to draw the sword in defense of righteousness. The following celebrated verse of the *Zafarnama* (Letter of Victory), written by Guru Gobind Singh to Emperor Aurangzeb, makes this point explicitly: "When all other methods have been explored and all other means have been tried, then may the sword be drawn from the scabbard, then may the sword be used."[27] The use of force is allowed in Sikh doctrine, but it is authorized only in defense of justice and then only as a last resort. Moreover, in the face of tyranny justice can be defended and maintained only through sacrifices. The *Zafarnama* stresses that no sacrifice is too great for the sake of truth and justice: "It does not matter if my four sons have been killed; the Khalsa is still there at my back."[28] For the Sikhs of the Khalsa the dominant ethical duty is the quest for justice.

Indeed, Sikhism is dedicated to human rights and resistance against injustice. It strives to eliminate poverty and to offer voluntary help to the less privileged. Its commitment is to the ideal of universal brotherhood/sisterhood, with an altruistic concern for humanity as a whole (*sarbat da bhala*). In a celebrated passage from the *Akal Ustat* (Praise of Immortal One), Guru Gobind Singh declared that "humankind is one, and that all people belong to a single humanity."[29] Here it is important to underline the Guru's role as a conciliator who tried to persuade the Mughal emperor Bahadur Shah (1643–1712) to walk the ways of peace. Even though Guru Gobind Singh had to spend the major part of his life fighting battles that were forced upon him by Hindu hill rajas (chieftains) and Mughal authorities, a longing for peace and fellowship with both Hindus and Muslims may be seen in the following passage from the *Akal Ustat*:

The temple and the mosque are the same, so are the Hindu worship [*puja*] and Muslim prayer [*namaz*]. All people are one, it is through error that they appear different . . . Allah and Abhekh are the same, the Purana and the Qur'an are the same. They are all alike, all the creation of the One.[30]

The above verses emphatically stress the irenic belief that the differences dividing people are in reality meaningless. In fact, all people are fundamentally the same because they all are the creations of the same Supreme Being. To pursue this ideal, Sikhs conclude their morning and evening prayers with the words "Says Nanak: may thy Name and glory be ever triumphant, and in thy will, O Lord, may peace and prosperity come to one and all."

Sikhism: Practice

Sikh worship

Ideally, the daily routine of a devout Sikh begins with the practice of meditation upon the divine Name. This occurs during the "ambrosial hours" (*amritvela*, the last watch of the night, between three and six in the morning), immediately after rising and bathing. Meditation is followed by the recitation of five liturgical prayers, which include Guru Nanak's *Japji* (Recitation). Similarly, a collection of hymns, *Sodar Rahiras* (Supplication at That Door), is prescribed for the evening prayers, and the *Kirtan Sohila* (Song of Praise) is recited before retiring for the night. These prayers are learnt by heart in childhood and later on they are recited as part of daily routine from memory. In fact, the memorization of *gurbani* (Inspired Utterances of the Guru) by heart has always been compared in the Sikh lore with the possession of cash money that is readily available for use (*gurbani kanth paisa ganth*).

In a *gurdwara* (Sikh house of worship), the main focus is upon the Guru Granth Sahib, which is newly installed ceremoniously every morning. Worship consists mainly of the singing of scriptural passages set to music, with the accompaniment of instruments. Professional and amateur *ragis* (Sikh musicians) lead the congregation in devotional singing. Indeed, the singing of hymns (*kirtan*) in a congregational setting is the heart of the Sikh devotional experience. Through such *kirtan* the devotees attune themselves to vibrate in harmony with the divine Word, which has the power to transform and unify their consciousness. It is based upon the assumption that the singing of *gurbani* (utterances of the Guru) invokes the divine Word, of which it is an earthly resonance. This practice also helps them cope with the added challenges and obstructions that a modern technological society puts in the way of their spiritual life.

The exposition of the scriptures, known as *katha* (homily), may be delivered at an appropriate time during the service by the official *granthi* (reader) of the gurdwara or by a traditional Sikh scholar (*giani*). At the conclusion of the service, all who are present join in reciting the *Ardas* (Petition, or Sikh Prayer), which invokes divine grace and recalls the rich common heritage of the community. The most significant point in the Sikh experience of accepting the Ādi Granth as a living Guru may be seen in the practice of "taking the Guru's Word" (*vak laina*) at the end of congregational prayer. The procedure functions in a liturgical

Figure 8.1 A group of three Sikh musicians (*ragis*) performing devotional singing at Gurdwara El Sobrante in California in June 2009. Photo taken by Pashaura Singh.

fashion by opening the scripture at random. During the process the first hymn at the top of the left-hand page (or when a hymn begins on the preceding page as is usually the case, one turns back to its actual beginning) is read aloud as the proclamation of the Guru's Vak (saying) for that particular moment or situation in life. It is then appropriated by the audience through "hearing." In the case of individual early morning prayers, the whole family gathers in the presence of the Guru Granth Sahib to receive the divine command which serves as an order of the day. This Vak becomes the inspiration for personal meditation throughout the day. Again during evening prayers, one takes the Vak to conclude the day with its particular joys and sorrows. Similarly in the corporate setting, the whole *sangat* (congregation) receives the Vak as a divine command at the conclusion of different ceremonies. Then follows the distribution to everyone of *karah prashad* (sanctified food), a cooked sweet porridge made of flour, sugar, and clarified butter. In larger *gurdwaras*, the free community meal (*langar*) begins after the service or concurrently in the basement hall. Sikhs and non-Sikhs alike sit together to share a common meal of traditional Indian vegetarian food, usually consisting of flat bread, bean stew, and curry. One can easily recognize a powerful egalitarian spirit in the meal and in the way it is served.

Life-cycle rituals

In the Sikh tradition, life-cycle rituals are inseparably connected to the text of the scripture. The performance of ritual is indeed the performance of text. That is, the central feature of the key life-cycle rituals is always the Guru Granth Sahib. When a child is to be named, the family takes the baby to the *gurdwara* and offers *karah prashad* (sweet porridge), sanctified food prepared in a large iron dish. After offering thanks and prayers through *Ardas*, the Guru Granth Sahib is opened at random, and a name is chosen beginning with the same letter as the first composition on the left-hand page. Thus, the process of seeking guidance from the sacred Word (Vak) functions to provide the first letter of the chosen name. The underlying principle is that the child derives his or her identity from the Guru's word and begins life as a Sikh. To a boy's name the common surname *Singh* (Lion) is added, and to a girl's name *Kaur* (Princess) is added at the end of the chosen name. In some cases, particularly in North America, people employ sub-caste names as the last elements of their names, like Grewal, Sethi, Kalsi, or Ahluwalia. For such Sikhs, *Singh* and *Kaur* become middle names. In addition, the infant is administered sweetened water that is stirred with a sword, and the first five stanzas of Guru Nanak's *Japji* are recited.

A Sikh wedding, according to the *Anand* (bliss) rite, takes place in the presence of the Guru Granth Sahib and the performance of the actual marriage requires the couple to circumambulate the sacred scripture four times to take four vows. Before the bridegroom and the bride make each round, they listen to a verse of the "wedding hymn" by the fourth Guru, Ram Das, being read by a scriptural reader.[31] Then they bow before the Guru Granth Sahib and get up to make the round while the professional musicians sing the same verse with the congregation. During the process of their clockwise movement around the scripture four times, they take the following four vows: (1) to lead an action-oriented life based on righteousness and to never shun obligations of family and society; (2) to maintain a bond of reverence and dignity between them; (3) to keep enthusiasm for life alive in the face of adverse circumstances and to remain detached from worldly attachments; and (4) to cultivate a "balanced approach" in life, avoiding all extremes. The pattern of circumambulation in the *Anand* marriage ceremony is the re-actualization of the primordial movement of life in which there is no beginning and no end. In fact, the memory of four marital vows internalizes the Sikh tradition's goal for the couple to lead a blissful life.

Finally, at the time of death, both in the period preceding the cremation and in the post-cremation rites, hymns from the Guru Granth Sahib are sung. In addition, a reading of the entire scripture takes place at home or in a *gurdwara*. At the conclusion of the reading within ten days, a *bhog* (completion) ceremony takes place when the final prayers are offered in the memory of the deceased.

Family, society and gender in Sikhism

Rejecting the ascetic alternative, Guru Nanak stressed the way of the householder as the ideal pattern of life for the person who seeks liberation. His successors upheld the ideal of family life, expressing it in their own lives as well as in their teachings. The third Guru, Amar Das, proclaimed, "Family life is superior to ascetic life in sectarian garb because it is from householders that ascetics meet

Figure 8.2 Sikh couple circumambulating the Guru Granth Sahib at the time of their wedding on June 6, 2009 at Gurdwara El Sobrante in California. Photo taken by Pashaura Singh.

Sikh initiation

The key initiation ceremony (*amrit sanskar*) for a Sikh must take place in the presence of the Guru Granth Sahib. There is no fixed age for initiation, which may be done at any time the person is willing to accept the Khalsa discipline. Five Khalsa Sikhs, representing the collectivity of the original *panj piare*, conduct the ceremony. Each recites from memory one of the five liturgical prayers while stirring the sweetened water (*amrit*) with a double-edged sword. The novice then drinks the *amrit* five times so that his body is purified from the influence of five vices, and five times the *amrit* is sprinkled on his eyes to transform his outlook toward life. Finally, the *amrit* is poured on his head five times to sanctify his hair so that he will preserve his natural form and listen to the voice of conscience. Throughout the procedure the Sikh being initiated formally takes the oath each time by repeating the following declaration: *Vahiguru Ji Ka Khalsa! Vahiguru Ji Ki Fateh!* (Khalsa belongs to the Wonderful Lord! Victory belongs to the Wonderful Lord!). Thus, a person becomes a Khalsa Sikh through the transforming power of the sacred word. At the conclusion of the ceremony a Vak is read aloud, and *karah prashad* is distributed.

their needs by begging."[32] To understand family relationships, one must address issues of caste and gender from the Sikh perspective.

In Punjabi society family life is based upon broad kinship relationships. Every individual is a member of a joint family, a *biradari* (brotherhood), a *got* (exogamous—marriage outside a social unit—group), and a *zat* (endogamous—marriage inside a social unit—group). Like most other Indians, Sikhs are endogamous by caste (*zat*) and exogamous by sub-caste (*got*). Descent is always patrilineal, and marriages link two groups of kin rather than two individuals. Within the framework of the patriarchal structures of Punjabi society, the cultural norms of honor (*izzat*) and modesty play a significant role in family relationships. The Gurus employed the term *pati*, which essentially refers to the core of a person, encompassing honor, self-respect, and social standing.

Guru Nanak and the succeeding Gurus emphatically proclaimed that the divine Name was the only sure means of liberation for all four castes: the Khatri, originally the Kshatriya (warrior), the Brahmin (priest), the Shudra (servant/agriculturalist), and the Vaishya (tradesman). In the works of the Gurus, the Khatris were always placed above the Brahmins in the caste hierarchy, while the Shudras were raised above the Vaishyas. This was an interesting way of breaking the rigidity of the centuries-old caste system. All of the Gurus were Khatris, which made them a top-ranking mercantile caste in Punjab's urban hierarchy, followed by Aroras (merchants) and Ahluvalias (brewers). In the rural caste hierarchy an absolute majority (almost two thirds) of Sikhs are Jats (peasants), followed by Ramgarhias (artisans), Ramdasias (cobblers), and Mazhabis (sweepers). Although Brahmins are at the apex of the Hindu caste hierarchy, Sikhs place Brahmins distinctly lower on the caste scale. This is partly because of the strictures the Sikh Gurus laid upon Brahmin pride and partly because the reorganization of Punjabi rural society conferred dominance on the Jat caste.

Doctrinally, caste has never been one of the defining criteria of Sikh identity. In the Sikh congregation there is no place for any kind of injustice or hurtful discrimination based upon caste identity. In the *gurdwara*, Sikhs eat together in the community kitchen, share the same sanctified food, and worship together. The *Sikh Rahit Maryada* (Sikh code of conduct) explicitly states, "No account should be taken of caste; a Sikh woman should be married only to a Sikh man; and Sikhs should not be married as children." This is the ideal, however, and in practice most Sikh marriages are arranged between members of the same endogamous caste group. Caste, therefore, still prevails within the Sikh community as a marriage convention. Nevertheless, inter-caste marriages take place frequently among professional Sikhs in India and elsewhere.

The Sikh Gurus addressed the issues of gender within the parameters established by traditional patriarchal structures. In their view an ideal woman plays the role of a good daughter or sister and a good wife and mother within the context of family life. They condemned both women and men alike who did not observe the cultural norms of modesty and honor in their lives. It is in this context that images of the immoral woman and the unregenerate man are frequently encountered in the scriptural texts. There is no tolerance for any kind of premarital or extramarital sexual relationships, and rape in particular is regarded as a violation of women's honor in Punjabi culture. Rape amounts to the loss of family honor, which in turn becomes the loss of one's social standing in the community. The notion of family honor is thus intimately linked to the status of women. It should, however, be emphasized that Sikh tradition does not allow any kind of "honor killings" of women.

The third Guru, Amar Das, proclaimed, "They are not said to be husband and wife, who merely sit together. Rather, they alone are called husband and wife who have one soul in two bodies."[33] This proclamation has become the basis of Sikh engagement and marriage, which traditionally emphasizes a spiritual commitment between two partners over any material or physical advantages of the union. At every step the traditions surrounding Sikh marriages aim to ensure the spiritual compatibility of the couple to be married. To this end Sikh marriages are arranged by the families of the prospective couple. While the involvement of the couple itself has increased over time, the involvement and input of the family has remained vital. This emphasis on family, reflected in every aspect of Sikh life, from the communal eating halls of the *gurdwaras* to the common practice of identifying oneself through one's parentage, is among the most important precepts of Sikhism. At every stage in the Sikh process of engagement and marriage, the opinion of the each partner's family is respected, considered, and valued.

The issue of gender has received a great a deal of attention within the Sikh Panth. It is notable that the Sikh Gurus offered a vision of gender equality within the Sikh community and took practical steps to foster respect for womanhood. They were ahead of their times when they championed the cause of equal access for women in spiritual and temporal matters. Guru Nanak raised a strong voice against the position of inferiority assigned to women in society at the time:

> From women born, shaped in the womb, to woman betrothed and wed; we are bound to women by ties of affection, on women man's future depends. If one woman dies he seeks another; with a woman he orders his life. Why then should one speak evil of women, they who give birth to kings?[34]

He sought to bring home the realization that the survival of the human race depended upon women, who were unjustifiably ostracized within society. Guru Amar Das abolished the customs among women of the veil and of *sati* (self-immolation) and permitted the remarriage of widows. He further appointed women as Sikh missionaries. Indeed, Sikh women were given equal rights with men to conduct prayers and other ceremonies in *gurdwaras*.

In actual practice, however, males dominate most Sikh institutions, and Sikh women continue to live in a patriarchal society based on Punjabi cultural assumptions. In this respect they differ little from their counterparts in other religious communities in India. Although there is a large gap between the ideal and reality, there is clear doctrinal support for the equality of rights for men and women within the Sikh Panth. In contemporary times the feminine dimension of the Sikh tradition has received considerable attention. Under the influence of feminist movements, for example, Sikh women have begun to assert themselves in addressing the bioethical issues of birth control and of abortion. Sikhism does not approve of abortion just because raising a child would be "inconvenient to one's lifestyle" or, in the case of female children, "uneconomical." When, however, the mother's life is in danger, or in cases of incest and rape, Sikhism allows abortion of the fetus by medical procedure. Again, if a child is an inordinate economic burden because of some disability, this should be carried by both the woman and the man together, not just the woman. On the other hand, Sikhism regards the cloning of humans as unethical since this is seen as "playing God rather than walking in His will."

Elite and popular expressions of Sikhness (Sikhi)

The modern religious and cultural transformation within the Sikh tradition took place during the colonial period at the initiative of the Singh Sabha (Singh Society) reform movement in 1873. The Tat Khalsa (Pure Khalsa), the dominant wing of this movement, succeeded in eradicating all forms of religious diversity at the turn of the nineteenth century and established uniform norms of religious orthodoxy and orthopraxy. They were largely successful in making the Khalsa ideal the orthodox form of Sikhism. They systematized and clarified the Khalsa tradition to make Sikhism consistent and effective for propagation. Indeed, the Tat Khalsa conception of Sikh identity was both old and new, an identity which was very much forged in the colonial crucible. In addition to the economic and military policy of the British, there were other elements that meshed together to produce a great impact on the emerging identity. These additional elements in the larger colonial context were new patterns of administration, a new technology, a fresh approach to education, the entry of Christian missionaries, and the modernist perspective based on the scientific paradigm of the Enlightenment. All these factors produced a kind of neo-Sikhism, characterized by a largely successful set of redefinitions in the context of the notions of modernity and religious identity imposed by the dominant ideology of the colonial power closely associated with Victorian Christianity. As such, modern Sikhism became a well-defined "system" based on a unified tradition, and the Tat Khalsa understanding of Sikh identity became the norm of orthodoxy.

The Tat Khalsa reformers further secured legal recognition of a distinctive ritual for Sikh weddings in the Anand Marriage Act (1909), and re-established direct Khalsa control of the major historical *gurdwara*s, many of which had fallen over the years into the hands of corrupt *Mahants* (custodians) who were supported by the British. Inspired by the Tat Khalsa ideal, the Akali movement of 1920s eventually secured the British assent to the Sikh Gurdwara Act (1925). The immediate effect of the Gurdwara Act was to make available to the Shiromani Gurdwara Prabandhak Committee (SGPC; Chief Management Committee of Sikh Shrines) enormous political and economic benefits that came from control of the *gurdwara*s.

The standard manual entitled *Sikh Rahit Maryada* was published under the auspices of the SGPC in 1950 after reaching a general consensus within the Sikh community. It has ever since been regarded as an authoritative statement of Sikh doctrine and behaviour. Ideally, the *Sikh Rahit Maryada* presents an image of a uniform Sikh identity. Based on Guru Granth Sahib and supplemented with teachings from revered Sikh leaders, this manual guides Sikhs in the moral, social, and religious aspects of everyday life. It enjoins Sikhs to cultivate a pure and pious inner spirituality (*bani*), symbolized by the adoption of the Five Ks as outward visible signs of virtuous conduct (*bana*). The *Sikh Rahit Maryada* forbids hair cutting, adultery, the use of intoxicants, and the eating of *kutha* meat, that is, Muslim *halal* meat, obtained through the slow bleeding or religious sacrifice of animals. Upholding belief in one God, the Guru Granth Sahib and the teachings of the ten Gurus, it encourages the worship of God and meditation on his name, undergoing Khalsa initiation and attending divine services. It calls upon Sikhs to earn a living honestly and truthfully; to share selflessly with the needy and less fortunate in order to further the well-being of all; to nurture such virtues as compassion, honesty, generosity, patience, perseverance, and humility; and to avoid superstitions, idols, and images. Not punitive in intent or effect, the *Sikh Rahit Maryada* encourages devotees to regulate their daily lives to the will of God, just as the discipline of *nam-simaran* is designed to attune Sikhs to the *hukam*. It calls for tolerance of those who stray or who are slow developers, suggesting that these Sehaj-dharis (gradualists), who follow the teachings of Guru Granth Sahib without accepting the full discipline of the code of conduct (*Rahit*), will slowly progress to become the Khalsa. The only code of conduct now sanctioned by the *Akal Takhat*, which is the highest seat of religious and temporal authority among Sikhs, the *Sikh Rahit Maryada* serves to unify the religious and social practices of Sikhism around the world. Distributed free of charge by the SGPC, the *Sikh Rahit Maryada* has been translated from Punjabi into Hindi and English, in acknowledgement of the needs of Sikhs living outside their historical homeland.

Although the standard manual of code of conduct (*Sikh Rahit Maryada*) tends to represent Sikhism as a single coherent orthodoxy, the actual situation at the popular level shows the existence of colourful diversity within the Sikh Panth. For instance, the Nihangs constitute a distinctive order within the Khalsa. They are recognized by their distinctive appearance. On their heads they wear a high turban known as a *damala*, surmounted by a piece of cloth called a *pharhara* (standard or flag). Their garments are always blue, with some saffron and white color combinations. They are rigorous in the observance of the Khalsa Rahit. Because they have renounced all fear of death, they are always ready to die for their faith. In North America some Sikhs occasionally wear Nihang dress and add color to the scene in any Sikh gathering. They are conspicuously visible at the time of Baisakhi celebration, particularly in Vancouver, Toronto, Montreal, New York, and California.

Further, the group inspired by Bhai Randhir Singh (1878–1961) constitutes the Akhand Kirtani Jatha (devoted to "continuous singing of the Sikh scriptures") that strictly follows its own special Khalsa discipline prescribed in the *Rahit Bibek* (discerning code of conduct). It includes a complete vegetarian diet, the insistence upon *sarab loh* (all iron), and the *keski* or small turban for female members. Although Bhai Randhir Singh refused to eat anything which had not been cooked in an iron vessel, his North American followers are not keen on this strict observance.

Furthermore, the followers of two nineteenth-century reform movements, Namdharis and Nirankaris, revere their lines of Gurus in opposition to the orthodox claim that after Guru Gobind Singh there can be no human Guru. In addition, there are inspirational figures (*Sants/Babas*, Sikh saints) who play an important role in the lives of Sikh devotees throughout the Punjab countryside. Because of their acclaimed piety they exert equally strong influence among the diaspora Sikhs.

The two important Sikh centers of authority outside the Punjab, *Takhat Sri Patna Sahib* in Bihar and *Takhat Sri Hazoor Sahib* in Nanded (Maharashtra), follow their own daily Sikh rituals which are significantly different from the ones routinely followed at the Darbar Sahib in Amritsar. For instance, there is a tradition of waving of lamps at the time of the devotional singing of *Arti* (Adoration) in the evening and a paste of sandalwood (*chandan*) is ritually prepared in the morning to apply as a frontal mark (*tikka*) on the foreheads of the Sikh devotees. These practices reflect the local Hindu influence in ritual and worship at Hazoor Sahib. Moreover, the sacrifice of a goat on religious festivals (*gurpurbs*) at Hazoor Sahib reflects the influence of the animal sacrifice so popular in South Indian religious traditions, including South Indian Catholic devotional life. This is by no means a universal Sikh phenomenon.

In fact, the Sikh Panth has never been a monolithic or homogeneous group. Among the twenty-five million Sikhs in the world today approximately 20 percent are the Amrit-dharis (initiated) who represent the orthodox form of the Khalsa. There is, however, a large majority of those Sikhs who "retain their hair" (Kes-dharis) and maintain a visible identity. In particular, the male Sikhs are easily recognized by their beards and turbans. They follow most of the Khalsa Rahit (code) without having gone through the initiation ceremony. Further, there are others who have shorn their hair and are less conspicuous, but their number is quite large in North America and the United Kingdom. They are popularly known as "clean-shaven" Sikhs, although they do not like the term "Mona" (shorn) as the designation of their status within the Panth. In order to overcome this difficulty, I propose to use the term Ichha-dhari (one who follows one's own desire or free choice) for them. I am using the term Ichha-dhari with two meanings in mind. In the first place, most of the Ichha-dharis "desire" to keep their hair intact, but cut it under the pressure of circumstances at a particular moment (which may be a temporary phase in their life). The moment they feel secure in their life they start keeping their hair again. Secondly, there are those Ichha-dharis who cut their hair because of reasons of their own choosing, but retain their affiliation with the Khalsa families. They use the Khalsa names "Singh" and "Kaur" without inhibition. Neither do they consider themselves as "lesser Sikhs" in any way, nor do they identify themselves with the "Hindus." In fact, there has emerged a new sense of identity among them in recent times. Being the majority in the diaspora, they participate with equal zeal in all Sikh rituals and in the management of the *gurdwaras*.

The Ichha-dharis are frequently confused with the so-called Sehaj-dhari (gradualist) Sikhs who have never accepted the Khalsa discipline. Although the Sehaj-dhari Sikhs practice *nam simaran* and follow the teachings of the Ādi Granth, they do not observe the Khalsa Rahit and, in particular, cut their hair. The number of Sehaj-dharis has continued to decline in the last few decades, although they certainly have not disappeared completely from the Panth. This impression, however, concerns only true Sehaj-dharis. It does not apply to those who violate the Khalsa Rahit and cut their hair after initiation. They are lapsed Amrit-dharis who are known as "Patit Sikhs" (apostates). They become apostates after committing any one of the following four prohibitions: "cutting the hair, using tobacco, committing adultery, and eating meat that has not come from an animal killed with a single blow."[35] This condition has occurred largely in the Sikh diaspora.

It should be emphasized here that all these five categories of Sikhs are not "fixed" permanently. The movement from one category to another takes place frequently and, therefore, it refers to their dynamic nature. For instance, all Amrit-dharis are Kes-dharis as well, even though all Kes-dharis are not Amrit-dharis. Also, there is internal differentiation in each category. Thus any one individual might go through different stages in one's life, each referring to a different status within the Panth. Therefore, to think of the five categories of Sikhs as "predetermined" or "fixed" permanently (as in the case of the caste system of the Hindus) would be misleading. Moreover, the actual numbers of different categories of Sikhs may show marked variations in different diaspora settings. For instance, the percentage of Ichha-dharis is much higher in North America and England than in Singapore, Malaysia, and East Africa. There is thus no single way of being a "Sikh," and Punjabi Sikhs move frequently between different categories according to their situation in life.

Authority structure within the Panth

Sikhism is strictly a lay organization, which makes the issue of religious authority within the Panth a complex one. The Sikh Panth recognizes no priesthood, and there is no centralized "church" or attendant religious hierarchy. At the inauguration of the Khalsa on Baisakhi Day 1699, Guru Gobind Singh chose five Sikhs (*panj piare*, the Cherished Five) of proven loyalty to receive the first initiation of the double-edged sword and then to administer it to the Guru himself and to others. He thus symbolically transferred his authority to the Cherished Five, who became responsible for conducting initiation ceremonies. Traditionally, Guru Gobind Singh conferred his spiritual authority upon the scripture (Guru Granth) and the community (Guru Panth) together when he died in 1708. Since then the twin doctrines of Guru Granth and Guru Panth have successfully provided cohesive ideals for the evolution of the Sikh community.

In 1925 the SGPC came into being as an elected body to manage shrines in the Punjab. As a democratic institution, it eventually became the authoritative voice of the Sikh community in religious and political affairs. In order to maintain its control over the large Sikh community, it invokes the authority of the Akal Takhat in Amritsar, which is the seat of religious and temporal authority among Sikhs. The Akal Takhat may issue edicts (*hukam-namas*) that provide guidance or clarification on any aspect of Sikh doctrine or practice. It may punish any person charged with a violation of religious discipline or with activity "prejudicial" to Sikh interests and unity, and it may place on record individuals who have performed outstanding service or made sacrifices for the sake of the Sikh cause.

The *gurdwaras* in the Sikh diaspora have their own managing committees. Each congregation (*sangat*) is a democratic community. Because there are no priests or ordained ministers, lay people actively participate in the various functions of a *gurdwara* on a voluntary basis. Each *gurdwara*, however has an official *granthi*, or "reader" of the Sikh scriptures, who is responsible for conducting its routine rituals. As with other Sikh institutions, *gurdwaras* play a central role in community life by making it more religiously and culturally homogeneous. They offer a wide variety of educational and cultural programs, such as the teaching and perpetuation of the Punjabi language and of Sikh music and songs among new generations. Some *gurdwaras* operate a Sikh version of a Sunday school, where children are given formal instruction in the tenets of Sikhism, while others support Sikh charitable and political causes.

Although Sikhism is an organized religion, the issue of membership within the Panth depends upon the personal choice of adherents of the faith. As a matter of fact, Punjabi society is kinship based, making most of the people Sikhs by birth. To a certain extent it is a closed society, and Sikhs are not ordinarily known as aggressively expansionist in urging their beliefs upon others. Despite the absence of an active agenda to proselytize non-Sikhs into the tradition, people may join Sikhism of their own free will. It is instructive to note that in Sikh society the idea of conversion does not carry with it the same notions as in Judeo-Christian societies, out of which the term originally evolved. On the one hand, Sikhism does not actively seek converts by knocking on people's doors, but, on the other, it does not refuse admission to any person who makes a conscious effort to join the Sikh fold.

Sikhs in the diaspora

About two million Sikhs have settled in foreign lands as a result of successive movements of emigration over the past hundred years. The overseas Sikh communities are to be found in the countries like Singapore, Malaysia, Thailand, Hong Kong, Australia, New Zealand, East Africa, the United Kingdom, Canada, and the United States of America. Wherever the Sikhs have gone they have carried their sacred scripture with them to practice their faith and have tried to build their own places of worship. It is not surprising to find the establishment of more than four hundred *gurdwaras* in North America and the United Kingdom alone. Living in new cultural environments has resulted in some adaptations: for instance, the congregational worship in diaspora *gurdwaras* takes place every Sunday, not because it is the holy day but because it is then that most Sikhs are free to worship. Another adaptation is the celebration of Sikh weddings at the weekend and the registration of civil marriages in the *gurdwaras* in the Western countries.

In fact, Western culture has added new challenges and obstructions to the spirituality of the Sikh tradition. Turban-wearing Sikhs have frequently faced discrimination by prospective employers, and the Khalsa Sikhs have to negotiate with various institutions to wear the *kirpan* (sword) as a religious symbol. Also, without an adequate knowledge of the Punjabi language the new generation of Sikhs is in danger of being theologically illiterate. The diaspora Sikhs are fully aware that a steady process of assimilation is in progress among second- and third-generation Sikhs. Notably, recent years have witnessed among them a revived interest in their inherited tradition and identity. This awakened consciousness has produced a flurry of activities in children's education at Sunday schools in the *gurdwaras*. Many Sikh parents have started home-based worship in both Punjabi and English in order to meet new challenges from the diaspora situation. They have introduced another innovative feature in the form of Sikh youth camps to pass on the Sikh traditions to the children. Through these camps a spiritual environment is created which provides the children with continuous exposure to Sikh values and traditions.

In the 1970s a group of white (*gora*) Americans and Canadians converted to the Sikh faith at the inspiration of their yoga teacher, Harbhajan Singh Khalsa (Yogi Bhajan). Both male and female Caucasian Sikhs wear white turbans, tunics, and tight trousers. They live and raise families in communal houses, spending long hours in meditation and chanting while performing various postures of yoga. They have introduced the Sikh tradition in a new cultural environment. Most of the Punjabi Sikhs have shown an ambivalent attitude towards these new converts, praising their strict Khalsa-style discipline but expressing doubts about their mixing of the Sikh tradition with the ideals of yoga. With the coming of a second-generation of these *gora* Sikhs, however, Sikhism has indeed moved beyond its cultural environment of Punjab and become a world religion.

Sikhism: Current approaches

The early twenty-first century continues to be a very exciting time for Sikh studies. Within the last generation scholars have begun to question the prevailing attitudes towards the study of Sikhism in both the West and India itself to the point that this least examined and perhaps most misunderstood of South Asia's religious and cultural traditions now occupies seven academic chairs within the United States of America and one in Canada, with more proposed. It should therefore elicit little surprise that undergraduate and graduate courses in Sikh studies, particularly Sikh history and religion, have been increasing dramatically over the last decade, a rise which corresponds in part to Sikh immigration into Canada, the United States of America, and the United Kingdom.

Until recently most of the academic works have been theoretically limited, following with little deviation what we may call the meta-narrative of the Khalsa and describing other ways of being Sikh, whether explicitly or not, as deviations from the "normative" Khalsa trajectory. The privileging of a normative Sikh tradition from which others diverge is in itself a Sikhism refracted through a Western Orientalist lens (as is the term Sikhism) and speaks nothing of the Sikh tradition's rich, plural, and inclusive past. In such a light, one clearly sees that even the religion of the Sikhs is interpreted through categories which are not intrinsically Sikh or Indic but rather Judeo-Christian (monotheism and violence are two such examples) thus leading to many of the misunderstandings. There is therefore an urgent need to look at the colorful diversity of the Sikh tradition through an inclusive lens which allows the multiplicity of Sikh voices throughout the Sikh world today and throughout Sikhism's history to be heard without privileging any singular one.

In sum, Sikhism has had and continues to have a seemingly unending number of dominant, institutional, regional, national, and local expressions of faith in constant dynamic relationship with one another, continually influencing each other and defining and redefining what it has meant and continues to mean to be a Sikh in different places around the globe. Most interestingly, the Sikh community has always been involved in the process of "renewal and redefinition" throughout the world. In fact, the question "Who is a Sikh?" occupies much of the attention in the online discussions among the various Sikh networks, although the debate frequently becomes acrimonious. Each generation of Sikhs has to respond to this question in the light of a new historical situation and to address the larger issues of orthodoxy and orthopraxy. Not surprisingly, the diaspora Sikhs have to respond to these issues from their own particular situation in different cultural and political contexts. In fact, they rediscover their identity in cross-cultural encounters as well as through their interaction with other religious and ethnic communities. They have to face new challenges which require new responses. It is no wonder that they are starting to provoke fresh responses to the notions of self, gender, and authority in the postmodern world. On the whole the process of Sikh identity-formation is an ongoing phenomenon of a dynamic nature.

Discussion questions

1   Do you think Guru Nanak intended to found an independent religion in the last phase of his life? If so, what is the evidence in his works? Describe the Kartarpur period of his life in detail.

2   Do you think the rural base of Punjabi society played a major role in the evolution of militant traditions within the Panth? What role did the martyrdoms of Guru Arjan and Guru Tegh Bahadur play in this direction? Is there any relationship between the rural background of Punjabi Sikhs and the spirit of factionalism in the *gurdwaras*?

3   Do you think the institution of the *gurdwara* plays a major role in the survival of the Sikh traditions in the diaspora? How will the second and third generation of diaspora Sikhs redefine Sikhism? Will they provoke new responses to the notions of identity, gender, and authority in the postmodern world?

Key terms (in Punjabi language)

Ādi Granth—Literally, "original book"; first compiled by Guru Arjan in 1604 and invested with supreme authority as the Guru Granth Sahib after the death of Guru Gobind Singh.

Akāl Purakh—"The One Beyond Time," God.

Five Ks—The five marks of Khalsa identity: *Keś* (uncut hair), *Kaṅghā* (wooden comb), *Kirpān* (sword), *Karā* (iron bangle), and *Kachh* (undergarment breeches).

Gurdwārā—Literally, "Guru's door"; the Sikh place of worship.

Gurū—"Teacher"; either a spiritual person or the divine inner voice.

Khālsā—Literally, "pure" or "crown estate"; hence an order of Sikhs bound by common identity and discipline.

Laṅgar—The term for both the community kitchen and the meal that is prepared there and served to all present in the congregation.

nām-simaran—"Remembrance of the divine Name," especially the devotional practice of meditating on the divine Name.

Panth—Literally, "path"; hence the Sikh community.

Vāk—"Saying"; a passage from the Guru Granth Sahib chosen at random and read aloud to the congregation as the lesson of the day.

Notes

1 Some of the material in this chapter has been adapted from my earlier published work, "Sikh Dharam," in Sushil Mittal and Gene Thursby, eds., *Religions of South Asia: An Introduction*, London and New York: Routlege, 2006, pp. 130–48.

2 M1, *Var Majh* 27, AG, p. 150. The reference means that the passage quoted from the twenty-seventh stanza of the ballad (*Var*) in the musical measure *Majh*, by Guru Nanak (M1), on page 150 of the *Adi Granth* (AG). The code word *Mahala* (or simply "M") with an appropriate number identifies the compositions of each Sikh Guru. The works by Guru Nanak, Guru Angad, Guru Amar Das, Guru Ram Das, Guru Arjan, and Guru Tegh Bahadur are indicated by "M' 1, 2, 3, 4, 5, and 9, respectively.

3 M1, *Ramakali Siddh Gost* 36, AG, p. 942.

4 M1, *Var Malar*, 1 (22), AG, p. 1245.

5 M5, *Bhairau* 3, AG, p. 1136.

6 M9, *Salok* 16, AG, p. 1427.

7 M1, *Japji*, AG, p. 1.

8 M1, *Sorathi* 6, AG, p. 597.

9 M5, *Majh* 24, AG, p. 103 and Gauri *Sukhmani* 4, AG, p. 268.

10 M1, *Maru Solha* 15, AG, pp. 1035–6.

11 M1, *Japji* 2, AG, p. 1.

12 M1, *Siri Ragu* 15, AG, p. 19.

13 M1, *Japji* 20, AG, p. 4.

14 M1, *Gauri* 18 , AG, p. 156.

15 M1, *Suhi Kafi* 1, AG, p. 751.

16 M5, *Var Ramakali*, 2 (21), AG, p. 966.

17 M5, *Asa* 12, AG, p. 374.

18 M5, *Asa* 4, AG, p. 15.

19 W.H. McLeod, *Guru Nanak and the Sikh Religion*, Oxford: Clarendon Press, 1968, p. 203.

20 Ibid., p. 199.

21 For detailed analysis of the five spirtual stages, see my *Life and Work of Guru Arjan: History, Memory and Biography in the Sikh Tradition*, New Delhi: Oxford University Press, 2006, pp. 276–80.
22 M1, *Var Asa* 20, AG, p. 474.
23 M1, *Japji* 1, AG, p. 1.
24. M1, *Siri Ragu* 14, AG, p. 62.
25 M1, *Dhanasari* 7, AG, p. 662.
26 M1, *Var Majh*, 2 (7), AG, p. 141.
27 *Zafarnama* 22, *Shabadarath Dasam Granth Sahib*, Vol. III, Patiala: Punjabi University, 3rd edn., 1995, p. 1240.
28 *Zafarnama* 78, ibid., p. 1246.
29 *Akal Ustat* 85, *Shabadarath Dasam Granth Sahib*, Vol. I, Patiala: Punjabi University, 1973, p. 28.
30 *Akal Ustat* 86, ibid., p. 28.
31 M4, *Suhi Chhant* 2, AG, pp. 773–4.
32 M3, *Var Vadahansu*, 1 (4), AG, p. 587.
33 M3, *Var Suhi*, 3 (9), AG, p. 788.
34 M1, *Var Asa*, 2 (19), AG, p. 473.
35 *Sikh Rahit Maryada: The Code of Sikh Conduct & Conventions*, Amritsar: Dharam Parchar Committee, SGPC, 1997, p. 38.

Recommended resources

British Broadcasting Corporation: http://www.bbc.co.uk./religion/religions/sikhism/
Guru Granth Sahib Resource: http://www.srigranth.org/servlet/gurbani.gurbani
Mandair, Arvind and C. Shackle (eds. and trans.). *Teachings of the Sikh Gurus: Selections from the Sikh Scriptures*. London and New York: Routledge, 2005.
McLeod, Hew. *Sikhism*. London: Penguin Books, 1997.
Sikh Foundation: http://www.sikhfoundation.org/
Sikhism Homepage: http://www.sikhs.org/
Singh, Nikky-Guninder K. *Sikhism: An Introduction*. London and New York: I.B. Tauris, 2011.
Singh, Pashaura. *Life and Work of Guru Arjan: History, Memory and Biography in the Sikh Tradition*. Oxford and New Delhi: Oxford University Press, 2006.

Index